A SIDELIGHT ON ANGLO-AMERICAN
RELATIONS 1839-1858

A

SIDE-LIGHT

ON

ANGLO-AMERICAN RELATIONS

1839-1858

Furnished by the Correspondence of Lewis Tappan
and Others with The British and Foreign
Anti-Slavery Society

EDITED WITH INTRODUCTION AND NOTES

BY

ANNIE HELOISE ABEL

AND

FRANK J. KLINGBERG

[1927]

AUGUSTUS M. KELLEY · PUBLISHERS

NEW YORK 1970

First Edition 1927

(Washington, D. C.: The Association for the Study
of Negro Life and History, 1927)

Reprinted 1970 by

AUGUSTUS M. KELLEY · PUBLISHERS

REPRINTS OF ECONOMIC CLASSICS

New York New York 10001

. . . .

I S B N 0 678 00650 4

L C N 73 117503

. . . .

PRINTED IN THE UNITED STATES OF AMERICA
by SENTRY PRESS, NEW YORK, N. Y. 10019

PREFACE

With respect to the contents of the present work on an exceptionally interesting phase of Anglo-American relations in the period between 1839 and 1858, it should be explained that the senior editor stumbled, so to speak, upon a certain number of the Tappan letters while engaged in an examination of the files of the *Anti-Slavery and Aborigines' Protection Society* in connection with her search for materials on *British Native Policy,* the said files being the consolidated manuscript records of the original *British and Foreign Anti-Slavery Society* and the *Aborigines' Protection Society,* which were amalgamated in 1909. The remaining Tappan letters, a very considerable portion of the whole, as well as the Sturge, the Alexander, the Scoble, the Leavitt, the Jay, and others, were the result of a definite, deliberate, and persistent investigation of those same files by the senior editor after she and her present colleague had resolved upon a work of joint authorship. The transcribing of the letters and of all supplementary and illustrative material was made possible by the generous research grant to the junior editor by the University of California for the comprehensive purpose of anti-slavery studies, the junior editor's interest in the history of British anti-slavery having been already manifested in a recent publication, issuing from the Yale University Press, entitled, "The Anti-Slavery Movement in England to 1833."

In offering this, their joint contribution, to the historical literature of Anglo-Saxon humanitarianism, the editors would have it clearly understood that they make no claim to an exhaustive investigation and that they have refrained from incorporating the materials they here offer into the general body of the history of the times. They have, however, made their investigation thorough as far as it goes. Indeed, their interpretation of the facts and of the inter-

v

relation of them is based upon a much broader study of the entire period of British and American philanthropic interests than might at first appear. They are and have long been engaged on cognate subjects of research, necessitating an examination, not only of manuscript records, private and official, but also of newspapers, periodicals, and pamphlets without number, the greater portion of which, for want of space, they have been obliged to leave unmentioned.

Of great kindnesses received they are most appreciative. To Mr. Travers Buxton, Honorary Secretary, and to Mr. John Harris, Parliamentary Secretary, of the *Anti-Slavery and Aborigines' Protection Society* their thanks are especially due and not alone for kindness and for courtesy but for unexampled privileges. To Dr. H. W. Meikle of the Institute of Historical Research and to Mr. F. D. Sladen and Dr. Henry Thomas of the British Museum they are likewise indebted for far more than official courtesy, while to benefactors like the University of California and the American Association of University Women they recognize an obligation that a mere prefatory acknowledgment is inadequate to express.

ANNIE HELOISE ABEL,
FRANK J. KLINGBERG

AT SEA, December, 1926

CONTENTS

INTRODUCTION

In the forward movements of the nineteenth century, British humanitarianism was one of the strongest of forces, despite the fact that in the history of those movements, as in all general social and political accounts, it has never yet been given its legitimate place. Much the same neglect has been shown the American but with less serious import; for, while the scope of the American was limited, that of the British covered a wider field than even the lands ultimately to be embraced within the far-flung empire. It reached out into every sea and into the most obscure corners of the earth, exposing first and then vigorously attacking every abuse of power, every form of injustice that might prove incident to colonization or to the increase of commerce. Its constant and tireless activity reacted, in turn, upon the national character, which had conditioned its own existence, and that character, strengthened in its natural bent, expanded and deepened its sense of responsibility until the time came when, as a matter of course and of right, Britain took the lead, within the League of Nations, as the staunch advocate of the claims of weaker peoples.[1]

[1] Numerous and varied were the contemporary expressions of American appreciation of the weight and wholeheartedness of the British sympathy for the oppressed weaker peoples of the earth. One only can be quoted here, the *Address of Colored Citizens of Boston to the Prince of Wales*, October 18, 1860:

"To His Royal Highness the Prince of Wales:

"The Colored Citizens of Boston respectfully beg leave to place in Your Royal Highness's hand this expression of their profound and grateful attachment and respect for the Throne which you represent here, under whose shelter so many thousands of their race, fugitives from American slavery, find safety and rest; and of their love for that realm which, noblest among modern nations, first struck off the fetters of her slaves; under whose law there is no race whose rights every other race is not bound to respect; and where the road to wealth, education, and social position, and civil office and honors is as free to the black man as to the white.

"God bless England while her law is Justice and her sceptre secures Liberty!" (*Anti-Slavery Advocate*, II, 403, no. 50, February 1, 1861).

At the base of British humanitarianism lay a deeply religious philanthropic spirit, which, although not altogether absent in the earlier period of colonization, came especially to the fore in the time of the evangelical movement and of the rise of the older missionary societies. As the years passed, it interested itself more and more in all sorts of good causes with the result that innumerable benevolent organizations sprang into being, to the activities of which the secular press gave space lavishly. And these benevolent organizations were, many of them, of political significance. To influence the ministry of the day and to shape public opinion they hesitated not to use all available methods of democratic agitation. Their executive committees were professional and, in course of time, highly experienced lobbyists. They petitioned, they memorialized, they protested, they interviewed. They endorsed policies. They championed or opposed parliamentary candidates; and members, like Buxton, Lushington, Pease, were in a very real sense their parliamentary spokesmen. Abroad, they had a corresponding membership through which they collected a surprising amount of information and they made every possible use of chance travellers. All this came to imply an intricate organization; but, in general, the organization was much simpler than it seemed. Most highly developed, perhaps, was that of the London Missionary Society, itself expressive of a universality and a broad liberalism commensurate with the imperialism and the internationalism which it helped to advance. A pioneer among Protestant institutions, it came to have its Home and Foreign offices—a nomenclature said to have been borrowed from it by the State Department—its general business agent like Marsden and Ross in New South Wales, its superintendent like Dr. Philip in South Africa, and its occasional deputations. For purposes of survey and investigation these deputations, comparable to royal commissions in their range and thoroughness, were sometimes on circuit for almost a decade. The Tyerman-Bennet journeyings were of that duration; and it is not without interest to observe that, in selecting this particular deputation, the London Missionary Society imitated, unconsciously no doubt, the Carolingian institution of the *missi dominici* by sending out a cleric and a layman together to make the required inquest.

After its formation in 1839, the British and Foreign Anti-Slavery Society had, similarly, its means of ferreting out information and this in the most remote places. Many were the special parties [2] sent out to the West Indies, following in the wake of Sturge, Harvey and Scoble,[3] who, with means largely private, had made, in 1837, that remarkable investigation which had resulted in the abolition of

[2] One of the most interesting of these was the Alexander-Candler of 1849 to which some letters in the text have reference.

[3] Although the three went out together, John Scoble continued his course to British Guiana, leaving Joseph Sturge and Thomas Harvey to make the investigation into the working of the apprenticeship system in the West Indies. The idea of the visit was Sturge's and the funds to pay for it were chiefly his; but he was no scholar, a fact to which such manuscript letters of his as are extant bear witness, and so the literary task of reporting their discoveries and observations fell upon Harvey. A manuscript copy of the report is at Denison House and corresponds closely to the same as published. A second edition, of 476 pages, came out in 1838.

Scoble's investigation of conditions in Demerara and Berbice made him the acknowledged authority on emancipation beyond the Caribbean. He made a second visit there and, both before and after, lectured and wrote extensively. One of his earliest speeches on British Guiana was delivered at the anti-slavery meeting in Exeter Hall, July 4, 1838, and later circulated in pamphlet form. The subject was a vital one, especially when it was claimed for Guiana as for Jamaica and other islands that emancipation had resulted in a shortage of labor likely to be disastrous, economically. The Sligo despatches at the Public Record Office furnish some clews as to the validity of the claim. To meet the supposed shortage it was at one time proposed that laborers should be brought from the greatly over-populated island of Malta, at another from India, and at yet another from the United States. Dr. Hodgkin, whose instincts were humane and who had personal knowledge of conditions in Malta, addressed a strong communication to the Colonial Office urging that the population be reduced by emigration before it had become completely demoralized. Being a friend of the American Colonization Society, he would probably have favored also the proposed emigration from the United States; but not so the American Anti-Slavery Society. On the contrary, it was most emphatically opposed to negro removal in any shape, manner or form and so expressed itself when William H. Burnley, a Trinidad planter and a member of the Legislative Council, inquired officially concerning the possibilities of the same (*Seventh Annual Report*, 1840, pp. 41–42).

the apprenticeship system. Of the special visits of the British and Foreign Anti-Slavery Society, those induced by the great General Anti-Slavery Conventions of 1840 and 1843 remained throughout the most conspicuous. Three in particular were made in 1841, the Scoble-Alexander to the countries bordering upon the North Sea,[4] the Sturge-

[4] At Denison House are a few Scoble letters bearing upon this deputation. Most of them were addressed to John Beaumont. On the thirtieth of October, Scoble reported from Rotterdam:

"We reached this City after a stormy passage of about twice the usual length yesterday afternoon at four o'clock, and found to our mortification that the Anti-Slavery Meeting had been held, and that the friends from a distance had departed in various ways. There were gentlemen from Amsterdam, the Hague, and other influential places in Holland to the number of twenty-four who assembled for the purpose of forming the Netherlands Anti-Slavery Society; but owing to difference of opinion on points of form . . . the Society can scarcely be said to have been formed and another Meeting, to be held at the Hague, a month hence, will I presume give it a constitutional existence. In the meantime, a Committee of three, one resident in Rotterdam, another at the Hague, and the third at Amsterdam, are deputed to draft a petition to the Netherlands Government praying for information on the state of slavery in the Dutch Colonies with a view to the promotion of its abolition. Of course this does not come up to our notion of what should be done, and whilst we are here we shall endeavor to give the cause an impulse by applying sound principles to it. Our business will be to visit influential persons, & to hold meetings where it can be effected. . . .

"If you intimate in the pages of the Reporter our departure for Holland do not publish this letter; but merely refer to the bare fact that we are here on Anti-Slavery business—that a meeting of influential gentlemen met in Rotterdam yesterday. . . ."

On the second of November, he wrote from the Hague and, on the fifth, from Leyden. He requested that the Leyden letter be not published. In it he told of a meeting that he and George William Alexander had held in Rotterdam "on Monday evening" and also of a "select meeting" held in their hotel at the Hague "on Wednesday."

"We spent," wrote he, "nearly three hours . . . and replied at length to the various questions that were put to us relating to the preparations necessary to prepare the slaves for freedom, the results of emancipation in the British Colonies. . . . We hope our interview with these friends will prove a good preparation for the anti-slavery meeting to be held at the Hague the last week in this month when friends from Amsterdam, Rotterdam, Utrecht &c. are expected to meet together. . . ."

In closing, he noted the fact that the Dutch seemed doubtful about bringing people of different religious faiths together as was quite feasible in England.

On the ninth of the same month, he wrote from Amsterdam. Alexander had been obliged to leave him and Scoble surmised that he must ere this have reached home. Of his own movements he wrote that he had reached Leyden on the fifth and Amsterdam on the sixth, at midnight. The next morning he made calls and arranged "with our friend Mallet to hold a meeting at our hotel . . ." at "1 p. m. the following Monday." "This we did. It was small, but. . . ." He further wrote,

Candler [5] to the United States, and the Alexander-Wiffen

"After a sitting of about two hours we parted, and I hope some good was done. But this is a cold and dead place. The pro-slavery influence is felt in every quarter, and *seen* as well as *felt*. Much labor is required here to give strength to the Anti-Slavery cause. Information is required and what be the first principles of Abolition needs to be taught in all directions. Yet there is a movement—the subject is the theme of conversation. It is felt that something must be done, and schemes are afloat proposing to emancipate the negroes without loss to the Planters! Some Planters who profess Christianity are bestirring themselves on the subject of education and religion; but I have told them in all the conversations that I have had with them that their schemes will all fail. Immediate and entire emancipation I have endeavoured to enforce on the ground of duty as well as policy wherever I have gone. . . . This evening I depart for Utrecht, and, after having finished my work there, shall proceed to Groningen, the Ultima Thule of my wanderings in Holland."

In a postscript he expressed a hope that he would be home again "the end of next week—Weather miserable for travelling."

From Groningen, he wrote on the thirteenth to Alexander,

"I trust you arrived home safely without mishap or misadventure, and found everything as you could have wished in both Lombard Street and Stoke Newington. Soon after your departure I went to Mr. Jamieson's to breakfast according to appointment. . . . From his house we proceeded to Mr. Gulcher's. . . . His father who was a slaveholder died about a year and a half ago, and left him and his sister the property. It is quite apparent that he is willing to do a great deal for his slaves in the way of education . . . but I did not find him advanced so far as to comtemplate their emancipation, at least not for the present. . . . He did not attempt to defend the system in principle and admitted that in practice it was bad; but thought it was necessary the slaves should be educated before they were entrusted with their liberty. . . . I gave him the results of my own experience and knowledge of the state of things in the West Indies and British Guiana. . . ."

Of yet other personal visits, he informed Alexander and of his meeting with a certain Englishwoman who had the temerity to argue that the evils of slavery had been exaggerated. Scoble considered, however, that he had changed her mind before he parted with her. He saw "one of the chief men among the Moravian Brethren" and conversed with him about Surinam.

"It is sufficient," wrote Scoble, "to say that they experience the greatest difficulties in doing good, and that but little good is doing. After I had obtained from this Brother all the information I wanted, I spoke to him on the subject of the Moravians in Surinam holding slaves, and soon found this to be a sore as well as a weak point with him. . . ."

The Moravian assured him that the free natives could not be made to work.

Of the meeting at Rotterdam on the thirteenth, Scoble reported to Beaumont on the fourteenth. At that meeting he dwelt again upon the "results of emancipation" while sketching the whole subject of slavery and the slave trade. The Dutch Protestant clergymen impressed him as "very cold, at present, in our cause."

[5] Of this visit, particular mention will be made in the text. Sturge's own published account of it is to be found in "A Visit to the United States in 1841," Boston, 1842. It was an especially active period of Sturge's life and the B. & F. A-S. *Reporter* teems with evidences of his exertions in the anti-slavery cause (See II, 52, 121, 150, 154, 164, 180, 188). After Scoble became

to Spain and Portugal [6]; in 1842, there was the Scoble-Alexander to France [7]; in 1843, the Alexander-Wiffen to

Secretary of the B. & F. A-S. Society—and perchance before—he wrote almost daily to the office in London, directing its movements and keeping himself, though in Birmingham, fully apprised of all its interests. John Candler, only slightly less well known, had already similarly acquainted himself with the state of affairs in distant and foreign parts. In 1839, he and his wife went to Jamaica on a missionary tour and coasted along the northern shores of Hayti, becoming so much enamored with the scenic beauty of the negro republic that, after visiting Jamaica and seeing there what they thought were the happy results of emancipation, they were enthusiastic enough to extend their journey to Hayti. In 1842, Candler published in London his "Brief Notices of Hayti with Its Condition, Resources, and Prospects." His letters on file at Denison House are neither numerous nor of much narrative value. They show, however, that his interest in the West Indies antedated the visit of 1839. One to Thomas Pringle, dated Chelmsford, 22d of 8th month, 1836, is as follows:

"The unwillingness of the London Press to take up the Anti-Slavery Cause is very evident. . . .
"There are West India Captains in this neighbourhood who are stung to the quick by what we are doing and a Physician here who has property in Barbadoes supports them in asserting the most atrocious falsehoods. They endeavour to run me down by private scandal in the manner of the John Bull newspaper and stick at nothing in the way of assertion—They have great influence at Card table parties, and almost persuade some of our elderly women that Slavery is really a good thing. . . .''

Another of Candler's letters was addressed to Thomas Clarkson, 30th of 5th month, 1840, and concerned itself with Jamaica. Altogether Candler spent about twenty months in the West Indies distributed over two separate visits. On the occasion of one visit, he was the representative of the B. & F. A-S. Society. This was the visit he made with Alexander in 1849 and his MS. report is on file at Denison House. He also visited, officially, Brazil and published a narrative thereupon in 1853. His Jamaica visit of 1839 is commemorated in a publication of 1840.

[6] Of the importance of this expedition, the best evidence is Alexander's own publication, 1842, "Letters on the Slave-Trade, Slavery and Emancipation; with a Reply to Objections made to the Liberation of the Slaves in the Spanish Colonies; Addressed to Friends on the Continent of Europe during a visit to Spain and Portugal." The letters are eight in number, seven written from Madrid to friends in France and one from Lisbon to a gentleman in Spain. They trace the history of the abolition movement in British dominions and are of much more than ordinary interest and value.

[7] Of Scoble's visit to France in 1842, again in the company of G. W. Alexander, there is little source material available. The friends crossed over to Boulogne, March 2 (Scoble to Beaumont, dated Dover, March 2, 1842). On the twenty-sixth of March, Scoble wrote to Beaumont from Paris reporting his interview that day with Louis Philippe, for which, as "Dr. Madden will have informed you," he had lingered. Sturge, wishing anxiously for Scoble's return, wrote the same day to Beaumont,

"Dr. Madden was here last night. . . . I was sorry to find from him &

Holland, Denmark, and neighboring countries [8]; and in 1844,

Jno. Dunlop who was also here today that J. Scoble was yet detained in Paris. I do not think the French King is worth stopping to see.''

[8] The intention of G. W. Alexander and Benjamin B. Wiffen to make this visit was announced at a special meeting of the British and Foreign Anti-Slavery Society Committee, August 4, 1843 (*Minute Books*, II, 100). It was of particular importance because of additional facts that had come to light relative to the holding of slaves by Moravian missionaries in the Dutch and Danish colonies (*idem*, pp. 72–73, 76, 92, 114–115, 127, 156, 262, 316–317, 403). Since the Scoble-Alexander visit of 1841, the anti-slavery cause had not progressed far in Holland. From a letter of J. J. Gurney's to Scoble, dated from Earlham, 1 mo. 21, 1842, it would seem as if the earnestness of the latter had run counter with his discretion and criticism of the Dutch enlistment of negroes for service in Java, appearing in the *Reporter*, had given great offense to the Dutch and to the abolition cause a set-back. These facts were communicated to Gurney by John S. Mollet (Mallet?), ''our steady friend & ally,'' and the news, said Gurney,

''has mortified me a good deal, & I fear that considerable injury has been inflicted, through want of caution in the cause.

''How my name came to be connected with it, I have no idea; as I never made any public statement or offered any particular proof respecting African enlistment by the Dutch authorities.

''All that I did was to mention the facts, as stated by thyself & Sir F. Buxton to the King of the Netherlands who promised me to desist from the practice; and I now find by a letter from . . . our minister to the Hague, that his promise has been fulfilled.

''I have not read the article as No. 26 has missed me.

''I will thank thee to send me the said number by return; also to return J. M.'s letter with thy remarks, as I wish to hear the explanation, before I answer it.

''In case of the correctness of his statement, I think the Reporter ought to make the amende honorable; also to express satisfaction at the conclusion of the affair.

''If thee wishes to retain J. M's letter to lay before the Comee which I think might be right, pray send me thy explanation without it; which will enable me to write to him. . . .''

The enclosed letter from John S. Mollet called attention to an article on the Dutch slave trade (B. & F. A.-S. *Reporter*, II, 270) and to its refutation by the Dutch Government in the *Staats Courant*, the official organ. The refutation amounted to a denial of the charge that African soldiers employed by the Dutch were slaves or bondmen of any kind. The account of the matter in the *Reporter* had been given by Scoble on the authority of J. J. Gurney who was said to have ''proved these appalling truths.'' Mollet took a very serious view of the affair and wrote,

''It will prove, I fear, a death blow to all the attempts which were going on to obtain a liberation of the slaves in our West India Colonies. . . .''

Although no letters have been forthcoming written by Alexander and Wiffen during the progress of their journey, such were certainly written and some idea of their contents may be gleaned from the entries in the *Minute Book* of the London Committee. At the meeting of October 27, 1843, it was

following almost immediately, as in the other cases,

recorded that the Committee had "learnt with deep regret from their friends Alexander & Wiffen. . . ." that the United Brethren "will have no disposition most likely to discontinue the practice of holding slaves in the West Indies" (*Minute Books*, II, 127). No better news on this subject came until Scoble and Alexander were about to depart for their visit to the countries concerned in 1844; but, in the interval, the anti-slavery cause did make some headway, after all, in Holland. This is vouched for in the letter subjoined:

"JOHN SCOBLE ESQ.
        London
                                        "ROTTERDAM 19th Dec. 1843
"Dear Sir:

        "I intended long since to have had the pleasure of writing to you, but I wished to wait till I could procure for you the enclosed staats courant, which Mr. Alexander had intimated a desire to have. This is the last information regarding the state of the Colony of Surinam that has been published in our Government paper.—

        "Our Committee have frequently corresponded with friends in other parts of the country in order to fall upon some plan for promoting the interest taken in the cause of emancipation in the Netherlands—many people, otherwise well intentioned, do not care about it, because they do not understand it, and will not take any trouble to read what is written upon it—besides the works published here hitherto upon Surinam are in part at least, not calculated to make converts to speedy abolition. We have at last got so far that an association has been formed at Utrecht, consisting of several professors at the University and other principal people, and to which our Committee intend lending all the assistance in their power.

The plan is to give out a Magazine, to appear at first every two months, which will contain all the information that the editors can collect relative to the Dutch Colonies, especially the West Indian, with a view especially to the abolition of slavery. The names of the Editors will be published with the first number, and a copy of this magazine will be regularly forwarded to you.

Perhaps it may appear already next month. The talent & weight and respectability of the leading parties in it, will secure for it an attentive perusal by many, and it is hoped that the Government may be induced by it to be a little more communicative regarding the affairs of the Colony.

        "In conjunction with the Utrecht gentlemen, we have been busily employed in collecting information of various kinds—the principal questions that occurred to us were the following:

1) What was the increase or decrease of the population in the *British* Colonies before and after emancipation? With a comparative statement of births and deaths.

2) What was the proportion of the increase or decrease of cultivated plantations before and after Emancipation?

3) A comparative statement of the imports and exports, and if possible of the use of spirituous liquors.

4) Was there any emigration of negroes since the Emancipation to any extent from one British Colony to another in consequence of difference in wages, and, if not, where might such have been expected?

5) A comparative statement of the instruction and number of schools before and after Emancipation.

6) The proportion of Marriages before and after Emancipation.

7) The number of churches before and after Emancipation, and the different sums subscribed for these and other similar purposes by the Negroes?

8) The sums remitted to Great Britain for Missionary purposes &c.

9) The changes that may have taken place in the population of the towns and plantations before and after Emancipation.

10) The value of the plantations before and after Emancipation.—

the Scoble-Alexander to Holland and France [9]—all told a

"A good deal of the information relative to these different queries we have already got together, in which your Reporter has been of no small service —a part still is wanting, especially as the Editors have to work upon a stiff-necked and unbeliev[ing] people, whose hearts are for the most part in their heads (I am an Englishman and so write to you just what I think) & it is therefore absolutely necessary that whenever it can be done a statement be given of the official sources whence the information communicated is drawn. We have the parliamentary documents up to 1839, but suppose there must have been some printed since, especially as the subject was brought forward by Lord Stanley so late as March of last year, and as we think we shall find in such parliamentary papers much of the information we still come short, you would much oblige us by forwarding to the address of 'D: Twiss Esq.., Rotterdam' any such papers there may be, and mention[ing] the expense incurred.—Your zeal in the cause will I dare say render it unnecessary for me to make any long apology about the trouble I am occasion[ing] you.—

"I am glad at least we are not to be any longer idle here in the emancipation cause—it is slow work, but still we are going to do something.—I must now end this long scrawl, and hoping to be favored with your reply.

"I remain,

"Dear Sir:
"Yours truly
"ALEX JAY
"Sec of the Eott Comm."

[9] On February 5, 1844, Scoble and Alexander set sail from Dover. "Our destination is Calais," wrote the former (Scoble to Joseph Soul, February 5, 1844). On the fifteenth, when he next wrote, he was in Paris and seemingly more concerned with the memorial to Lord Aberdeen then being prepared by the B. & F. A-S. Society than with French affairs and in some of the subsequent days his labor was "impeded by an attack of a disorder called the Grippe." William Forster was of the party and he and Alexander were soon discouraged by the attitude towards the cause in France, but Scoble was not. He, more sanguine, saw something to hope for from the fact that the French were ready to accept the British contention that, in principle, "Slavery is a crime." It was the "application of the principle" that bothered them (Scoble to Beaumont, dated Paris, March 6, 1844). On the sixteenth of the third month, Alexander wrote a "private" letter, "the contents not to be noticed in the Reporter," reporting an interview that he and Scoble had had that morning with Guizot, which seems to have inspired him with more confidence.

"Guizot," he wrote, "distinctly says without being asked by us that the Government intends to make a commencement by doing something this session. He also informed us that the English Govt. had communicated to theirs copies of the documents forwarded to it by the B&F A-S. Sy including the Add[s] to Sir R. Peel on the subject of the sugar duties. He also expressed intention as we understood, of asking our Com[ee]. its views on the subject of the slave trade & slavery. The whole of this must of course be considered confidential. It is satisfactory thus to find that some importance is attached to & we hope some good done by our Ass[n]. not only at home but in foreign countries. . . .''

From a letter that Scoble wrote to the Reverend J. H. Hinton and Joseph Soul, on the thirtieth, and from the extant evidence at Denison House, Alexander had done most of the writing of the intervening days, Scoble himself

few only of the many that justified the insertion of "foreign" in the patronymic of this most worthy of benevolent societies.

Although the humanitarian body of the British world was a large one, it at no time represented nearly so many distinct families as, from the largeness and importance of its undertakings and achievements, one might conceivably surmise. Large families were an ordinary phenomenon in the England of the early and middle nineteenth century and often, as in the case of the Sturges, the Forsters, the Gurneys, the Frys, practically all members of a family were committed to several identical reform movements. Yet further be it noted that the families were frequently related by blood or connected by marriage with each other, the Stephen with the Wilberforce; the Buxton with the Gurney and the Forster, the Hoare and the Hanbury; the Gurney with the Fry; the Howard with the Hodgkin; the Hodgkin with the Backhouse and the Haughton; the Denman with the Macaulay and so on. And a goodly number of the leading philanthropists were of the Society of Friends which would account for the fact that many of them were bankers and merchants and in a position, therefore, to contribute liberally to humanitarian needs. The Evangelicals, likewise, were largely represented and even by men of Clapham Sect traditions.

And, across the Atlantic, enthusiasts like the Tappan brothers [10] and Jay and Leavitt and Goodell were to America what Clarkson, Wilberforce, Buxton and many another were or had been to England. They, too, were devotees of evangelicalism and arrogated to themselves the distinc-

having "been employed in writing a pamphlet on—it can hardly be called a review of—the Duc de Broglie's report." This was doubtless the same that was published in Paris the same year, under their joint authorship—

"Liberté immédiate et absolue, ou esclavage,

Observations sur la rapport de M. le duc de Broglie, président de la commission instituée par décision royale du 26 mai 1840, pour l'examen des questions relatives à l'esclavage et à la constitution politique des colonies françaises, addressées à tous les français amis de la liberté et de l'humanité. par Geo. W. Alexander et John Scoble. . . . Paris, 1844.   55 p.''

[10] For a short sketch concerning the Tappans, see pp. 176, 177.

tion of being its chief American representatives. Such being the case, it is not surprising that British and American philanthropists kept in close touch with each other or that they identified themselves with the same beneficent causes, among which stood, first and foremost, *anti-slavery*. If a religious or a benevolent society originated in the United Kingdom, its counterpart soon appeared in the United States, the result being, that the two sections of the English-speaking world, within the realm of all that indicated high endeavour, thoroughly understood each other. They spoke in the same terms and had the same lofty ethical conception of their individual or joint responsibility for the world's concerns.

And yet there was between them a great difference, notwithstanding this unity of interest and this identity of feeling and of expression, a difference which, as the years went on, became more and more striking. It was a difference of breadth of outlook, the American being narrowly provincial and the British not simply imperial. Trans-Atlantic conditions made for self-absorption on the part of the Americans. They were engaged in territorial expansion, in conquering a continent at their very doors. The British were also expanding but on the sea, which meant an ever-widening contact and the growth in complexity of commercial and political interests. And it was because of the enormous variety and extent of these interests that the British outlook became, not merely imperial, but world-wide as it has continued to the present day. Furthermore, slavery in the United States was a home institution, seemingly bound up with the economic prosperity of a large part of the country, recognized by the constitution, and utilized politically. Because of vested rights and of states' rights it was a thing not easily to be dealt with or to be disposed of. In the British Isles it was non-existent and there because of parliamentary supremacy over the colonies, where it was, and because of the static and perhaps decaying condition of such of them as were sugar-producing, of absenteeism,

which meant divided interests, of distance and of detach-
ment, it had been a comparatively easy matter to develop,
through the philanthropists, a public opinion sufficient to
destroy it by partially compensating the owners.

At the time of the formation of the United States constitution (1787), the American *slave* system seemed likely to
disappear of its own ineptitude, whereas the British *slave
trade* system—on the increase ever since the Asiento concession—was so much a part of the commerce of the country
that it was able to resist all assaults for another twenty
years.   After 1807, universal slave trade abolition became
a practical part of the creed of all Britons and, from the
date of Buxton's famous motion of 1823, there was, within
Britain, an increasing sentiment favoring slave liberation
in the colonies.   In 1833, the British emancipation law was
enacted and, by that time, the American slave system had
become intrenched just as formerly, with the British, the
slave trade had been; and the views of Thomas Jefferson
were gradually replaced by those of John C. Calhoun.   The
growing strength of slavery in the United States, in Cuba,
and in Brazil, economically considered, more than counter-
balanced the growth in philanthropy on both sides of the
Atlantic and neutralized the attack that had already been
made successfully upon the slave system.   The great day
of the African-Atlantic slave trade was between 1830 and
1860.

Confronted by an increasing slave system which seemed
impregnable, the men of Sturge and Tappan type fought on,
sustained as was James Stephen in earlier days, even in
the face of unrequited effort and of defeat, by a religious
conviction, by a consciousness of duty that permitted no
wavering, no cessation of toil, no possible drawing back.
They contended against fearful odds.   To them the annexation of Texas was a terrific blow [11] and the Mexican

[11] Some idea of the intensity of feeling with which it was viewed, even in
prospect, may be derived from what these letters convey:
  (a) From Judge William Jay to the *Liberty Press*, October 21, 1843.
  "My Dear Sir,— . . . Recent demonstrations convince me that the fate of

War, succeeding, seemed wellnigh to mock their efforts. Upon British philanthropists of British and Foreign Anti-Slavery Society association, the events just mentioned had

our country depends on the ensuing Congress. A mighty effort is to be made to bring Texas into the Union. If that accursed republic is received into our bosom, farewell to every hope of freeing our country from the plague of slavery. If we remain united—which, in that case, God forbid!—Slavery may in time be extended from Maine to Panama. Rather than be in union with Texas, let the confederation be shivered. My voice, my efforts, will be for dissolution, if Texas be annexed. My dear Sir, the country is in great peril. I have a large family of beloved children. I tremble at the misery to be brought upon them, and upon my fellow citizens generally, by this horrible project. We of the North will become serfs of the slaveholders. And yet the nation is in a state of stupor. Our politicians will sacrifice anything and everything for votes. We shall certainly have a slaveholder for President, or Van Buren, who is as bad.

"If we can keep Texas out for the next two years, all danger will be over, and the fate of slavery will be sealed. The slaveholders are driven to despair, and, if necessary, they will bribe high. . . . Nothing can save us but a strong expression of public opinion. . . . God bless you and save our country! . . .'' (British and Foreign Anti-Slavery *Reporter*, December 27, 1843, p. 240).

(b) From John Quincy Adams to Miss Anna Quincy Thaxter, July 29, 1844.

". . . The abolition of slavery in the Colonies of Great Britain, by the Parliament of that realm, was an event, at which, if the whole human race could have been concentrated in one person, the heart of that person would have leaped for joy. The restoration of eight hundred thousand human beings from a state of grinding oppression to the rights bestowed upon them by the God of nature at their birth, was of itself a cause of rejoicing to the pure in heart throughout the habitable earth. But that is not the only nor the most radiant glory of that day. It was the pledge of power and of will of the mightiest nation upon the globe, that the bondage of man shall cease; that the manacle and fetter shall drop from every limb; that the ties of nature shall no longer be outraged by man's inhumanity to man; that the self-evident truths of our Declaration of Independence shall no longer be idle mockeries, belied by the transcendent power of slavery welded into our constitution. It was the voice of the herald, like that of John the Baptist in the wilderness, proclaiming, as with the trump of the archangel, that the standing, fundamental policy of the British empire was thenceforth the peaceable abolition of slavery throughout the world.

". . . My unwillingness to participate in it (August First celebration) arose only from shame for the honour and good name of my country, whose government, under a false and treacherous pretense of co-operating with Great Britain for the suppression of one of the forms of this execrable system of slavery, has been now for a series of years pursuing and maturing a counteraction of the purpose of the universal emancipation, and organizing an opposite system, for the maintenance, preservation, propagation, and perpetuation of slavery throughout the world . . . (He here mentions Mexico, Texas, California).

"Their (the conspirators) foul and filthy purpose has at length been extorted from them. It is, by an exterminating war to rob Mexico of her provinces and to defend and perpetuate slavery by open war against England, for undertaking to abolish it throughout the world. A self-styled president of the United States, and two successive secretaries of state of his appointment, have, with shameless effrontery, avowed that their project of wholesale treachery, robbery, and murder, was undertaken and pursued for the deliberate puran effect so depressing that they came to regard the annexation of Cuba [12] and, perchance, of all Mexico by the

pose of overreaching, overturning, and destroying the system of policy of the British nation to promote the abolition of slavery throughout the world. I have long foreseen and watched the progress of the two systems towards this issue, and have given formal warning to my countrymen of it, by speeches in the House of Representatives in 1836, 1838, and 1842, by addresses to my constituents, in 1837, at Quincy, in 1842 at Braintree, and 1843 at Dedham, and by an address signed by twenty-two other members of Congress and myself to the people of the free States at the close of the session of 1843—an address falsely charged by the forty-bale weathercock hero of Texan annexation, nullification, and the blessings of slavery, as threatening the dissolution of the Union. I have seen the steady and gradual approaches of the two systems to the conflict of mortal combat, in all their phases, from the strictly confidential letter of Andrew Jackson, of 10th December, 1833, to the secretary, not governor, of Arkansas Territory, to that consummate device of the slave-holding democracy, the two-thirds rule of the late Democratic convention at Baltimore, and to the casting down of the glove of defiance, by our present secretary of State, in his letter to the British plenipotentiary, of 18th April last. The glove was indeed not taken up. We are yet to learn with what ears the sound of the trumpet of slavery was listened to by the British queen and her ministers. We are yet to learn whether the successor of Elizabeth on the throne of England, and her Burleighs and Walsinghams, upon hearing that their avowed purpose to promote universal emancipation and the extinction of slavery upon the earth is to be met by the man-robbers of our own country with exterminating war, will, like craven cowards, turn their backs and flee, or eat their own words, or disclaim the purpose they have avowed. That, Miss Thaxter, is the issue flung in their faces by President Tyler and his secretary, John C. Calhoun. And that is the issue to which they have pledged, to the extent and beyond the extent of their power, you and me, and the free people of this Union, and their posterity, for life and death, for peace and war, for time and eternity.

"Shall we respond affirmatively to that pledge? No! by the God of justice and mercy! No! ... Proceed, then, to celebrate and solemnize the emancipation of eight hundred thousand British slaves, whose bonds have been loosened by British hands. Invoke the blessings of the Almighty, with prayer that the day may speedily come when the oppressed millions of our own land shall be raised to the dignity and enjoy the rights of freedom, and when the soil of Texas herself shall be as free as our own. I cannot be with you, for age and infirmity forbid; but for every supplication breathed by you for the universal emancipation of man and the extinction of slavery upon earth, my voice shall respond Amen!

"From your faithful friend & kinsman
"JOHN QUINCY ADAMS"

(B. & F. A-S. *Reporter*, September 18, 1844, pp. 183–184).

[12] Selected from the many things that would indicate this, are three of dissimilar origin. One is from a letter written by a certain James White of Plymouth to John Scoble, January 23, 1846; another from the B. & F. A-S. Committee *Minute Book;* and a third from a map, a sort of moral map one might well call it, published, in 1846, with J. B. Estlin's "A Brief Notice of American Slavery and the Abolition Movement. . . ." In this map the slave states were colored red with red lines running from them into the free states and Cuba was also represented and colored red as if it were already a part of the American Union.

James White was an ardent anti-slavery man who must have had developed within him a strong animosity towards the slavocracy of the United States

slavocracy of the United States as almost inevitable. In America, however, although Lewis Tappan had similarly his hours of despondency, they were short ones and, as calamity succeeded calamity, his energy remained unabated. Indeed, if anything, it increased and he became more politically alert and his policy more and more aggressive so that, by 1855, he had advanced to the position that slavery might be interfered with, under the constitution, even in the so-called sovereign states.

Aside from the Texas question which, until closed by events, was always a prominent topic in the Anglo-American anti-slavery correspondence, three other subjects chiefly engrossed the attention of the British and Foreign and the American and Foreign Anti-Slavery societies. These were, the position of the black man, fugitive slave or free, in the United States, in Canada, and in Liberia; the coastwise slave trade; and the attitude towards slavery of the churches, their ministers, and their missionary boards. An additional one, a fourth, towering above all the others, explicit or implicit, was the question, how best could Britain help the United States in her anti-slavery struggle.

On one occasion he wrote that the burning of a Negro, of which he had read, "must show the horrid state of society in the Southern States of America . . ." and asked, "Is it not desirable some enquiry sh^d be made into this history, so disgraceful in every way?" (Letter to John Scoble, July 18, 1842). With regard to Cuban prospects, he wrote:

". . . I hope the Society will do far (*sic*) possible to prevent Cuba falling into the hands of the Americans. If they will go to war may the slaves of the South be emancipated. The Americans are the chief proprietors of the Brazilian vessels engaged in slavery & now the Brazilians are going to make restrictive laws on Englishmen dying in their country or rather on their property all owing from their faithless regard to treaties—Spain also will sufer (*sic*) until she is faithful. I sh^d not be surprised if the wretches who controul Spain would sell Cuba or anything else to make a (?)

"The Hudson Bay Company will be too strong for the American squatters on the Oregon . . ." (Letter to John Scoble, January 23, 1846).

The apprehensions of the London Committee were expressed, at its regular meeting, October 12, 1849, thus:

"The proposed annexation of the Island of Cuba to the United States having engaged the attention of the Committee, the Secretary, when in possession of the general facts of the case, is requested to draft a memorial to the Spanish Government in relation thereto, suggesting the abolition of slavery as the best mode of defeating the design. He was also requested to call Lord Palmerston's attention to the subject" (*Minute Books*, III, minute 308).

If, in the past, much misunderstanding has existed respecting British intentions regarding things affecting the United States in the middle years of the last century, there need be none henceforth; for this is a subject upon which the Tappan correspondence throws considerable light. The idea has obtained that Britain had aggressive designs upon Texas and, possibly, upon other Mexican territory; but the Tappan letters show that for some reason, not easily ascertained, she resisted pressure brought to bear upon her to be aggressive. And, considering how great that pressure was, great because communicated from one group of philanthropists, American, to another, British, the marvel is that the Foreign Office remained so quiescent. A more extended research than the editors have been able to make may warrant the conjecture that the fear of encounters with Russia and France contributed to an ignoring of humanitarian issues. Moreover, there were reasons, strong commercial ones, why Great Britain and the United States should maintain the peace. In the light of that peace and its maintenance, an aggressive policy on the part of either would have been exceedingly unwise.

As the easiest way out of all difficulties connected with Texas, many Englishmen advocated its colonization by free people. They advised, in fact, what Americans of slave-holding interests actually accomplished—possession by peaceful occupation. Under English auspices, a Texan Land Company [13] was organized on the model of the many

---

[13] *The Texas Land and Emigration Company.* In the spring of 1841, the B. & F. A-S. *Reporter* published several letters concerning the character and objects of the company, pro and con. One of the writers, N. D. Maillard, took the stand that colonization on anti-slavery principles was impracticable (*Reporter*, II, 38). Henry Prater, Secretary of the Texas Land and Emigration Board, was more keen for colonization than for anti-slavery and he contended that the abolition of slavery ought not to be made a condition of the recognition of independence and that Texas was likely to be to England on the south what Canada was on the north. The chairman of the Board, by the way, was a West India proprietor but a man who frankly admitted that he would like to see that done in Texas which had been done in the Barbadoes (*idem*, p. 47). Charles T. Torrey wrote in reply to Prater, April 26, 1841. To his way of thinking anti-slavery was the chief object in view (*idem*, pp. 123–124).

designed for territory already British and the cause of colonization was championed by men at once prominent and nobly disinterested, Dr. Thomas Hodgkin, the chief founder and, for more than a generation, the mainstay of the Aborigines' Protection Society, being at their head. The movement, however, was viewed askance by the British and Foreign Anti-Slavery Society and at times vigorously opposed, the contention being, that no such device could, by any manner of means, make headway against slave interests already established inside and outside of Texas.[14] The free German emigration thither that Lewis Tappan approved of would have been confronted by the same barrier.[15]

As it happened, he and Leavitt had yet other solutions of the problem to offer. In the beginning of the contest, they urged that Great Britain recognize the independence of Texas on condition of her doing away with slavery and, later, that Britain relieve the usual frontier stress by making a huge money loan. British philanthropists, the medium of these urgings, responded [16] to them by preparing

[14] The B. & F. A-S. Society Committee would seem to have been very chary about endorsing anything and everything proposed. A Mr. H. G. Martin, by letter, dated November 29, 1839, had submitted to its consideration a plan for circumventing the designs of so-called ''Texian Pirates.'' It was ''the formation of a small Colony of free Blacks and the coloured race generally on the Mexican territory under the protection of the Mexican Government and authorities.'' The Committee commended Mr. Martin's ''benevolent and laudable object,'' but declined to furnish him or it any material support (*Minute Books*, I).

[15] At a meeting of the B. & F. A-S. Society Committee, November 24, 1843, it was decided that the matter of German emigration to Texas, considered at the meeting of September 29, 1843 (*Minute Books*, II, 115), was to be left in the hands of G. W. Alexander (*idem*, p. 130).

[16] They also considered such matters, unsolicited, as did various of their auxiliary bodies. This was not to be wondered at since the Texas question had been before Parliament and thoroughly aired there (See *Quarterly Anti-Slavery Magazine*, II, no. 3). The Darlington B. & F. A-S. Society Committee, at a meeting in the autumn of 1839, took very decided action with reference to the claims of Texas and passed the following resolution:

''The important subject of the possible recognition by the Government of this Country of the independence of the territory of Texas, having been considered, it is the judgment of this Committee that such an act is strongly

memorials [17] that rivalled genuine state papers in point of

to be deprecated, and this Committee hereby enters its protest against it,—believing it would be a measure fraught with the greatest danger to the cause which the people of Great Britain have for years struggled to promote, that of the universal abolition of Slavery and the Slave Trade.

"Texas by its very constitution avowing itself a Slave State and offering openly and unblushingly a ready market for the superabundant Slaves of Virginia and of the Slave breeding States of America."

The resolution was forwarded to London and its receipt acknowledged at a Committee meeting in November (*Minute Books*, I). Scoble's pamphlet, "Texas: Its Claims to be Recognized as an Independent Power by Great Britain; Examined in a Series of Letters," had already been resolved upon and was expected shortly to appear. The Convention of 1840 asked that Texas be not recognized until certain laws on slave manumission be rescinded (*Reporter*, August 12, 1840, p. 205); and later in the year, December 2, 1840, the B. & F. A-S. Society Committee itself passed resolutions embodying strenuous objections to recognizing Texas while Hayti remained unrecognized. These were published in the *Reporter*, December 16, 1840, as also a letter from J. H. Tredgold, the secretary. Even a commercial treaty had been objected to, notwithstanding that Palmerston had argued that such a treaty would mean the mitigation of slavery.

[17] That to Lord Aberdeen is here cited in illustration. It was presented by a deputation at an interview asked for by John Scoble in the name of the Committee.

"TO THE RIGHT HON: THE EARL OF ABERDEEN &C.

"My Lord

"The position which the Government of this Country has happily taken in relation to the great question of Human freedom is such as to warrant the expectation of the people of Great Britain and of the Civilized world, that whenever and wherever its influence can be legitimately exerted to advance it, that influence will be promptly and efficiently put forth. It is on this ground the Committee of the British & Foreign Anti Slavery Society solicit your Lordship's serious attention to the remarkable state of things at this time existing in the Republic of Texas, which they are firmly convinced present an opportunity—such as never occurred before—for the extinction of Slavery, and which if properly and promptly seized by the Govern. of this Country cannot fail to lead to the happiest results.

"Whatever opinions may be entertained with regard to the severance of Texas from Mexico and the relations established between these Republics and this and other Nations, it must be conceded that its situation—natural resources & Institutions render it a Country of Great importance to the whole of the human family. If it continue to be a Slave State the hopes cherished with regard to the speedy extinction of Slavery would be greatly depressed. Should it, on the contrary, become a Free as well as an Independent state, those hopes would be realized in the extinction of that giant evil, and consequently of the Slave trade in those parts of the Western World where it now unhappily prevails.

"Recent intelligence from various quarters shew that the embarrassed state of Texas arising from its difficulties with Mexico—its financial perplexities—the depressed prices of its produce &c, have forced upon its inhabitants a discussion of the question whether the alarming state of things under which they suffer, could not be remedied, and the prosperity of the Country permanently secured, by the voluntary abandonment of the system of Slavery, and the adoption of a constitution ensuring freedom to all its inhabitants.

dignity and of clearness of diction and argument. They
also prepared personal letters and sent them out over the

The enterprizing and intelligent portion of the Texas Community appears
to be aware that unless some change is effected, immigration, which has already
subsided, may entirely cease; and that they will be utterly unable to bring
the vast resources of the country into profitable use. Their attention is consequently directed to the consideration of such measures as they apprehend
will relieve their country from its desperate condition. Annexation to the
United States is one of the measures contemplated. This, it is said will
enhance the value of the land, induce immigration of Planters with their
slaves, and create a new market for the slaves reared in the Slave-breeding
portion of that country. Another measure proposed is the abolition of Slavery.
This, it is argued, would invite the hardy yeomanry of Europe and the Free
States of America, and give even greater value to the land and stability to
its Institutions. It is scarcely necessary to suggest to your Lordship, that
these are questions of the highest interest, not only to the people of Texas,
but to the Friends of Freedom and peace throughout the world.

''With respect to the annexation of Texas to the United States, the
Committee would deprecate that as one of the greatest evils that could befall
the human race, inasmuch as it would serve to insure the extension and perpetuation of slavery in both Countries. But they are not without hope that
this catastrophe may be prevented by the timely interposition of the British
Government, as they (sic) are indications, not less striking than cheering, of
a great movement in Texas in favour of liberty, which if now judiciously
strengthened and encouraged, will lead, they believe, to its triumphant establishment.

''Supposing this important point gained, the people of this country, and
the friends of free institutions throughout the world, would regard with feelings of the liveliest interest the tide of immigration of free settlers which
would then rapidly flow into Texas. Such a population, carrying with them
the blessings of freedom, civilization and religion—rapidly increasing in number, and as rapidly developing the resources of the Country—would prove not
only of immense commercial value to this country, but to the world at large;
and in advancing its own prosperity and greatness. Texas would then eminently promote the freedom and happiness of millions now held in bondage,
and add to the general progress and welfare of mankind.

''It must however be confessed, that while the discussion of this question
is going on in Texas, an influential portion of the Slaveholders of the United
States,—many of whom possess lands in that country, now of but nominal value,
—are making a renewed, vigorous, and desperate struggle, in unison with
that part of the people of Texas whose interests lie in the same direction, to
have it annexed to the United States, either by legislative enactment, or by
the more summary mode of treaty.

''In reference to this point, the Committee feel it to be their duty to apprize
your Lordship that facts have come to their knowledge which afford grounds
for serious apprehension that unless the British Government speedily interpose
with Texas, either directly, or through Mexico, to relieve its people from
the overwhelming pressure of their present difficulties, the event so much dreaded
may occur. The Committee presume not to suggest to your Lordship how
the influence of this country should be exerted; but they would fail in the
duties imposed on them by the Anti Slavery body of this country, as well as in
the discharge of their obligations to humanity, and to the God of the oppressed, if they did not respectfully and strongly urge an immediate consideration of this weighty subject, in all its important bearings, on Her Majesty's
Government, believing that they have it in their power to aid Texas in freeing itself from the curse of a system which has blighted its prosperity, and
ruined its prospects, and of establishing a state of things which would ensure
its future strength & prosperity.

''Nor do British philanthropists stand alone in these views. At the late

signature of Clarkson, now commonly called, "the Venerable," addressed to President Houston [18] of Texas, whose

Anti Slavery Convention, embracing the representatives of the sacred cause of human freedom from various parts of the world, the contemplated annexation of Texas to the United States was viewed as an evil of the greatest magnitude, which ought to be strenuously resisted by all the friends of Justice and freedom throughout the world; and that the feeling now prevailing in that country in favour of free institutions ought to be encouraged by the British Government and people as a great duty they owed to mankind. In accordance with these views, and the increasing feeling of the people of this country on the subject, the attention of your Lordship is earnestly invoked to its early consideration; and the Committee would cherish the expectation, that it may result in such efficacious measures as will redound to the honour of Her Majestys Government, and the fame the nation has acquired by its past efforts for the suppression of Slavery and the Slave trade.

"I have the honor to be on behalf of the Com^e.

"My Lord

"Your Lordships obedient humble Svt

(Signed) "THOMAS CLARKSON

"July 7, 1843

"27 New Broad Street"

(*Memorials and Petitions*, 1840–1843, pp. 215–216; B. & F. A.-S. *Reporter*, July 26, 1843, pp. 141–142).

18 "TO HIS EXCELLENCY SAM. HOUSTON, President of the Republic of "Texas

"*Sir*,

"We have learned with gratification by the recent proclamation of your Excellency that an armistice has been agreed on between the Republic of Mexico and the Country over which your Excellency presides, thus affording a reasonable expectation that the effusion of more blood may be prevented, and a permanent peace established between the two countries.

"But this pleasure we derive from this source has been greatly augmented by the more recent announcement in the British House of Lords on the part of the Minister of foreign affairs in reply to a question from Lord Brougham, of the gratifying intelligence that this first step towards an amicable adjustment of the existing differences was by the friendly offices of Great Britain, and that negotiations are now pending, by which it is hoped that the total extinction of Slavery in Texas may be effected simultaneously with the conclusion of peace.

"An event like this while it would be most auspicious for the rapid advancement and future prosperity of Texas is one in which the anti Slavery body in this Country cannot but feel the most intense interest. We hope therefore that *we* the Committee of the British and Foreign Anti Slavery Society shall be pardoned by your Excellency for presuming to address you upon this subject.

"We utterly disclaim all political motives and influences. We come before you solely for the purpose of pressing the claims of humanity in the most respectful, but yet in the most urgent manner. We are encouraged in doing so by the sentiments which your Excellency has heretofore expressed in your published documents, in which you have unhesitatingly recognized the existence of Slavery as a great evil, as it is undoubtedly a flagrant violation of the rights of man, and of the spirit and precepts of the Gospel.

"It is perhaps within the knowledge of your Excellency, that this Committee have felt it to be their duty hitherto to discourage in every proper manner emigration and the investment of capital in Texas, and to abstain from every thing which might tend to foster the growth of a country which had adopted a system so hostile to the true interests of mankind; nor can we doubt

position on the question was so generally unknown that he

that our efforts have been in some measure instrumental in disseminating a general sentiment of repugnance to the institutions of your Country, both here and abroad. We have however no quarrel with Texas. It is with slavery alone, and with that in every country, that we contend, and must continue to contend while slavery continues to exist. Abolish it and nothing would give greater pleasure to the numerous body of Britons who unite in combating Slavery in every part of the world, stand not only to witness, but to aid by every means which they may have in their power the growth and prosperity of Texas. By the extinction of Slavery the prosperity of your country would be greatly promoted, her character elevated, and her relations with the rest of the world rendered far more intimate and agreeable.

"Permit us to speak with frankness. Texas by re-establishing the system of Slavery in the midst of the light and knowledge of the present day, offended against the Spirit of the age. By embodying slavery in her constitution, thus proclaiming her determination to render it perpetual she seemed to court the ill opinions of mankind, or at least to defy the public sentiment of the world upon a subject in which all christendom was deeply interested. She had not even the miserable apology which is urged for the continuance of Slavery in the United States of America, viz:—that it is not an institution of their choice, but one entailed upon them by a past age, to change which is a work of difficulty. Texas adopted Slavery, invited its augmentation and decreed its perpetuity.

"We rejoice to believe that some among her people have always deplored the step, and would gladly retrace it, & that your Excellency clearly perceives the extremely injudicious nature of that measure.

"The unwavering firmness with which Your Excellency is said to have espoused the cause and defended the rights of the oppressed Indian tribes within the Texian territory gives us much reason for encouragement to hope that Your Excellency will entertain equal considerations for the rights of the still more hapless and oppressed descendants of Africa.

"We feel well assured that in no country can slavery at the present day be regarded as a permanent and settled order of things. All the tendencies of the age are obviously against it and we look forward with confident expectations to the near approach of the time when the arrogant assumption of property in man shall be tolerated in no part of the world.

"Within the past year, freedom has been restored to more than twelve millions of our own fellow subjects in the possession of the East India Company in Singapore, Malacca Penang and Ceylon. At the same time the great work of emancipation has been progressing in various other countries with astonishing rapidity, and the indications are daily becoming more convincing of the decrepitude and incipient decay of Slavery as a system even in those countries where it appears the most vigorous.

"Why should Texas by her adhering to Slavery cut herself off from the sympathies of the rest of the world and plant at the same time the seeds of early decay in their own political constitution? The advantages of soil and climate; of an extended territory, and of political independence may all be neutralized by this one baleful ingredient. Proclaim liberty on the other hand to all the inhabitants of the land, and you will secure the elements of strength. A contented and happy population at home; institutions attractive instead of repugnant to the people of other nations; the gradual establishment and growth of agriculture, commerce, and manufactures, and a density of population, and the scientific and religious training of the people would result in the formation of a national character such as would ensure respect abroad, and tranquility and prosperity at home.

"It is probable that the question of Slavery or freedom is soon to occupy the serious attention of the people of Texas, & it is our earnest desire that God in his infinite mercy may incline them to adopt measures of Wisdom and justice.

"The position at present occupied by Your Excellency is one of great responsibility & importance, a right issue on this momentous question may rest

was supposed to be hostile to slavery, and to Santa Anna,[19] President of Mexico.

greatly with yourself. The eyes of the world will be upon you: expectations will be aroused which we anxiously hope may not be disappointed. Should your Excellency be enabled to conduct a peaceful revolution in Texas upon the subject of Slavery forward to a result favorable to the great cause of human freedom and human happiness, such an achievement would be worthy of more honor than a thousand victories
                    "On behalf of the Committee
                        (Signed) "THOMAS CLARKSON
"27 New Broad St London
    "Oct 6. 1843
                "(sent pr Lewis Tappan Esq.)"

(*Memorials and Petitions*, 1840–1843, pp. 230–231; this letter was published in the B. & F. A-S. *Reporter*, December 27, 1843, p. 235.)

19 "TO HIS EXCELLENCY GENERAL ANTONIO LOPES DE SANTA ANNA, President of the Republic of Mexico

"Most Excellent Sir

"Learning by the public announcement of the British Minister of Foreign Affairs, and from other sources, that an armistice has been proclaimed between the extensive Republic over which your excellency presides and the province or Republic of Texas, with a view to the opening of negociations for the conclusion of hostilities upon such terms as (*sic*) conditions as may be hereafter agreed upon; and hailing as the friends of peace the prospect of thus seeing a termination of bloodshed, and the numberless evils of war, we feel impelled at the same time by the duty which specially devolves upon us as the Committee of the British & Foreign Anti Slavery Society to avail ourselves of this opportunity (while we distinctly disclaim all political motives & influences) to press upon your Excellency with respectful urgency the consideration of the actual existence & possible extinction of personal Slavery in Texas.

"Encouraged by the noble sentiments which have been heretofore expressed by your Excellency upon the subject, and by the prompt and early rejection of the horrible system of Slavery by the entire Mexican Nation, we cannot but be confident that your excellency and the Government of Mexico will cordially coincide with us in feeling that the continuance of Slavery in Texas whether she shall be restored to her connexion, as integral portion of the Mother Country, or her independence acknowledged, will be a deplorable calamity to the human race, and thus its extinction would be a benefit conferred upon mankind of corresponding magnitude.

"The different positions occupied before the world upon this great question by the two Countries have largely contributed to enlist the sympathies of all good men, during the recent struggle on behalf of Mexico, and to arouse their just indignation against the rapacious and Slave-holding spirit of the people of Texas. From the documents issued by this Committee your Excellency will have learnt, that they have felt convinced upon the most conclusive evidence that the severance of Texas from Mexico was planned, and the means for accomplishing that object contrived within the Slave-holding portions of the United States and the annexation of the Province to that Republic ardently sought, for the express purpose of extending and augmenting the dominions of Slavery, with the hope of maintaining that system of abomination, against the encroachments of the spirit of freedom at home and of opening an unlimited outlet for their own surplus slave population on its fertile plains.

"The extinction of Slavery in Texas would assimilate the institutions of that Country with those of Mexico, thus tending to consolidate and render permanent such amicable relations as may be established by the existing negociations and while it would completely dissever the people of the former Country from their present close connexions and sympathies with the Slave

At this stage it may not be out of place to call attention to the great political detail of the Tappan and Leavitt let-

holders of the Southern States, it would tend to bring in a more virtuous law-abiding population upon whom Mexico might rely as a barrier interposed against the encroachments of the Slaveholders and their predatory attacks.

"Your Excellency will—the Committee trust, permit these allusions to well known events and tendencies in certain quarters which they have ventured to refer to, hoping that it may appear that the true policy of Mexico is not only compatable (*sic*) with, but highly favorable to the same procedure, which as the friends of oppressed humanity they wish to urge upon the Mexican Government.

"They are most deeply penetrated with the desire that no arrangements shall be made with Texas on the part of Mexico, which shall in any manner sanction the continuance of Slavery; but, on the contrary, that the present most favorable occasion should be seized to impose terms upon that Country which shall result in its immediate and total abolition. The desire of the people of Texas for peace, the comparatively unprofitable character of Slavery, especially at the present time and some existing indicatives that a conviction of the evil nature of the institution is becoming prevalent among them, encourage the hope, that it is at this moment in the power of your Excellency to secure the accomplishment of this glorious object, an achievement which all Europe would regard as conferring a more lasting honor upon your name than a thousand victories.

"The Committee therefore respectfully but earnestly address your Excellency, as the representatives of the great Anti Slavery body of this Country, that the abolition of Slavery in Texas may be peremptorally insisted on in any negociations which may be had with that Country; and that no effort be left untried to bring the people of Texas to agree to so just an arrangement. Such an arrangement would moreover be hailed with the utmost joy by all the friends of the Slave in every part of the world, not only from considerations connected with the personal liberation of those now held in bondage in Texas, but from the immense influence which it would exert upon the continuance of Slavery in the United States themselves. Instead of Texas then becoming as has been feared by the Committee and intended by the Slaveholders, a new and extended theatre for the employment of Slave labor, and for carrying on the nefarious traffic in human beings, it would as a country, enjoying free institutions, such as Mexico has proclaimed to the world, become the source of a most powerful counter-influence upon the very borders of the Slave regions, threatening the speedy downfall of the system even there.

"That such a result is greatly desired by large numbers of the most respectable and excellent citizens of the United States we are well aware—men who sympathise in no degree with the Slaveholding and Slavery propagating portion of the population, and the bare possibility that it may be secured renders Texas at the present moment however unimportant in other respects, a country of great interest to the friends of abolition.

"Trusting therefore that your Excellency may be impressed with the importance of the subject, and be enabled by the over-ruling hand of God, and in the exercise of great wisdom to produce out of the present unhappy and unpromising condition of affairs in Texas, indescribable and permanent blessings to the world.

"On behalf of the Committee
(Signed) "THOMAS CLARKSON

"27 New Broad Street
        London
    "October 6th. 1843.
        "(Sent through the medium of
                "Thomas Murphy Esq
        "The Mexican Minister)"

(*Memorials and Petitions*, 1840–1843, pp. 225–226.)

ters, a detail that indicates how the American propagandists aimed and managed to keep their British friends thoroughly well informed of all conditions at home likely to affect the cause they mutually had at heart. As a matter of fact, the British of those years, at least the philanthropists, manifested an interest in and knowledge of American life and politics such as has, from that time to this, if equalled, assuredly never been surpassed. Their means of gaining intelligence were manifold. Besides the correspondence of Tappan and Leavitt, they had that of many others. One group of them heard regularly from the Society of Friends, another from the American Colonization Society, another from the original American Anti-Slavery Society, Garrison's, the great rival of the American and Foreign Anti-Slavery Society and the body from which the Tappan brothers and their friends had seceded. Then, too, practically every British newspaper had one or more American correspondents.[20] This was true of the religious press as of the secular. George Thompson, on the occasion of his first visit to the United States, 1834–1835, supplied himself with some twenty-four hundred distinct publications on American slavery. The practice of acquiring American anti-slavery literature, if not actually begun then, was continued from that time and the Tappan letters bear unquestioned testimony to it. The solicitation for everything published was mutual. It came with earnestness and without a pause from both sides. The space it occupies in the letters under review is, for the appraiser of their value, almost discouragingly large.

[20] Some of the American newspapers had, similarly, their regular London correspondents. "J. K.," for example, contributed letters to the New York *Emancipator*, when Joshua Leavitt was the editor-in-chief, and George W. Alexander to the *National Era* of Washington City. *The Christian Times,* an English weekly, had two regular correspondents in the United States, who, differing in their own views, reflected divergent public opinions. In the issue of July 23, 1852, p. 473, the two men are thus described:

" . . . both gentlemen of standing in the estimation of the Churches there, and, as it happens, although both are hostile to slavery, yet the opinions of one as to the duties and responsibilities of Christian men in that land, in relation to slavery, are precisely opposite to those entertained by the other."

To the coastwise slave trade is accorded the initial position in the Tappan correspondence. It is the subject matter of the first letter here given and deserves, on its own
merits, a prominent place in any such discussion as the
present. The form it took, involving as it did the whole
question of the immunity of neutral commerce, the right of
search, carries us back to the origins of the War of 1812
as well as forward to the American Civil War, to the Great
War, and to the contraband liquor traffic of today. But
for the time with which we are dealing it was all important
on account of the British interest in the suppression of the
slave trade. In criticizing Britain for encroaching upon
the rights of other seafaring powers and in resenting the
arrogance implied in her well-earned title of "Mistress of
the Seas," there is a disposition to lose sight, even to ignore
consciously, the real philanthropy that lay behind the whole
movement. It was a philanthropy that cost her millions of
pounds. She retained armed cruisers on the coast of Africa and mixed commissions in places like Havana; she
sent out special agents, at no small monetary outlay, to in-
vestigate conditions on the spot and she extended her benevolent interest even to individual Africans, the expense
of whose return home she was more than willing to incur.

The difficulties in her way were by no mean wholly those
incident to the attacking of neutral flags. The famous clipper ship had come to sail the seas and against it the heavy
armed cruiser was no match in swiftness. The clipper had
a speed, a lightness of motion with which the fleetest
merchant ship afloat could not compete. And Britain was
confronted by difficulties created by the avaricious within
her own camp; for, while in many places the capital engaged
in the slave trade was largely American, considerable British was likewise employed.[21] To deal with her own un-

[21] The following editorial from *The Patriot*, July 24, 1851, p. 476,
expressed the extreme anti-slavery view relative to British connivance in
connection with the obnoxious and illegal traffic:

"We have never entertained a doubt, that the African Slave-trade might
be speedily extinguished, provided only that our Government was believed

regenerate citizens was a far harder task than might at first appear.[22]   So lucrative was the trade that its prosecution warranted a resort to every conceivable subterfuge and disguise.

Finally, there was the division in the Anti-Slavery ranks, due to the fact that the British and Foreign Anti-Slavery Society was bound by its constitution to attack the slave system by peaceful means only.[23]   As Sturge and his

to be in earnest in suppressing it. Not that we have suspected Lord Palmerston of insincerity. In and out of office, His Lordship has uniformly given every proof of his solicitude to put a stop to this accursed traffic. But it is no secret, that he has been ill suported, if not actually thwarted, by other departments of administration; and more care has certainly heretofore been taken to make the preventive service *productive*, than to render it effective.''

[22] The Zulueta Case of 1843 brought out very pointedly the extent to which British capitalists were prepared to go in order to evade the law and, secretly, to profit by the nefarious traffic. Sir George Stephen prosecuted this case and earned for himself a vote of appreciation of his philanthropic zeal taken by the B. & F. A-S. Society Committee (*Minute Books*, II, 140). Several letters that he wrote, while the trial was in progress or immediately afterwards, are of interest. Extracts from one or two are here given:

(b) ''It results from this trial that a British merchant may through the agency of a slave captain, purchase a slave ship in a British port, for a foreigner whom he knows to be a notorious slave trader, and. . . . Is there a man in England except the Jury, and the witnesses to Zulueta's character, that could lay his hand upon his heart, and say that he believes him to be innocent? or, is there one who could read the disgraceful comments of the Times & Morning Herald, after the trial, without feeling ashamed that the press of this country could in the face of decency & common sense, and in outrage of humanity, thus prostitute its influence to the gratification of their personal malice and sordid cupidity? The guilt, the horrible and murderous guilt of slave trading, is not even yet, generally appreciated in this country, or these things could not be . . .'' (Letter to John Beaumont, December 25, 1843).

(a) '' . . . The case not only brought out the fact that while 'Our efforts have not been wanting to detect the traffic on the African coast, or to expose its prevalence in foreign colonies—but we at length have it confessed that it is in our own country that the capitalists are to be found by whose instrumentality alone, this infamous traffic can be supported. . . .'

''If a clear case could be established against British subjects in our African settlements, and supported by such evidence as would ensure a conviction, I entertain little doubt of being able to bring the charge home to those merchants in this country of whom these offenders were notoriously the Agents'' (Letter to John Beaumont, December 18, 1845).

[23] It was not in its constitution only that this idea had been emphasized. At their preliminary proceedings, held at the Guildhall Coffee House, February 27, 1839, the founders of the B. & F. A-S. Society clearly stated that they had met ''to take into consideration the propriety of the formation of a Society for promoting the abolition of the Slave Trade and Slavery throughout the World by moral and religious influence, and such means only as will not

fellow Quakers became more and more convinced of the righteousness of this course of action, the philanthropists not of the Society of Friends and the British Government itself were as strongly convinced of its absolute inefficacy and were more than ever determined to use the armed cruiser to the uttermost.[24]

So vigorous was the illicit traffic that it undoubtedly broke down with ease the barriers of the United States where the coast-trade was alone legal. Charges were made that slaves were still being introduced into the States and, although Jay, and Tappan after him, strenuously denied them, they probably did so without sufficient knowledge and the suspicion once aroused was never quite allayed. In the West Indies there were various avenues by which British vigilance, even if we presume it always honestly exercised, could be circumvented. Elsewhere, the same was true of the vigilance of the cooperating American armed squadron. Concerning all the more important coastwise cases, the Tappan correspondence yields something and, with respect to the two best known, the *Amistad* and the *Creole,* it yields

directly or indirectly sanction the employment of an armed force for its prevention or suppression'' (*Minute Books,* I). So vividly did Joseph Sturge, at whose invitation they had met, remember this fact and so rigidly did he stand by it himself that he felt that no man holding opposite views had any right to take or to retain a place on its Committee. He wrote to Scoble to this effect, in 1847, when the son of the greatly revered Sir Thomas Fowell Buxton was about to be asked to serve (See letters of December 9 and 30, 1847, and November 20, 1849). Dr. Lushington had withdrawn from the Committee because he had come to disagree with it on this matter involving a fundamental principle.

[24] Lord Denman, as much a philanthropist by nature as was Sturge but not a pacifist, was the great parliamentary pleader for the retention of the African Squadron and won the day. His son, Captain Joseph Denman, was a part of the squadron and could personally testify to its effectiveness in particular instances. An American missionary on the Gaboon River, the Reverend J. Leighton Wilson, had also faith in it and wrote in its defence when he learned that a House of Commons Select Committee report was in favor of withdrawing it (Wilson, J. L., "The British Squadron on the Coast of Africa''). Mr. Hutt, the Chairman of the Committee, had had preconceived notions hostile to the squadron (See correspondence of Lord Denman with his son published in Arnould, Sir Joseph, *Memoir of Thomas, First Lord Denman, formerly Lord Chief Justice of England,* II, 253, note 13).

much. It, moreover, illustrates forcibly in connection with them the fullness and the extent of Anglo-American coöperation.

Second in our list of important subjects stands the position of the black man, fugitive slave or free, in the United States, Canada and Liberia. His position in the United States was so much one of prejudice that the American Colonization Society could make out a remarkably strong case in advocacy of his return to Africa and in England this measure was strongly, though unavailingly, suported by Dr. Hodgkin.[25] Opposition to it in England came chiefly from members of the British and Foreign Anti-Slavery Society influenced by Tappan, who was its inveterate enemy, or by memories of the unfortunate Sierra Leone experiment. And there were some who pretended to see in it a menace to British commerce, an impediment to an easy control of African resources, likewise a beginning of a colonial rivalry. To offset all objections, the British African Colonization Society was established, working to the same end as the American and, territorially, not far distant from it. Yet other opponents of the colonizing scheme were George Thompson and his friends, influenced by Garrison, who abhorred it, as did Tappan. Wherever there was opposition, it was vindictive opposition, which the presence of slaveholders within the ranks of the colonizers scarcely justified. Something was gained, no doubt, when Dr. Hodgkin discovered that to the colonization scheme the Buxton

[25] Thomas Clarkson had shown it, originally, some favor also; but, after Elliott Cresson had visited England in its behalf, he became one of its most violent opponents. On his later views, see letter of John Scoble's published in the B. & F. A-S. *Reporter,* I, 241. Dr. Hodgkin was, until the death of Cresson, his very faithful friend. Many of his letters, as well as some of his pamphlets, notably two, "On Negro Emancipation and American Colonization" and "An Inquiry into the Merits of the American Colonization Society . . . ," reveal how intensely he was prepared to advocate the removal of the Negroes from the land where so bitter a prejudice against them prevailed. James Cropper and William Allen were, from the start, convinced that the American Colonization Society was downright pernicious in its objects and its influence, and they never lost an opportunity to expose it (Allen, William, *Life and Correspondence,* III, 154).

scheme for African civilization presented points of remarkable similarity if not identity.[26] The failure of the Niger expedition was, therefore, indirectly a blow to Liberia.

In Canada the position of the black man, satisfactory at first, came to be comparable to that in the United States. This was when his numbers increased sufficiently to make segregation seem desirable. The change in feeling towards the refugee blacks was nothing if not a proof that color prejudice is inherent and is bound to force itself to the surface whenever two distinct races enter into economic competition with each other or the integrity of the superior of them be threatened. Once made apparent in Canada, it developed rapidly and plans were made for the removal of the unfortunate blacks to the West Indies where the labor demand was ever present. To those who found Canada barely tolerable Jamaica was presented as a genuine Negro paradise.

To the West Indies also were destined the blacks rescued from slavers and Earl Grey had some idea of being able to colonize there the free blacks of the United States. Some preliminary steps he took but the plan itself came to nothing. As a matter of fact, great uncertainty prevailed in the United States as to the real state of affairs in the West Indies. It was quite commonly believed that the apprenticeship system still flourished there. There was also doubt as to the disposition actually made of the Negroes rescued from slavers. With the Southern planters that disposition became a favorite point of attack for there was much reason to think that under the guise of apprentices liberated Africans were consigned to bondage. The Mixed Court was not without its traducers and Dr. Madden who, for a time, belonged to it himself made the charge that its benefits were not unalloyed since men declared free by it and allowed to remain in Cuba were soon deprived of their liberty and thenceforth adjudged to be slaves.

[26] Sir Fowell's son, however, denied most emphatically that his father had ever recognized this similarity or changed in any way his views regarding the vicious character of the Liberia project (Pennsylvania *Freeman*, February 6, 1840; New York *Emancipator*, February 13, 1840).

How to explain the Irish antipathy to the free black
so much complained of is difficult.[27]   At home the entire

[27] One of the earliest references to this subject is to be found in an address delivered by Dr. R. R. Madden before the Dublin Anti-Slavery Society.
It was published in the Dublin *Register*, February 1, 1840, and copied into the
April sixteenth issue of the New York *Emancipator*.   Madden contended, from
a presumably intimate knowledge of the writings of the Church Fathers, that
anti-slavery was the sounder doctrine and urged the Roman Catholic Church
to inculcate it among the Irish emigrating to the United States; the existing
situation in which those already there found themselves was, he claimed, most
regrettable.

The situation to which he had reference remained, however, unchanged
and is thus described in the *Anti-Slavery Advocate*, II, 301 (February 1, 1860):

"In the north the most vehement upholders of slavery are the Democratic
party, which includes a large portion of the working classes in the towns, and
nearly every individual of Irish emigration—the very class who have been all
their lives, while in their own country, complaining of tyranny and oppression,
and have looked to the United States as a haven of liberty, fraternity, and
equality.   There are very few instances known of poor Irishmen in the United
States who are not thick and thin supporters of slavery, as 'the corner stone
of the republican edifice,' whose overthrow would be the certain ruin of the
Constitution and the Union.''

Some Roman Catholic priests there were who preached abolitionism and
one at least there was who shared with Daniel O'Connell a great contempt for
America because she prated about the Declaration of Independence and its
boon of natural rights yet held human beings in bondage.   The one priest
thought of was Father Theobald Mathew, who, in conjunction with Daniel
O'Connell, and, in the name of seventy other inhabitants of Ireland, sent a
long message to their countrymen and countrywomen in the United States of
which the following is an extract:

"Slavery is the most tremendous invasion of the natural, inalienable rights
of man, and of some of the noblest gifts of God, 'life, liberty, and pursuit of
happiness.'   What a spectacle does America present to the people of the earth!
*A land of professing Christian republicans uniting their energies for the op-
pression and degradation of three millions of innocent human beings*, the
children of one common Father, who suffer the most grievous wrongs and the
utmost degradation, for no crime of their ancestors or their own!   Slavery is
a sin against God and man.   All who are not for it must be against it.   None
can be neutral. . . . We call upon you to unite with the abolitionists. . . .
Join with the abolitionists every where.   They are the only consistent advocates of liberty!   Tell every man that you do not understand liberty for the
white man, and slavery for the black man; that you are for liberty for all, of
every color, creed and country. . . . Irishmen and Irishwomen!   treat the
colored people as your equals, as brethren.   By all your memories of Ireland,
continue to love Liberty—hate Slavery—cling to the Abolitionists,—and, in
America, you will do honor to the name of Ireland'' (*The Liberator*, November 21, 1851).

Harriet Beecher Stowe was another who remarked upon the Irish indifference or hostility to Negro freedom.

"She warmly approved of the efforts of the Dublin Ladies' Anti-slavery
Society to circulate anti-slavery information amongst Irish emigrants previous

Irish population was one with the rest of the British in its anti-slavery proclivities and Roman Catholics like Daniel O'Connell and Dr. R. R. Madden were among the staunchest anti-slavery supporters. It was Madden, indeed, who argued that the cause would gain much by soliciting and securing the personal approval of the Pope. Daniel O'Connell, whose hatred of America was so intense because of what he regarded as her gross hypocrisy, memorialized his countrymen in America praying them to stand fast by the black man. This appeal was wholly without effect and Garrison charged that emancipation was seriously delayed by the Irish who broke up anti-slavery meetings and showed

to their embarkation for America; saying that this class were likely to exercise a very powerful influence, for good or evil, in the United States'' (*Anti-Slavery Advocate*, October, 1853).

The feeling of William Lloyd Garrison on this matter manifested itself in a way that was almost vindictive. It was on the occasion of an Irishman's having been whipped in the South and he said, ''I am glad they caught an Irishman; (laughter) and though I wish well to every Irishman in the world, I shall not object to their catching some more of them . . .'' (*idem*, July 2, 1860). He commented further upon the Irish lack of sympathy for the slave, upon the contrast between the native and the foreign born, and upon the indifference or contempt with which the O'Connell-Mathew address, years before, had been received:

''We have had a great deal to contend with, so far as the Irish population of our country is concerned. I have often said that if this were a fair stand-up fight between native-born Americans, we should soon settle the question. But the calamity has been that the millions who have come here from the old world in quest of homes, have been used by the Slave Power of the country to perpetuate the chains of those in bondage. . . . But it is a tremendous political and religious power exerted in one direction, and that is against the anti-slavery enterprise. A few years ago, O'Connell, Father Mathew, and seventy thousand other Irishmen, a considerable portion of them priests of the Catholic Church in Ireland, put their names to an anti-slavery address, calling upon Irishmen in this country to be true to the anti-slavery enterprise, and to regard the abolitionists as the only true friends of freedom in America. And it was received with indifference, contempt, nay, even with hostility, by the great body of Irishmen here. I am very glad, therefore, if it must be so, that through their own sufferings they are made to understand and feel what slavery is.''

To some extent the pro-slavery affiliation charged against the Irish immigrant was chargeable against immigrants from other sections of the British Isles and was explained by the fact, said the *Anti-Slavery Advocate*, October, 1852, that slavery is so intrenched in the United States that it is extremely rare to find ''emigrants from the middle classes of these countries, risking their fortunes in their adopted country by identifying themselves with the unpopular and uncompromising abolitionists.''

in yet other ways how virulent was their detestation of the Negro. The explanation was probably a fear of economic competition.

The question of remanding the fugitive slaves finds its best discussion in the Tappan letters in connection with alarm over the tenth clause of the Webster-Ashburton treaty. Against this tenth clause Tappan's suspicion was early aroused and he lost no time in communicating it to his overseas friends in whose minds it grew and strengthened. Some of the very best of the British and Foreign Anti-Slavery Society memorials were written on this subject; for the clause seemed to put into jeopardy much of what had already been accomplished and boded disaster for the future. And their insistence on its modification or complete abrogation is not to be wondered at, notwithstanding all Ashburton's attempts at reassurance. In his letters he conveyed the impression that, personally, he had no misgivings, let alone fears, as to the interpretation that would be given to the clause in America; but he was not convincing. The philanthropists, therefore, continued to give expression to their alarms and to give utterance to their indignation. Clarkson, in particular, was not to be put off and wrote on his own account to Ashburton, citing remarks of Senator Benton which revealed the fact that the dreaded interpretation had already been given to it. In replying to Clarkson, Lord Ashburton ascribed to Benton decided anti-British sentiments to which, indeed, he himself would attribute the Missourian's entire opposition to the treaty and again his lordship expressed confidence in the Americans in general.[28]

[28] Clarkson to Ashburton, February 11, 1843. To this Ashburton replied ten days later. On March eighteenth, Clarkson wrote to Scoble or to Beaumont about still further correspondence that he had had with his lordship:

"I wrote to you two days ago," said he, "and informed you I had written again to Lord Ashburton in order to shew him from Mr. Benton's speech in the Senate of the United States that our *fears had been realized*, for it was evident from thence, that the Americans had begun *in consequence* of *the new Treaty*, to turn their (?) to Canada as a Place from which their fugitive Slaves might be reclaimed and therefore to make him take a serious and active part in preventing the evils from it, which might arise, he being,

The animosity to Britain, credited to Benton, was easily believed in; for the period furnished many issues that created discord. Webster, however, was thought to be friendly and the British philanthropists reciprocated by entertaining for him a respect that was very general and very sincere.[29] Considering this, it was a little strange that

as *the author* of the Treaty *responsible* for the *miseries* it might produce. I have already had an answer from him, which my wife has copied for me, and which she has thus enabled me to send you. It contains nothing new but that Benton is not of an amiable character, but extremely prejudiced against this Country, from whence his opposition to the Treaty originated—I should suppose that Lord Ashburton, when in America got hold of his character. I think however we may infer one thing from the kindness and tenour of his Letters, which is, that his attention has been called to the Treaty so as to *create a more than ordinary Interest* in the fate *of it*, and that he will exert himself, I believe to the utmost of his Power, *in aiding us all he can* to avert the Evils of it, and to move in the House of Lords for with-drawing *the obnoxious* article *altogether*, should the Americans be found to commit outrages in using it. . . .''

Lord Ashburton's letter of the seventeenth, the enclosure referred to, was as follows:

"PICCADILLY 17th March 1843
''Sir,

''Pray accept my thanks for the communication by your obliging letter received yesterday of the further information which has reached you from America on the subject of the extradition article of my Treaty—

''I believe you attach too much importance to the opinions expressed by Mr. Benton, who in finding fault with every part of the Treaty rather proved his hostility to arise from a general dislike to whatever promoted Harmony & good feeling between the two countries. The opinion you mention of this Gentleman seems however to tend rather to the belief that the authorities in Canada would deliver up slave criminals with great caution—I have no doubt they will do so but at the same time I trust & believe that this like every other condition of the Treaty will be fairly & honestly acted upon.

''It is perfectly true that in the surrender of real criminals no distinction can or will be made with respect to colour & condition & therefore the Slave committing crime will be treated like any other person. It being always understood that acts necessarily connected with the fact of emancipation cannot be dealt with as crimes.

''I am not fearful of difficulty in the working of this provision so necessary in the general interests of humanity, but I can but repeat if by experience this should be found not to be the case, the remedy is easily at hand by the abrogation at any time of this article.

''It would give me great pleasure if we lived nearer to each other, to call on you to discuss this question more at large, feeling as I do the greatest respect for your opinions on a subject to which your zeal & enlightened good sense have for so many years been devoted. I am with great esteem, Sir
''Your very obedient Servant
''ASHBURTON.''

[29] Very early in its history, the B. & F. A-S. Society exhibited its regard for Daniel Webster. At the meeting of the Committee on July 26, 1839, it was resolved that Joseph Sturge, George Stacey, William Allen and the Secretary, J. H. Tredgold, should form a deputation to wait on Webster to explain to him the object of the newly organized society and to solicit his ''support and cooperation in the promotion of its important design'' (*Minute Books*, I).

in objecting to the one article of the treaty that touched their peculiar interests they should shut their eyes to what, under other circumstances, they would have hailed with joy; for the treaty of 1842 was felt, on both sides of the Atlantic, to have averted a war. Webster continued to command the respect of anti-slavery zealots in his attitude towards the Mexican War and the Wilmot Proviso; but he lost it, eventually, by his Seventh of March speech. The betrayal of the cause, as Tappan saw it, produced a bitter revulsion of feeling extending to the American Civil War. Tappan was unable, apparently, to appreciate the deeper meaning of the speech, and since he himself could not, it is not surprising that the British failed to do so or that they sometimes saw reason to develop conflicting views of American patriotism. To men who, seemingly devoid of all patriotic motives, could calmly urge Britain to prevent the annexation of Texas by any and all means, unionism—although they did not exactly advocate its opposite— was not the prime virtue, or its maintenance the ultimate goal of American state policy that it was to Webster, the man who had of all others most consistently argued for a unified federal state. There is abundant evidence in the Tappan correspondence of the very dangers Webster pointed out—splittings taking place everywhere. Too surely was the country dividing against itself. The ten years of grace that the Compromise of 1850 gave saw the influence of large numbers of people following in the wake of those driven thither by the Irish Famine and the German Revolution of 1848 that strengthened the man power of the North almost to the extent of the total white population of the seceding states. For these newcomers there were no states' rights. For them a divided sovereignty had no meaning. They were, from the outset, *nationalists*. To them, as to the native born Americans who grew to manhood between 1850 and 1860, the thundering orations in which Webster for a generation had clothed his pleas for nationalism became a very Bible. Had the counter doctrine

gained the day, the North separating itself in the interests
of anti-slavery and going its own road, there would have
been created two rival countries and slavery would still
have continued in the South—at least, for a period.
George Thompson, infected with the Garrison view, thought
otherwise, notwithstanding that even free Negroes like
Frederick Douglass were of the different way of thinking
and believed that even a servile insurrection would not be
possible. To understand this divergency of view, one must
never forget that British philanthropists persistently
thought of the Negro as of a white man enslaved.

The Garrison-Thompson viewpoint that, without the
economic and political support of the powerful North, the
South could neither maintain slavery nor pursue an aggressive foreign policy was presented in such a way as to
appear both plausible and reasonable and it helped to make
for that confusion of thought which made British public
opinion so peculiarly varied a thing at the outbreak of the
American War. Again let us remark that, to those who
had believed with Garrison, disunion was but the royal
road to emancipation. The amazing thing is, that the
strongest adherents of this view in England, George
Thompson and his following, comprehended the situation at
once and became immediately, like the Garrisonians themselves, loyal supporters of the Union cause.

When the economic argument for disunion is reduced
to terms of cotton, the confusion of thought in Britain is
even more understandable. The country that for so long,
in and out of season, had preached and practiced abolition
became, through her continued and ever larger use of slave-
grown American cotton, a supporter, though an unwilling
one, of the "peculiar institution" itself. Four million
British people, it is estimated, were dependent on the cotton industry and cotton became King, not only in the Southern States of the American Union, but in Great Britain as
well.[30] George Thompson's intimate acquaintance with

[30] The following press comments from the *Anti-Slavery Advocate* are indicative of this:

India made him the leading exponent of the non-slave-grown cotton doctrine just as earlier James Cropper had been of the non-slave-grown sugar and, as a consequence, the Thompson-Garrison group of abolitionists were its advocates to a far greater extent than were the Sturge-Tappan. Indeed, there is some slight evidence for the view that strong anti-slavery men such as John Bright and Richard Cobden were not able to determine to their own satisfac-

(a) Anti-slavery in England "is little more than a sentiment; and we are much disposed to agree with an opinion expressed some time since in the *Saturday Review*, that if you take an Englishman and send him abroad, deprived of those institutions and freed from those restraining influences which surround him in his native land, you make him an American—as selfish and unprincipled; as ready to trample under his feet those whom he deems to be an inferior race. The pro-slavery course of the London *Times* and the radical *Leader*, and the cotton influence which may be traced in the speeches of Messrs Cobden and Bright, and the columns of their chief organ, the *Manchester Examiner and Times*, show that motives of mere humanity have little restraining influence even in England, when political or commercial interests interfere" (January, 1859, p. 193).

The same issue, but quoting from *Household Words*, said, with reference to the 8,572,000,000 miles of cotton estimated to be spun in England each year,

"Ninety years ago, at the commencement of our manufacturing career, the population of Britain was about eight millions. Now it has reached twenty-one millions. . . . If it were not for cotton, we could not clothe them; and, if it were not for cotton, we could certainly not feed them."

Early in the century little cotton came from the United States but from thirty other countries; but "We depend now almost entirely on the United States; that is, we receive from them nine-tenths of our supply. . . . England, then, with her vast requirements, not only for prosperity and political pre-eminence, but for the very daily bread of millions of her inhabitants, is not in a better position than Ireland was before the famine; for cotton is to the English more than the potato to the Irish. We must remember that if a blight should fall on cotton like that which converted the potato-fields into a grave-yard, . . . our manufacturing and trading classes would be involved in hopeless ruin, and millions would be deprived both of work and food."

(b) In 1786, out of a total importation of 20,000,000 pounds of cotton, Barbadoes and Demerara sent us about 5,000,000. Some continued to be sent but it was of inferior quality and the question was rightly raised, *Though cotton might be widely grown*, could any *other regions compete successfully with the southern states of America?*

"But," it is said, "the spinner ought to have expected the time when slavery would come to an end, and with it the growth of cotton on the Mississippi plantations. Why should he? . . . even if insurrection, anarchy, civil war, and social disorganisation should for a time so curtail and imperil the cotton crop of America, as to induce us, and make it worth our while, to found establishments, . . . yet, as the American disturbance and confusion, however sad and serious, can with such an energetic and shifty people be only temporary, as soon as order was restored and work resumed on the plantations (however the organisation of labor might have been modified) all our artificially fostered establishments *might probably have to be abandoned*, . . . because, in a word, Alabama *can*, and Australia and Africa *cannot* send us 'fair Orleans' at six pence per lb. in any quantities,—and can make a profit by doing so" (*Anti-Slavery Advocate*, April 1, 1861).

tion whether emancipation might not eventuate in servile insurrection and the destruction of the cotton industry.

The economic alliance which had come about naturally between Great Britain and the slaveholding states of the American Union helped still further to make for confusion in British thought. It must always be borne in mind that the Republican party was not only committed to the non-extension of slavery but also to a high protective tariff policy, which, in the very nature of things, would be more or less an economic menace to the United Kingdom. The truth of this was shown in the first American tariff legislation. Because of the long drawn out anti-Corn Law agitation and its resulting enactments, free trade had become to the British as much of a creed as the cause of anti-slavery itself. They looked for universal free trade as, for years, they had looked for universal freedom. The Morrill Tariff of the United States was to them a backward step.[31]

[31] The *Anti-Slavery Advocate* printed various items of interest on this matter:

(a) ''It really looks as if the Republicans themselves were playing with disunion. Mr. Morrill's Tariff Bill could never have passed the Legislature at Washington, with any idea that the Southern States would re-unite upon its terms. It is the most bigotted, intolerant, we might almost say, furious piece of protectionist legislation that any body of short-sighted monopolists ever perpetrated. . . . To this madness of greed Abraham Lincoln, the new President, openly bows. . . . He tells his manufacturing hearers that because the carriage from foreign countries is an extra and needless cost on such articles as can be produced at equal rate at home, therefore the importation should be further discouraged by duties, not seeing or not avowing that the cost of transport is protection enough, and that if the articles which could be produced at equal rates at home and abroad are arbitrarily kept out when foreigners offer them, the home producer will soon raise his price above the natural one. . . . If he (Lincoln) knows that he is telling economical false-hood to curry favour with unjust supporters, then there is no more political honesty in the North than in the South, and the parties may be left to settle their disputes or keep them open, as may best suit their partisan knavery. Mr. Jefferson Davis on this point is far more clear and well-informed than his rival. He describes his confederates 'as agricultural people, whose chief in-terest is in the export of a commodity required in every manufacturing country,' and whose 'true policy is peace, and the freest trade which their necessities will permit.' . . . If it is intended for anything but a makeshift, in our opinion it confirms the division unalterably, and in one most important regard makes industrious Europe the friend of the seceders'' (April 1, 1861, p. 414, quoted from the *Saturday Review*).

(b) ''. . . it is not unlikely that several more of the remaining slave States will withdraw and join the Southern Confederacy. We wish they may. The more that secede the better— We wish they were all gone. If they were all gone, with their population of 11,000,000 of whites—nearly threefold the

All the foregoing would seem to justify our contention that English uncertainty, instead of being due to ignorance, was due to a multiplicity of items of knowledge. The great confusion of American opinion had been reflected in Britain and intensified there by purely British issues, interests and modes of thought—and by remoteness also. Under the circumstances, the remarkable thing is, that such men as John Bright, W. E. Forster, and George Thompson so quickly realized the true situation and so far manifested their enthusiasm in it as to take the field at once in behalf of the Northern cause.

In no aspect of the anti-slavery agitation had the earnestness of the British philanthropists more forcibly expressed itself than in the trouble that arose over the peculiar position of the American churches. The splittings that Webster deplored were in some cases occasioned because of the determined stand taken by anti-slavery men in compelling churches to declare themselves and if they were not united in opinion then to effect a schism. When missionary boards similarly circumstanced were similarly approached and refused to declare themselves a rival organization was started. A striking example of this rivalry was

population of the thirteen colonies at the time of their revolt from Great Britain in 1776—it is difficult to see how they could be compelled to come back; or if they were compelled how they could be retained to any profitable purpose in a national political or military point of view. . . . As far as we have at present the means of judging, the President and the better portion of the Northern people will not give in to Southern dictation, and if the remaining slave States withdraw, all will be well; for slavery, while standing alone, exposed to the concentrated digust, contempt, and horror of the civilized world, will be doomed to speedy extinction. The rapid advance of free cotton cultivation in other countries, and the glorious results in every sense of our own West Indian experiment, must before any great lapse of time act upon the obtuse perceptions of all classes of the Southern people. . . .

"The strange Morrill Tariff Bill that has just passed the American Congress will have the effect of a prohibition of trade with other countries, especially Great Britain and Ireland. The framers and advocates of this act, while apparently having in view the protection of Northern manufacturers, are really playing into the hands of the Southern seceders. Free trade is the direct interest and policy of the South, and if they can maintain their independent national existence, free trade they will certainly have—and not only for their own consumption, but with a view to a smuggling trade with the Northern Union, they will have prodigious imports from England which will rapidly raise the Southern ports of Charleston, New Orleans, and Mobile into places of very great commercial importance. Nakedly viewed this Tariff Bill seems one of the most foolish and retrograde steps ever taken by a great commercial people . . .'' (April 1, 1861—*editorial*).

the formation of the American Missionary Association
which became the protesting opponent of the American
Board of Commissioners for Foreign Missions, the American Home Missionary Association, and other Missionary
boards.   Tappan was its chief sponsor and its treasurer
and, in his letters, he gives interesting details of its rapid
growth, extended activities, and flourishing state.

Because of Tappan's relations with the Evangelical
group in England there came an opportunity for a new
development in his propaganda that virtually amounted to
an outlawing in England of all who were not of his way of
thinking.   This method of attack by means of social os-
tracism affected seriously several prominent ministers, the
Baptist, Dr. Belcher,[32] the Congregationalist, Dr. Chickering, and others.   The case of Dr. Chickering presented an
interesting phenomenon in social psychology.   Dr. Chickering, at his home in Maine, was evidently a neutral or non-
professing anti-slavery sympathizer.   This was in New
England but in Old England he found it to his advantage to
pose as a vigorous anti-slavery man.   His conduct was a
sort of thing that Lewis Tappan deeply resented and lost
no time in denouncing; but the championship that Dr.
Chickering found in Dr. Campbell, the editor of the British
Banner, and like Chickering, a Congregationalist, proved
that instances were possible where denominationalism
might be found immeasurably stronger than even fanatical
humanitarianism.

The organization of Lewis Tappan's propaganda permitted the sending of something like accredited representatives, furnished with regular credentials, such credentials
as Tappan was not willing to issue indiscriminately and
hesitated to issue at all when he found that his word in
the Chickering case had not accomplished altogether its

---

[32] The Reverend Doctor Joseph Belcher, an Englishman by birth, but a
Baptist minister of Philadelphia, was one of those who attacked Mrs. Stowe
and her *Uncle Tom's Cabin.* F. W. Chesson took up the cudgels against him.
For material on the case in controversy, see *The Patriot* for 1853, January 20,
p. 46; March 28, p. 199; May 2, p. 277; and July 18, p. 471.

purpose. The expense, irritation and discomfiture, even
grief, which that incident caused him made him extremely
wary of giving more than positive introductions henceforth.
The British thereafter took over more and more of the
work that Tappan had initiated, scrutinizing every visitor
that sought Christian fellowship with ministers or with
active philanthropists.

Never did Tappan's strong disposition to divide the
sheep from the goats more manifest itself than in the
stand he took in the matter of the collecting of money from
slaveholders by commissioners of the Free Kirk of Scotland. To the Moderator and Assembly of the Free Kirk
he himself protested and he urged the British and Foreign
Anti-Slavery Society to protest likewise. The result disappointed him and his disappointment was heightened when
the letter addressed by Dr. Thomas Chalmers of Glasgow
to Dr. Thomas Smyth of Charleston appeared, acknowledging the indebtedness of the Free Kirk, financial and otherwise, to America. Tappan believed that the evil effects of
such a letter would be most far-reaching and much greater
than a similar letter from an American divine of prominence would have been. America was still in a position of
intellectual dependency upon the old mother country and,
despite much American bluster and self-complacency, there
was everywhere a very great respect for, and sensitiveness
to, British opinion.

The depth of the sensitiveness revealed itself in the
reaction to the so-called Stafford House Address.[33] That

[33] "The Affectionate and Christian Address of many Thousands of the
Women of England to their Sisters, the Women of the United States of
America,

"A common origin, a common faith, and, we sincerely believe, a common
cause, urge us, at the present moment, to address you on that system of negro
slavery which still prevails so extensively, and, even under kindly-disposed
masters, with such frightful results, in many of the vast regions of the western
world.

"We will not dwell on the ordinary topics—on the progress of civilization, on the advance of freedom everywhere, on the rights and requirements
of the nineteenth century—but we appeal to you very seriously to reflect and
to ask counsel of God, how far such a state of things is in accordance with His
Holy Word, the inalienable rights of immortal souls, and the pure and merciful
spirit of the Christian religion.

"We do not shut our eyes to the difficulties, nay the dangers, that might

British ladies should presume to admonish American women for their backwardness in recognizing a moral issue hurt to the point of arousing the bitterest animosity. Most tart were some of the letters, addresses [34] and newspaper com-

beset the immediate abolition of the long-established system; we see and admit the necessity of preparation for so great an event; but in speaking of the indispensable preliminaries, we cannot be silent on those laws of your country which, in direct contravention of God's own law, 'instituted in the time of man's innocency,' deny, in effect, to the slave the sanctity of marriage, with all its joys, rights, and obligations; which separate, at the will of the master, the wife from the husband, and the children from the parents. Nor can we be silent on that awful system which, either by statute or by custom, interdicts any race of man, or any portion of the human family, education in the truths of the Gospel and the ordinances of Christianity.

"A remedy applied to these two evils alone would commence the amelioration of their sad condition. We appeal, then, to you as sisters, as wives, and as mothers, to raise your voices to your fellow-citizens, and your prayers to God, for the removal of this affliction from the Christian world. We do not say these things in a spirit of self-sufficiency, as though our nation were free from the guilt it perceives in others. We acknowledge, with grief and shame, our heavy share in this great sin. We acknowledge that our forefathers introduced, nay compelled, the adoption of slavery in those mighty colonies. We humbly confess it before Almighty God; and it is because we so deeply feel, and so unfeignedly avow, our own complicity, that we now venture to implore your aid to wipe away our common crime and our common dishonour" (*The Christian Times*, December 3, 1852, p. 769).

[34] Two only can be given here and these only in part:—

(a) "Affectionate and Christian Address of many Thousands of the Women of the United States of America to their Sisters, the Women of England,

"Sisters, your land is filled with slaves—slaves to ignorance, slaves to penury, slaves to vices

". . . The entire amount of your annual Parliamentary appropriations for the education of your people is less by thousands of pounds than the annual public expenditures made by the city of New York alone. . . . (Then follows comment upon the fact that in England one person out of every eight is a pauper; one-third of the population of the State of New York is in school, while only one-eleventh of that of England is; ten thousand people in London have never been inside a church; thousands live there in gross immorality; thousands live together unmarried and so forth).

"But, sisters, we have said enough; and we now appeal to you very seriously to reflect, and to ask counsel of God. . . . How are you discharging your duties—your peculiar duties as women of education and influence?

". . ." (*The Morning Advertiser*, January 14, 1853, p. 3).

(b) Extracts from the reputed Address of Mrs. Tyler, wife of ex-President Tyler,

". . .

"Go, my good Duchess of Sutherland, on an embassy of mercy to the poor, the stricken, the hungry, and the naked of your own land—cast in their laps the superflux of your enormous wealth; a single jewel from your hair, a single gem from your dress, would relieve many a poor woman of England who is now cold and shivering and destitute. Enter the abode of desolation and want, and cause squalid wretchedness to put on one smile of comfort, perhaps the first one which has lighted up its face for a life time. Leave it to the women of the South to alleviate the sufferings of their dependents while you take care of your own. The negro of the South lives sumptuously in comparison with the 100,000 of the white population of London. He is

ments elicited in response. The counter attack upon English labor conditions and class distinctions deflected, for a time, interest from the anti-slavery cause. Lord Shaftesbury's courteous rejoinder [35] was as balm to a wound. He

clothed warmly in winter, and has meat twice daily, without stint of bread. Moralists and dealers in fiction may artfully overdraw and give false colouring, as they are licensed to do; but be not deceived into the belief that the heart of man or woman, on this side of the Atlantic, is either more obdurate or cruel than on your own. There is no reason, then, why you should leave your fellow-subjects in misery at home in order to take your seat by the side of the black man in the plantations of America. . . . Go, and arrest the proceedings of your Admiralty. Throw your charities between poor Jack and the press-gang!

". . . if, instead of cultivating good feeling with us, she (England) chooses rather to subject us to taunt, to ridicule, to insult in its grossest form; and, above all, improperly to interfere in our domestic affairs; if she scatters her nobility among us, first to share our hospitality and then to abuse us; if what is still worse, she sends her emissaries, in the persons of members of Parliament, to stir up our people to mutiny and revolt; if, which is quite as objectionable, her public press shall incite her women—the more illustrious for birth the worse it makes the matter—to address us homilies on justice, humanity, and philanthropy, as if we had not like themselves, the advantage of civilisation and the lights of Christianity, with all the desire to cultivate relations of undying unity, the men of the United States, deriving their spirit from their mothers and their wives, may be forced into the adoption of a very different feeling with regard to Great Britain" (*The Christian Times*, February 25, 1853, p. 114).

[35] Lord Shaftesbury, who was believed to be the author of the Stafford House Address (*The Christian Times*, December 17, 1852), wrote two letters in this connection. The one, which was in response to the American Women's address, was first published in the London *Times*. It was, however, written from Genoa and dated January 20, 1853. In it, after commenting upon the fact that the evils mentioned by the Americans were more largely true twenty years earlier than then, he observed that he might recriminate but forbore to do so because "we have far different objects; we have a real regard and kindness for our brethren in the United States, and we heartily and respectfully entreat their co-operation.

"The long and the short of the case is this:—We have had, and we still have, in England many evils, but we are now doing our best to remove them. They have had, and they still have, in America a great evil, which they not only will not endeavour to remove, but they make it daily worse (witness their Fugitive Slave Law), reviling, moreover, and persecuting every one who ventures to jog their memories on things of vital importance to the temporal and eternal interests of the human race" (*The Patriot*, January 31, 1853).

The second Shaftesbury letter was written from Nice in February and was in answer to a defender of the *Fugitive Slave Law*. It was based upon Charles Sumner's Senate speech of August 26, 1852, and ended thus:

"And yet we are to be told by your (*Times*) Correspondent that this monstrous act of legislation is the bond of the Union, the basis of the compromise, the security of the Confederation, the strength of America! We will not believe it. Who, born on this side of the Atlantic, would have presumed—I say not to utter, but—to imagine such a libel on the origin and virtue of the United States? What! is the greatness of such an empire;—is the power of such

admitted the evils that the American attack condemned but pointed to the great reforms already made and in process—all indicative of a desire to get rid as soon as might be of a bad heritage from the past, whereas the Americans, contrariwise, seemed bent upon defending their bad heritage as a beneficent institution. It is well to note that Lewis Tappan, although thoroughly aware of the glaring defects [36] in the English economic and social system, defects that often made the British philanthropists appear very inconsistent and even hypocritical, was yet so ardent in his own great cause and so keenly alive to the motives behind the American attacks that he refused to have his attention, even for a moment, diverted and advised his British friends to ignore the attacks likewise.

During the twenty years of propaganda and agitation, covered by these letters, the great outstanding question, often asked and often answered was, *How can Britain help*

political and social ordinances as have produced, almost in the infancy of the nation, a marvellous succession of statesmen, patriots, warriors, poets, divines, and men of science;—is the restless spirit of enterprise among her citizens;— are their singular skill, energy, and perseverance—the true sources of their mighty dominion—all dependent upon a statute to enable the Southern slaveholder to recapture miserable girls and heart-worn victims, and force them back to the sufferings from which they had escaped?

"If this be true, which it cannot be, the sun of America will never reach its meridian" (*idem*).

[36] The defects, however, were a favorite theme of travellers and critics. Colton, in his *Four Years in Great Britain*, insisted that the characteristic vice of English society was class distinction; Dr. Baird, in addressing the Evangelical Alliance went farther and stated that a State church was much worse for morality than slavery (*The Patriot*, August 28, 1851); and yet another observer wrote thus:

"Our peculiar institution, slavery, has proved a rock of offence to many of the nobility, and from Exeter Hall and certain *salons de noblesse*, no uncertain sounds have been wafted across the Atlantic. The English noble and his imitators in other castes have also their rock of offence, perhaps equally disagreeable to American eyes; that peculiar institution called *flunkery*. Whether James in his powdered flax, and his master's new and gaudy plush, who is even ready to fall down voluntarily and lick the dust of any titled shoe, or Pompey in his wooly greased head, and the cast-off clothes of his master, who says what impertinence he pleases to massa or missus, and cares not one cent for any other niggers's of the white man, is the more respectable being in the sight of angels and men, or has the greater and better founded feeling of self-respect, with an absence of that self-degradation, I leave to the abler casuists to decide" (*The Morning Star*, June 18, 1856).

America? [37]   The help described as needed was always given

[37] H. Taylor, who gathered together a good deal of information about Jamaica and Cuba, was also interested in the United States and in ways and means of helping her. As early as October 21, 1839, he wrote on this subject to the London Committee,

". . . During my recent visit to Scotland I had an opportunity of conversing with an influential minister of the Scottish Establishment, who takes a warm and deep interest in the extinction of slavery, and upon him I pressed the expediency of endeavouring to influence the General Assembly of the Church of Scotland at its next session in May to remonstrate with the Presbyterian ministers of the United States on their criminal participation in the guilt of slavery. A favourable opportunity for doing this will I believe be afforded in a letter which I understand is to be addressed on other subjects by the Scottish Assembly to that in America. The individual alluded to cordially responded to my suggestion, and I therefore anticipate should he be supplied with sufficient information, some movement on his part toward as it seems to me so desirable an end.

"Among other modes of attacking it has occurred to me during my summer tour that public lectures in our large towns would be a very efficient one. There are many Americans travelling in different parts of the kingdom in summer. And were therefore the British public accurately informed touching the nature of slavery in the United States many a remonstrance I conceive, might be addressed to an American traveller who having his own mind awakened to enquiry on the subject might on his return communicate a similar impulse to some of his countrymen. For after all the most powerful operation in the matter is the conversion of slave-holders themselves to sounder views. And this I conceive can only be accomplished by stating the question will all imaginable fairness—that is by giving due prominence to any circumstance which may appear to be favourable to them; such as individual cases of. . . . Were Bristol and Liverpool alone the scene of such lectures great good might I think be expected; as from the steam navigation between those parts and America there is a greatly increased and very frequent intercourse between the two countries—and thus many a Southern Planter visiting our shores who will not listen to expostulation in his own country might be compelled to hear it in this land where anti-slavery advocates can speak their sentiments.''

The *Anti-Slavery Advocate*, October, 1852, thought that advantage might be taken of American sensitiveness to European opinion,

"They assert," argued it, "that their nation is ever much influenced by the deliberate opinion of the intelligent and benevolent of ours; . . . Exhortations from the various religious bodies of this country to societies of the same communion in America . . . are considered as an important mode of aiding the efforts of the abolitionists. . . . The high-toned, consistent, persevering rebuke of Europeans, and especially those of England, Ireland, and Scotland, is keenly felt there.''

Horace Greeley, present at a B. & F. A-S. Society Soirée, claimed that Britain could best help America by being determined in her own attitude resisting slavery in theory and in practice (*The Patriot*, May 22, 1851); and the Reverend E. Mathews, missionary from Wisconsin, declared that,

"The means of removing Slavery were the same as they used to get rid of intemperance, namely, by lectures, prayer, the press, and the ballot box'' (*idem*, September 8, 1851).

Yet another opinion, one expressed in an editorial on "The American Churches," was

and that most readily. It took various forms, solicited and unsolicited. Money was occasionally sent but Tappan seems never to have asked for it. Indeed, he said on one occasion that he had always been opposed on general principles to seeking funds abroad. This was in contradistinction to many other sponsors of great causes both in Europe and America. The Tappan brothers gave lavishly of their own means to anti-slavery, thus helping to establish the present American practice of large giving.

Consistent with himself throughout in the matter of seeking pecuniary assistance, Tappan was quite otherwise in other aspects of his policy. A statement of the policy, explicit or implicit, appears from time to time in the letters. In twenty years he developed politically; for, by 1855, he had arrived at the notion that the "peculiar institution" might well be interfered with, constitutionally, even within the limits of the sovereign states. How far he took this idea we cannot from the letters say; but the letters do give us an account of the formation of a much more radical body than the American and Foreign Anti-slavery Society had been and to this Tappan transferred his activities; for he felt that the mission of the old organization was almost done. The radicalism of the new seems indicative of the view that the anti-slavery opinion of the North would soon have outstripped the platform of the Republican party. The nationalism that Webster had fostered, combined with the new radicalism of the Tappan men would, within a comparatively short time, have annihilated slavery. The South, therefore, was not misled in choosing the time for its secession.

"Our British friends, with all their desire to help us in our conflict with slavery, can do more for us by taking care to civilize and elevate the emancipated population in the West Indies than in any other way!" (*The Independent*, February 15, 1855, p. 52).

Had the writer been deemed serious in this, he might have had his attention called to the noble efforts made by the Trustees of the Mico Charity, the early records of which are at Denison House, and to those made by various missionary bodies, the Baptist, the Wesleyan, the Moravian, and, even more conspicuously, the London Missionary Society.

To the American anti-slavery opinion British cooperators had contributed largely, giving help according to the suggestions many times made by Tappan and summarized by him in 1854. In the matter of the first of his suggestions practically nothing had been effected, but rather a situation, most curious, created—a situation of economic support and humanitarian attack. The hope of the production of competitive free grown cotton in Texas, Africa, India had failed to be realized much to the disappointment of economists like Adam Hodgson, propagandists, and agitators.

Only slight allusion has been made in this *Introduction* to the existence of friction among the various American anti-slavery bodies, friction that reflected itself with equal force in Britain. So influenced had the British philanthropists, in their several groups, been by the bitter partisanship of the American factions that each and every one of them had its own way of interpreting events and forecasting the future. Being outsiders they all failed, however, to appreciate the fact that even under the Garrisonian attack upon the constitution there was an instinctive love of country that was bound to assert itself in the face of grave national danger.

On the British side, too, there was a very real fear of an undisciplined democracy such as America, to their view, presented, and with which not a few individuals among them had come into contact. And it was not alone that these British philanthropists thought America destitute of a national morality, but they, as practical business men, anticipated her becoming a definite menace to the dearest of British interests. John Bright [88] with clearer vision

[88] Whether it was that he saw with clearer vision or was more tactful, more politic, more of an opportunist one can scarcely say. The abolitionists were not always very sure of him. On one occasion, in 1853, he covertly criticized them and was, by them, well reprimanded. The *Anti-Slavery Advocate* of February, 1853, is our authority for the whole affair. It quoted Bright's criticism from the *Times*.

"'I am for viewing the institutions and course of America with a vigilant but friendly eye. I would copy, as far as I could, all that is good in that

could see an America purged of slavery—a strong moral force.

Of some of the writers of the letters we publish and of the recipients of them, a few concluding remarks may be made. Out of the obscurity in which they had been left because of the brilliance surrounding others, more fortunate in the possession of biographers, we have taken several of the loyal anti-slavery workers of the last century.[39] Although memories of them be held sacred at Devonshire House [40] or at

country, and if there is *anything I thought evil*, I would remark upon it with regret, but in the *most friendly spirit;* and the very last thing I would attempt to utter, would be *any comment* that should have a *tendency to irritate the people* of that country.'

"So spoke the champion of the spinning jenny at Manchester, on Friday last. When Kossuth was in Manchester, and John Bright was selected to give the Hungarian exile a welcome to the head quarters of slave grown cotton, he did not deem it necessary to comment 'in the most friendly spirit' upon the conduct of Austria and the exploits of Haynau. John Bright's Christianity is a commercial one. The marginal notes of his Bible are to the prices of yarn, and the prospects of the cotton crop. . . . If a professed democrat and a Quaker, will thus launch a rebuke against the abolitionists of this country . . . we cannot be surprised at the sneers of the *Times* and the invectives of Cass.''

On the doctrine of secession, John Bright expressed himself more wisely.

"If the thirty-three or thirty-four States in the Union can separate whenever they like, I cannot see anything but disaster and confusion throughout the whole of that continent. I say that the war, be it successful or not, be it Christian or not, be it wise or not, is a war to sustain the government and to sustain the unity of a great nation; and I say that the people of England, if they are true to their own sympathies, and to their own country, and to their own great act of 1834, to which reference has already been made, will have no sympathy with those who wish to build up a great empire on the perpetual bondage of millions of their fellow-men'' (*Anti-Slavery Advocate*, September 2, 1861, p. 458).

[39] It is not only the less prominent of the anti-slavery men who have suffered for lack of biographers or of the right kind of biographers. Zachary Macaulay, George Thompson and even the great Clarkson himself are among those to whom history has done scant justice. The life of Wilberforce was written by his sons, sympathetically, and while the records were still full. The Buxton family has kept Sir Fowell's memory green by following in his footsteps and devoting time and thought to the same high calling. Would that there were more biographers like Coupland to appraise rightly the deeds of national heroes or to rescue, as the Hammonds and Mr. Bready have lately done, the character of men like Lord Shaftesbury from interpretations, false or prejudiced.

[40] Until this year, 1926, *Devonshire House* was synonymous with the headquarters of the Society of Friends in London. The Society has now its own building, in the Euston Road, where its library is and its records are. The condition of the inadequately-ventilated vaults obliged those in charge to

Denison,[41] there is not a great deal of biographical data to be obtained regarding many of those who, in their day, gave unsparingly of energy, of time, and of means that their fellow men of a different colour might be free. Many of them have found no place in the *Dictionary of National Biography,* notwithstanding the fact that the work they did and that their successors are still doing ranks among the greatest of British achievements. Without the help of men like Tredgold, Hinton, Stacey, Bolton, and Beaumont—to mention only a few of the many and those the even less well known—the great abolitionists like Wilberforce, Clarkson, Macaulay and Buxton would have found their task too great for human accomplishment. To George W. Alexander, a banker and the Treasurer of the British and Foreign Anti-Slavery Society, to John Scoble, its Secretary, to James Stephen and his son, Sir George, to John Hodgkin, father of the renowned historian, one Thomas, and younger brother of that truly noble physician, another, to John Candler, to William Allen, to Dr. Stephen Lushington and to his brother Charles, as well as to the Gurney [42] brothers and to the Forsters, father, son and brother belongs a meed of praise that full appreciation of their work, and worth makes unstinted. George Thompson and his son-in-law, F. W. Chesson, Charles Stuart, and Dr. R. R. Madden are instances of men who though they could not be ignored in the day of their labours, have been, comparatively speaking, strangely forgotten since and the amount of their literary contribution to the great cause left entirely unestimated. Were we to depend for our knowledge of Joseph Sturge upon Richard's *Memoirs* and Hobhouse's biography

refuse access for research purposes when this study was under way. The editors had hoped to find among the old Devonshire House archives additional materials relative to the many Quakers whose names and deeds are here mentioned.

41 In *Denison House,* in the Vauxhall Bridge Road, are the present offices of the still gloriously active British *Anti-Slavery* and *Aborigines' Protection Society.*

42 Joseph Sturge once wrote that it was upon the Gurney family circle that the B. & F. A-S. Society most depended for pecuniary support.

alone, that knowledge would be most inadequate. To supplement what the biographers give is difficult; because so many of his letters have disappeared; but contemporary newspapers, periodicals, and private journals are teeming with references to him. His was the driving force of the great machine.[43]

Among the Americans there were, likewise, great figures and some of them have been almost forgotten. John Greenleaf Whittier, the poet, is widely known; but Whittier, the editor of the Pennsylvania *Freeman,* the anti-slavery propagandist, the writer of splendid political essays like that on Daniel O'Connell [44] is not. Any memory that there may be of Judge William Jay [45] is lost in the greater memory of his distinguished father. In addition, William Goodell,[46] the jurist, S. S. Jocelyn, Joshua Leavitt, and Amos A. Phelps were conspicuous in the anti-slavery crusade as were Garrison and Birney and the Tappans. Lewis Tappan has been overshadowed by his brother, whom he himself made the more famous of the two. Contemporaries, however, seem to have known the brothers as they really were and to have regarded Lewis, as J. B. Estlin did, as the "prime mover and principal member" of the American and Foreign Anti-Slavery Society.[47]

The Tappans of Northampton, that town of western Massachusetts that is yet redolent with memories of Jonathan Edwards and of his cousin, Joseph Hawley,[48] were of a rather remarkable family. Their mother was a grand-

---

[43] For an adverse criticism of Sturge because of his hostility towards the American Anti-Slavery Society, see *Anti-Slavery Advocate,* June, 1859, p. 238. He was said even to have been a serious hindrance to the development of anti-slavery help for America in England.

[44] Published in the *Emancipator,* April 23, 1840.

[45] For an appreciation of Judge Jay, see *Anti-Slavery Advocate,* December, 1858, p. 187.

[46] See *In Memorian-William Goodell,* 1878, for an account of his last years and an estimate of his services to the anti-slavery cause.

[47] *A brief Notice of American Slavery and the Abolition Movement.*

[48] One of the well-nigh forgotten worthies of the pre-revolutionary period of American History until Miss Mary Clune, while a graduate student at Smith College, rescued him.

daughter of Benjamin Franklin's sister Mary [49] and they themselves, Arthur and Lewis, were two out of seven sons in a group of eleven children, but they were not the only ones who attained prominence in a business or a national way. Their brother Benjamin, for instance, was a United States Senator from Ohio and, subsequently, Associate Justice of the United States Supreme Court. Lewis Tappan like his brother John was a business man in Boston as Arthur was in New York. Later on, he joined Arthur and, henceforth, was more closely identified with New York than with Boston, although he remained essentially a New Englander. Arthur Tappan had, early in his career as a philanthropist, united himself with the American Colonization Society and, when a branch of the same was projected in Massachusetts, Lewis was inclined to follow suit; but both he and Webster, who was chairman of the organization meeting, became convinced that it was but a device for ridding the country of free blacks for the benefit and convenience of slaveholders and withdrew forthwith, never again to endorse it.[50] His connection with the American Anti-Slavery Society was of longer duration and, although he and Phelps were regarded by some as dissentient spirits,[51] they really parted company with it only when it had come to associate with anti-slavery other issues like woman's rights and to take on the character of what seemed to the evangelicals a non-religious or almost atheistic body. With the men who were to be the founders of the British and Foreign Anti-Slavery Society Garrison, in the early thirties, was intimate and friendly; but he was repudiated by them, later on, for the selfsame reasons that he and the Tappans became estranged.[52] The

[49] Tappan, Lewis, *Memoir of Mrs. Sarah Tappan*, p. 10.

[50] Bowen, Clarence W., *Arthur and Lewis Tappan*.

[51] American Anti-Slavery Society, *Annual Report*, 1840, p. 73.

[52] Although several of the British philanthropists who came to form the B. & F. A-S. Society, notably T. F. Buxton, Joseph Sturge, and John Scoble, had been personally friendly with Garrison, they were very much more in accord, intellectually and temperamentally, with his subsequent opponents. With the ideas here quoted, attributed to Judge Jay and to Whittier as their reasons for participating in the secession movement of the late thirties, they were in deepest sympathy,

two societies with which we are most concerned in this publication were first, last and always fundamentally, religious. Their anti-slavery creed was, perhaps, never more vigorously and eloquently formulated than by the following from the pen of John Quincy Adams:

"The extinction of *Slavery* from the face of the earth is a problem, moral, political, religious, which at this moment rocks the foundations of human society throughout the regions of civilized man. It is, indeed, nothing more nor less than the consummation of the Christian religion. It is only as *immortal* beings that all mankind can in any sense be said to be born equal; and when the Declaration of Independence affirms as a self-evident truth that all *men* are born equal, it is precisely the same as if the affirmation had been that all men are born with immortal souls. For take away from man his soul, the immortal spirit that is within him, and he would be a mere tameable beast of the field, and like others of his kind would become the property of his tamer. Hence it is, too, that by the law of nature and of God man can never be made the property of man. And herein consists the fallacy with which the holders of slaves often delude themselves, by assuming that the test of property is human law. The soul of one man cannot by human law be made the property of another. The owner of a slave is the owner of a living corpse; but he is not the owner of a man." [53]

ANNE HELOISE ABEL

AND

FRANK J. KLINGBERG.

"Persuaded as I am," wrote Jay, "that the society under its present control is exerting an influence adverse to domestic order and happiness, inconsistent with the precepts of the Gospel, and exceedingly injurious to the anti-slavery cause, I deem it my duty to request you to erase my name from the roll of its members" (Tappan, *Life of Arthur Tappan*, p. 306),

and Whittier, in a letter to the Reverend Joshua Leavitt, June 6, 1840, regretted thus:

"The original cause of the difficulty—a disposition to engraft foreign questions upon the single stock of immediate emancipation, I early discovered, and labored to the extent of my ability to counteract" (*idem*).

[53] Letter from John Quincy Adams to Asa Walker, C. A. Stackpole, and F. M. Sabine, Esqs., of Bangor and vicinity, dated July 4, 1843 (B. &. F. A-S. *Reporter*, September 20, 1843, pp. 169–170).

THE TAPPAN PAPERS

(Copy)[1]

"New York July 5th 1839.

"To

"Joseph Sturge Esqr.[2]

"Honored Friend,

"In the absence of our corresponding Secretaries,[3] Birney & Stanton it falls on me to convey to you the gratification caused to our Committee by your letter of the 6th Ult received here by the Liverpool on the Ist Inst.

"It would be very gratifying indeed could some of us be spared to participate in the exercises of the 1st of August at Birmingham. There is excitement in the very idea. But as we are situated it seems impracticable.

"The labour of renewing our armament of Agents, the intense efforts and labour required to row against all these winds and storms, the preparation for the approaching national convention at Albany, and the fewness of the hands to do all this, forbid our sparing any one at this time.—especially as it seems quite desirable that who ever goes should be very intimately conversant with all our views. It is not certain that we shall be able to send as we could wish, even in the Autumn. The Committee have expressed a desire that I should be one of the deputation and I fear my family

---

[1] The letters at Denison House that were originally intended for others than those who, like Tredgold, Scoble, Soul, were regularly attached to the B. & F. A-S. Society office force, are almost invariably copies only.

[2] Sturge was not Leavitt's only English correspondent. In the *Emancipator*, which he edited, are to be found letters from a man who signed himself, "J. K." Their frequency is indicated thus: In the issue of December 12, 1839, there is one letter, in that of December 26, there are two, in that of March 5, 1840, one, and so on. In the issue of January 16, 1840, is a letter from the Reverend John Clarke, a Baptist missionary from Jamaica, then in London; and in that of the January 23, one from Thomas Harvey, dated at Leeds, December, 1838, a rather important letter, apprising Leavitt of the fact that some Americans create prejudice in England against abolitionists by calling them "fanatics."

[3] James Gillespie Birney and Henry B. Stanton.

and other circumstances will detain me until the Spring of 1840. In the mean time we shall rely with much confidence on the wisdom and fidelity of our brethren the Committee in London, to correspond with philanthropists of the continent of Europe and also with the West Indies and make all other needful preparations for the occasion.

"I highly approve of your view, that Slavery is the parent of the Slave trade, and the *guilty* cause of all its evils. Thos. Fowell Buxton has given [4] a most appalling view of the Slave trade, but has come entirely short of the exigency in proposing a remedy.[5] He

[4] Buxton, Thomas Fowell, *The African Slave Trade and Its Remedy.*

[5] The remedy was, of course, all that was hoped for from *The Society for the Extinction of the Slave Trade and the Civilization of Africa.* This, usually designated as "Buxton's plan" was decried by Sturge and Scoble and others of the B. & F. A.-S. Society; but very much approved of by others, among whom, as we learn from Scoble's letters, were Sir George Stephen and Captain Stuart. It was the military aspect of the plan to which many of the Quakers objected and they objected, not from a fractious spirit but from conscientious scruples. From the following letter, it is to be inferred that Samuel Gurney, to whom all acrimonious discussions were distasteful, was not of the number,

"LEAMINGTON—11 mo 11 1840

"Dear Friend

"In the remarks I made to Joseph Sturge I was entirely ignorant that they applied to thee—they were made under no other desire than that the advocates of the great cause of the abolition of slavery & slave trade, being united as in one heart in the object should abstain from all detraction of each others plans. I undoubtedly differ from thee in respect of the operations of the African Civilization Society— I esteem them very highly as bearing directly upon a great question. Notwithstanding this difference I hail all honest steady abolitionists as my friends & brothers amongst whom I cordially include thyself.

"I also esteem highly the objects of the British & Foreign Anti-Slavery Society and although I sometimes feel agrieved (*sic*) if not a little nettled at the conduct of some of its members towards the other Society and which I greatly disapprove yet I shall hardly debar myself from the privilege of contributing to its funds.

"Most heartily desiring thy labours in this great cause may experience the blessing of the most high I subscribe myself with much sincerity as thy Friend & Brother in this great cause

"Saml Gurney"

It was a cause for regret and criticism with many people that the British and Foreign Anti-Slavery Society Committee abstained for so long from declaring its opinion of the African Civilization Society, officially. William Leatham was one who would have preferred that a definite stand should be taken. He himself approved of the plan and wrote to Scoble, 12 mo. 16, 1840 that if he were to be forced to decide between the British and Foreign Anti-Slavery Society and Buxton, he would probably adhere to Buxton,

"I shall lament," wrote he, "over being driven to any act that may endanger this sacred cause by what appear to be hardly fair, and to say the least of it, uncharitable conduct towards our eminent, the most eminent Brother in the cause. . . ."

first shows that the Slave trade has annihilated legitimate commerce in Africa, and then he proposes to make legitimate commerce annihilate the Slave trade.

"I wish your Lushingtons, Buxtons, Broughams, O'Connells,[6] Eardley Wilmots and other statemen who feel that the British Nation has a call in Providence to care for bleeding human nature would turn their thoughts to the simple idea developed in your letter and confirmed by Buxton's book; that it is idle to think of suppressing the Slave trade, while Slavery continues to make it profitable, and then let them urge the Government to direct their efforts and shape their diplomatic and commercial arrangements against Slavery itself, wherever it exists, that is the only way and whatever right the Laws of Nations give to a Government in regard to Slave trading, must be equally valid with regard to Slavery. Great Britain cannot enjoy her rightful commercial advantages in Africa, as long as Spain, Portugal, Brazil and the United States hold slaves. She cannot protect her West Indian subjects from the liability of being kidnapped. Her coloured seamen and other subjects, coming in her ships to the port of Cuba or of the United States are at once treated like felons, and imprisoned, and if by any oversight left in prison, are sold as slaves.

"Why should she be at all this immense expenditure of wealth and life on the Coast of Africa, when she has it in her power to coerce every Slave trading power but the United States to abolish Slavery, and thus annihilate the Market?

"I hope your friends in Parliament will sift Lord Palmerton's concessions to Mr. Stevenson[7] with regard to the Slaves shipwrecked on the Bahamas, also keep a good look out with regard to Texas and Cuba.

[6] Not all connected with the Anti-Slavery cause in Britain were proud or even tolerant of association with men like Brougham and O'Connell. E. Bickersteth, writing from Walton Rectory, Ware, May 20, 1835, to the Secretary of the London Anti-Slavery Society then in existence, the predecessor of the B. & F. A-S. Society said,

"I have been, I believe, almost from the beginning a member of the Anti-Slavery Society though I have always regretted the union with men of the avowed principles of Lord Brougham & Mr. O'Connell. . . .
"The object of the Society I consider to be most truly Christian & benevolent; but the course of public events has more deeply than ever impressed upon my mind the importance of attention to the plain Christian principle, 'Be not unequally yoked with unbelievers.' The Committee having therefore chosen to call Lord Brougham & Mr. O'Connell to take so leading a part in the proceedings of its Anniversary, I must beg them to withdraw my name from the members of an Institution so completely under such influence."
[7] Andrew Stevenson.

printed in season to send by this opportunity instead of taxing you with the postage of the original.

"Mess[rs] Andrews & Bullard visited the Buzzard, & saw her prizes. I sent an artist down the harbour, and he has made a beautiful drawing of the vessels. Fitzgerald was arrested the other day by a man whom he had employed to get one of the prizes afloat, and who failed in accomplishing it. It was a mortifying thing to us. Capt. F. told me the Spanish minister, he might have intended Consul, had intimated to him that although he felt much esteem for him it would be agreeable to him not to receive any recognition from Capt. F. as they went to and fro from Staten Island to this city, frequently, alleging that public opinion was such here among Spaniards &c., that it would not do for him to be known to be on sociable terms with the commander *of the Buzzard!* Capt. F. appears to be a meritorious officer, & has I believe, acquitted himself so as to do honor to himself and his country since his Brig has been in our waters. He expects to sail in a few days, with his prizes as this Gov[t] will not receive them.

"I have received a farewell letter from Mr Andrews dated Boston Oct. 15, written just as he was on the point of sailing for New Orleans. He thinks it his duty to return to Texas forthwith, but says it is possible he might go to Cuba sometime in the winter. I did not hand him your letter to Dr. Madden.[12] Why cannot this

Lewis Tappan and under the editorship of William Goodell. (Tuckerman, Bayard, *William Jay and the Constitutional Movement for the Abolition of Slavery*, p. 40). After the secession, however, of the Tappans and others from the old American Anti-Slavery Society, that Society held that the paper had originally belonged to it and, at its annual meeting in 1840, passed the following resolution:

"Resolved, That we consider the New York City Anti-Slavery Society are, under the peculiar circumstances of the case, morally and honorably bound to re-transfer the Emancipator to this Society . . . " (*Seventh Annual Report*, p. 15).

[12] Richard Robert Madden (1798–1886), an Irishman of the Roman Catholic faith, a doctor of medicine, and an author of considerable repute in his own day. Between 1824 and 1827, he travelled extensively in the Levant and, in 1833, went out to Jamaica, preparatory to taking office there as one of the special magistrates, under the Marquis of Sligo, Governor, appointed to administer the British *Emancipation Act*, which was to go into effect in August, 1834. Difficulties connected with the working of the apprenticeship system brought him into collision with the planters of Kingston and, in consequence, he resigned his magistracy in November, 1834 (*Dictionary of National Biography*). *En route* for England, he visited the United States and

gentleman obtain all the information you desire from Cuba? If made himself somewhat acquainted with conditions there, incident to slavery. In 1836, he was appointed judge arbitrator in the Mixed Court of Commission at Havana and continued about three years in Cuba, "first as a commissioner of the Mixed Court, and second as H. B. M. Superintendent of Liberated Africans" (New York *Emancipator*, November 7, 1839, p. 110; The B. & F. A-S. *Reporter*, I, p. 3).

Of his connection with the Amistad Case, he himself gives us the origin. He was about to leave for England "when I ascertained that the trial was about to take place of upwards of forty individuals charged with murder and piracy, as Cuban slaves, whom I knew to be Bozal Africans recently introduced into Cuba, and therefore illegally held in slavery there— I determined to proceed to America at once, and give on their trial the only evidence which I supposed could be procured for them, with respect to that important fact. In taking this step I encountered some opposition, and assurance of disapproval of it, on the part of my superiors. I felt, however, that I had a duty to perform, and a right to expect it would be approved by the Secretary of State for the Colonies. In that expectation I was not disappointed . . ." (*Memoirs*, etc. *of Richard Robert Madden*, edited by his son, Thomas More Madden [1891], pp. 82–83).

Soon after his return home, which was in time to take part in the Special Meeting of the British and Foreign Anti-Slavery Society Committee, January 17, 1840 (*Minute Books*, I), he was sent to Egypt and, later, in 1841, to the West Coast of Africa, there to institute a special inquiry into the administration of the British settlements.

In March, 1843, he announced the necessity of severing his official connection with the anti-slavery cause (*Minute Books*, II, 53), ostensibly because of his intention to proceed to Portugal as a newspaper correspondent in Lisbon. The Committee expressed its regret and took steps to record formally its appreciation of his services and, particularly, of his West African. At the Committee meeting, March 31, 1843, he was cordially invited to maintain an official connection by becoming an Honorary Corresponding Member (*idem*, p. 61) and, at that of April 28, 1843, it was decided that he "be especially invited to be a Delegate to attend the next Anti-Slavery Convention (*idem*, p. 72).

In 1847, Dr. Madden was again in British employ, having been appointed to a post in Western Australia, which included that of *Protector of Aborigines*. It was in the year of this appointment that he wrote the letter, to which incidental reference has been made in the *Introduction*, advising an enlistment of the sympathy and help of the Pope in the cause of anti-slavery (Letter to the British and Foreign Anti-Slavery Society Committee, April 10, 1847). Between 1850 and 1880, he was Secretary to the Loan Fund Board at Dublin Castle.

Of the writings of Dr. Madden, published and unpublished, the following, relative to slavery and emancipation, additional to some elsewhere noted, are of particular interest:

Letter to R. W. Hay, March 14, 1835, on the Working of the Abolition of Slavery in the West Indies.

Mr Andrews should go he will only want his expenses paid. You can write what you think about it, & if, on further consideration you authorize it I will write to Mr. A. via New Orleans. If he goes to Cuba it must be incognito. I showed yr last letter to me to Mr A.—

Mr Andrews writes, "Mr. Sturge speaks of the *Abolition party* "in Texas & I may have led him into the error of supposing that "such a party exists by saying that there would, upon a favorable "opp^y for expressing such views effectively, be many individuals "to take the side of freedom. It must not however be understood "that there is at this moment any party or even individuals who, "with present prospects, are willing to hazard the attempt openly "to advocate abolition. I spoke of an undercurrent of feeling, "such as is expressed in private & confidential conversation, and "which would find its way to the public if any occurrence (such "as the interference of England) should render the discussion "inevitable. But too much dependence must not be placed upon "co-operation at home in the first instance. There is no country "more destitute of moral principle. The feeling that there is "against Slavery is mostly based upon interest. Of course it has "not the boldness and disregard of personal consequences requisite "for leading in great enterprises. The grounds of hope are the "weakness of Texas, particularly as respects money capital and "resources. Her anxiety to increase her population, the capacity "of G. B. to supply these wants, the possibility of making it her "interest to abolish slavery, or of convincing her that it is already "so, by opening an avenue for discussing the subject, on the ground. "Perhaps a good deal might be effected by sending out a pretty "full diplomatic representation to consist of persons of high rank "or character to treat expressly on the subject of abolition. In "this way the discussion of the advantages & disadvantages of "slavery to Texas would commence under the protection of the

Letter of July 19, 1835, on Lord Sligo's Injustice to Dr. Palmer and Dr} Chamberlain, Stipendiary Magistrates.

Letter to W. E. Channing, D. D., on the Subject of the Abuse of the Flag of the United States in the Island of Cuba, and the Advantage taken of it Protection in Promoting the Slave Trade, 1839.

A Twelvemonth's Residence in the West Indies during the Transition from Slavery to Apprenticeship (2 vols., 1835).

Address on Slavery in Cuba, presented to the General Anti-Slavery Convention, London, 1840; The Island of Cuba: Its Resources, Progress and Prospects, London, 1849.

"British flag—would find its way into the public prints and at all
"events break the dead silence which it is the policy of all slaveites
"to preserve. My plan is for the British nation to buy up Texas,
"which I think she can do, and would do if she should perceive
"the immense importance of the move. Let her lavish money upon
"the undertaking for she can never take a step so directly tending
"to the extinction of slavery, and the slave trade throughout the
"world. What I mean by buying is, that she shall, in some way,
"and at all cost, make it most obviously the interest of Texas to
"abolish slavery."

"Yesterday we had Ruiz & Montez, the two Spaniards of the
Amistad arrested, and not choosing to give bail they are now in
prison. They are arrested at the suits of some of the captured
Africans for assault & battery, and false imprisonment. The pro-
slavery press, and the Southern slaveholders now here, are greatly
exasperated & I doubt not it will exasperate the tyrants & their
abettors throughout the country. But we shall try the question
in our courts, & see if a man, although he is black, cannot have
justice done him here.

"Ever your's
"LEWIS TAPPAN."

Duplicate

"NEW YORK, Dec 10, 1839.

"JOHN SCOBLE, LONDON
"My dear Friend,

"Your esteemed favor of 11th Nov. was received
on the 6th inst.

"...

"Mr. Leavitt went to Hartford [13] to attend the trial of the
Africans for the Amistad, & a large number of persons attended
the court. As Dr. Madden attended as a witness [14] he will be

---

[13] *The Emancipator*, November 28, 1839, pp. 122–123.

[14] "It was the intention of Dr. Madden to proceed to England immediately,
but the counsel for the captured Africans of the Amistad have advised to his
remaining to attend the District Court on the 19th inst., as a witness, to which
he has cheerfully consented. . . .

"Dr. Madden says that the negroes brought here in the Amistad were
Bozal negroes, that is recently imported; that they were purchased by Montez
and Ruez at the Baracoon, or public receptacle and slave market for Bozal
negroes; that Ruez bought on account of his uncle, Saturnino Carrias, a merchant of Puerto princepe; that they were bought, *not for any estate of his,
but for sale at that place;* that these Africans were sold on account of Peter
Martinez, a nortorious slave-importer at the Havana, and had been recently
landed from one of his slavers, . . ." (*idem*, November 7, 1839).

able to give you all the particulars. He sailed hence for England a few weeks ago. The trial was postponed to 7th Jan[y] owing to the illness of James Covey the African lad, who speaks the English language and whom Cap[t] Fitzgerald [15] of H. B. M. Brig Buzzard kindly consented to send to New Haven to act as interpreter. The Spaniards did not appear even by counsel. Montez had previously departed for Cuba and Ruiz remained in prison.[16] Some one asked him why he lay in jail—he replied—'it is a national matter.' He expects to excite sympathy & to embroil this Government with Spain in consequence of one of the liege subjects of Her Catholic Majesty being incarcerated in prison merely for stealing half a hundred men and women! I blush to tell you that the U. S. District Attorney appeared as counsel for the Spanish minister by order of this government! ! And filed a libel on behalf of the minister who had made a formal claim for the Africans. It happened that a Cap[t] Green also filed a claim alleging that *he* captured the Africans ashore, on Long Island, previous to their capture by the officers of

Dr. Madden sailed on the twenty-fifth of November "leaving his deposition . . . in the Court of Common Pleas in this city. The substance (from the *New York Commercial Advertiser*) will be found in another column. Doctor Madden has visited Washington, and laid before the President of the United States, and the British Minister, important testimony with regard to the captured Africans, and the iniquitous proceedings in the island of Cuba . . ." (*idem*, November 28, 1839, p. 122).

In the Madden *Memoirs* (pp. 95–97) is given a fairly detailed account of an earlier visit to Washington, on which occasion the Doctor discussed with President Jackson—in whom he recognized great social graces—the results of emancipation in the British West Indies, Old Hickory appearing much interested. The following is from Dr. Madden's own account of what passed between them:

". . . 'The sooner, General, you adopt a similar measure in the United States the better. It would be a fitting finale of a great career like yours to connect it with such an act of emancipation.' The President burst out laughing, and addressing his guest on either side, said, 'This gentleman has just come from the West Indies, where the British have been emancipating their slaves. He recommends me to make myself famous by following their example. Come here, Donaldson (turning round to his private secretary), put the poker in the fire, bring in a barrel of gunpowder, and when I am placed on it give the red poker to the Doctor, and he will make me famous in the twinkling of an eye.' . . ."

[15] Dr. Madden carried with him to England a letter from Birney to John H. Tredgold, transmitting the resolutions, commendatory of the conduct of Lieutenant Fitzgerald, which had been passed November 6, 1839, by the Executive Committee of the American Anti-Slavery Society.

[16] In the *Emancipator*, November 21, 1839, is an interesting editorial on the Amistad Spaniards and Judge Inglis, who authorized the discharge of Montez and Ruiz on their filing common bail.

the U. S. brig Washington. Thus he is opposed to Lieut. Gedney. It is well that it is so, for Lieut. G. has manifested a willingness to withdraw his libel should it be any obstacle to the action of this Gov*. in surrendering the Africans to the Spanish authorities. Should Gedney's libel & the libel filed by the District Attorney be withdrawn (and there be no other libel) the Africans would be delivered over to the Executive of this country—but Capt. Green will not withdraw his libel & therefore the poor foreigners cannot be taken out of the jurisdiction of the court unless it be done by some monstrous act of usurpation. We hardly think our Government will attempt it. Still they may, & we should be prepared for it. I hope your Gov*. will interpose.

"Some of our enlightened lawyers think the act of seizure by the U. S. brig Washington was an illegal act. The trial comes on 7 Jan*.

"Great efforts are making to form an abolition political party in this country. You will (see) the question is discussed, pro and con, in the Emancipator.[17] The number of abolitionists is now so large here, and their views on many points of policy so various, that it will be impossible, I think, to have them united long. In fact they are disunited already. There will probably be an abolition political party—a religious association—a Garrison party, &c, &c. We shall, I hope & pray, get along without quarrelling, for it will be a sad sight to witness the friends of human rights contending *angrily* among themselves.

"I hope you will send me any excellent pamphlet or book that may be published respecting the great cause in which you are engaged, with a memo. of the cost, & I will repay you. If there is a small work on the West Indies, giving statistics, history &c I should be glad to have it.

"I have been reading, with delight, George Thompson's splendid Lectures at Manchester.[18] I wish we had a man of his peculiar power in this country.

[17] In *The Emancipator*, November 21, 1839, this matter is opened up by reference to Lewis Tappan's recent letter on political action. In the issue of December 5, 1839, are Whittier's remarks upon the same as quoted from the Pennsylvania *Freeman* and a letter from Gerrit Smith to William Goodell, of date, November 12, 1839, quoted from Goodell's paper, *The Friend of Man*. Whittier was seemingly pretty much in agreement with Tappan in deprecating the formation of a political party by abolitionists. In *The Emancipator* of December 12, 1839, was published the letter on the subject written by Lewis Tappan to J. G. Birney on the sixth with Birney's reply of the ninth.

[18] Thompson, George, *Lectures on British India*, Delivered in the Friends' Meeting House, Manchester, England, in October, 1839. With a Preface by

"The financial difficulties of this country press with great severity upon the anti-slavery cause. We can hardly keep our press going & have been compelled to withdraw most of our lecturers. We have difficulties also with the State Societies who wish to controul anti-slavery matters in their geographical limits, & do not like to have the Parent Institution send agents to collect money.[19] We have notified a meeting of the American Anti-Slavery Society to be held in this city Jan 15th & shall endeavor to arrange all these difficulties, & hope that the State Societies will not drive us to withdraw from that Society & establish an independent Board to carry on the enterprise, so far as we can, as a moral and religious point of View. I have sometimes thot such a Board would do much good however. We have in the press an Anti-Slavery Hymn Book compiled by Rev. E. F. Hatfield [20] of this city.

"Yours L. TAPPAN."

Wm. Lloyd Garrison. Pawtucket, R. Is., 1840. The first lecture was actually delivered, September 25, 1839, and it appeared in *The* (New York) *Emancipator*, December 26, 1839.

Thompson, who had been engaged as a public speaker by the Aborigines' Protection Society, became so enthusiastic over the subject of India that he helped to bring about the organization of a separate society, "The British India Society," with which he henceforth identified himself (*Life and Correspondence of William Allen*, III, 302). It is worthy of remark that the B. & F. A.-S. Society was not so well pleased with what he had to say at Manchester as was Lewis Tappan and, at the meeting of the Committee, November 29, 1839, John Scoble brought to its attention certain remarks of Thompson's to which he felt great exception might be taken (*Minute Books*, I).

[19] This was one of the points at issue between the Garrison group and the Tappan. For other points and a discussion of the same, see Tappan, Lewis, *Life of Arthur Tappan*, p. 301; *Seventh Annual Report* of the A. & F. A.-S. Society; Garrison, W. P. and F. J., *William Lloyd Garrison*, II, 258–365; Birney, William, *James G. Birney*, p. 295 ff.; McMaster, John B., *A History of the People of the United States*, VI, 570.

[20] Hatfield, Edwin Francis, *Freedom's Lyre; or Psalms, hymns, and sacred songs, for the slave and his friends* (1840). The compilation of this work was undertaken at the request of the Executive Committee of the American Anti-Slavery Society; but, for lack of funds, was published privately (*Seventh Annual Report*, 1840, p. 38). A few years before, Joshua Leavitt had published a collection of hymns under a title somewhat similar, *The Christian Lyre*.

"New York,
"December 14, 1839.

"JOSEPH STURGE
"Birmingham
"My dear Friend,

"When Dr Madden was here he, in conjunction
with the counsel for the poor Africans brought here in the schooner
Amistad, addressed a letter to the British members of the Mixt Commission at the Havana, requesting them to procure certified copies
of the Treaties between England and Spain of 1814 and 1815 and
Annexes. Yesterday a letter was rec^d from the British Commissioners stating that it was very doubtful whether they should be
able to procure them—as the Govr would not probably affix his
signature—that it was an extra-judicial act in them to apply for
it—they might be censured by their own Gov^t as well as the authorities of Cuba, &c. Still their letter was very civil & concluded
thus:—'We cannot conclude without expressing our gratification
to observe the truly British feeling which animates your community
on the subject of the wrongs to which those unhappy victims of the
Slave trade have been exposed, and the peculiar zeal and ability
you manifest in their behalf.' We shall write to Mr. Fox,[21] the
British minister in this country to apply to the Spanish minister
here for certified copies of the Treaties and the Cedula or Royal
Decree of Spain but we have little expectation of procuring them
in this way—as the Spanish minister, like the Govr of Cuba may
wish, instead of facilitating us to throw every obstacle in the way
of obtaining the papers wanted. We have in books (our own law
books and in British books) copies of said Treaties &c, but they
cannot be received in Courts of Justice. Certified copies are indispensable. It would be desirable to obtain them from Spanish
sources, but if this cannot be done we must obtain them from the
British authorities. To ensure copies at any rate and as speedily
as possible, Theodore Sedgwick Esqr, of counsel for the Africans,
has, by this vessel, written to William Sharpe Esq. of the firm of

[21] Henry Stephen Fox. The communications passing between Mr. Fox
and Secretary of State, John Forsyth; viz., Fox to Forsyth, January 20, 1840,
and Forsyth to Fox, February 1, 1841, communicated to Congress by President
Van Buren, were published in full in the B. & F. A-S. *Reporter*, II, 58–59
(March 24, 1841). For additional information on the Amistad case, see
Memoirs of John Quincy Adams, . . . Ed. by Charles Francis Adams, X, 132
ff., 367 ff.; XII, 186; Moore, J. B., *International Law Digest*, V, 852–854.

Taylor, Sharpe, Field & Jackson, Solicitors, 41 Bedford Row, London for certified copies of the Treaties between England & Spain of 1814 and 1815 and Annexes, and by my permission has directed him to apply to you for the fees &c. I will thank you to advance the sum, & on your informing me the amount I will immediately reimburse you. I will thank you to see, before paying them, that the sum charged is reasonable. If you can get Dr. Madden or Mr Scoble to see Mr Sharpe, and urge him to thoroughness & despatch we shall be greatly obliged. We hope also that Dr Madden will get instructions sent from the proper authority to the British Commissioners to afford every facility in their power in this case. We are most unfortunate in attempts to procure testimony in several respects. Our own Sec. of State (Mr Forsyth) is a Slaveholder— we get no facilities from our own Government—and the British Commissioners even are afraid of offending the Spaniards or their own Gov^t by performing an act not strictly, as they conceive, within the line of their duty.

"Dr. Madden's letter [22] to Dr Channing on the Slave trade &c,. is published & I hope to send you a copy by this opportunity. It is a severe thing, but justly deserved, & will, I hope, do much good. I shall send it to the care of Messrs Cupper, Benson & Co, as I do not know your regulations about postage on pamphlets. When I was in England the postage on newspapers & pamphlets was enormous. Postage on newspapers & letters is now reduced. How it is on pamphlets I shall be glad to be informed.[23]

"I perceive in a letter in the Journal of Commerce [24] of the 13th

[22] Madden, Richard Robert, *A Letter to W. E. Channing . . . on the Abuse of the Flag of the United States* in *. . . Cuba, and the advantage taken of its protection in promoting the slave trade,* (Boston, 1839).

A Calm Observer, writing to Dr. Channing after Madden's letter to him had become public, accused Madden of being always unreliable, a hypocrite, and of making a pretense to learning; but he, none the less, admitted the truth of Madden's main contention that the Americans were engaged in and facilitating the slave trade (See pp. 25–27). He claimed, however, that, as the law stood, it was impossible for the United States Consul to do anything about it and he begged of Dr. Channing that he would make a moderate appeal to the American people. A second Madden letter against Trist was addressed to Ferdinand Clark of Havana, dated September 6, 1839, and published in the *Emancipator,* December 19, 1839, copied from the New Orleans *True American,* where the one to Channing was also published.

[23] As a general thing, hereafter, all references to postal rates will be omitted from the letters.

[24] The Havana letter, dated November 22, 1839, is on p. 2. The New York *Journal of Commerce* was founded by Arthur Tappan.

from their correspondent at Havana, Nov. 22d that it is supposed that the pacification of Spain will have an effect of increasing not only the commerce of Cuba, but of all South America, in as much as the Spaniards now will extend their voyages.to that Continent &c. Is is not probable that the Slave trade between the Coast of Africa and Cuba and S. A. will greatly increase?

"Mr. Clay has been defeated in not obtaining the nomination for the Presidency at the great Convention at Harrisburg, Pennsylvania. Gen¹ Harrison of Ohio was his successful competitor. It is not disguished (*sic*) that Clay's defeat was owing chiefly to the increase of abolitionists in this and other States, who would not vote for him. It is a most righteous blow after his pro-slavery speech in the Senate of the U. S. last year. Harrison lives in a free State, is not a Slaveholder, has once taken a decided stand when brother Weld [25] was lecturing in his neighborhood in defence of free discussion &c. It is very doubtful whether he is elected. Van Buren will have the votes of all the Slave States, I fear, and many votes in the free States. He will probably be re-elected though the Whigs profess to believe that their candidate, Harrison will be elected.

"I have read George Thompson's Speeches at Manchester, respecting affairs in British India, with great satisfaction, & pray God to prosper the undertaking in which he is engaged.

"It is desirable that those friends of human rights who are devoting themselves to the improvement of Africa should expose whatever is wrong in the American Colonization Society.[26] This Society, taking advantage of the momentary sensation occasioned in this country by the capture of so many slavers by British Cruisers are endeavoring to obtain funds &c under pretense that the Col. Soc. is laboring for the suppression of the Slave trade, and with the money, thus obtained, are shipping off to Liberia a few slaves conditionally emancipated to go to Africa if the requisite funds are raised from a deluded, & as O'Connell would say, a bamboozled community.

[25] Theodore D. Weld.

[26] The allusion here is probably to the fact that the leading men in the American Colonization Society were seeing, in the African Civilization scheme, a project similar to their own and one of them, R. R. Gurley, at a meeting of the Pennsylvania Colonization Society, November 11, 1839, had delivered an address from which the inference might be drawn that Sir Fowell Buxton was now adopting and adapting ideas that he, in conjunction with Wilberforce, S. Lushington, William Allen, Samuel Gurney, and others, had publicly repudiated years before (B. & F. A-S. *Reporter*, I, 234; II, 55).

"Amidst all the obstacles & difficulties with which we have to contend (and they are many and oppressive) we should utterly despair did we not know that the promises of the Almighty are unfailing. He *will* cause the wrath of man to praise Him, & the remainder of wrath he will restrain. He *will* break the rod of the oppressor, and let the oppressed go free. He will give efficacy to truth, & cause it to take deep root. These considerations sustain us, in the moral conflicts with the enemies of our cause, amidst the scorn & abuse that are heaped upon us, in the apathy of the christion church, and in the knowledge of the fact that slavery has entwined itself around the American church & the state so closely. We are also sustained amidst the defection of professed friends of the cause, the apostacy of a few, and the waywardness of others.

"Affec[y] & truly your's
"LEWIS TAPPAN."

"STOKE NEWINGTON. 3 mo. 11. 1840.

"Respected friend," [27]

"The letter bearing thy signature as Chairman of the Hibernian Anti-Slavery S[y]. was read at our Committee on 6th Day in last week, when I volunteered to write a reply. In doing so I can scarcely refrain from expressing some surprise at remarks which appear to reflect strongly upon the character of the Committee of the British & Foreign Anti-Slavery Society, & which I do not think deserved, but I proceed to advert to the principal subject of the letter. This appears to be a demand that the Committee should assign the reasons for its conduct relative to J. A. Collins.[28]

[27] James Haughton.

[28] John A. Collins was one of the most influential members of the American Anti-Slavery Society and one of those who had, in the recent factional disputes (1839–1840), most vigorously resisted the claims and the pretensions of the secessionists, who had had the Tappan brothers, Leavitt and Phelps at their head. For an appreciation of the work of Collins, especially as General Agent of the Massachusetts Anti-Slavery Society, see the *Twelfth Annual Report* (1844) of that body, pp. 39–42. The allusions in Alexander's letters are intelligible when one recalls that *woman's rights, states' rights,* or the relative position of the main society and its auxiliaries in the matter of raising funds, and what might, for lack of a better name, be called *religious orthodoxy* were the chief points in controversy between Garrison and Collins on the one hand and the secessionists on the other. Ulterior motives were, however, ascribed to the latter. Charles Tappan is said to have admitted that the real object of the secessionists was "to put down Garrison" (*Seventh Annual Report of American Anti-Slavery Society,* 1840, p. 70).

On this point I may remark that the British & For^n Anti-Slav^y S^y feel very strongly the importance of anti-Slavery Societies confining their attention to the simple objects of the abolition of the slave trade & slavery, and on this account think that those Societies in America which have connected with this great end the advocacy of what are called women's rights or other extraneous subjects have adopted a course seriously injurious to the cause of emancipation. The opinion I have expressed has not been weakened by the opportunity of noticing the conduct of persons connected with the party referred to in America, at the late Convention, and regarding J. A. Collins as the Representative of a portion of this body we did feel bound to withhold giving him our confidence & support. In making known this sentiment we do not consider that we have done anything derogatory to the personal character of J. A. C. We do not indeed impute improper motives to many of those who have blended the advocacy of the rights of the slave with that of other objects, while we are seriously apprehensive that some such indiscreet friends are doing the work of an open enemy & possibly in some cases a greater injury than these are capable of effecting. In reference to extracts copied in M.S. & sent anonymously the Com^{ee} were not aware that such a circumstance had occurred until thy letter was read to them. It appears to have been done with the cognizance of two of their number & I may express my opinion that it would have been better avoided. It was deemed best by our Sec^y after the correspondence which had passed relative to J.A.C. to forward for your information the letter which contains an allusion among other matter to an anti-Sabbath Con^n but in this step I do not think the Com^{ee} are committed to any opinion on the subjects to which the letter refers. It may not be improper to state that there is one part of J.A.C's conduct since his coming to England which the Com^{ee} must disapprove, that of his imputing to J. G. Birnie [29] & H. B. Stanton conduct in America which it was said if it had been committed in this land would have subjected them to imprisonment.

"This was done at a Meeting at Chelmsford & may have occurred in other places. This is indeed a personal accusation of a most serious character against individuals who had come amongst us with high credentials & whom we had no ground to believe were unworthy of them. The charge too was made after Birnie &

[29] James G. Birney.

Stanton had left England & could not consequently reply personally. We have only in conclusion to express with you our hope that that cordial & friendly cooperation which has existed amongst us may continue. Our object is we trust the same, & we hope it ever will be while the occasion remains, the abolition of slavery & the slave trade. Should any alienation occur while cemented by this single bond of union it must assuredly give us much pain, but while we are united in our object we think such a circumstance almost impossible. Surely we are brethren & are not about to do wrong to the other.

With kind regards to thyself & each member of the Com⁰⁰

"Thy sincere friend

G. W. ALEXANDER"

"New York,
May 5th 1840

"JOHN SCOBLE
"London.

"My dear Friend,

"I am indebted to you for a gratifying letter accompanied with D. Turnbull's valuable work on Cuba,[30] for which please accept my best thanks. In return allow me to present to you (in care of Mr Birney) a small book by Richard Hildreth Esq of Boston entitled "Despotism in America".[31] He is not a member of the Anti-slavery Society, but is an independent thinker, a friend of human rights & a fearless writer. You will not fail to be delighted with the work.

"You will see in our Emancipator of April 30th & May 7th a report of the proceedings in the Circuit Court at New Haven,[32] in the case of the Africans of the Amistad. The cause goes up to the

[30] Turnbull, David, *Travels in the West; Cuba with Notices of Porto Rico and the Slave Trade* (1840).

[31] Hildreth, Richard, *Despotism in America; or, An inquiry into the nature and results of the slave-holding system in the United States* (1840).

[32] Lewis Tappan himself attended the trial and his account of each day's proceedings was published in *The Emancipator* (See the issue of January 9 and of January 16, 1840). In the January 16 issue there appeared, also, an interesting letter on the Amistad case, written by John Quincy Adams, November 19, 1839 and one from the Reverend H. G. Ludlow, commending the efforts of Staples, Sedgwick and Baldwin. Baldwin's plea at the trial, as copied from the *New Haven Palladium*, is in the issue of January thirtieth and the court decision is in that of the twenty-third.

Supreme Court of the United States which will sit at Washington January 1841. As Judge Thompson learned that the case would go up, whichever side he decided, he advised the counsel not to argue the matter at length, but to let it go up to the highest judicial tribunal in the country with as little delay as possible. The action of this government is decidedly against these Africans and they will send them to Cuba if they dare.

"More anti-slavery men intend going to your great convention than I was aware of. There will be a very good representation of the cause I think, and rejoiced should I be if they were all harmonious. Unhappy dissentions have arisen in our ranks, of which you saw and heard something when you were here. I see not but Garrison [33] & his party must act by themselves, and those who can not go with them will act by themselves. For one, though I can not act with Garrison I am determined to do what I can for the poor slave without abusing those abolitionists who differ from me, and to receive abuse, if it must be so, with meekness. The *cause* is advancing in this country, be assured, although the organisation is odious in the eyes of the many, owing chiefly I think to the dissentions to which I have alluded.

"Rejoiced should I be could I possibly attend the Convention. May you have a harmonious meeting, & may great results spring from it.

"Assuredly yours,

"LEWIS TAPPAN

I send a newspaper *The Evening Post,* containing some account of Consul Trists letter." [34]

"NEW YORK, August 20, 1840.

"J. H. TREDGOLD, ESQ.

"Secretary, &c.

"My dear Sir,

"Yesterday I had the pleasure of receiving your letter of 1st August, enclosing a copy of the Resolutions passed at the several sittings of the Anti-Slavery Convention, for which please accept

[33] For Garrison and the Convention of 1840, see Garrison, W. P. and F. J., *William Lloyd Garrison,* II, 366–420.

[34] Nicholas Philip Trist studied law under Jefferson, whose granddaughter he married. He became President Jackson's private secretary and negotiated the peace with Mexico which closed the war.

my thanks. I have also received by the hands of Friend Fuller,[35] a packet containing a letter [36] to each of the Governors of States and Territories. These will be forwarded. A previous packet, containing circulars signed by Mr. Clarkson for the respective Governors, was duly sent to their destinations. Allow me to suggest that it would be better not to have such circulars superscribed in London, but here, as several mistakes are made in the names, residences, &c. The Governors of the States are elected by the people, some for one, some for two, and some for three years from different periods—and the Governors of Territories are appointed by the President, with the concurrence of the Senate. You will see therefore that changes are frequently occurring.

" . . .

"The intelligence from your side, since the meeting of the Great Convention, has given much joy to the abolitionists of this country, and additional accounts of the proceedings will be looked for with deep interest.

"Our new association meets with considerable favor, although we can do but little until our Secretaries Messrs. Birney [37] and Stanton return.

[35] James Cannings Fuller of New York State was a delegate to the Convention of 1840, took an active part in it, and wrote a letter, dated July 15, 1840, on *Slavery and the Methodist Church in America*, published in B. & F. A-S. *Reporter*, August 12, 1840 pp. 198–199. He was also present in the Convention of 1843 and listed as General Agent for Fugitive Slaves, North America. In the B. & F. A-S. *Reporter*, II, 243–244, is an article, "Gerrit Smith's Slaves," described as extracted from a letter dated, New York, September, 1841, addressed by Fuller to Joseph Sturge and published in the *Emancipator* and *National Anti-Slavery Standard*.

[36] One answer, at least, to this letter was forthcoming. It was from William Pennington, Governor of New Jersey (B. & F. A-S. *Reporter*, September 9, 1840, I, 231).

[37] Not long after the Convention of 1840 closed its sessions late in the evening of June 23, (B. & F. A-S. *Reporter*, I, 153), Birney and Stanton started out with Scoble on a lecturing tour throughout the length and breadth of the British Isles. From letters written at the time chiefly by John Scoble, their itinerary can be ascertained and, likewise, their own impressions of what they were accomplishing.

On July 18, Scoble wrote to Tredgold from Northampton, reporting the unexpected success of the meeting at Cambridge the day before, where Birney was one of the speakers and where two resolutions were adopted. "The first resolution had reference to our own proceedings—the second was meant for America. Mr. Birney spoke admirably. . . ." On the 21st, writing from Leicester, he similarly described to Tredgold the meeting at Northampton the preceding evening which

"The whole country is now agitated with the Presidential elec-

"went off much better than I expected, as the attention of the people was divided between the Judges who came to Town to the Assizes, a Lecture delivered on some popular subject, and the Anti-Slavery cause. The Meeting was in the Wesleyan Chapel and was well attended. . . . The speech of Mr. Bennett (Independent) was admirable. Resolutions approving of our Society, and condemnatory of American Slavery, were passed unanimously, and, I trust, our cause is now firmly established in Northampton, and will be zealously supported there. I had an interview with the leading friends in the morning at the house of Mr. James Atkins, a member of the Society of Friends, and the feeling displayed was excellent. I have hopes that a Ladies' Auxiliary will be formed in addition to the Gentlemen's Society already in existence.

"Mr. Birney and myself reached here this afternoon at three o'Clock, and found the Meeting is to be held in the theatre. Mr. Knibb has preceded us both at N'Hampton and here, and unfortunately has taken with him to Birmingham two of our best friends and best speakers, the Revds Messrs Mursell and Miall, so that matters look rather gloomy. We find also a shyness existing here among many of the 'Liberals' on our Subject. I hope, however, the Meeting will not prove a failure.

"We proceed to Nottingham tomorrow morning, and to Derby on Thursday morning. Friday we expect to be at Birmingham.

"Please forward me a copy of the last Patriot, and any other Papers which contain full particulars of the late Riots in Jamaica."

Scoble's next letter was dated from Newcastle, August 7, 1840.

" . . . in consequence of letters from Edinboro' and Glasgow Birney and myself will not go thither. . . ."

"We have been obliged to hurry on from place to place so rapidly that we have scarcely had time for proper meals or rest. I shall therefore, be glad of a quiet day tomorrow or Monday to write you. . . ."

In some of the Scoble letters occur references to Stanton's movements. In a letter to Tredgold, written in London, September 22, 1840, Scoble wrote,

"Agreeably to the arrangements made previously to my leaving Town I proceeded to Chelmsford on Tuesday the 9th Inst. and in company with my excellent friend Mr. Stanton, held an Anti-Slavery meeting in the Shire Hall on the evening of that day. . . ." On this occasion, Stanton seems to have made a "powerful address." "On Wednesday we proceeded to Colchester where we were most kindly received and entertained by Thomas Catchpool, Esqr. . . ." There was a good meeting at Colchester in the evening at the Friends' Meeting House. "On Thursday evening we were at Ipswich— meeting in new and commodious Temperance Hall. Thos. Clarkson in Chair & Clarkson astonished many by speaking—he spoke about twenty minutes— moved hearts of all.

" . . . he was able to remain until nearly the close of Mr. Stanton's speech, which was a powerful one, and which drew from the audience alternately tears and bursts of indignation. I confined myself to the results of emancipation. . . .

"On Friday we paid a visit, by request, to Mr. Clarkson at Playford, where we spent several hours in conversation with him on Anti-Slavery subjects, and were both gratified and surprised at the amazing vigor of his intellect, the extraordinary retentiveness of his memory, and the freshness of his feelings. It was truly delightful to find that he has not materially suffered by his recent very great exertions.

"On Saturday we left Ipswich for St. Ives, Huntingdonshire, which we reached late at night. The refreshment of the Sabbath in some measure prepared us for the meeting which was held on Monday evening. . . . On the following day we proceeded to Boston, in Lincolnshire, in the expectation of

tion, and the abolitionists, as well as others, are absorbed in the

holding a meeting there the following evening but owing to the evening having been pre-occupied by the Wesleyans we were obliged to defer. . . .

"On Thursday (?) I returned to Town exceedingly unwell from a severe cold on my chest which confined me to my bed on Wednesday, and Mr. Stanton proceeded to Lincoln and Gainesbro' to hold meetings at those places. . . ."

On the fourteenth of October, Scoble arrived in Edinburgh and the self-same day wrote to Tredgold, of the very fatiguing journey thither that he had had and of the preparations already made for a public meeting that evening and for a public breakfast the next morning.

"I think," wrote he, "I discover a good feeling towards us notwithstanding all the Garrison party have been doing to produce a contrary state of things— Stanton arrived yesterday— Birney is just arrived from Glasgow. . . . We all dine at our friend John Wigham's— and Thompson is invited to meet us— Gurley, the Colonizationist, is also here endeavouring to make a favorable impression, so that our visit is well-timed. Things do not look quite so promising at Glasgow, but I hope all will pass off well, though I learn that our friend Smeal is exceptionally sore about the Women's question. I shall act purely on the defensive and confine myself to explanations merely, for the purpose of justifying the Committee, and exonerating myself and others from blame. "..."

On the fifteenth, he wrote again, intending, as he said, "to give you (Tredgold) a succinct account of Birney's and my anti-slavery tour through part of the West of England. . . ." According to this, they were at Devizes, September 25, and had held a meeting there in the morning, which was mostly "attended by ladies who appeared deeeply and painfully interested. . . ." They would have preferred an evening meeting and would have liked to linger a few days had their plans permitted. At the meeting on the twenty-fifth, the Dissenters wanted "to make appeal against Jamaica Marriage Act which is so flagrantly unjust, and so entirely opposed to that in force in this Country." As it was a *Memorial* was adopted, bringing to the attention of the Government the state of law in Jamaica and the Barbadoes (See *Wiltshire Independent*). On the twenty-eighth, at a meeting in Bristol, Birney and Scoble were followed by Captain Charles Stuart, who had accompanied them from Bath and, "in Bristol," Scoble was of the opinion, "we may calculate upon effective support." A second meeting was held there on the twenty-ninth and Scoble had cause to write,

"Stuart, I regret to say, still continues to oppose our views on the subject of East India Slavery, altho' at the meeting he did not contradict my statements. I was also pained in a conversation with him after the meeting, to learn that he is so favorably inclined to Mr. Buxton's scheme that he proposes, conjointly with Mr. Blair, who appears entirely to agree with him, to attempt the formation of an auxiliary Society during the Winter! This must be prevented, if possible, as it would be a mischievous precedent. I say not this in the spirit of opposition to the African Civilization Society but because I am thoroughly convinced that it is vain to expect any good to Africa to accrue from the scheme. On this point however I shall write more at large to Joseph Sturge."

From Bristol, they went to Taunton and discovered, to their great sorrow, that several of their old and tried friends were no longer among their supporters, "in consequence," wrote Scoble, "as I am informed, of a change in

question. A portion of the abolitionists—a small portion probably

their religious views.'' At Exeter, they had a good meeting and from there Scoble went to his boyhood home at Kingsbridge to spend the "Sabbath." On the Monday succeeding, at Plymouth, so large a concourse of people came to hear them that the Mechanics Institute was insufficient for their accommodation. From Plymouth they journeyed to Reading and there came into conflict, most unexpectedly, with Buxton's scheme again, Sir George Stephen having visited the place previously. Scoble was much mortified and confided to Tredgold,

''. . . To me it is exceedingly unpleasant and embarrassing not to have a fixed course of action in reference to the African Civilization Society. I am quite aware that the Committee must feel the question 'How to act in the matter?' a difficult one, yet I cannot help thinking that something ought to be done. Against any hostile movement I am as much opposed as any one, yet surely we ought to have an opinion about the matter. For want of it I am often placed in great difficulty, as I cannot answer the question 'What does your Committee think of the Scheme?' ''

At Oxford, on October eight, their meeting "was a splendid one.'' It was held in the Town Hall and was "Such a meeting (as) was never before held at Oxford.'' "Though the Term had not commenced, several Gownsmen were present,'' and the Reverend Mr. Cox, "Vice Principal of one of the Colleges, would have taken part in the proceedings had he not been obliged to quit at an early hour.'' "Thus we finished this series of meetings. . . .''

"On Saturday Birney and I returned to London . . . (and) started for Edinburgh on Monday last. Birney parted with me at Liverpool preferring to finish his journey to the Northern Capital by Steam Boat whilst I proceeded onwards by land. I arrived in Edinburgh at two o'clock Wednesday morning —he in the afternoon. Stanton was in Scotland before us, and met us at the hospitable home of our friend Mr. J. Wigham.''

Of the work in Scotland, the lecturers had reason to be most hopeful. Scoble wrote,

"Our Scotch friends gave the deputation a warm and cordial reception. Birney and Stanton made two capital speeches. I followed them in a short address making way for our Mr. Anderson from Jamaica who, though his speech was long, much interested the audience by the testimony he bore to the negro character, and the beneficial results of Emancipation. The Resolutions were ably moved and seconded. . . . The breakfast meeting will be on friday morning, when I am expected to speak on the general results of Emancipation in the West Indies, and the duties which still devolve on British abolitionists. . . .

"I have thus brought to a close a rapid and very imperfect account of the interesting and important Meetings . . . in all of which the proceedings of the Committee of the British and Foreign Anti-Slavery Society, and of the late Anti-Slavery Convention have been fully sustained; and even those persons who feel an inkling after other Societies have generally admitted that our objects and mode of operation are worthy of their regard and support. This is encouraging. But what I principally hope for is the effect that will be produced by them on America. In this respect I feel we may go on and take courage. The testimonies gathered up in our journeys, and sent to the United States must work conviction into the minds of many, and, at all events, will greatly strengthen the hands of our friends who are so zealously laboring in the cause of the Oppressed.''

This was not, however, the end of their tour or of Scoble's observations. On the twenty-first of October, Scoble wrote to Beaumont,

—will vote for Mr. Birney, but 99/100ths of the people will cast

". . . My arrangements at present are, Carlisle tomorrow evening (Thursday) 22nd.—Kendal 23rd. Liverpool 24th.—embark for Dublin—26th. Meeting there 27th—ditto—(28th.) 29th Belfast—Birmingham 1 Novr—Cheltenham Meeting 3rd Novr. Norwich Meeting 6th Nov.— pretty sharp work this. . . .

"Our Scotch Meetings are finished and have gone off well—particulars in my next.

"I shall have much to tell you when I have the pleasure of meeting you in London—in the meantime I may say that our visits to Edinbro' and Glasgow have produced an excellent moral effect; and I think I may now say we have nothing to fear from Garrisonism.

". . ."

On the thirtieth of October, Scoble sent to Tredgold another of his succinct accounts. It was dated from Belfast.

"At length we have brought to a termination the projected series of Anti-Slavery Meeting in Scotland and Ireland. . . ." There would be only two more meetings he thought, Cheltenham, November 2 and Norwich, November 6, "unless Birney and Stanton should be still further detained in this Country. . . ." The meeting at Glasgow, on the twentieth, had been well advertised by William Smeal and John Murray. Dr. Wardlaw presided. "Mr. Birney and Mr. Stanton were both exceedingly happy and effective in their addresses on American Slavery and the duties of British abolitionists . . ." The resolutions "were exceedingly well drawn up, and were carried unanimously," perchance, because George Thompson, present at the meeting, had had a hand in them. "An excellent Report of the Speeches together with the Resolutions will be found in the Glasgow Argus of the 28th Oct. . . ." "I should have stated that C. L. Remond made a good speech against the American Colonization Society."

On the twenty-first of October, there was another meeting, the occasion being, a public breakfast in the Trades Hall. As Dr. Wardlaw was indisposed, Robert Kettle presided and the impression made upon Scoble then and earlier was that from all he "could learn by enquiry and observation I am extremely happy to say that Garrisonism has made but little way in Scotland, and that even his warmest admirers are by no means prepared to advocate his extreme views—indeed I may say that they are more inclined to repudiate them. As opportunity was afforded the Deputation did not fail to give such information as our Scottish friends desired upon the matters at issue.

"I may just mention that during the late sitting of the British Association in Glasgow, the African Civilization Society held a meeting. . . .

"Mr. Gurley has also been in Glasgow advocating the claims of the American Colonization Scheme. . . . He could obtain only an audience of fifteen. With his usual address, however, he managed to get a favorable report of his meeting inserted in one of the papers; and I perceive by an American Journal that he boasts of having made Converts, and that his Cause progresses well!

"22nd. Oct. Started for Carlisle, and were disappointed to find that a public meeting was not to be held for fear of the Chartists. . . ." A private meeting was, however, held at the home of G. H. Head. At Kendal, the evening meeting that had been hoped for had to be postponed, the Tract Society having a prior claim. On the twenty-fourth, they set off for Liverpool and, when there, embarked by the mail packet for Dublin. The "night was very stormy and wet, and Mr. Birney and I suffered much. . . ." Dublin was reached about nine Sunday morning and there they found Stanton and his wife already lodged at James Haughton's.

On the twenty-sixth, at a meeting of the Hibernian Anti-Slavery Society, "the deepest interest was taken in the addresses of our American friends, and the enthusiasm of our Irish friends was not a little heightened when they heard that Mr. Birney was of Irish descent both by his father's and his mother's side." A second meeting was held on the twenty-seventh and, at that, Dr. Madden was one of the speakers. On the twenty-eighth, they journeyed to

their votes for Van Buren or Harrison.[38]   Both of the great parties

Belfast and held a meeting with the Belfast Anti-Slavery Society the next day. ''Mr. Stanton, in the absence of Mr. Birney, delivered a manly and heart stirring address. . . . I followed him on the Results of Emancipation. . . .'' At a dinner on the thirtieth, given in the Victoria Temperance Hotel, Stanton and Scoble again spoke and together they set out for Liverpool, arriving there on the morning of November first. They were soon *en route* for Birmingham.

Scoble's next letter, so far as the present files go, was written to Joseph Soul on the eighth of November. Various untoward circumstances had prevented some of their meetings from being held, that at Yarmouth and that at Lynn. On the twelfth, he wrote to Soul from Bury St. Edmund's. He had had a note from William Forster announcing a meeting at Wisbech at noon the next day. He and Stanton were due at Spalding on the Saturday but were not sure they could get there. They were then about to proceed to Cambridge by fly since no coaches were obtainable, ''all being taken up by the election for High Steward.'' On the fourteenth he wrote to Tredgold that the meeting at Bury St. Edmunds had been an exceedingly interesting one. It had been held in the Town Hall and the Mayor, George Creed, had presided. From Wisbech, Scoble and Stanton went to Spalding, although the meeting there had been cancelled, thence to Boston, where they entered upon their return tour, which was to end at Hitchin on the following Friday.

The incidents of his comings and goings Scoble, undoubtedly, communicated as regularly to Sturge in Birmingham as to Tredgold in London and Birney and Stanton may have done the same. There are Sturge letters still extant that indicate they all continued in pretty close touch with each other. Take, for example, the following, addressed to Beaumont, October 23, 1840:

''I am obliged by thine of yesterday and though I have a letter from Birney today from which it appears very doubtful if he does not go to America without visiting Norwich yet I mean to write this evening to J. J. Gurney to fix a meeting there for the 6th as there appears little doubt Scoble & Stanton will be able to be there— I will try to drop a line to Dr. Madden— I fear he will think we have rather neglected his poem & I am sure he deserves every attention we can shew him. We cannot be silent much longer I think on Sir T. F. Buxton's plans— A paper is coming out in Liverpool in a few days that I hope will do some good— I fear our friend Tredgold will be too much discouraged with his want of success in getting money— I have written to encourage him as much as I can— It is possible I may reach London by 5th Day. Scoble writes a bright acct. of their doings at Glasgow.

''Very sincerely thy affectionate friend,
''Jos. Sturge.

''Birmingham 10/23, 1840.

(P. S.)
''Thou wilt please to have summoned all the Sub-Committee on publication. . . . Johnson the Reporter must do his best to get all ready & what is wanted we must fill up afterwards— I fear we shall get little from Birney, Scoble & Stanton till the 2nd. when I expect them here— I write to fix a meeting at Cheltenham for the 3rd— We must not let this Brazilian Mining business drop—''

[38] Some of Birney's later movements may be determined from two of his letters on file at Denison House. The later, written on the seventh of No-

are sanguine of success. Both are unfriendly to the Anti-Slavery cause.

> "With much regard,
> > "Your fellow-laborer in this righteous cause
> > > "Lewis Tappan."

vember, indicates that he was then in Bristol, the earlier, written, when he was with Scoble and Stanton in Edinburgh, October 16, 1840, refers to one or two things of interest and may as well be quoted in full. It was presumably addressed to Tredgold as the later was to Soul.

"There is in the Sep. no. of the American & For. A-S. Reporter a letter of mine which any person may see from its face was never intended for publication—be good enough to say to Mr. Hinton, that I do not want it in whole or in part to appear in the B. & F. Reporter.

"We had a good meeting here. We go out this morning to the public breakfast.

"I am obliged to you for the Morng Chronicle. Dr. Madden's letter is one of the most remarkable—indeed one of the noblest productions, we have had in the progress of the whole A-S. cause. . . ."

On the separate movements of Stanton, at this time, the letters of G. W. Alexander, who was occasionally his companion, are an authority,

(a) "In accordance with the wish wh has been expressed I propose to visit a few places in Kent & Sussex in company with H. B. Stanton. The following is nearly as much as I can calculate on performing—2nd Day next—Chatham, 3rd Rochester, 4th Maidstone, 5th Canterbury, 6th Margate, 2nd day week, Dover, 3rd Hastings, 4th Lewes, 5th Brighton— We may take one more place on 6th Day probably Tunbridge Wells—My object in writing this was not however simply to refer to the above particulars but to call your attention to the circumstance that the acct of the Sy. is already overdrawn £500 & to request your attention to this matter. I think if J. Beaumont & some other friend were to call on the Marquis of Westminster, the Duke or Duchess of Sutherland & the Duke of Devonshire the last of whom has accepted the office of Prest. of an auxy Sy & they were informed of our pecuniary wants some money might be obtained. The Marquis of Westr gave £500 to the African Sy. May I also suggest the propriety of giving some notice of the meetings held & any interesting particulars that may arise in each number of the Reporter. I felt some disappointment in not observing an allusion to the interesting & important meetgs wh have lately been held in the North at one of wh the Bishop of Chester was present & many Wesleyan ministers on the same or another occasion . . ." (Letter to B. & F. A-S. Society Committee, dated Rochester, 8 mo. 13, 1840).

(b) "I intend writing in this some report of the proceedings of H. B. Stanton & myself during the past week. . . ."

Evening of 24th—good meeting Dover, Wm. Horsnaill (Quaker) in Chair. As no preparations made at Hastings for meeting on 25th. Independent minister Davies invited a few friends to meet them the next morning.

26th. Lewes— Thos. Dicker Banker in Chair.

27—. Brighton— no meeting—friends there not considering time suitable— 28th good meeting at Tonbridge Wells notwithstanding short notice . . .(From Letter to Jno. Morgan, dated Rochester, 8 mo. 31, 1840).

NEW YORK,
Janʸ 28/41

"J. H. TREDGOLD, ESQʳ

"London

"My dear Sir,

"I am indebted to you for the Resolutions [39] respecting Texas, which have been copied into many of our papers, and to the Resolutions respecting the services of Messʳˢ Birney & Stanton which will be published forthwith.[40]

"Mr. Turnbull took the letter you sent by him, to the Havanas from which place I have received it.

"My B. and F. Anti-Slavery Reporter does not reach me frequently until the date is quite old. You will do me a favor to have it expedited as I wish to use it sometimes for the columns of our Reporter. I shall be glad also of the London *Patriot*.[41] If they will not exchange for the Reporter have the goodness to subscribe for it for me. It will also subserve the interest of the cause here if London & other newspapers containing valuable articles on the great subject are occasionally forwarded. Whatever expense may be incurred respecting all the above matters please charge to the Society here and we will adjust accounts annually. Will it not be a good plan to notice in your Reporter the titles of the

[39] Evidently those accepted, finally, at the meeting of the B. & F. A.-S. Society Committee, December 2, 1840. As early as September, 1839, Lord Palmerston had been memorialized on the subject of Texas, the Committee being exceedingly anxious to obtain a full knowledge of the state of affairs. The (New York) *Emancipator*, November 28, 1839, contains the text of the *Memorial*, copied from *The Liverpool Mercury*. The exact contents of the projected commercial treaty could not be ascertained since, as Lord Palmerston notified the Committee, access to the document was not permissible, until ratification had taken place. The treaty was signed November 16, 1840, and, at the Committee meeting of November 27, George Stacey, John Scoble and Josiah Forster were appointed a sub-committee to protest against it. For remarks upon the treaty, appearing in the A. & F. A.-S. *Reporter* and comments upon the same, see B. & F. A.-S. *Reporter*, II, 41–42 (February 24, 1841).

[40] In the B. & F. A.-S. Society *Minute Books*, (I, 377), it is recorded that at the Committee meeting, April 16, 1841, a letter was read from Lewis Tappan with resolutions from the A. & F. A.-S. Society, acknowledging the B. & F. A.-S. Society vote of thanks to Birney and Stanton.

[41] The first number of this London daily appeared, rather significantly, on the one hundredth anniversary of George Washington's birthday, 1832. On the third of January, 1867, *The Patriot* was incorporated with *The Independent*.

principal valuable papers published on the great subject in Great Britain, whether in newspaper Reviews or Pamphlets for the information of abolitionists throughout the world.

We hope that anti-slavery principles are fast pervading the minds of the people.

Very respectfully yours
"LEWIS TAPPAN"

"NEW YORK
"June 18th 1841.

"J. H. TREDGOLD ESQ.
　"27 New Broad Street
　　"London.

"My dear Sir,

"By the bearer, Mr W. W. Patton [42] of this city, a young gentleman whom I can recommend to you as a staunch abolitionist, I send you a parcel containing a few copies of R. S. Baldwin Esq's argument [43] in the Amistad [44] case for distribution. *It is a most*

[42] From the B. & F. A-S. Society *Minute Books*, (I, 432), it is to be inferred that W. W. Patton went to England in the interests of the New York City Vigilance Committee. He applied to the B. & F. A-S. Society Committee for pecuniary assistance in replenishing funds "for the purpose of assisting fugitive slaves in their flight from the Southern States to Canada." W. Johnston, Secretary of the Vigilance Committee, was concerned in the application; but the B. & F. A-S. Society was obliged to fall back upon a previous resolve (*idem*, p. 429) and answer, "that whilst the Committee could not devote any portion of its funds to the object proposed, they sympathized with it, and cordially wished it success."

[43] For Roger Sherman Baldwin's argument before the United States Supreme Court, see *Memoirs of John Quincy Adams*, X, 395, 430. He contended that the Court dismiss the case, "on the ground that the United States having no interest in the case, have no right to appeal from the decision of the District Judge."

[44] For documents relating to the Amistad case, see A. & F. A-S. *Reporter*, nos. 12 and 13. In no. 14 is a statement respecting American public opinion of the case. See also February twenty-fourth issue of B. & F. A-S. *Reporter*, 1841 (II, 41). Other important references to the later phases of the Amistad case to be found in the B. & F. A-S. *Reporter* are the following, all in the second volume:

(*a*) The Amistad case "now being argued in the supreme court at Washington. Mr. Baldwin, one of the original counsel. . . . John Quincy Adams has already spoken two days, about four hours each . . ." (p. 61).

(*b*) " . . . All British sense of justice is outraged by the prejudgment of the case in long newspaper articles, abounding with pro-slavery virulence and denunciation; the worst of these, too, being written, as is said, by a

able argument. In the parcel are a few copies of the "American Intelligencer" a paper started by an active individual in Philadelphia. He has published a large edition—to be scattered gratuitously over the land—and proposes to follow it with other publications. It is a cheap mode of doing good on an extensive scale.

"I am sorry that the June number of the A. and F. Anti-Slavery Reporter[45] is not out. It contains an account of the annual meeting of the Society & will be published this week. By the way your Reporters are generally a long time reaching this country. I could wish that two copies might be expedited to the Editor of the A. & F. Anti-Slavery Reporter regularly.

"Our friend Joseph Sturge [46] attended a large meeting in the Friends' Meeting House in this city last week with John Candler [47]

person of no less official importance than Mr. Forsyth, the secretary of state to the Van Buren administration . . ." (p. 61).

(*c*) Appeal for public thanks because the Amistad negroes have been adjudged free men—signed by Jocelyn, Leavitt, and Lewis Tappan and dated, New York, March 11, 1841 (p. 73).

(*d*) Letter from Jocelyn, Leavitt and Lewis Tappan to Alexander, dated, New York, March 25, 1841, extending thanks to the British for help rendered and expressing the desire to bring certain other facts brought out by the case to the attention of Her Majesty's Government (pp. 76–77).

(*e*) A full account of the Amistad trial (pp. 89–96).

(*f*) The correspondence of the American and Foreign Anti-Slavery Society with Lord Palmerston (pp. 129–130).

[45] Concerning the origin of the A. & F. A-S. *Reporter*, the B. & F. A-S. *Reporter* had this to say:

"*New Anti-Slavery Organization.*—The last papers inform us that the American Anti-Slavery Society has suffered a division. Dissatisfied with some of its proceedings, several of its most distinguished members have seceded from its ranks and organized themselves anew, under the designation of the American and Foreign Anti-slavery Society. Among its officers we observe the names of Arthur and Lewis Tappan, James G. Birney, Henry B. Stanton, and other eminent men. They have originated, as the organ of the society, a periodical entitled the *American and Foreign Anti-slavery Reporter*, in size and appearance the very copy of ourselves . . ." (July 1, 1840, I, 151).

[46] " . . . Sturge was touring the eastern states of America on Anti-slavery business from April to August, 1841 . . ." (Stephen Hobhouse, *Joseph Sturge*, p. 70). Hobhouse further says, p. 95, that Sturge's visit to the United States was a following up of the Convention of 1840 and, p. 98, that Sturge "aspired . . . to rouse the apathy and heal the divisions of his brethren across the Atlantic. He was away between March and August, 1841. His journal of impressions . . . was published . . . under the title of 'A Visit to the United States in 1841' . . ." In the B. & F. A-S. Society *Minute Book*, I, 348, is an entry, February 26, 1841, to the effect that Sturge was expecting to sail by the British Queen steam vessel from Portsmouth, March tenth. It was resolved that Hinton and Scoble should prepare an address to the President of the United States which Clarkson should be solicited to sign. The address was considered at the meeting on March 5, 1841 and was finally dated, London, March 8, 1841.

[47] At the time when the visit to the United States was resolved upon John Candler was yet in the West Indies. In the B. & F. A-S. *Reporter* for

& wife. Messrs Candler & Sturge spoke at length, and with great effect. Mr. Sturge is now in Philadelphia & proposes to proceed to Washington with the Address [48] signed Thomas Clarkson for the President of the United States.

"Charles Stuart [49] arrived here a few days since, and is in good health. He brought a pamphlet from John A. Collins, which I can not but look upon as a vile production—full of misrepresentations and calumny.

With kind regards to Mr. Scoble I remain, My dear Sir,
"Most truly your's

"LEWIS TAPPAN."
"BEDFORD—25th July 1841

"Dear Sir

"Accept my thanks for your letter of the 21st Inst. & the accompanying circular— Your address to our American Friends is excellent both in sentiment & temper— May it do great good. I have reason to believe that West India emancipation would not have been effected without the efforts and cordial coöperation of your Society.

April 21, 1841 (II, 80) is a letter written by him from Jamaica to Sturge reporting on conditions there. About a year before he and Captain Stuart had protested vigorously against the enlistment as soldiers of recently captured Africans, a matter so serious that, at the Committee meeting, March 30, 1840, it was the consensus of opinion that extracts of their letters detailing the same ought at once to be transmitted to the Colonial Office (*Minute Books*, I).

[48] The text of this Address is to be found in various places, British and American. For one of the former, see B. & F. A-S. *Reporter*, II, 73.

[49] Captain Stuart, who was an extremist in the Anti-Slavery cause, had recently made himself conspicuous by a letter, written by him from Bath, dated January 7, 1841, to the Editor of the B. & F. A-S. *Reporter*, condemning the attitude of British religious deputations to the United States and particularly that of which Dr. James Matheson was a member (*Reporter*, II, 7). He had made a like charge at the General Convention in June, 1840, to which Dr. Matheson's letter to the Reverend Thomas Scales, dated Wolverhampton, June 17, 1840, was more than an answer. According to Stuart, Dr. Matheson's conduct was most reprehensible; because, upon his return, he had not borne testimony against America and the churches as "the chief bulwarks of this inexpressibly nefarious system." The Reverend Dr. Reed, Dr. Matheson's colleague in the deputation to the United States, immediately by way of answer, retorted that he objected "to the policy and the right of making the slave question a test and term of Christian communion . . . "(*Congregational Magazine*, January, 1841; B. & F. A-S. *Reporter*, March 10, 1841).

"The Mgs [Mss?] on peace to which you are pleased to refer, has been written some years. In the mean time circumstances have occurred, & statistical facts have been collected which strengthen the positions taken in that paper. I therefore propose revising the Essay & making a few additions to it, & then submitting it to the press.[50] I am obliged by your kind offer to publish it in Eng⁴ & would be gratified by its appearance there under your auspices. Will you be so good as to give me your address in England, & to point out a way in which I may forward you a pacquet without subjecting you to postage. I revert with pleasure to the visit with which you favoured me, & beg you to be assured of my sincere wish for your safe return, your continued usefulness, & your personal welfare.

"Yours very respectfully
"WILLIAM JAY"

"Joseph Sturge Esqr

"P. S. Suffer me to remind you of my desire to receive all the publications of the Br. & Fo. A. S. Soc⁷. Payment will be made for them in any mode you may indicate."

"P Britannia

"NEW YORK, Sept, 15/41.

"JOHN BEAUMONT, ESQ.

27 New Broad St., London,

"Dear Sir,

"Your favor of 3/7 was duly received, enclosing Rev. John Clark's letter [51] relating to the Colony of Liberia. I had it printed & extensive circulation will be given to it. It is a true statement without doubt. Corroberations come in from various sources.

---

[50] Jay, William, *War and Peace* (London, 1842).

[51] The Reverend John Clarke, who had served as a missionary in Jamaica for a number of years, went, in 1841, to Africa on an exploring expedition for the Baptist Missionary Society. He wrote, April 5, 1841, from Clarence, Fernando Po, the letter referred to. The text of the letter is to be found in B. & F. A.-S. *Reporter*, August 11, 1841, pp. 169–170. The letter tells of the conflicts, war at times, between the colonists, sent from the United States by the American Colonization Society, and the natives of Liberia. "The desire manifested by the colonists to return to America," said Clarke, "is so great, that, if the vessels were supplied, such a number would leave in them that those willing to remain would find themselves too few to protect themselves from the natives, and would therefore leave on this account."

"Mr. Sturge, after a visit of much importance in the country, has returned followed by the grateful thanks of a large number of friends.

"Resp^y your's

"LEWIS TAPPAN."

NEW YORK Sepr 25 1841.[52]

"The Com^{ee} who have been charged with the defence, support & education of the Africans late of the Amistad, have determined on sending them back to Africa as soon as possible. Their country Mendi or Kaasa is from 60 to 150 miles east or south east of Sierra Leone—some of them have been to Sierra Leone—some have relatives there—& they are confident if they can reach S—L— in safety they would soon be able to reach their homes. Two or three colored & white religious teachers, will, we expect accompany them to take up their abode in Mendi or Kaasa.

"We have applied to the President of the United States for aid to send them back, hoping that he would grant a national vessel for

[52] The original of this letter was evidently sent to Joseph Sturge, who, under cover of the following, sent a copy of it to John Beaumont, October 9, 1841:

"I send thee a letter which I rec^d from New York this morning respecting the Mendians. Will thou be kind enough to let me know whether you can see that all Lewis Tappan's wishes are attended to and if T. F. Buxton is not in town see (sic).

"I have a letter from W. W. Anderson from Woods Hotel Furnivel's Inn from which it appears he will not finally leave London until 3d Day. I write him tonight to ask him to call at the Office in Broad Street on 2nd Day afternoon. I wish you to talk over the Amistead case—in a letter I had from him this morning he says 'I have seen Sir Geo. Stephen. He thinks well of clothing the Mendians with the Character of British Subjects but suggests it must be done by an act either of the British or Jamaica legislature. The Jamaica would be the easiest & he thinks it would certainly be confirmed by the Home Government. In that case the Mendians would have to go to Jamaica & abide there for such time as the act might fix—perhaps 60 Days. I think the Jamaica Legislature would readily pass such an act—an act giving the immunities & privileges of British Subjects to every son of Africa that had been so many days within the Island territory! ! That would encourage Emigration fast enough. I am delighted with the idea of the possible benefits that might arise from such a proceeding— Do think of it & write me—' I am obliged by thine of yesterday which I mean to forward to Bath tonight. " . . ."

Tappan's letter was brought before the B. & F. A-S. Society Committee at its meeting, October 29, 1841, and the Committee informed that, in consequence of Tappan's application, a deputation had already waited upon Lord Aberdeen (*Minute Books*, I, 465–466). The report made of the visit was substantially the same as that reported by Scoble to Tappan in the undated letter, on pp. 211–215.

that purpose. But we have no great expectation that our request
will be granted. He may think that he has not authority, & that
it will require an act of Congress. It will not do to wait for this.
They ought to leave here before the 1st of December.

"Will you confer with Mr Buxton, Capt John Washington, H—
M— S Shearwater Harwich, & others, and ascertain whether the
British Government would probably lend its aid to re-convey these
people to Sierra Leone? Jno W— is sec— of the Geographical
Society & has lately been acting as joint sec— of the Society for
the Civ^n of Africa. We shall be glad to know very soon what the
probability is of aid from your Govern^t. If we send them in a
Merchant vessel we fear the Spaniards will be on the look out &
re-capture them. What a triumph they would have if they could
re-enslave Cinque & his companions [53] . . .

"LEWIS TAPPAN."

The Amistad Captives.[54]

"To LEWIS TAPPAN of New York.

"My Dear friend,

"I have just returned from an interview which a deputation
of our Committee have had with the Earl of Aberdeen respecting
the Mendi people.

"The two points submitted to his Lordship were the safe con-

[53] Because of his services rendered in their cause, Cinque and his companions presented to John Quincy Adams, a Bible. His acknowledgment was
as follows:

"My Friends,—I have received the elegant Bible which you have presented
me through your true and faithful friend, Mr. Lewis Tappan. I accept it,
and shall keep it as a kind remembrance from you, to the end of my life. It
was from this book I learned to espouse your cause when you were in trouble,
and to give thanks to God for your deliverance. . . ."

The letter is dated, Boston, November 19, 1841, and is to be found, along with
one on the same subject from Adams to Lewis Tappan, in B. & F. A.-S. *Reporter*, III, 7–8. The appreciation of the B. & F. A.-S. Society Committee was
expressed in a letter prepared by the Secretary, intended to accompany a set
of the publications of the Society. The letter contained a very touching reference to the nobility of his efforts (*Minute Books*, I, 467). Considering that
the decision of the Supreme Court, in line with the argument put up by ex-
President Adams, had set the Mendians free, it seems very odd that J. B.
McMaster should refer to the interference of Great Britain as "unwarranted"
and as justifying strained relations between her and the United States (*History
of the People of the United States*, VI, 605).

[54] B. & F. A.-S. Society *Memorials and Petitions*, 1840–1843, p. 76.

veyance of Cinque and his companions to Sierra Leone, and whether on their arrival in that British colony the Government would naturalize them, and thus throw over them the shield of British protection. Though I cannot speak with absolute certainty that the Government will order a vessel round to take the Mendians home, yet I do not think it improbable, if no circumstance should arise to render it inexpedient. Of course the moment we obtain the final decision of the government upon the point we shall inform you. Whether the Government will be able, in view of certain precedents, to naturalize the Mendians, is doubtful; the subject will however engage the attention of the proper authorities and if it can be done it will be done. This will be a great point gained, if it be consummated.

"We found Lord Aberdeen exceedingly well disposed towards Cinque and his companions.[55] Whilst we were with Lord Aberdeen we called his attention to our present relation with Texas. Of

[55] The documents here subjoined are self-explanatory and indicate what was the outcome of the affair:

(a) "To THE RIGHT HON. THE EARL OF ABERDEEN
&c   &c   &c
"My Lord,
   "Since I had the honor of an interview with Lord Canning respecting the safe conveyance of the Africans taken on board the Amistad, from the United States to Sierra Leone, the Committee of the British and Foreign Anti-Slavery Society have received communications from their friends at New York stating, that, in consequence of the state of health of the Mendians and the approach of winter which they are unable to endure, it had been resolved to forward them to their native home at the earliest possible period; that the Barque 'Gentleman' had been engaged for that purpose; that they will be accompanied by 'William Raymond and James Steele, both pious men, abolitionists; attached to the people of colour, and preachers of the Gospel,' and 'Henry Richard Wilson, a colored man (a native of Barbadoes) as Catechist;' that it is the intention of Messrs. Raymond and Wilson, 'to take up their abode in Mendi, as long as the Providence of God may direct;' and that the vessel which had been engaged was expected to leave the United States some time in the month of November; that this arrangement was made previously to the arrival of the intelligence that your Lordship had favorably entertained the proposition submitted by the Deputation of the London Committee; and, that all that now remains to be done is respectfully to request your Lordship to forward instructions, by the earliest opportunity, to the British Consul at Cape de Verde, to the Acting Governor of Sierra Leone, and to the Admiral on the Station, to afford the Mendians and their companions all the aid in their power, in order to secure their safe arrival in their own Country.
   "In making this communication to your Lordship I do but express the feeling entertained by the Members of the Committee of the British and Foreign Anti-Slavery Society and the friends of the Mendians in the United States, when I say that we all feel deeply obliged for the considerate kindness of your Lordship in giving a favorable answer to our united request for the safe conduct of these poor people to Sierra Leone; and that we shall feel still further obliged, if, during their stay there, they can be naturalized. Such a measure, we venture to think, if it can be carried into effect, will not only

course the reserve of office prevented his Lordship from saying what the Gov^t. intended to do upon the point. We however may mention that the independence of Texas is not yet recognized by

throw the shield of British protection over these people in future; but operate most favorably on their countrymen, by showing them the deep interest which the Government and People of this Country take in their welfare, and their deep-rooted hatred to the Slave-trade. The Mendians are 35 in number, Cinque, who is regarded as their headman, is the son of a Chief. Since their residence in the United States, they have been taught to read and write, and their progress in useful and Christian knowledge has been very remarkable. Their Country, Mendi or Kossa is said to be from 70 to 100 miles from Sierra Leone. This contiguity to the British Settlements when coupled with the extraordinary circumstances under which they are restored to their Country, it is hoped will facilitate every proper measure that may be adopted in that direction for the suppression of Slavery and the Slave-trade and for the introduction of Christian civilization into that part of the African Continent.

"I have the honor to be
"My Lord
"Your Lordship's most obedient servant
(Signed) "JOHN SCOBLE.
"27, New Broad Street
Decr. 10th. 1842" (1841?)
(*idem*, pp. 77–78).

(*b*) "TO THE RIGHT HON. THE EARL OF ABERDEEN
&c &c &c

"My Lord,

"Since my last communication respecting the Mendian negroes, the Committee have been favored with information from New York respecting their embarkation for Sierra Leone, the substance of which they have the honor to convey your Lordship.

"'Last Saturday' (the 27th. Nov^r.) writes their Correspondent, M^r. Tappan 'all the Mendian Africans (35 in number) sailed from this Port for Sierra Leone, on board the barque 'Gentleman,' together with five Missionaries and Teachers, viz. the Rev James Steele, the Rev. Wm Raymond, Mrs. Elizabeth Raymond, and infant, M^r. Henry R. Wilson and M^r. Tamar Wilson, the two colored teachers. M^r. Wilson a native of Barbadoes. They have had a fine breeze and are now we hope, well on their way. The Anti-Slavery public have generously responded to our appeal, and sent the means to enable us to fit them out well, to pay their passages, supply them with many useful articles and to give the Missionaries money to sustain themselves for a while'

"'The British Consul here and M^r. Fox, the British Minister, kindly furnished the Missionaries with letters to the Authorities of Sierra Leone. We hope that on their arrival there they will find that instructions have been sent out from London by the British Ministry to aid the Mendians to reach Mendi or Kossa their home'

"'Mr. Haensel' (a Reverend gentleman who formerly resided at Sierra Leone, and with whom M^r. Tappan had been in correspondence) 'says, he thinks there will be no physical difficulty in their making their way to their native land when once arrived at Sierra Leone, provided the Country be not distracted by War, and security be obtained for their passage through the territory of a hostile tribe. On this subject he says there is some reason to apprehend, as the latest printed intelligence he has had from Sierra Leone, mentions, under date of September last year, the existence of a war between the Queah tribe of Timmanees (or Timnahs) adjoining the British territory on its Eastern junction to the main land, and the Kossas.'

"'Mr. H says further that the road of the Amistad Africans would be, he thinks, E b S, through the territories of the Queah chief, Mohammed, and that consequently it would be a hazardous undertaking for them to attempt

Great Britain, and will not be, at least for some time to come. Whether the Gov^t. may make its recognition to depend on that of

it until such a state of peace shall have been restored, as shall admit of a guarantee being given by the native chiefs to the Colonial Government of Sierra Leone for the undisturbed transit of these expatriated Kossas to their native land'

" 'We hope that the friends in England will do all they can to insure to these Mendians and their Teachers, on their arrival at Sierra Leone, or soon after, all the protection, aid, convoy &c they will need. If not already done despatch will be important.'

"In submitting the foregoing extracts to your Lordship's attention,
"I have the honor to be
My Lord
"Your Lordship's Obed^t. hble Servant
(Signed) "John Scoble

"Decr. 20th. 1842." (1841?)
(*idem.* pp. 78–80).

(Reply)

" (c) Sir,

"I am directed by the Earl of Aberdeen to acknowledge the Receipt of your letters of the 10th and 20th Inst, respecting the Mendian Africans now on their return to Mendi by way of Sierra Leone; and I am to request that you will inform the Committee of the British & Foreign Anti-Slavery Society, that his Lordship has taken measures for procuring for the Individuals in question every aid which can, with propriety, be given to them by the British Admiral on the African Station, the Senior Officer on the West Coast of Africa, the Lieutenant Governor of Sierra Leone, and Her Majesty's Consul at the Cape Verde Islands

"With regard however to the suggestion contained in your letter, that these Negroes should be naturalized, during their stay at Sierra Leone, I am to inform you, that the subject is under consideration, but that Lord Aberdeen is not at present prepared to state whether or not the wishes of the Society in this respect can properly be complied with

"I am, Sir
"Your most obed^t hble servant
(Signed) "Canning

"Foreign Office
"December 23rd 1841"
(*idem,* pp. 80–81).

(d) Extract of a letter from Lewis Tappan of New York to J. H. Tredgold dated New York, Decr. 18 1841:

"Since the departure of the Mendians on the 27th. Nov we have received a letter from Lieut. Governor Fergusson of Sierra Leone saying that on their arrival they would be hospitably received and sent to Mendi at the public expense. This is noble and characteristic of your Government."

The following is a copy of the letter:

"Gentlemen,—I have to acknowledge the receipt of a letter addressed by you to the late Sir John Jeremie, governor of this colony, under date New York, 25th. March, 1841, relative to thirty-six persons, the survivors of the kidnapped Africans, who some years ago found their way to the United States in the schooner Amistad, and whom you are desirous of having returned to their native country.

"While I am happy in being able to afford you satisfactory information as to the locality of Mendi (the country to which these persons are said to belong), I can confidently assure you of the cordial cooperation of the government in aid of the endeavour to restore them to it.

Mexico or not, there does not appear at the present moment any very friendly feeling towards Texas.

"Very truly yours

(Signed)   "JOHN SCOBLE"

"Washington, Jan. 28–42 [56]

(To Joseph Sturge)

" . . .

"The spirit of liberty I am happy to say is rising.   Henry M. Wise has been entertaining the House with your letters—astonished that a *monarchist* should presume to intermeddle with our elections or other affairs.

"Mr. Adams now has the floor for a full vindication of himself if the House will allow it— He is charged with contempt, & the charge will either be dismissed & thrown out or he *will* be heard.

"I wish to receive the earliest & fullest intelligence of whatever

"Mendi is situated on the banks of the Rokelle, or Sierra Leone river and may be reached in three or four days from Free Town. Bey Fonti, its chief, is a party to a treaty of alliance existing between this government and the confederate chiefs of the Timmanee country.

"Sierra Leone is thus, from vicinity and facility of intercourse with Mendi, preferable to Monrovia or Gallinas (as suggested in your letter), as the place to which these persons should be brought, in order most conveniently to insure their return to their own country.

"With respect to their removal from America, and their voyage across the Atlantic, I cannot, for these purposes, promise any aid of a pecuniary nature from this government. I may, however, assure you that, on their arrival here, they and their teachers will be cordially received, adequately maintained and provided for, and safely conducted to their own homes, under the protection of government, and at the public expense. It is not likely that a two years residence in America will have effected such changes in the constitution of those Africans as to render their arrival here at any season hazardous; but, as their teachers are to be Americans not acclimated to this country, certain precautions may, in respect to them, be necessary. I would therefore recommend their arrival here at any period between the 1st of December and the 1st of May; and I think it would be more adviseable for them to return all together than in small companies.

"I have the honor to be gentlemen &c

(Signed) "W. FERGUSSON, Lieut Governor

"Messrs. S. S. Jocelyn, J. Leavitt, L. Tappan"

(*idem.* pp. 81–82).

56 This document and the next are from copied extracts, transmitted by the recipient, Joseph Sturge, to Beaumont, February 17, 1842. The following is the letter of transmittal:

"I enclose an extract or two from my last American letters, a copy of which thou canst please to send to the Reporter } also to any portion of tho Daily press thou thinks fit."

Joseph Sturge had his own symbol, or glyph, for *and.*

is communicated to Parliament [57] respecting the Creole—or Texas —or the Right of search.

[57] That the B. & F. A-S. Society Committee was already engaged in endeavours to influence the Government is shown by the *Minute Books*, I.

P. 480. (Meeting, January 7, 1842).
The Case of the Creole, Capt. Ellson from Richmond, Virginia, to New Orleans with Slaves &c. recently reported in the Bahama Papers, having been brought under the attention of the Committee, it was ordered that the draft of a Memorial be prepared embodying the facts as far as they can be ascertained for presentation to Lord Aberdeen.

P. 492 (Meeting, January 28, 1842).
The Copy of a Memorial to Lord Aberdeen was read, relative to the Slaves on board of the American ship – Creole – and was referred to Dr. S. Lushington for his opinion on some points involved in it.

P. 498. The Memorial to the Earl of Aberdeen respecting the Negroes taken into custody at Nassau, Bahamas, from on board the Creole, as revised by Dr. Lushington was read and adopted and ordered to be presented by Deputation to his Lordship at such time as might suit his convenience.
It having been suggested to the Committee by Dr Lushington that a writ of Habeas Corpus should be sued out in the Bahamas in behalf of the Creole Negroes, it was concluded by the Committee that J. H. Hinton, J. Beaumont and J. Scoble be a sub-committee to take steps for the accomplishment of this object, as soon as they have received definitive information from Dr. Lushington on the subject.

P. 500. Letters from Viscount Canning appointing Saturday the 12th Inst. at ½ past 3 o'Clock in the afternoon for the Deputation to see the Earl of Aberdeen respecting the *Creole* Negroes, was read; and a suggestion made that the Legislature should be petitioned on the same subject when it was resolved that the propriety of petitioning should be made dependent on the result of the forthcoming interview with Lord Aberdeen. Its further consideration was therefore deferred.

P.—(Meeting, February 25, 1842).
The Deputation who waited upon Lord Aberdeen with the Memorial respecting the Negroes from on board the Creole, reported that Her Majesty's Government have sent out orders to Nassau for their immediate release. Resolved That this Committee receive with the highest satisfaction the intelligence communicated as above relative to these Negroes, by which Her Majesty's Government recognized the undoubted right of their immediate freedom.

The text of the *Memorial* to Lord Aberdeen is to be found in *Memorials and Petitions*, 1840–1843, pp. 82–86. It was published in various papers; e. g., *The Nonconformist*, February 23, 1841, p. 124. It is here reproduced in full:

CASE OF THE CREOLE NEGROES

The following memorial was presented to the Right Hon the Earl of Aberdeen, Her Majesty's Principal Secretary of State for Foreign Affairs &c &c by the Committee of the British and Foreign Anti-Slavery Society, on Saturday, 12th. February 1842

My Lord—However much the Committee of the British and Foreign Anti-Slavery Society may regret the existence of any causes of irritation between the governments of Great Britain and the United States arising out of the existence of slavery in the latter country, and of the slave-trade on the coast of Africa they cannot but rejoice, that in the eyes of enlightened hu-

"Lord Ashburton will accomplish nothing with the poor im-
manity and of christian philanthropy, the cause of human freedom, civilization
and happiness, is earnestly sought to be promoted by the former; and that a
large portion of the citizens of the United States, in common with the people
of England, are uniting their best efforts for the removal of those causes of
irritation, by the universal extinction of the evils, to which, unhappily they
owe their birth.

The case of the *Creole*, like that of the *Amistad*, is exciting not only the
profound attention of public men, but stirring the deep sympathies of the
public mind on both sides of the Atlantic. In common with the friends of
humanity at large, the Committee feel the deepest solicitude as to the ultimate
fate of the negroes now in the custody of Her Majesty's authorities at the
Bahamas for the part they are reported to have taken in the affair of the
Creole. That solicitude induces them to lay before your lordship, conclusions
to which they have arrived after a careful review of this deeply interesting
and important case, and which they venture respectfully to submit to the consideration of Her Majesty's government.

There are two versions of the *Creole* affair, one derived from the protest
of certain persons who formed part of the crew of that vessel, made before a
notary at New Orleans; and the other, founded on private information from
Bahamas. From the first, it appears that the *Creole* left Hampton Roads in
the State of Virginia, on the 30th. of October last, "laded with manufactured
tobacco in boxes, and slaves,"—for New Orleans; that whilst on the voyage,
a part of them, nineteen in number "rose on the officers, crew and passengers,
killed one passenger, severely wounded the captain and a part of the crew, and
compelled the first mate to navigate said vessel to Nassau, New Providence."
It appears also from the same protest, that after they had accomplished their
object, they were guilty of no excesses; but treated all the whites on board
with great humanity, dressing the wounds of those that were injured, supplying them with their usual food, and only keeping them apart and under such
restraints as were necessary to secure their safe arrival in a British port; and
to use their own simple but emphatic language, "all that they had done was
for their freedom." On their arrival at Nassau, they were charged with
mutiny and murder, and placed under the custody of the authorities of the
island, until the government shall decide whether they shall be tried there or
elsewhere for the alleged crimes.

From the latter account, it appears, that the negroes having discovered
their proximity to a British island, demanded to be landed there; that this was
resisted by the captain, passengers and crew; that thereupon a struggle for
the mastery commenced which terminated in the triumph of the negroes, and
the loss of two lives, one a passenger on board the *Creole*, who had the care
of a portion of the slaves, and one of the negroes who died of the injuries he
received on his arrival at Nassau, where those implicated in the rising, were
given into custody, and the remainder of the slaves allowed to go free.

Whichever of these accounts be the true one, or whatever may have been
the means by which the negroes achieved their liberty, the Committee presume
it cannot alter the decision of Her Majesty's government in the case. They
are persuaded that, under the circumstances which took place, neither the
charge of mutiny or murder can be sustained in a British court of justice.

becile at the head of our Government & the poor debauchee his

If these offences have been committed, they have been committed against American citizens, on board an American vessel, and can only be dealt with in American courts. The negroes of the *Creole* were forcibly placed on board that vessel as slaves—they were forcibly detained on board as slaves—they were detained for the New Orleans market as slaves. This they knew, and to avoid the horrors and degra. of the condition that awaited them, as well as to relieve themselves from the bondage in which they were held, they rose upon those to whose custody they had been committed, asserted their natural rights, and after a short but severe struggle, secured their freedom. That homicide was committed during the affray is justly to be deplored and deprecated— but that homicide is to be traced to the resistance made by those who endeavoured by force of arms to retain them in slavery, not to a spirit of revenge on the part of the negroes. They sought not life but liberty; and that obtained, their subsequent conduct must be regarded as an admirable specimen of forbearance, self-government, and humanity. In confirmation of the views of the Committee, they refer to the dcisions of the United States courts, in the case of the Mendians found on board the *Amistad*, in which it was held that the alleged offense of murder, with which they stood charged, having been committed on board a *foreign* ship was without their jurisdiction, and such they have full confidence will be the decision of the British courts also.

The only question which remains to be noted, is whether the United States have a right to claim these negroes, either as slaves or as felons. The Committee conceive the first point as finally settled by the British Government; they cannot and will not be delivered up as slaves; and with respect to the other point, they conceive it is equally clear, that these negroes cannot be delivered up, merely because they have been charged with a capital crime by some American citizens. They are not felons by the laws of England nor by the laws of nations; but even if they were so, the United States have no authority, under treaty with Great Britain, to require them to be delivered over to the vengeance of their laws; and the uniform custom of that country runs counter to such a demand. They will not deliver up criminals to the demands of this country, whatever the offence may be with which they stand charged.

The Committee feel themselves, therefore, at liberty to consider the negroes, recently taken from on board the Creole, and now in the custody of Her Majesty's officers in Bahamas, to be safe; and they have respectfully, yet earnestly to request, on their behalf, that Her Majesty's government will be pleased to afford them such protection, as their circumstances may require—On behalf of the Committee

(Signed)   JOSEPH STURGE
Chairman.

The above memorial was presented to the Earl of Aberdeen by a deputation from the Committee consisting of the following gentlemen viz.—Messrs. William Allen, Joseph Sturge, J. Scoble, J. H. Hinton, J. Beaumont, Henry Tuckett, Benjn. Wiffin and John Dunlop of Edinburgh. They were very courteously received and his lordship led them to hope that a measure would be adopted by the government for the immediate liberation of the eighteen persons detained in custody; which hope has since been fully realized.

prime Minister.[58]   (Joshua Leavitt).
   " . . . "

(To Joseph Sturge)   "AMESBURY, 1 mo 31, 1842
   " . . .

"By the Papers sent by this Packet thou wilt see that we have
a good deal of discussion in Congress in spite of all attempts to shut
out the dreaded subject. The Creole case mentioned in my last has
caused much excitement throughout the Country and has called
forth some debate in both Houses of Congress. The general impression in this section is that the prisoners at Nassau will not be
given up to our Government & that *they ought not to be*. The
news of the late treaty on the Slave Trade [59] has fallen like a
thunder bolt amidst the Slavery party; they scarcely know what
to say or do, in reference to it. The New York Herald [60] & other
prints charge the whole of the abolition movement here to the
machinations of England—I send thee a paper—'The Liberty
Standard' containing some *marked* articles—also the New York
Herald of last week, containing the debate in Congress on the presentation of a petition from some persons advising a peaceful dissolution of the Union— This was taking the blustering Southerners
at their word, as they have all along threatened to dissolve the
Union. Adams stated in presenting it that he wished the committee to report against it. Thou wilt see that they name is pretty
freely used in the debate. Lord Morpeth was present during the
discussion. I feel anxious that all difficulties between this country
& Great Britain with the exception of the slave question should
be speedily settled—
   "The Land Agent in Maine has communicated a Report to the
Legislature of that State in which he proposes to *waive the claims*

   [58] Webster wrote two important dispatches in the Creole case (*The Writings and Speeches of Daniel Webster* . . . National Edition [1903] XIV, 372–
381; XI, 303–318). They were addressed to Edward Everett, January 29,
1842, and to Lord Ashburton, August 1, 1842. He made the following distinction: "If slaves, the property of citizens of the United States, escape into the
British territories, it is not expected that they will be restored. In that case
the territorial jurisdiction of England will have become exclusive over them,
and must decide their condition. But slaves on board of American vessels lying in British waters are not within the exclusive operation of English law;
and this founds the broad distinction between the cases" (*idem*, XI, 311).
   [59] Reference is to the Quintuple Treaty for the suppression of the slave
trade negotiated by Great Britain, France, Austria, Russia, and Prussia.
   [60] Anti-Slavery men regarded the London *Times* and *The New York Herald*
as their chief newspaper enemies.

of the State and accept in lieu of that claim another portion of the territory or rather the navigation of the St. John— I have not yet seen the report but it evidently places the matter in a more *adjustable* form. The Reporter is not yet out—but we are in good spirits. Never was there a time when our principles were so powerfully moving the public mind as at the present. The New York Liberty Convention on the 19th numbered from 800 to 1000 delegates. Stanton writes me that it was a glorious meeting— Charles T. Torrey has been tried as an *Incendiary* in Maryland & acquitted on the ground that he had *not* distributed Anti-Slavery publications in the State. Thou & I narrowly escaped a ten years sojourn in the Maryland Penitentiary for distributing books &c. in Baltimore. I should scarcely risk it again. . .''

(J. G. WHITTIER).

"NEW YORK,
"April 1st 1842.[61]

"JOHN SCOBLE, ESQ,
27, New Broad Street,
London.

"My dear Friend,

"Your letter of February 3d was not received until about the middle of March. Since that period I have been endeavoring to find the document for which you wrote. My efforts, so far, have not been successful. You state that it bears date somewhere about the year 1828. Are you sure it was in that

[61] Simeon S. Jocelyn, corresponding secretary of the A. & F. A-S. Society, also addressed the B. & F. A-S. Society on April 1. His letter is to be found in the *Nonconformist*, April 27, 1842, pp. 275–276. It expressed gratitude and gratification that the British Government had no intention of surrendering the Creole negroes, either as felons or as slaves. In the same issue of the *Nonconformist*, p. 275, is an extract of a letter from John G. Whittier, March 31, 1842, commenting upon the American attitude towards the Creole affair and the censure passed on J. R. Giddings of Ohio for the stand he had made in favor of the captives. Judge Jay had written to Sturge, on the sixth of January, with reference to the possible legal status of the Creole negroes and had said that they could not be surrendered as murderers because there being no extradition treaty in existence as between Great Britain and the United States, murderers of any color were not being surrendered. "If you cannot surrender them as murderers, can you as fugitive slaves? If you surrender these men, on what plea can you afford protection to the 12,000 fugitives in Canada?" (*The Non-conformist*, February 9, 1842, p. 92). For further enlightenment on Jay's views, see his pamphlet, *The Creole Case and Mr. Webster's Despatch*, New York, 1842.

year or near it? I send you a pamphlet on the Creole case. By looking on page 36 you will see a notice of the late Mr Wirt's report 20 Nov, 1821. This may be what you want. I will, however, pursue my enquiries although the matter being settled by your Gov^t there may now be no special need of further information. The Creole case has been amply discussed in the American newspapers and in conversation from one end of the land to the other. Hon. Joshua R. Giddings, one of the members of the House of Representatives, in Congress, from Ohio, has resigned his seat in consequence of a vote of censure for introducing a set of resolutions relative to the Creole affair. These resolutions [62] contain an admirable and incontrovertible statement of the law in the case, but being in opposition to the views taken by this Gov^t they excited great heat in Congress, & the mover was virtually expelled. He has returned to his constituents & it is hoped they will return him in a few weeks with an increased vote. I am happy to say that public opinion at the North is opposed to the hasty & unconstitutional act of the majority that censured Mr Giddings, but few have the moral courage to defend his act, or the argument of his resolutions.

"Many thanks are due to your Com. for their prompt & efficient action in the case of the Creole. That case may be considered as terminated with the exception of the claim of this Gov^t *for compensation!* Most disastrous will it be if any is given. The great danger now is war with Mexico and union with Texas. May God avert both.

"Sincerely & truly yours,
"LEWIS TAPPAN."

"TO THE SECRETARY OF THE BRITISH & FOREIGN ANTI-SLAVERY SOCIETY

"NEW YORK 1st April 1842.

"Dear Sir,

"I am instructed by our Committee to express to you their high gratification at the determination of your government not to surrender the negroes of the Creole, either as felons, or as slaves. It is now understood that their *surrender* will not be insisted on by our Cabinet, but that a pecuniary compensation for the loss of these human chattels will be peremptorily demanded.

"We are consulting the interests not merely of humanity, but also of our country, when we unhesitatingly declare our earnest wish that this demand may be promptly and resolutely refused. It

[62] *Congressional Globe*, 27th Congress, 2d Session, pp. 342–346.

would tend greatly to strengthen & perpetuate slavery among us, were other nations to recognize our property in human beings beyond the actual jurisdiction of our slave code.

"By acceding, moreover, to this demand, your Gov⟨t⟩. would become, in fact, to a very great extent, *insurers* of our American Slave Traders against shipwreck & revolt. This American slave trade is a most inhuman & detestable traffic, little if any inferior in atrocity to the African trade, & our slave holders are exceedingly anxious to compel Great Britain to recognize & respect it as a legitimate commerce. If Portugal still authorised the slave trade, & a cargo of Africans should happen to be brought into London under circumstances like those under which the Creole negroes were carried into your West Indies, would the British Nation condescend to participate in the accursed commerce by calculating and paying the market price of men, women & children?

"We are happy to assure you that Anti-Slavery principles are rapidly extending at the North, & are gaining converts even at the South. The Anti-Slavery *Organisation* is from various causes less efficient than formerly, but the tone of public opinion is decidedly improved, while the opposition to us has diminished in strength & virulence.

"We perceive at present but one obstacle to our ultimate and entire triumph, & that is the possible annexation of Texas with the United States. Should this renegade Republic be received into the Union, not only would the permanency of slavery be secured in this country, but the curse would probably be spread over Mexico, & perhaps far beyond it. The annexation is the last hope of the Slaveholders, and to effect it, their agents at Washington will endeavour to involve this country in a war with Mexico,—a measure which they justly believe would result in a union with Texas. The abolitionists will do their best to avert so dire a calamity, but it is uncertain how far success will attend their efforts.

"We shall be happy to receive frequent communications from you, & to co-operate with you in promoting the great cause of human liberty.

"I am, Sir, very Respectfully

"Y⟨r⟩ Ob⟨t⟩ Serv⟨t⟩, SIMEON S. JOCELYN

"Cor⟨s⟩. Sec⟨y⟩. of the Am. & Foreign A. S. Society."

"J. H. Tredgold Esq, Secretary &c

"No. 27 New Broad Street

"London."

"Pr Great Western.

"NEW YORK,
"April 28th 1842.

"JOHN SCOBLE, ESQ. 27 New Broad St.
London.

"My dear Friend,

"Your letter, owing to the putting back of the Steamer, did not reach me until a long time after it was written. The *document* you wrote for was not at hand, and after some correspondence & searching I am unable to obtain it. Judge Jay thinks the paper wanted issued from the Department of State some years earlier than 1828, & he promised to find it if possible. As this Gov^t has virtually abandoned its claim for the Creole *men*, and now restricts itself to a demand for remuneration the document may not be so much wanted as it might be under a different view of the case. I hope no remuneration will be allowed. If it should be our Southern slaveholders will find a market for their slaves in the West Indies.

"I send you by this opp^y a copy of Dr. Channing's popular little work, 'The Duty of the Free States or remarks suggested by the case of the Creole.' [63]

"Very aff^ecy & truly your's
"LEWIS TAPPAN."

"NEW YORK, June 16. 1842.

"J. H. TREDGOLD ESQ
27 New Broad St. London

"My dear Sir,

"Rev. James Steele, one of the missionaries who accompanied the Mendians to Sierra Leone, wrote to me April 20th that he was to leave in 12 days for London, on his way to this country. If he has arrived, please hand him the enclosed. If he has not arrived, and is expected, the letters can be retained at your office, with the exception of that directed to Rev. Wm. Raymond, and the one for Dr. Ferguson, which please forward to those gentlemen by first opportunity. Can you afford to send Mr. Raymond regularly your Reporter, and occasionally some other paper—pamphlets—or tracts?

[63] This was published in London and in Glasgow in 1842. It went through several editions, the same year, in the United States.

"Our Reporter is resumed & copies were forwarded some days since. Another number will be out on Saturday.

"With much regard, Yours truly,
"LEWIS TAPPAN.

"I read the account of your Anniversary with great interest."

"New York, July 11/42.
"WILLIAM ALLEN,[64] ESQ
          Chairman of the Com. of the B. and F. Anti S. Soc^y.
"Dear Sir,

          "The Circular bearing date June 13/42, from your office announcing that the Com. have fixed on the 13 June '43 [65] for the meeting of the Second General Conference of Abolitionists, is rec^d. It was laid before the Executive Com. of the Amer. & For. Anti-S. Soc. at their meeting on the 6th inst. The Com. directed that the Circular should be published as extensively as possible—that delegates should be appointed immediately—that measures should be taken to ascertain the names of American citizens who expect to be in London next June who are favorable to the anti-slavery cause that they may be induced to join this Society and be appointed delegates—and that a Correspondence should be opened with such persons in this country as it is desireable should attend the Conference.

"Be assured the Ex. Com. rejoice at the announcement made in the Circular, and will do all they can to forward the views of your Com. with respect to it.

[64] William Allen, one of the most revered of British philanthropists and one of the fathers of the anti-slavery movement, as of the aborigines' protection, was asked by the B. & F. A-S. Society Committee to stand in readiness to be the presiding officer of the Convention of 1843 in the event the aged Clarkson might not be fit or available for the post. Should anything transpire to prevent Allen's discharging the duty, it should devolve upon Samuel Gurney (*Minute Books*, II, 83).

[65] The question of the time of the next convention had been under consideration a long time. There is some indication in the Sturge correspondence that the Americans had originally wished to hold it in 1842; but, in July, 1841, Joshua Leavitt reported that, at a meeting of the Executive Committee of the A. & F. A-S. Society, July twenty-first, a preference had been shown for 1843, the date already resolved upon by the Committee of the B. & F. A-S. Society (Letter to Scoble, July 22, 1841). Further correspondence in anticipation of the Convention was arranged for in early December, 1842 (*Minute Books*, II, p. 17).

"They have already appointed seven of their number as delegates to represent the Com. & the Society.

"We have learned with grief of the death of Mr Tredgold, your esteemed & valued Secretary, but are yet unapprised of the name of his successor.[66]

"It will be very gratifying to the Com. to receive frequent communications from your Com. We wish you abundant success in your labors, and pray that the Almighty may be pleased to crown them with His benediction.

"Referring you to the annexed copy of the Constitution of our Society & the list of Officers I remain,

"Dear Sir, most cordially & respectfully

"your's

"LEWIS TAPPAN,

"*Cor. Sec.*"

" NEW YORK, July 15/42.

"By Caledonia.

"JOSEPH STURGE, ESQ.

"My dear Friend,

"Circumstances beyond my controul have prevented me from replying to your kind letter of June 2ᵈ. until this moment, which is only a few minutes before the post leaves for the Steamer, at Boston.

"I have read in the English newspapers, with great pleasure, the doings with reference to the election, and am daily expecting to hear of your election to Parliament.[67]

"The circular from your Comᵉ. respecting the London Conference has given much satisfaction. Our Comᵉ. have appointed six Delegates & the Circular will be extensively published.

" . . .

"Truly & affecly yours

"LEWIS TAPPAN"

---

[66] James Carlile took charge of the office temporarily (*Minute Books*, II, 116). In the B. & F. A-S. *Reporter*, III, 172, is a statement, concerning the permanent appointment of John Scoble, reprinted from the *Leeds Mercury*. His salary was fixed at £300 per annum (*Minute Books*, II, 5). The official notice of Tredgold's decease and services was singularly meagre.

[67] Had Sturge been elected—which he was not—he would have been one of the first members of the Society of Friends to sit in the House of Commons, Joseph Pease, elected in 1832, being the first. Interesting questions with respect to etiquette and procedure were raised at the time he, Pease, took his seat.

"NEW YORK,
"July 23d 1842.

"JOHN SCOBLE, ESQ.
London.

"My dear Sir,

"Yesterday I had the pleasure of rec⁵ yʳ'ˢ of the 2d.

"Respecting *Nelson Hackett*, the fugitive slave, given up by the Govʳ Genˡ of Canada,[68] on the requisition of the Executive of Arkansas Territory, much alarm and indignation were manifested at the first announcement of the intelligence, and there are reasonable doubts now whether under all the circumstances the giving up was not an impolitic, inhuman, and dangerous procedure. The material facts[69] are said to be these:—In July 1841 N. H. the slave of Alfred Wallace, Washington Co. Arkansas, took a horse valued at $300, a gold watch and chain valued at $200, with some minor articles, and fled towards Canada. He was about 30 years old, and a man of prepossessing address. He traveled through Illinois, Ohio, & Michigan to the Canada line, which he found no difficulty in crossing, and arrived in Sandwich, in September.

"During all this time 'the officers of justice' were in hot pursuit, the slaveholder having relinquished all claim to the negro. Ten days after N. H. had arrived at Sandwich he was overtaken by his pursuers. The horse and watch were found in his possession and the owner of the former being one of the pursuers it

[68] Sir Charles Bagot.

[69] B. & F. A-S. *Reporter*, III. Before the receipt of Tappan's letter, the case had come before the B. and F. A-S. Society Committee. At the meeting of June ninth (*Minute Books*, I, 543), it was resolved,

"That a letter be drafted embodying the facts of the case to be forwarded to Lord Stanley, and that J. H. Hinton be requested to draft the same."

In October, at the Committee meeting of the twenty-eighth, it was announced, inferentially, that all the materials in the case were not yet available inasmuch as papers laid before Parliament at the close of the last session had not yet been published (*idem.* II, 2). Two days before, there had appeared in *The Nonconformist* a letter from an American Quaker to Clarkson, dated September 17, 1842, containing the comforting intelligence that the cause in the United States was prospering because fugitives were making their escape to the North and being given a jury trial there; and the writer added, that the recent panic in the country was a just punishment on the United States for its guilt in slavery.

was given up to him. The watch was retained till further evidence could be obtained. Nelson was committed to jail, to await a requisition from the Governor of Arkansas [70] to the governor of Canada. This requisition was rec^d in February. Nelson was then brought over to the United States delivered into the custody of a Mr. Davenport who committed him to the jail in Detroit until the opening of navigation on the upper lakes. A few days previous to such opening a Mr. Evans arrived from Arkansas, with full power from the civil authorities to take him in charge. Engaging Mr. Davenport to accompany him, they left in one of the first vessels. They fell in with four men, from this State, bound to Iowa. Nelson contrived to escape at Princeton, Illinois. It was supposed that one of the New Yorkers aided him. Davenport & Evans offered a large reward for the apprehension & delivery of Nelson. After wandering about for two days & nights through the prairie and timber, and losing his way, he was taken only 7 miles from Princeton, by a man into whose house he went for the purpose of obtaining something to eat. His captor received his reward.

"If you have read the 'Address of the Peterboro' State Convention to the Slave' (written by Gerrit Smith) you will have seen that the ground is boldly taken that it is not stealing for a slave to take all along his route, in the free as well as in the slave State, so far as is absolutely essential to his escape, the horse, the boat, the food, the clothing, which he may require. This advice is viewed differently by abolitionists, and the pro-slavery part of the people are greatly excited by it. Many of our best men heartily approve the advice. If the Governor of Canada did he would not surely have given up Nelson. And if he did not I see not why he felt it incumbent on him to comply with the requisition. It is not an unusual trick for slave holders to accuse fugitives of stealing in the free States, and thus get possession of them, and the forms of the law may be prostituted in slave States to enable slaveholders to recover their slaves when they have escaped into free States. The governor might have waited until it was clearly shown that Nelson had been guilty of felony, or he might have refused giving him up even if he had been. Why should not the person of an American fugitive slave be as safe in Canada as in Nassau?

"I know of no other similar case.

[70] Archibald Zell.

Your letter shall be communicated to Mr. 'Weld. I will endeavor to make a good use of the pamphlets when they come to hand.

"Very truly your's
"LEWIS TAPPAN"

"NEW YORK, Oct. 21/42.

"JOHN SCOBLE, ESQ
London
"My dear Friend,

"Your letter informing me of your appointment as Secretary to the B & F. A.S. Soc. is received. I rejoice in this appointment.

"I send you by this opportunity some Reporters, No 7 for November, & will send the copies regularly that you desire.

"We have found it very difficult to get letters hence to Sierra Leone. Mr. Steele, who arrived here safely a few weeks since, says letters sent via London will reach soonest. I enclose a letter for Mr. Raymond which please send. The postage charge to the 'Union Missionary Society.' I am Treasurer of this Society & will be responsible for all you may pay.

"Please send Mr. Raymond a copy of your Reporter regularly.
"In great haste
"very truly your's
"LEWIS TAPPAN

"Please put the enclosed in an envelope & direct &c.
"I fear the Reporters will not be ready."

"NEW YORK, October 25/42.

"JOHN BEAUMONT, ESQ
27 New Broad St
London
"My dear Friend,

"I duly received your kind favor of 9/9 month, with the two copies of Queries.[71] I sent one copy to T. D. Weld, and inserted

[71] QUERIES RELATING TO SLAVERY IN THE UNITED STATES
(Issued 7th of 9th Month 1842)

1. From which of the Slave-holding States are slaves exported, specifying, as near as can be ascertained, the number sent from each State and the proportion that the males bear to females, and the adults to children?

the other in the Reporter N° 7 for November, just printed—a copy of which I send you. The Queries are admirably written & will, I hope, attract attention and induce replies. I have spoken to some influential abolitionists respecting them, and hope they will reply & give the needed information.

> "Very truly & affectionately your's
> "LEWIS TAPPAN

"Yours of May 3ᵈ. was duly received, for which I felt much obliged."

2. To which of the Slave States are they exported, and the proportion sent to each?

3. What is the average price of adult slaves, male and female?

4. Does the price of slaves vary with the fluctuations in the price of the produce they are employed in raising?

5. What are the chief productions of each of the slave-holding States, and the proportion that cotton, sugar, rice, tobacco and grain bear to each other in these States?

6. What is about the average annual expenditure of a planter for food, clothing, shelter, medical attendance &c for a slave?

7. Is the food and clothing for slaves imported either wholly or in part into any of the Slave States?

8. Is the mortality among slaves greatest on the sugar, rice, cotton or tobacco plantations?

9. Comparing the census of 1841 with that of 1831, in which of the Slave States has there been the greatest decrease in the Slave population, and in which the greatest increase—stating the causes, if they can be ascertained?

10. What is the lowest rate at which cotton, rice, sugar, tobacco and corn, can be grown in any of the Slave-holding States?

11. Have any experiments been made in these States, to grow the above articles by free labour—to what extent have they been carried, and how have they succeeded?

12. Are the plantations in the Slave-holding States much encumbered with debt, and what is the effect of this on cultivation and the price of produce raised?

13. Is there a general want of capital in the slave-holding States—on what terms do they borrow money, what guarantees do they give for its repayment, and how are the loans repaid?

14. To what extent are the slave holding States indebted to the free and to foreign countries?

15. What is supposed to be the average annual amount of goods, sent by the free to the slave-holding States, and how are they paid for?

16. What proportion does the foreign trade with the slave-holding States, bear to that with the free?

17. To what extent has the cultivation of land by the labour of slaves tended to deteriorate its quality and lower its price, and, in an economical point of view, interfere with the general prosperity of the States in which Slavery exists?

18. What has been, and is, the political effect of the existence of Slavery, on the institutions, the public men, and the people of the United States?

19. What has been the general financial effect of Slavery on the United States, considered as an element of national prosperity or decay?

20. What has been the moral and social effect of Slavery, on the general habits, modes of thought and feeling, of the people of the United States, especially what has been its effect on the various sections of the Christian church in that country?

"NEW YORK, Oct. 26/42.

"JOHN SCOBLE, ESQ
27, New Broad Street, London

"My dear Friend,

"My lad was a few minutes too late in his attempt to get the copies of the Reporter on board the vessel that took my letter of the 21st. I send you 20 copies of Nos 4, 5, 6 and 7. There are none left of Nos. 1, 2 & 3.

"Please send 2 or 3 copies of the N° 7 Reporter to Rev. Wm Raymond, York, Sierra Leone care Capt Wm Laurence, Sierra Leone. Will you bear him in mind & send him papers &c as op-

21. What has been the effect, morally and religiously considered of Slavery on the slave population generally—on the slave-holders and their families, and their connections in the free States?

22. What sections of the Christian church in the United States, are mostly distinguished by their hostility to Slavery and which are most remarkable for giving it countenance and support?

23. What has been the progress of the Anti-Slavery cause in the United States since the Convention held in London in 1840, in the State Legislatures, in Congress, in the action of religious bodies and particular churches, and in the public press and general periodical literature of the country?

24. What is the number of State anti-slavery societies, and their auxiliaries, at present in existence—what number connected with religious bodies—and what number not connected with either, but having peculiar organizations of their own?

25. What number of agents have these societies, actively engaged in disseminating anti-slavery principles and information throughout the United States?

26. What number of newspapers are either wholly or in part devoted to the anti-slavery case,—how are they supported,—what is their circulation, and, is there any demand for them in the Slave-holding States? (*Memorials and Petitions*, 1840–1843, pp. 135–137).

MISCELLANEOUS

1. Can you procure authentic copies of laws or parts of laws, passed in the Slave States which affect the free people of colour of the United States or of foreign countries resorting thither on their lawful occasions?

2. Can you procure copies of laws or parts of laws, in the several States of the Union which prohibit the education and religious instruction, either wholly or in part, of the slave population and people of colour?

3. What are the present relations of the United States with Texas, and what probabilities at present exist either for, or against, its annexation?

4. What measures have been taken by the United States government for the suppression of the Slave-trade on the part of its citizens, or others illegally employing its flag?

5. What progress has the liberty party made in its organization, and how are its efforts likely to tell on future elections to the State legislatures and to the general Government?

6. Are any African negroes surreptitiously introduced into any of the Slave states at the present time—in what number and by what means?

7. Are there any means of ascertaining the number of slaves, who have either been sold to planters in Texas, or who have been taken thither by their owners or who have been run into that republic by fraudulent debtors? (*Idem*, pp. 137–138).

portunities occur. He will be pleased to receive your Reporter, and any spare paper &c you have from this country. I will have 3 extra copies of the Reporter sent to you that you may send them to him by different opportunities. He is a dear brother & complains that he has received but few letters and little intelligence from America since he left.

"I enclose another letter for him. Please send it by a different opportunity from that by which you will forward the letters sent to you with mine of the 21st. We shall trouble you some in this way, & you may do so to us. I will thank you to keep an account of postage &c, letting me know how much is paid for the Mendi mission—both ways—& how much for other objects.

"It will be better to send all your communications directly to this city & none via Boston, as the postage is greatly increased when they come by the way of Boston.

"I have rec^d a bill of some £5 due from me to your office. Will you send me the particulars, when I will see that it is paid & charged to the proper accounts? I requested C. Stuart to pay what was due & he wrote that he did. He did not send particulars & I fear there is some mistake.

"Please inform me what publications should be taken by our Com^e to keep them well informed relating to all matters connected with the anti Slavery cause.

"My address is *L. T. New York*. Leave out 122 Pearl St or 143 Nassau.

"NEW YORK, Novr. 17/42.

"*Pr. G. Western.*

"JOHN SCOBLE, ESQ
      London.

"My dear friend,

"Your acceptable letter of Oct 3^d was duly received. I rejoice to learn that you have accepted the appointment of Secretary, as successor to the lamented Mr. Tredgold, and feel sure you can render valuable services to the great cause in this position.

" . . .

"Your remarks about British India I handed to the editor of the *Standard*,[72] as the Novr Reporter was printed a few days before your letter arrived. I am on so good terms with the editor, Mrs.

[72] See The New York *Standard*, November 3, 1842, p. 86.

Child,[73] as to do such favour readily. A more kindly feeling prevails on the part of the active members of the two divisions than formerly, at least it prevails with some of them.

"We have sent 20 copies of each of the Reporters that are on hand by a previous opportunity. Hope to hear they arrived.

"Mr. Weld has never published anything on the *New* Testament. Mr. Green [74] was about his Chattel Principle about the time Weld had finished his investigation of the Old Testament, & therefore forbore to touch the same subject. He may take hold of it at some future time. I will send you some of each very soon. We have about 300 of Weld's on hand.[75]

"I must break off or I shall be too late for the Gt. Western.

"With much regard your's
"LEWIS TAPPAN."

"pr. Great Western.

"JOHN BEAUMONT ESQ[r].
27 New Broad Street,
London.

"NEW YORK,
"Nov 17/42.

"Dear Sir,

"Yours of 20th/10 was duly received, with the book & pamphlets. Those for Judge Jay are delivered to him. This and the former similar present are very acceptable, & are on the shelves of the Ex. Com.

"Be so kind as to separate the half sheet for Mr Alexander.[76]

". . .

"After our interview with Lord Ashburton our fears respecting any action in Canada adverse to the safety of fugitive slaves subsided. If he was sincere—which we could not doubt—it seems to us impossible that your Government will allow any practice contrary to the intentions of the framers of the Treaty in Canada.[77]

[73] Mrs. Lydia Maria Child, who retired from the editorship of the *Standard* at the Annual Meeting of the American Anti-Slavery Society, May 9, 1844.

[74] Green, Beriah, *The chattel principle, the abhorrence of Jesus Christ and the apostles; or No refuge for Americans in the New Testament* (New York, 1839).

[75] Weld, Theodore D., *American slavery as it is: testimony of a thousand witnesses* (1839).

[76] George W. Alexander, Treasurer of the British and Foreign Anti-Slavery Society.

[77] How very unfortunate can the gaps in this correspondence be considered

Should they do so it will be a foul blot upon the fair fame of Old England. Fugitives are fleeing to Canada in all directions. The obstacles to their escape are lessening every day. Great alarm is felt in the Slave States contiguous to the free States. Still some very oppressive cases occur of hindrance opposed to the fugitive in the free States on the part of the hired agents of the Slaveholders & their sympathisers.

> "With much regard,
> "Your's resp^y & truly,
> "LEWIS TAPPAN.

"Copies of the Reporter (20 of all on hand) have been forwarded to 27 New B^d St as requested & will be hereafter while the Reporter is continued."

—gaps frequently not to be accounted for—is obvious here. Conceivably, this could not have been Lewis Tappan's first allusion to the great treaty that Lord Ashburton and Daniel Webster had negotiated, although, if we are to judge from a letter of his, originally published in the *Liberator* and commented upon in the B. & F. A-S. *Reporter* of the nineteenth of October, 1842 (III, 172), he was slow to develop misgivings as to the dangers that might lurk in the significant tenth article, the famous extradition clause. Clarkson's suspicions, on the other hand, were early aroused (*idem*, p. 175), as were those of Charles Stuart. At the B. & F. A-S. Society Committee meeting of thirtieth September, a letter was read from the latter,

> referring to the 10th clause in the recent boundary treaty with the United States having for its object the extradition of criminals . . . and the subject having been considered it was ordered that a letter be addressed to Dr. Lushington requesting an interview with him for the purpose of ascertaining whether by a forced construction or otherwise that clause can be brought to bear on fugitive slaves who have sought refuge in Canada or any other part of the British dominions (*Minute Books*, I, 571).

Pending a report from Dr. Lushington, the Committee resolved (Meeting of October 28, 1842, *idem*, II, 4) to follow the example of the Executive Committee of the A. & F. A-S. Society, and seek an interview with Lord Ashburton that his personal intentions as one of the negotiators might be determined.

By November 28, Scoble was able to report that he and John Beaumont had waited upon Dr. Lushington and that he had said, substantially,

> "that by nothing short of the most forced and 'treasonable construction,' could the clause be made to bear on fugitive slaves finding refuge in Upper Canada; but that nevertheless he would recommend the Committee to memorialize the British Government to the intent that no fugitive slave charged with any offence whatsoever should be given up by the Canadian Authorities; but only on the Authorities at home so deciding after the case had been fully submitted to them.—

"New York, Dec. 14/42.

"P^r. Virginia,
  L'pool.

"John Scoble, Esqr.
  London

"My dear Friend,

"Since mine of Novr 17th I am without anything from you.

"I enclose two letters for Rev. Wm. Raymond, Sierra Leone, which please forward as early as possible *by different opportunities.* I shall send another by the steamer Columbia tomorrow. As they contain, in triplicate, a letter of credit, I am anxious they should reach their destination as soon as possible. We have letters from Mr R. as late as Oct 28th. He remained at York, Sierra Leone, with 13 of the Mendeans who cleave to him. Mr & Mrs R. had both had the fever & have lost their only child. He is encouraged in the belief that Providence will open the way for the establishment of a mission. He & Mr Raston, a Wesleyan Methodist were about proceeding to the Sherbro in quest of a suitable location. I will thank you to send Mr Raymond the Reporter &c and any American papers you can spare. Please keep all the postages you pay on letters &c. to & from Africa distinct from other charges, holding me responsible.

"I have received a minute of £5. 7. 5 due from me to your office for the Patriot &c. I requested Charles Stuart to pay what was due from me & he wrote that he had done so. I have written to him for an explanation and when it is received will attend to the payment.

"The Latimer case in Boston, has aroused old Massachusetts. The results will be most propitious to the cause.[78]

Whereupon it was resolved:—

That the Secretary draft a Memorial, embodying the recommendation of Dr. Lushington, the same to be submitted to him for his approbation, and to be laid before the Committee at its next sitting" (*Minute Books,* II, 11).

[78] The importance of the George Latimer case is pointed out by Mc-Master (VII, 257). Massachusetts was, indeed, so aroused by the application by Justice Shaw of the decision in the Prigg case to the Latimer that her legislature passed "An Act further to protect personal liberty." Other states followed her example and thus the *personal liberty laws,* in contravention of the constitution, became the regular thing.

"Mr. J. Q. Adams has moved for the abolition of the famous 21st rule of the H. of Rep. in Congress which excludes petitions on the subject of Slavery, but his motion has been laid on the table. Vote of 106 to 102, so you see we are gaining ground there.

"I have rec⁴ a letter from Mr Dunlop, member of the Parliament in Canada respecting the case of Nelson Hackett. He wishes to know if he is delivered up to his master in Arkansas, a question I cannot at present answer. Should it be found that he has been, Mr. D. intends to move that the Legislature request the home Gov' to claim him.

"By a Packet to sail this day I shall send you 20 copies of Weld's [79] Bible vs Slavery, & 5 copies of the Chattell Principle in a box to be forwarded by Wiley & Putnam, Booksellers, of this city to their house in London, Amen Corner, St. Paul's. I think these establishments afford the best opportunities we, and our friends, have of sending pamphlets to our respective countries.

"Respy and very truly your's
"LEWIS TAPPAN."

"WASHINGTON CITY, Dec. 27. 1842
"JOHN SCOBLE ESQ.
        Sec. B. & F. A. S. Soc.
"Dear Sir,
          "I hasten to communicate to you an interesting piece of information I have just obtained from the Hon. Mr. Cross,[80] Representative in Congress from Arkansas. It is that Nelson Hackett, the colored man who was surrendered by the Governor of Canada on a requisition from the Governor of Arkansas, to answer to a charge of stealing, was taken to Arkansas, and without trial restored to the possession of his former master as a slave;—that he escaped again and was retaken, but finally escaped the third time & has not been heard of since—& whether he has gone over or is destroyed is not known.

"As it is reported that systematic measures have been adopted here for the recovery of the vast numbers of slaves that are escaping, by claiming them as felons, the exasperation and

[79] In a duplicate of this letter, also at Denison House, this work is referred to as Welsh's *Bible on Slavery*.
[80] Edward Cross.

dismay that exist here are indescribable, and if they should recover even one man, they would hope, by making him an example, to deter those that remain. The Canadian authorities ought to be expressly instructed to give up no colored man to the Slave States, on any pretext whatever. There is no other security.

"From a perusal of Mr. Benton's speech [81] in the Senate, against the ratification of the Ashburton treaty, I have no doubt the idea was seriously entertained that the 10th article would secure the surrender of slaves from Canada. He exposes its insufficiency for that purpose, & makes it a main ground of objection to the treaty itself, that it abandons the South. He says 'The South, left alone by the separate treaty now made for the Northern States, & with the sympathies of half the Union & all the rest of the world against her, must now expect greater outrages than ever, in all that relates to her slave property.' None of the slaves that have escaped from this neighborhood have been recovered. Probably the loss in value is at best a hundred thousand dollars in the last six months.

"We are expecting some exciting debates on the subject whenever the treaty shall come before Congress. I have no doubt the London Committee will exercise due vigilance in regard to the regulation of Parliament to carry the treaty into effect. Mr. Benton, in his speech recites the *proviso* of Art. 10, & proceeds to say,

" 'This reduces the engagement to the merest hoax. The offence is to be one for which the fugitive could be arrested and tried, if committed at the place of apprehension. And who supposes that in the abolition dominions of Great Britain, the murder or robbery of a master by his slave will be admitted to be a crime for which the perpetrator should be delivered up to justice? Even admitting that, under the common law of England, there may be a killing of a master by his slave, under circumstances which would amount to murder, yet who would expect, in the present state of British feeling, that the law would be executed by a British judge? Who would expect even such a murderer to be given up, much less when the killing takes the form of defence against violence, or escape from oppression?'

"I shall be happy to hear from you. Address to Boston. We

[81] *Congressional Globe*, XII, 27th Cong., 3rd Sess., Appendix, p. 12 ff.; for Benton's attitude on the quintuple treaty see *Idem*, p. 63 ff.; Dec. 20, 1842. He argued that this treaty was a threat by England, France, Russia, Prussia, and Austria to compel the United States to maintain its own African squadron.

are beginning to flatter ourselves that the plot for annexing Texas
to the United States has been defeated by exposure, for this year.[82]

"Yours sincerely

"JOSHUA LEAVITT."

"WASH^{GTON}. City
"29 Jan. 1843

"JOHN SCOBLE ESQ.

(acknowledging Scoble's letter of December 30, 1842, which
was forwarded to him in Washington), "where I have been in attendance several weeks, for the purpose of watching over the interests of the Anti-Slavery cause as connected with the action
of our Federal Government. It is my present expectation that I
shall attend the London meeting, & I need not assure you that I look
forward to it with the deepest interest. It is probable that owing
to the prevailing scarcity of money, the attendance of delegates
from this country will be small — I shall, however, take immediate measures to call the public attention to it, by inserting
your circular again in the Emancipator & by copying also your
able list of queries to solicit information on various subjects. . . .

". . .

"JOSHUA LEAVITT"

NEW YORK, January 30th 1843

"JOHN SCOBLE, ESQ. SEC. &C.
       London.

"My dear Sir,

"Your favour of 30th Dec. was received a day or two since. I
tender to the Committee my most grateful acknowledgements for
their kind invitation [83] to attend the proposed Convention in Lon-

82 For additional information on the British attitude regarding Texas,
see Adams, Ephraim Douglas, . . . *British Interests and Activities in Texas,*
1838–1846 (1910); *British Correspondence Concerning Texas* (1912–1917);
and for the British attitude on the Civil War, see his *Great Britain and the
American Civil War* (2 vols., 1925). This is a monumental work.

83 The following were men to whom a special invitation to attend the
Convention would seem to have been sent; Lewis Tappan, S. S. Jocelyn,
G. Smith, Samuel Webb, William Goodell, B. Green, J. G. Birney, H. B.
Stanton, J. C. Fuller, William Dawes, C. P. Grosvenor, A. A. Pennock, A.

don next June, but my business and engagements are such that I do not see how it will be in my power to be absent for the time it would require. Last year I looked forward with considerable hope & expectation that I should be able to attend the Convention. Were I able to do so it would gratify me exceedingly. The sacrifice I should be obliged probably to make to go would seriously affect the business in which I am now engaged.

"At the last meeting of our Ex. Com. I was instructed to make enquiry as to the number of persons who would probably go from this country to attend the Convention. After inquiry & correspondence I fear the number will be few. The pecuniary affairs of the country are such that few comparatively can afford the expense. This circumstance will undoubtedly prevent many from going who would otherwise be pleased to attend. The state of Mr. Weld's family will prevent him from going this year at least, Mr. G. Smith's affairs will prevent him from going, & I know others who feel as if it would be impossible for them to be absent the present year. Under these circumstances many American abolitionists would undoubtedly be pleased if the proposed Convention could be postponed one year. I make the suggestion. Still if the London Committee, with the information given, think it important or desirable that the Convention sh^d be held as proposed they can rely, I think, on seeing Joshua Leavitt, Amos A. Phelps and William Shotwell, and perhaps others.

"With true regard sincerely your's
"LEWIS TAPPAN."

"Pr. Geo. Washington via Liverpool, with 2 & 3d to Mr. Raymond enclosed.

"NEW YORK,
"Feb. 7/43

"JOHN SCOBLE, ESQ.
27 New Broad St,
London.

"My dear Sir,

"Referring you to my last, of Jany. 30th, respecting the expected Anti-Slavery Convention—stating that probably but

A. Phelps, Elizur Wright, Joshua Leavitt, Charles Osborn, J. T. Norton, N. Fowler, Elon Galustia [Galusha?], Dr. Brisbane (B. & F. A-S. Society Committee Meeting, December 6, 1842, *Minute Books*, II, 17).

few would go from this country, and that many of our friends
would be gratified if the Convention could be deferred to another
year—I now enclose two copies (duplicate & triplicate) of a letter
to Rev. Wm. Raymond which I will thank you to enclose and forward by the first two good vessels for Sierra Leone, charging the
postage to the Mendi mission. We feel very desirous that they
should reach him as soon as possible. Please forward him the Reporter, and any other newspapers &c., that will be useful to him.

"We have in press an Address [84] to the Non-Slaveholding citizens of the Southern States, to be issued by the Com. of the A. &
F. Anti-S. Society, that contains very valuable information & wh
will be sent to you when published (It is from the pen of Judge
Jay, at the suggestion of S. S. Jocelyn).

"I have done what I could to disperse the sets of Queries received from the office in London, but I fear no one will do the subjects justice. Mr Weld promises to do something. Both he & Mr
Leavitt are at Washington where they will remain until the close of
this short session of Congress. Nothing of importance will be
done in Congress, this season, on the Anti-Slavery subject. The
session will end the 3d of March.

"We have in this State a 'democratic' government & majority
in both houses of the Legislature, and it will be their policy, it is
feared, to undo as much as they can of ex-governor Seward's acts
—noble acts—on behalf of the free people of color & fugitives from
slavery. Apropos—you will be pleased with gov-Seward's replies [85]
to the addresses of colored citizens on his retiring from public life.
He retires at an early age being but little over forty, but he will
be called back at some future day probably.

"The *cause* is decidedly onward in this country malgre the dis-
cordances of abolitionists—their personalities & splitting up into unfriendly parties.

"Very truly yours

"LEWIS TAPPAN."

[84] This address anticipated many of the arguments of Helper, H. R.,
Impending Crisis of the South, 1857.

[85] *The Works of William H. Seward*, ed. by George E. Baker (1887)
III, 437–438.

"JOHN SCOBLE, ESQ^r.   "NEW YORK,
27, New Broad St.   "March 1. 1843.
London.

"My dear Friend,

      "I thank you for the copies of the notes [86] between you and the *honest* Lord Ashburton. If your country &

[86] The following, although of considerably earlier date, may have been some of those referred to:

(a) "TO THE RIGHT HON. LORD ASHBURTON
      &c   &c   &c
                    "27, NEW BROAD STREET, LONDON
"*My Lord*,   "29th. October 1842

"The deep anxiety felt by the friends of the Anti-Slavery cause, on both sides of the Atlantic, as to the true interpretation of the 10th. Clause of the Treaty, which your Lordship recently negotiated with the American Government, whether by any construction, forced or otherwise, it can be made to bear on the security, at present enjoyed, by fugitive slaves who have fled from oppression in the United States, to the British Territories in Canada, the Committee of the British and Foreign Anti-Slavery Society offer as their apology for troubling you on the subject. But feeling that, in a merely written communication, they could not do justice to so important a matter, and anxious to bring under the consideration of your Lordship some important points relative thereto, I am directed by the Committee respectfully to solicit for a deputation of that body the honor of an interview with your Lordship at such time as may be convenient for your Lordship to receive them.
        "I have the honor to be
              &c   &c
      (Signed) "JOHN SCOBLE, *Secv.*"

(b)   R e p l y
                   "THE GRANGE, ALRESFORD.
"Sir,   4th. Novr. 1842

"The letter you did me the favor of addressing me on the 29th. Ult^o., having by some accident been detained in Town reached me only yesterday. It needed no apology and I beg you will assure the Gentlemen who take so laudable an interest in the objects of the Anti-Slavery Society that they would not be more disappointed and grieved than I should be if any part of the Treaty lately concluded by me with the United States of America should tend to impair in any way the protection which fugitive slaves receive when they take refuge in any of our Colonies. I have had this subject anxiously in my mind throughout my negotiation and I have no doubt of being able to satisfy the Committee of your Society; but as you properly observe, this is a question better considered by a conference than by letter, and it will give me much pleasure to meet your deputation not only with a view to this particular case, but generally to confer with them on the state of things connected with the objects of their association. I am not aware that there is any pressing necessity requiring very early attention or that the subject may not rest until we all meet in Town after Xmas; but if the Gentlemen on your Committee think otherwise I will take the earliest opportunity of being in Town for a day or two and give you notice when it may be in my power to see them.
        "I am very truly, Sir,
          "Your very obedt. Servant
            (Signed) "ASHBURTON
"JOHN SCOBLE ESQ
  Secy. to the B & F. Anti-Slavery Socy."

mine would always depute such men to negotiate treaties and maintain harmonious correspondence there would be perpetual peace & mutually advantageous commercial intercourse. Interested politicians may call such treaties 'capitulations' but they (are) founded upon the Divine system of christianity & more honorable to nations than battles won at Trafalgar or Waterloo.

"You invite me to a regular correspondence & promise to return letter for letter. The inducement is great, but in the multiplicity of my affairs I fear I should be an inconstant & unsatisfactory correspondent. I am acting as Cor. Sec. because I write faster (I know no other good reason) than my colleagues and I have not time to record one quarter of the interesting intelligence that comes to my knowledge. However, I accept your proposal, expecting you will make generous allowances for a merchant & make me liberal compensation by your own frequent & interesting Letters.

"The cause is onward in this country. We are steadily & surely approaching a crisis. The Slave-holders are beginning to find out that emancipation has taken place in the West Indies and that amidst unavoidable difficulties, it works well.[87] They are realizing

(c) "To THE RIGHT. HON. LORD ASHBURTON
&c &c &c

"27, NEW BROAD STREET, LONDON
Nov. 10th. 1842

"My Lord,
"I beg to acknowledge the receipt of your communication of the 4th. Inst, and to tender to you, on behalf of the Comme. their best thanks for the same.
The Committee cannot propose that your Lordship should come to Town expressly for the purpose of seeing them on the subject referred to in their letter of the 29th Ulto., anxious as they are for the interview, but should you have occasion to be in Town any time before Christmas they will feel obliged by an intimation of it when a Deputation from the Committee will do themselves the honor of waiting upon you.
"I take the liberty of stating that there is no question in which the Correspondents of the Committee, take a deeper interest at the present time, than that of the 10th. Article of the late Treaty negotiated by your Lordship with the Foreign Secretary of the United States, or one on which they are more anxious for correct information.
"I have the honor to be
&c &c
(Signed) "JOHN SCOBLE, Secv."

[87] Scoble, who so frequently spoke and wrote on this subject, regarding himself as an authority, had only very recently said that the results of emancipation within the British colonies were good, public affairs were tranquil, crime diminishing, the negroes industrious. Women had been withdrawn from field labor, the children were in school, the men had now a variety of occupation. It was the droughts and not emancipation that had affected the production

too that slavery compared with requited labor is a losing business— a ruinous affair. Information is penetrating the Slave States—the consciences of not a few are moved—and an increasing apprehension is felt that the days of slavery are determined. The desperate slaveholders are now looking with intense interest to the hope of having Texas annexed to this Union. If Texas can be annexed slavery, they think, will live one more generation but if they can not they almost despair of its outliving the present one. Towards the close of the late Session of Congress a secret movement was made by the slaveholding members, and what might be termed a Plot was devised to have some definite action on the subject. The friends of Liberty ascertained what was going on & took measures to oppose the attempt. They did not content themselves with this but appointed one of their number to write an Appeal to the People of the United States warning them of the Plot. This address was prepared & received the signature of the venerable Adams and several others. They intend to have it circulated among the members and after getting all the signatures they can to publish the Appeal. The friends of universal freedom must be wide awake, to use a Yankee expression, to detect & expose schemes for the annexation of Texas. Should such a disastrous event ever take place it must be in consequence of the votes of Northern men who will sell liberty for office & must surely end in the dissolution of the Union of these States. Gr^t Britain can do much to avert the dire calamity. Christians can do much in their beseechings of the Great Ruler of Nations to avert a measure that must be calamitious to the whole human race.

"The contest for the Presidential chair will be, principally, between Mr. Van Buren & Mr. Calhoun, for I do not think that Mr. Clay, after all, will be very strongly supported. The Whig party is divided & will not be reunited. Its power is gone. But the democratic party, heretofore united, seems about suffering disunion. There are several prominent men who have been partisans, Messrs. Benton, Cass, Buchanan, &c., but Van Buren & Calhoun will, it is believed, finally be the only candidates of that party. Each is straining every nerve to obtain the object of his ambition. The man that will make the most promises will probably be the suc-

of sugar in Jamaica, Barbados, and British Guiana. Moreover, British exports had increased one-third in value since 1834 (B. & F. A-S. *Reporter*, III, 49).

cessful one. If Van Buren will promise to use all his influence
for the admission of Texas, he and Calhoun hesitate on that point
he will probably succeed. On the contrary if M^r. Calhoun goes
out and out for the annexation of Texas and makes satisfactory
promises to Northern democrats respecting points in which they
feel a local & peculiar interest he may succeed. Not improbably
the great question that will decide the matter will be Texas. In
this view of the case the next Presidential contest is one of immense importance to the cause of human rights, & may be decisive
of the Union of these States. Mr. Calhoun is a man of great capacity, experience, & industry, and is for perpetual slavery. Mr.
Van Buren is more insinuating & popular, with less principle. He
would sell the North to obtain the suffrages of the South, and rivet
the fetters around millions of his fellow-men to obtain personal
advantages for a brief period.

"You can not but have noticed the strong desire manifested on
the part of Mr Calhoun to maintain peace with England. He
doubtless feels that war would not only endanger his own prospects but endanger the stability of the slave system. He is too wise
a politician to indulge even in vaporing against G. B. at such a
crisis. I am rejoiced to see that your Statesmen maintain the right
ground on the subject of visitation of ships at sea.[89] . It is to be
hoped that they will stick to that point. They may be assured that
there are Statesmen and intelligent citizens in this country who
hold to the same doctrine and also that the so called slaves of the
Comet & Endymion [90] as well as of the Enterprise & the Creole
were free by the operation of our National Constitution the moment
they passed from the local jurisdiction of a Slave State into National jurisdiction on the High Seas. It is, in the language of a

[89] President Tyler's First Annual Message, December 7, 1841 (Richardson, J. D., Messages and Papers of the Presidents, IV, 74–89) had reviewed
the correspondence between Stevenson and the British Foreign Office on this
subject and an article in the B. & F. A-S. Reporter, January 12, 1842, embodying the gist of it re-stated the British position with exactness, especially
as it affected the anti-slavery cause. In this and subsequent years, there was
occasion for frequent repetition of this sort of thing; for it was not only
as between Great Britain and the United States that the right of search
was a matter in controversy. With France, likewise, it was a diplomatic
issue. In this connection, Clarkson's letter of March 1, 1845, and Canning's
reply of the twentieth are of interest.

[90] It would seem that this should be the Encomium. For an account of
these various cases, see McMaster, J. B., VI, 241–243.

friend in Ohio, whose letter is now before me, a disgrace to our Government that any negotiation was ever set on foot for indemnity in either of these cases for the negroes were free long before they reached British Territory. It is, he says, a deep disgrace that indemnity for the human cargoes of the two vessels first named was actually received into our National treasury. Not a few in this country, who feel it to be so have cleared themselves of participation in it by an emphatic protest against it. G. B. can hardly injure the cause of the American slave so much as by allowing preposterous claims set up by this country with regard to slaves. Your country should interpret the American Constitution literally, and in connection with the Declaration of Independence, & allow nothing, unless obligated to do so by treaty that these instruments do not justify this Gov^t in requiring. No question of policy, no desire to extend commerce, should ever induce them to take the side of American slaveholders & their abettors against those who here advocate the cause of human rights & against those who are suffering the galling yoke of slavery—We look to Gr. B. to to be the bulwark of Liberty, and distressing is it to the friends of freedom in this land whenever she stoops from the high moral grandeur on which by the Providence of God she has often stood to perform acts of oppression or inhumanity. Oh that G. B. so enlightened & so powerful would ever employ the great resources the Almighty hath imparted to her in ameliorating the condition of mankind, in diffusing peace, liberty, knowledge, temperance, learning, & religion throughout the world without a single act of oppression, violence or inhumanity to stain her escutcheon.[91]

"You will have noticed that a large number of influential merchants & persons interested in the coastwide navigation of this

[91] While it is true that the settlement of the slavery question probably cost the American people more lives than all the wars of Great Britain combinded up to the Great War, England cannot be held to blame for the American Civil War. The responsibility which Tappan and his followers throw upon Great Britain for the eventual outcome of the anti-slavery struggle in the United States strikes one, at this distance of time, as having been almost absurd and would have been so regarded then by any one not of the anti-slavery persuasion. These American letters have to be read with the strength of the slave power and the desperate situation of American anti-slavery in mind. British anti-slavery leaders accepted all criticisms in the right spirit. Had they been petty or resentful the B. & F. A-S. Society would not now be working in that same great cause of freedom, long after all interest in world anti-slavery has been dead in America.

country, in Boston, New York, Cincinnati, &c, have sent to Congress memorials against the laws of the Southern States which authorize the imprisonment of colored seamen, cooks, stewards &c. A capital Report in favor of the prayer of the memorialists was made in the House of R. by Mr Winthrop,[92] of Boston, but the Southerners contrived to have it laid upon the table after ordering its being printed. Still, Congress will not be likely to have much rest from the exciting theme.

"The law granting trial by Jury to persons arrested in this State as fugitives from Southern slavery will probably be speedily repealed. The administration in this State has been recently changed. The new Governor, Bouck, (pron. Bouke) willing to please his party & those of them who live at the South, adopts a policy on this subject somewhat at variance with that of the late excellent Governor, Seward. These things are distressing, but they do not indicate that free principles are on the retrograde. Party leaders keep up false fires to deceive.

"It is quite certain that the number of those at the South who are enquiring, reading & reflecting upon the subject of the abolition of slavery is greatly on the increase. Mr. Leavitt, on his return from Washington, informed us that the Hon James J McKay, Elizabethtown, Bladen Co, N. Carolina, who is one of the ablest and most upright members of Congress, & who takes an interest in the question of the Slave Trade &c lately applied to him at Washington for statistical information on the subject of the Slave Trade. He also wished for precise information as to the manner in which the British Gov^t dispose of the recaptured Africans. Mr. Leavitt thinks that a systematic attempt is going on to create odium against the English Gov^t for converting the recaptured Africans into soldiers & 'apprentices' and remarks that the slaveholders always give a significant curl of the lip to the latter word. Will you give in the Reporter full & precise information on this subject? Mr. McKay has a copy of the 2nd Report of your Com. & I think I shall send him one of the 3rd lately received.

"Mr. Gurney sent to me the copies of the Report directed by you to several individuals, they have been mostly forwarded according to direction. It is a valuable document.

"Congress adjourned without receiving the Latimer petition

[92] Robert C. Winthrop.

which Mr. Adams made several attempts to present. Its appearance however—as large as a bomb—on his desk for several days, attracted much attention, & the moral effect of a presentation was accomplished. As the next Congress will contain an increased number of 'northern men with Southern principles' it has been feared the gag Rule in Congress, the 21st rule, would be continued, but a letter to an abolitionist from an influential & conspicuous slaveholder, of recent date, says in substance that the progress of public opinion would soon rescind the rule; that then would come the abolition of slavery in the District of Columbia and the total insufferance of slavery beyond the borders of Slave States; that then Kentucky, Tennessee, Missouri & perhaps Maryland & Virginia awakening to a sense of their true interests would abolish slavery of their own accord. No doubt says the friend to me to whom the letter was addressed there are many, very many slaveholders who believe slavery to be a curse and a grievous violation of the code of equal rights & who would willingly concur in putting an end to its existence by legislative enactment, who do not regard it as a sin or moral wrong & have no scruples on the point of slaveholding, simply because they are not religious men & therefore will not emancipate though willing to vote for emancipation. This friend of mine hints these men look to the Liberty Party in the U. S. with great interest & hope. They wish, he says, to see it become so powerful, that they may safely move towards emancipation by law at home, without the fear of being crushed by the weight of the local Slavery party backed by the public sentiment which has been made almost universal by the almost universal array of the people in the ranks of pro-slavery parties. It is said by my friend that there are not a few such men, & he thinks that if the people of the free States could be brought to a clear perception of their own connexion with responsibility for National Slavery and would act as Liberty men against National Slavery consistently unitedly & efficiently they wᵈ find themselves soon reinforced by the friends of Liberty in Slave States who would act, not only against National but against State Slavery and the overthrow of both would then be near.

"The Address to non-Slaveholders by our Ex-Com. is exciting considerable attention. The facts embodied in it are very valuable. The fact disclosed that so small a proportion of the white citizens of the South are Slaveholders astonishes people here at the North who have been accustomed to look upon most of the white inhabitants of [the] South as Slaveholders or in the families of Slaveholders. Slavery does not appear so formidable when it is considered how few the number of Slaveholders is, & the danger and 'loss' of abolition dwindles when it is seen that a small comparative number are directly interested in the system.[93] The attention of the small farmers, mechanics, merchants, &c of the South, who are not Slaveholders will be attracted to this subject I doubt not; & they too will begin to consider that the majority suffers for the interests of the minority, & that real estate, business &c, suffer throughout the community to enrich a few nabobs. We intend to publish this Address far and wide in the hope it will exert a powerful influence.

"I will give you a fact that shows the prevalence of anti-slavery principles at the North. A professor of a college in New Hampshire (Dartmouth College) called upon me to-day and solicited on behalf of a literary institution near the College a donation of one copy of each of the publications of the American Anti-Slavery Society for its library. He says the President & all the professors are abolitionists. There is little sale of such publications at present unless they are in the form of newspapers or pamphlets. Book reading seems in a great measure to be superseded here by newspapers. All the popular new works are published in this form and distributed over the country at a very cheap rate. The two volumes of Dickens Notes, for example, were published here in pamphlet form and sold for 12 cts a copy (about sixpence sterling)! —The Anti-Slavery matter that will be henceforth read will be anti-slavery newspapers & pamphlets in addition to articles in magazines & newspapers.

"The time has come, I think, when we may advantageously use many of the magazines & newspapers, which have hitherto refrained from publishing much of anything on the subject of anti-slavery instead of being at the expense of publishing in papers &c, of an exclusive anti-Slavery character. Many editors will now admit anti-Slavery matter who would not have done it heretofore. The money necessary to support one anti-Slavery paper would be sufficient to feed many commercial, literary & religious newspapers. For one I have always been of the opinion that we had too many anti-Slavery newspapers in this country.

93 The extent to which this work of Judge Jay's anticipated Helper's *Impending Crisis* fourteen years later is well worth noting.

"Not being able to attend the approaching London Convention I have offered to aid three brethren by contributing what would be my own expenses should they conclude to go. I hope there will be a respectable delegation from this country.

"I perceive this morning in a leading Virginia newspaper the frank & explicit avowal that Slavery is inconsistent with Democratic principles! The editor says no Slave holder can consistently be a democrat. He is a Whig, & is taunting his opponents. Still the avowal, considering its source, is an important admission.

"The warfare between the Old organisation—which is in possession of the *name* of the Amer. Anti-Slavery Society—and the New Organisation, including the Liberty Party—is unrelenting. They denounce us without reserve, and have no sympathy either with us or English abolitionists who sympathise with us. All hope of reunion is out of the question. The N. Y. Standard, edited by Mrs Child, is the organ of the A. Anti. S. Soc, but she is moderate compared with the Liberator, Herald of Freedom &c. My brother Arthur I understand has been denounced in the Liberator. They make anti-S. *organisation* here almost a stench.

"I have written, I think, more than you will have patience to read, & remain very truly your's,

"LEWIS TAPPAN."

"BOSTON, March 9, 1843.

"JOHN SCOBLE ESQ.

"My dear Sir—

"Your letter of Dec. 3, sent I believe through our friend Lewis Tappan, reached me at Washington, about the first of this month. Please direct to me, direct, by the Liverpool & Boston steamers. If your government will do justice in the case of the poor hunted colored people, they must resolve to surrender no person of color without the most indubitable proofs that he is free, & that enslavement forms no part of the penalty of the offence charged, by the laws of the State where he is to be tried—nor of any other offence for which he may be liable to prosecution when once in the power of his pursuers. In short, I think no person of color can be righteously delivered into the power of American authorities on any allegation whatever.[94] I

[94] To this very conclusion the B. & F. A-S. Society had already arrived. At a special meeting, called for the sixth of February, it was resolved to

have heard, since my arrival from Washington, that Mr. Fuller
has gone to England to collect funds for the Canadian seminary
established by Hiram Wilson. It seems to me that if the Christians
memorialize Lord Aberdeen "with a view to preventing" the application
of Clause 10 "to that class of Persons under any circumstances or pretext
whatsoever" (*Minute Books*, II, 41). At another special meeting of the
Committee, on the thirteenth of February, the draft of a memorial was
considered and adopted (*idem*, p. 42):

"On the Extradition Clause of the Treaty of Washington
"My Lord,
      "I beg to forward to your Lordship copy of a Memorial agreed to
at a Special Meeting of the Committee of the British & For. A. S. Soc⁷ relative
to the extradition clause of the Washington Treaty, with a request that your
Lordship will be pleased to allow them to present it by deputation, at such
time as may suit your Lordship's leisure and convenience to receive them.
                    "I have &c
                    (Signed) "Jno Scoble, Sec."

              "The Right Hon. The Earl of Aberdeen
"Her Majesty's Principal Sec⁷ of State for Foreign Affairs
"My Lord,
      "Deeply impressed with the importance of the subject, and convinced
that it requires and deserves the most mature consideration of Her Majesty's
Government, the Comme. of the B. & F. A. S. Soc⁷, venture respectfully to
call your early and serious attention to the bearing of the extradition clause of
the Treaty recently negotiated between the Government of this Country and
that of the United States on the case of fugitive slaves who have sought
a refuge from oppression within the British Dominions.
      "It has long been one of the chief glories of this land, as it is now
of all its dependencies in the Western World, that the moment a slave touched
its soil, he was free, and became entitled to protection for his life, his liberty and his property. The Committee, however, conceive that the Clause referred to may become a weapon in the hands of the Slave-holders for destroying
the dearest rights of humanity—for violating the sanctuary of freedom in
this Country—and for compelling British Functionaries of every class to become
to the oppressor instruments of tyranny in restoring to perpetual bondage
his lost and highly coveted prey. The operation of the clause extends to every
part of the British dominions including Great Britain and Ireland. Besides
Murder, *Assaults* with intent to commit murder, Piracy, Arson, and Forgery,
it embraces every imaginable offence comprehended within the term robbery.
It provides that a single Justice of the Peace shall be competent to decide
on the committal of the accused, on *ex-parte* evidence—it may be the oath
of a single witness, or the attested affidavit of a suborned in the United States.
Moreover, it gives no power to the Executive to withhold the warrant of
surrender in any case where the terms of the clause have been complied with.
All that it requires is such *prima facie* evidence of criminality as, according
to the laws of the place where the fugitive is found, would justify his apprehension and commitment for trial; and the surrender follows as matter of
course.
      "In the case of a freeman charged with a criminal offence, the barest
amount of evidence is sufficient to warrant commitment and delivery; but,
in his case, ample provision is made by law for his trial before an impartial
tribunal, by a jury of his peers, with every possible means of defence that
equity and humanity can afford. If innocent, he is acquitted—if falsely
charged he has his remedy—if guilty he suffers that amount of punishment

of England intend to sustain that institution, they should hold its conductors responsible to them. I think Wilson has done great good as a most laborious pioneer in looking after the poor fugitives

only awarded by the law against all similarly circumstanced with himself. The case is otherwise with the fugitive slave—on the barest amount of evidence he also may be committed and delivered. But no impartial trial awaits him—no jury of his peers pronounces on his guilt or innocence—no means of defence are provided for him—his fellow-slaves may be witnesses against, but not for him—nor against his master. His accuser may be a Slave-holder—his Jury Slaveholders—his Judge a Slave-holder. Thus circumstanced, though he may be innocent his escape from conviction is next to impossible, but should he be honorably acquitted, he is not therefore liberated from suffering. He falls into the hands of an infuriated master to suffer the degradation and horrors of perpetual slavery, and the infliction of punishments the most terrible and revolting. But if found guilty he is subjected to a far heavier punishment than if he were a free-man. In Virginia, an old Slave State, wilfully setting fire to any barn &c, or advising &c, the perpetration of such offence, in the case of a slave *death*—in that of a free-man, payment of the value of property destroyed and imprisonment for not less than *two* nor more than five years. Breaking into any Warehouse or Storehouse and taking money or goods to the value of four dollars, in the case of a Slave *death*—in that of a free-man, imprisonment for not less than one nor more than ten years: Horse-stealing, in the case of a slave, *death*—in that of a free-man, restoration of property stolen, and imprisonment for not less than five or more than ten years: *Attempting* to commit a rape on a white woman, in the case of a slave, *death*—in that of a free-man not a statutable offence, but punishable as an assault and battery, by fine and imprisonment at the discretion of the Court: Burglary, in the case of a slave, *death*—in that of a free-man imprisonment for not less than five nor more than ten years.

"In Mississippi, a new Slave State, wilfully burning a barn or stable, in the case of a Slave *death*—in that of a freeman, imprisonment not exceeding six months and paying damages: *Assault* with intent to commit murder, in the case of a slave *death*—in that of a free man, a fine at the discretion of the Court and imprisonment not exceeding one year, and exaction of surety of the peace: Attempting to commit rape, burglary and robbery, in the case of a slave, death—in that of a free-man, imprisonment not exceeding one year: Horse-stealing, in the case of a slave *death*—in that of a free-man not provided for by statute.

"These are given by way of specimen; but in looking over the various codes of Laws, now in operation in the United States, the Comm^e. find that there are no less than seventy one crimes punishable with death in the case of Slaves, whilst in that of free-men the highest penalty is imprisonment in the penitentiary. Surely my Lord, it were the height of injustice as well as cruelty to surrender slaves to the vengeance of such Laws, especially when it is considered that in the event of capital convictions taking place, the value of the slave is paid for by the State so that the master is no loser by his death; but a gainer, in every case where the slave is surrendered for an alleged infringement of the Laws. This leads the Comm^e. to observe that in the case of venial or it may be even of grave offences committed by free-men, the injured party may not for various reasons pursue them, but the motives on the part of Slave-holders to pursue their slaves are of the strongest kind; they have a large pecuniary stake in fugitive slaves—they fear the contagion of example, and will take every means for recovering them, that they may not only demonstrate the insecurity of British territory as an asylum of liberty but for the purpose of striking terror into their miserable companions in bondage by the severity of their punishments or even by their death. It may therefore be fully calculated upon that if they have the least ground on which to found a charge they will avail themselves of it, to regain their victims; and it may be feared that when no offences against law, has actually

from American oppression, but I confess I do not feel so much confidence in his ability to manage an institution of learning or any other matter involving a large expenditure of money.   I there-

been committed, or can be maintained before any competent tribunal, attempts will be made to obtain them by the thousand ways in which iniquity often triumphs over justice.   Moreover as the recovering of fugitive Slaves is deemed a matter of serious importance by Slave-holders generally they will be ready to sympathize with and eager to aid any of their fellows in accomplishing, to them, so desirable and necessary an object.   The clause of the Treaty referred to enables them to do this, by affording them the best, because the easiest, the least expensive, and most effectual way of satisfying their cupidity and glutting their vengeance.   That Clause enables them to seize fugitive slaves even in the streets of London, to place them in custody, and by false accusations and the foulest means, to obtain possession of their persons for the purpose of hurling them back again into a bondage more dreadful than that from which they had escaped at the peril of their lives.   Surely, my Lord, the British Government can never be parties to so fearful a result as this.

"The Committee enter not into the discussion of the policy or impolicy of the general principle involved in the extradition clause—they refer that to the wisdom of the Government and the Legislature—but they cannot willingly be parties to any arrangement which involves the possibility of the restoration of fugitive Slaves to bondage, or which renders any part of the British Dominions less the asylum of Liberty, than it is at present.   They therefore beseech your Lordship, that, in the contemplated act of Parliament for giving that clause effect, the Government will be pleased to provide that it shall not, under any circumstances, or under any pretext whatever, apply to the case of fugitive slaves, but that they shall be wholly excepted from its operation.

"On behalf of the Committee

(Signed) "THOMAS CLARKSON, President.

"27, New Broad Street,
"13th. Feby. 1843"

(Memorials and Petitions, 1840–1843, pp. 188–193).

Of the immediate result of the interview, accorded by Lord Aberdeen, there are two Committee records, one from the volume of Memorials and Petitions, 1840–1843, and the other from the Minute Book.

(a)

The Earl of Aberdeen having appointed Wednesday the 22nd. Feby. to receive the deputation the following gentlemen waited upon him, vizI :— Messrs. G. Stacey, J. Forster, G. W. Alexander, J. Beaumont, W. Ball, S. Fox, H. Tuckett, S. Gurney, E. N. Buxton, Revs. J. H. Hinton & J. Carlile, Drs. Madden and Rolp (Rolph?) and M. L'Instant, and presented the Memorial.

The noble Earl received them with great courtesy, and intimated that he took the deepest interest in the security and welfare of the fugitive slaves who have sought and found refuge in Upper Canada.   He stated also that the greatest care would be taken to prevent, in their case, the abuse of the extradition article; but stated that, as the Treaty had been ratified, the prayer of the memorial could not be acceded to without vitiating the whole of its stipulations (p. 193).

(b) At a meeting of the Committee on Friday, February 24, 1843,

The Deputation appointed to wait on Lord Aberdeen . . . to present Memorial to him on the bearing of the 10th Article of the Washington Treaty, having reported, through the Secretary, that, though his Lordship could not agree with the Prayer of the Memorial, inasmuch as it would vitiate the whole

fore feel bound to say to you that I wish not to be understood as in any way recommending Fuller's mission to your country.

"Your views of the 10th article of the treaty are undoubtedly

Treaty, he nevertheless assured them not only of his intention to watch the operation of the article in the same spirit as that which animated the Deputation, but of his intention, should an evil use be made of it, in the case of fugitive slaves, to propose its abandonment by the Government, it was resolved, considering the deep importance of the subject, to petition both Houses of Parliament, that fugitive slaves should be wholly exempted from its operation and that the Secretary draft petition to that effect.

It was also resolved, that a deputation composed of Geo. Stacey, Wm. Ball, Jos. Forster, Robt. Forster, Jno. Beaumont and John Scoble, should wait, as early as possible, on Dr. Lushington and Lord Brougham to consult with them relative to the course the Committee had best adopt, in bringing their views under the attention of the Legislature.

It was further resolved that Copies of the Memorial to L^d. Aberdeen and form of a Petition to Parliament be forwarded by Circular to the Friends of the Anti-Slavery Cause throughout the Country, inviting them to petition the Legislature and to address their representatives on the subject to which they refer (II, 46–47).

The day following, being the twenty-fifth, the Committee held a special meeting further to consider the matter and took the decision that a Preamble and Resolutions should be prepared also (*idem*, p. 49). These were ready for an adjourned meeting on the twenty-seventh, were altered, added to and agreed to, together with the Petition and Memorial. It was decided that the Petition should be presented to the House of Commons by Hawes and to the House of Lords by Brougham and that the Preamble and Resolutions should be forwarded to the Earl of Aberdeen and a copy of the Memorial and of the Resolutions to each member of the two houses of Parliament (*idem*, pp. 50–51). The Petition was as follows:

To the Honorable the Commons of the United Kingdom of Great Britain and Ireland, in Parliament assembled,

The humble Petition of the Committee of the British and Foreign Anti-Slavery Society,

Sheweth,

That your Petitioners, greatly alarmed on perceiving the evil uses which may be made of the tenth Article of the Treaty of Washington, by the Slave-holders of the United States, for the recovery of fugitive Slaves; deeply impressed with the necessity of maintaining inviolate the right to liberty, acquired by every human being who may have obtained an asylum within the British dominions; and most anxious that, under no circumstances and upon no pretext whatsoever, this right should be abridged or modified,—

Your Petitioners earnestly and respectfully entreat, that in any measure your Honorable House may be called upon to pass to give effect to the said Article of the Treaty, provision may be expressly made, that in no case shall fugitive slaves, surrendered on the demand of the Federal Government of the United States for alleged criminal offences, be again subjected to the incident of slavery.

And your Petitioners will ever pray,

On behalf of the Committee

(Signed)   JOHN SCOBLE, *Secy.*

(*Memorials and Petitions*, 1840–1843, p. 204).

Some letters of individual members of the British and Foreign Anti-Slavery Society, particularly of Clarkson and Alexander, are of interest here:

correct in fact, but the experience we have of the unprincipled
character of slaveholders is such that they will make a fraudulent
use of every provision—no matter how much perjury and other

(a) On February 8, Clarkson wrote to Beaumont relative to his "letter to
Lord A. on the American treaty." On the 15th, he wrote of Lord Brougham
in the same connection, expressing a desire to write to him himself "for
whom," he says, "I believe he has an esteem greater than for any other
person. I must persuade him to take up our Cause in the H. of Lords—He
is, I think, the only man who can carry Us through that House." Between
these two dates, he addressed himself to Lord Ashburton on the matter of
the *10th Article;* but Lord Ashburton was unavoidably prevented from replying until ten days later.

(b) The Alexander letters are two in number, one of the 25th of February,
the other of the 1st of March—both to Scoble, presumably, the first certainly
to him. It was dated from Bath.

(1) "I called on Wm. Blair & saw him as well as Capt. Stuart on 5th day
evens. I found that they entered fully into the objectionable character of
the 10th Clause of the Ashburton treaty on which I suppose the Com°° has
received a letter from one or both of them. Yesterday morning I called on
Lucy Townsend who with her husband is at present visiting Captn Townsend
who resides near Bath. She also feels very strongly the importance of ex-
cepting slaves from the general operation of the clause already referred to
& suggested that it might be desirable to memorialize the Queen on the
subject. I replied that if this were done, I thought that it should be the act
of Ladies' Societies. I met the Ladies Com°°. here this morning & proposed
the subject for their consideration & adoption or otherwise as they might
deem best. . . . I believe the members of the Bath Gentleman S^y. will address
the town & country members in reference to the clause in the Ashburton
treaty, a measure respecting which there can I think be little or no doubt of
its propriety as Roebuck ought, from his late appointment in connexion with
Canada, his talents & professional habits to lend important help in exposing
the danger & impolicy of the measure to be brought under his notice. . . . I
had considerable conversation with the few gentlemen I met on the subject
of free labour produce. I regret to find that W. T. Blair has not agreed
with us on this subject. . . ."

(2) The second Alexander letter was written from Cirencester:—

"I met yesterday at Christopher Bowley's a room nearly filled by the
friends of the slave in this place who entered warmly into the subject of the
10th Clause of the Ashburton treaty & intend to forward to the Representatives
of the Town & County a statement of their objection to its confirmation by
the Legislature so far as relates to refugee slaves. . . .

"Our friends at Cirencester wish to be furnished with some copies of
the Memorial to Lord Aberdeen in order that they may forward one to each
of their representatives. . . ."

(c) Some other letters of Clarkson's, on the same subject, might well
be inserted here, they being of rather special interest. On the 17th of March,
he wrote to 27, Broad Street, intimating that he would like a certain letter of
his "with the addition made to it about the Senator Benton" to be printed
and distributed even in preference to the Committee's *Circular.*

"Recollect," wrote he, "that in my Letter is a *History* of the *Rise*
of the *fugitive* Colony, which cannot but *excite* the sympathy of the Reader,
which is not in your circular, and with which members ought to be acquainted—

crimes may be involved—to bring their slaves back into their power —when the criminal proofs will at once be abandoned and the claim of ownership revived.

"I have been unable to find out what has hindered the regular reception of the Emancipator in England—of which I am much mortified to have so many complaints. I will re-examine the matter & see what remedy can be applied. From it you will gather the most material points of information respecting the state & prospects of our cause. I intend also to write you a letter which you may publish if you please.

"Allow me to call your particular attention to the proofs of a grand conspiracy involving France, Spain &c. I hope the Convention will be prepared to throw light upon the continental movements, Thiers, Gov. Cass, Wheeton, &c.

"I have inquired as to the detention of your papers, & now send you some of the arrears to Dec. We can find no reason why you should fail of receiving them by the monthly steamer, as they are carefully sent. As soon as the steamers run semi-monthly we will forward papers accordingly.

"The provision of means for my projected voyage to England comes in slowly, but I still trust it will be furnished so that I may take the steamer of May 16, which I think will be in season to get off my sea legs by the 13th June. I shall employ all the time I can command to collect & prepare materials for the Convention, & have one or two friends employed, in certain branches of the subject. The intelligent friends of the cause in this country will look with much interest to that Convention. I trust you will be

recollect that I give probable Reasons why the Americans will consider fugitive Slaves to be comprehended in the Treaty, and that Bentons little Speech determines the Point, & that the Americans themselves have begun to think so, so that the Treaty will be acted upon, whether we like it or not, if ratified. This ought to be known. Benton's Speech ought to be known because it shows that the *Die* is cast. Now having stated this, your Circular will come greatly in aid of our wishes. I *show* that the Americans will positively take advantage of it *to get back their fugitive Slaves;* and *your Circular shows* that, when they are *brought back into Slavery*, what dreadful Punishment they will have to undergo. . . I wrote yesterday to Lord Ashburton again, just to send him what Benton said in the Senate, that he may see, that all our conjectures about the Treaty will be realized, and that he may see the dreadful Responsibility, which hangs over his head for having made it and that he may make every Effort with the Government which sent him out, to do it away or make it harmless— Pray do you know anything of J. Leavitt— Is he a respectable person. . . ."

On the 18th, Clarkson wrote again to 27, Broad Street, presumably to Scoble or to Beaumont. See Introduction, pp. 159–160.

able to procure good evidence in regard to Cuba, Martinique, France, Germany, relative to the conspiracy. May I ask a letter from you by the steamer of the 19th? I am this moment (March 31) going on an excursion to lecture. Will *endeavour* to prepare an article for the Reporter on my return in season tomorrow morning to send by the steamer tomorrow.[95]

[95] TO THE EDITOR OF THE A. S. REPORTER.

BOSTON, April 1, 1843.

Sir—

The aspects of our glorious cause were never so cheering in our country as at this time. The treaty of Washington has totally destroyed the power of the Slaveholders and their northern "allies" to plunge your country and ours into a war for the protection of slavery & the slave trade. There will probably be a good deal of altercation for years to come, but no war. Every attempt in Congress to create an effective opposition to the treaty failed. In the Senate, Benton's motion to strike out of the appropriation bill the allowance for the African—80 guns squadron, was supported by only five votes. In the House of Representatives, the bill for carrying into effect the other provisions of the treaty was carried without a division & almost without debate. The only noticeable circumstance in the brief discussion which took place was the remark of Mr. Cushing, that "the United States had ample cause to regret that they had ever given in to sentimental legislation," that "we had taken a false step when we gave a false name to the slave trade," for "the only debatable point in this whole matter was a question under the law of nations, which might arise on the piracy statute." Mr. Cushing then expected to become a member of Mr. Tyler's cabinet, but the Senate rejected his nomination. He is now returned to his old district in Massachusetts, where the Liberty party has hitherto prevented a choice of representative, and is now waiting an opportunity to present himself to the people for a re-election to Congress. The only paper that now sustains his pretensions, in publishing the speech above referred to, left out the paragraph from which I have quoted! A striking testimony to the spirit of Liberty.

In the Legislature of the State of Maine, a series of resolutions condemnatory of the treaty were rejected by an overwhelming majority. This shows how hopeless is the effort to reproduce exasperation on this subject. The nice point relating to the right of visit will, I think, gradually become cleared up by the discussions so as to bring the parties together—especially as the design of the slavery party in France & the United States to restore the Slave Trade shall become more manifest to the world.

With this subject, the African Emigration schemes of your countrymen, & the Texian annexation project of ours, are both intimately connected. The utter failure of the African Civilization project, as well as of our kindred Colonization humbug, disproving the idea that negroes are a *race* distinct from the human race, by showing that selfishness & depravity reign in their hearts as absolutely as in white men, will ultimately drive all true philanthropists to our policy—of removing the evil by removing its cause—slavery.

The tone of the slaveholders in Congress during the late session was

"I remain, very truly
"Your friend & brother
"JOSHUA LEAVITT."

materially different from that which hitherto prevailed. They no longer evinced that overbearing and dictatorial manner which had formerly caused so much disgust, but rather took the attitude of complainers, whining & begging for pity & protection. Nothing would provoke them to make a speech, so that, with the single exception of a speech by Mr. Cushing in reply to Giddings, the latter had the debate all to himself. It is impossible now to foresee what will be the temper of the next Congress. As it will contain an overwhelming majority of the Democratic party, called "the national allies of the planters," it is probable enough the slaveholders will reap some advantage, but it will be shortlived.

The legislature of Massachusetts have passed all the measures that were proposed in consequence of the Latimer case—and passed too, without division or debate. An Act to prohibit the officers of the State from taking any part in the recaption of alleged fugitives from slavery, & denying the use of our jails for their detention, an act repealing the intermarriage prohibition which was enacted by our ancestors a century ago to prevent connections with heathen; a resolve authorizing the Government to vindicate the rights of colored citizens imprisoned in Southern seaports; resolves against the annexation of Texas; & resolves demanding an alteration of the U. S. Constitution so far as it allows the Southern States an additional number of representatives in Congress for their slave property, all passed by the general consent of both parties. The tardiness of the Democratic legislature of New York to comply with the advice of Gov. Bouck, & humble the State to the dictation of Virginia, evinces the force of public opinion which restrains the servility of unprincipled politicians. The Democratic legislature of Maine has passed resolutions for the protection of colored seamen in Southern seaports. What is your government doing on this subject?

The Legislature of Ohio have repealed the base Statute enacted some years since at the dictation of the Legislature of Kentucky, rendering it highly penal to afford aid or sustenance to a fugitive from slavery. To balance this, however, they have passed an act prohibiting the children of colored persons from attending the public schools, although the parents are taxed for their support. They have also virtually overthrown a decision of their Supreme Court, that persons of a lighter hue than mulatto (half-blood) are entitled to vote or to give testimony the same as white persons. This shows how the elements are striving. A person has recently been convicted in that State of kidnapping a free person who was carried across the Ohio river into Kentucky & sold as a slave. This is the first case of conviction in that State, & it was effected by the efforts of William Birney, Esq of Cincinnati, Attorney at Law, the second son of our honored James G. Birney.

These movements in the political & civic circles are accompanied, pari passu, by corresponding advances in the press & in the religious communities. The number of Churches declining communion with slave holders, is constantly on the increase, & the tone of sentiment in our newspapers, both

(NEW YORK, April 22 1843)[96]

"My dear Sir

"I lately rec^d. from you the 3rd Report of the B. & F. A. S. Soc^y and thank you for it. It is a very able & useful document & I will be obliged to you for the preceding reports having never seen them.

"I enclose a paper, from which you will perceive the use I have made of the parliamentary documents you forwarded to me. You will confer a favor on me by keeping me supplied with such papers & pamphlets as from time to time appear, connected with the anti-Slavery cause. I shall always be glad to bear the expense of them.

secular & religious, in all questions connected with slavery, is manifestly rising towards the true standard.

George Latimer, the fugitive from slavery, whose case created so much interest, is lecturing in this State. The two Clarke's from Kentucky, white slaves, having no other title to liberty than the seal of the sea, of the Almighty on their manly foreheads are lecturing with great effect, Lewis in the State of Maine, & Milton in the State of New York.

Efforts are making to send a respectable delegation to the London Convention. I have already heard that the following persons expect to attend:

Rev. H. H. Kellogg, Galesville, Illinois.
Rev. J. W. C. Pennington, Hartford, Conn.
William Shotwell, Esq. New York City.
Joshua Leavitt, Boston, Mass.
Nathaniel Abner (?) Ditto.
Amos A. Phelps,—Ditto.

There will doubtless be others.

There is a division taking place in the Methodist Episcopal Church, connected with the question of slavery, which bids fair to push that great branch of our religious community to take higher ground on the whole subject. The American Board of Commissioners for Foreign Missions is in difficulty with the missionaries of the Sandwich Islands, on the same account. It is believed that the sensitiveness of the managers of that society on the subject does not grow out of a desire to secure pecuniary support from the South, for only a very small amount is realised; but rather from the fact that so many influential members & friends of the Board at the North have unthinkingly committed themselves against the doctrines of the inherent unjustness of slaveholding and the imperative duty of immediate emancipation, & hence the pride of consistency requires them not to yield anything to abolition. Let us hope they may learn that for a Christian to acknowledge error is noble.

[96] One of Tappan's letters to Scoble, of date March 20, 1843, not found at Denison House, was published, with one indicated omission, in the B. & F. A.-S. *Reporter*, May 17, 1843, pp. 75–76.

"I have been long an attentive observer of the state of public opinion in this country respecting the slave question, & hazard little in saying that anti-Slavery sentiments are making rapid, indeed wonderful progress. I have never since the agitation commenced, felt so much encouraged as at the present moment. If we can only keep Texas out of the Union, Slavery may & probably will cease within the next 20 or 30 years, perhaps much sooner. May God hasten its fall.

"Yours very respectfully
"WILLIAM JAY

"John Scoble Esqʳ.
  Secʸ. &c
    New York"

"JOHN SCOBLE ESQ,   "NEW YORK,
London.   April 25/43
"My dear Friend

"Your letter of March 14th and April 3rd gave much satisfaction. I procurred the insertion of an extract respecting the venerable Clarkson in two of our daily papers, and sent several copies of them to the principal anti-slavery publications. Last evening I read portions of your letter at an anti-slavery meeting. The facts communicated afforded much gratification to the friends of the cause, who rejoice in the activity, watchfulness & wisdom of the London Committee, & in the advancement of the cause so dear to our hearts. Be assured there are many indications here that the cause is advancing. Some abolitionists (when) they see an abatement of effort in their personal associations and among anti-slavery friends, feel discouraged and do not notice the more general indications of the prevalence of anti-slavery principles among those hitherto opposed to them.

"In the legislature of this State, now loco foco, strenuous efforts have been made to procure the repeal of the law which allows a jury trial to persons arrested here as fugitive slaves. Near the close of the session the repealing-bill passed the lower house by a majority of only five, the speaker voting with the minority, but the Senate refused to take up the bill at all. Mr. Van Buren, who was at Albany, was supposed to use personal influence among the members of the legislature to induce them to pass the bill as an offering to the South with reference to his claims for their support

to the Presidency.   Considering this fact & the character of the legislature the non-repeal of the act is considered by us as a strong
indication of the prevalence of anti-slavery principles.

"The New-World,[97] a weekly publication in this city, which has
extensive circulation, the editor [98] of which accompanied Dr. Channing's Lenox Discourse [99] with a most humble apology, has recently
published some long anti-slavery articles without hesitation.

"Arnold Buffum can tell you some encouraging facts with regard
to the lectures of Mr Smith at Cincinnati—his being invited to lecture in Kentucky and the anti-slavery writings of Mr C. M. Clay,
himself a slaveholder, in Ky.

"Mr Gates,[100] member of Congress, lately sent me a proof sheet
of a Remonstrance [101] against the admission of Texas to be signed
by several members of Congress.   It is a strong document & headed
by the venerable J. Q. Adams.   When published I hope to send
you a copy.

"I send you a copy of a letter [102] recently addressed to me by

[97] *The New World*—A Weekly Family Journal of Popular Literature,
Science, Art and News.

[98] Benjamin Park.

[99] Channing, William Ellery, *An Address at Lenox*, August 1, 1842, the
anniversary of emancipation in the British West Indies (Lenox, 1842).

[100] Seth Merrill Gates.

[101] Joshua Leavitt was the instigator of the Remonstrance.   See *Memoirs
of John Quincy Adams*, XI, 41, 313.   The later volumes of this work are, of
course, a mine of information for the American Anti-Slavery Movement.

[102]   "PERTH AMBOY
                                                       "Apl 18th 1843

"MR LEWIS TAPPAN.

"Dear Sir,

        "I embrace the first leisure moment to answer your enquiries of
yesterday relative to my disconnexion from the A. B. C. and the more readily
as others besides yourself have manifested some interest in the subject.   Your
first inquiry is relative to myself and secondly as to others.   Of the reasons
of the other members of the Sandwich Islands Mission who have recently
been disconnected from the American Board, I do not feel sufficiently informed to pretend to give a full account nor should I feel at liberty to do
so without consulting them if I were.   But I have no hesitation in saying
that with some of them, the course which the Board has hitherto pursued
in relation to Slavery constituted in part the reason of their asking a dismission from its service.

        "In regard to myself I may premise that my disconnection was entirely
of my own seeking.   Individually I have received none other then the kindest
treatment from those officers of the Board to whom my transactions have been

Dr. Lafon who has recently returned from the Sandwich Islands. This gentleman was once a slave holder, & is now President of the Hawaiian Anti-Slavery Society which is composed of a majority of the American Missionaries at the Sandwich Islands.

"Rev. W^m. Raymond, missionary to Mendi, has recently returned from Africa on a visit. He expects to return in a few months & to locate at Kau-Mendi which is about 30 miles from the sea, & perhaps a hundred miles south of Sierra Leone. King Henry Tucker has consented to the mission being located in his dominions. The Committee charged with the superintendence of this mission

confined. A difference with the Board in sentiment upon the following points induced me to ask a dismission from their service.

"(1) The laws of the Board especially the one in relation to the return of missionaries which reached the Islands in 1838.

"(2) The Common stock system of support.

"(3dly) In relation to Slavery.

"In regard to the first two reasons it is needless to remark because the law alluded to has been virtually repealed and the Common stock system is done away. And without pretending to speak to any extent of the merits of the question of slavery or of my own views of it, I may say that the latter are such that I could not approve of the Board's receiving without reproof or rebuke the wages of slave labor, whereby they countenance the keeping in heathenism 2½ millions to send the gospel to reclaim from heathenism a few thousands. The slave population at home and the heathen population abroad require substantially the same works for their civilization and their christianization. Nothing in my estimation is gained if we have to elevate the one at the expense of the other.

"But in addition to that objection, it should be remembered that one of the greatest impediments to the success of the gospel at the Sandwich Islands has been slavery as it existed there until the year 1839 and oppression as it has existed there ever since. Slavery is universal oppression— Oppression is partial slavery. Since the S. Islanders have enjoyed a Constitution and printed laws imperfect as they are and partially as they are executed, they cannot strictly be said to be slaves. They have improved under the change. The lowest degree of intelligence—the most abject poverty without enterprize, industry or economy must necessarily be the attendants of slavery. All that I ever wished or expected of the Board upon this subject was that they should let it be known distinctly that they were opposed to the system. No missionary under their care so far as I know, ever thought that duty required them to make a *business* of preaching against Slavery. But surely the inconsistency is palpable, to be receiving the wages of slave labor here (& in such a way as to countenance and keep the system in existence) for the purpose of sending the gospel abroad for the good of those who are in substantially the same condition.

"Yours truly,

(Signed) "THOS. LAFON."

will make soon an appeal to the christian people of this country to sustain this mission on account of its anti-slavery principles.

"We propose publishing another edition of the Address to Non-slave holders, by Judge Jay. It has already done great execution.

"I should write more but the fact that delegates to the Convention will accompany this letter, and give you the state of things here seems to render it unnecessary.

"The new British consul has received his exequatur. It is a notorious fact that his wife holds a considerable number of slaves.

"All the Reporters you sent have been forwarded as directed & the extra copies have been sent to persons indicated by you.

"I earnestly hope that you will have a large gathering in June & we shall look with deep interest for an account of the proceedings. Mr Weld & others will I trust make answers to the Queries which were widely circulated.

"Truly & affec⁷ yours,

"LEWIS TAPPAN."

"BOSTON, May 1, 1843.

"My Dear Sir—

"Another absence from the city & an unlooked for detention in returning, has prevented my giving you as much time as might have been agreeable. The public mind has evidently advanced somewhat, if we may judge by the tone of the political press of both parties, in regard to the evil of slavery. The Legislature of New York have adjourned without repealing the law, passed in 1841, securing a trial by jury to all persons claimed as fugitive slaves. The Democratic party, now in power, was fully pledged to the slaveholders, to effect that repeal, but it is believed the revulsion among their own party particularly in the Western part of the State, has deterred them from consummating their design. The Courier des Etats Unis, a French newspaper published in the city of New York, has published our official correspondence and circular of the Colonial Deputies in Paris, summoning a 'World's Convention' of planters, to be held in New Orleans in September next, to take measures for the protection of their hideous 'institution'— It appears that France is now the battle ground of slavery, which the supporters of that interest are fortifying with political 'barricades,' with the conviction that as soon as slavery is conquered there, Spain & Brazil must follow, & then the planters of the United States will stand forth *alone*. Let us learn from our enemies.

"The Rev. A. A. Phelps takes his passage in the Britannia this day, to attend the London Convention, on the 13th of June. Mr. Phelps, who is an able & esteemed minister of the Congregationalists, has been intimately conversant with the Anti-Slavery cause in this country from a very early period, & was one of the first ministers that dared to take sides publicly with the advocates of immediate emancipation. His faithful judgment & truehearted devotion to the cause, with his aptness for the transaction of business, will make him a highly useful member. The veteran Arnold Buffum has already sailed from New York in the Siddons, packet ship. I have a letter from him, replete with noble sentiments and wise suggestions in reference to the convention. He represents the State of Indiana. I think the prospect is that there will be a good delegation from the United States, notwithstanding the extreme difficulty of raising money for any public object. The pro-slavery party press is just beginning to show its apprehensions in regard to the convention. The American Daily Sentinel, a paper in Philadelphia, devoted to the Tyler administration, has sounded the alarm, and in justification of the charge of sinister motives in Great Britain, copies a very long article from Fraser's Magazine, for April, 1841, on 'War with America a blessing to mankind.'[103] The American writer says of the men who attend these 'World's Conventions,' that 'These *philanthropic* Americans have told our most deadly foe that we have three millions of enemies burning for revolt in our very midst'—I do not think the people of the United States will be very much alarmed. . . .

"(JOSHUA LEAVITT.)"

"NEW YORK,
"May 13/43

"JOHN SCOBLE ESQ,
Sec &c.

"Dear Sir,

"It is now in my power to answer your Queries respecting Texas.[104] Presuming you retained a copy, I proceed to answer according to the numbers.

[103] The author advocated the British annexation of Cuba as a means of abolishing the slave trade (*Fraser's Magazine*, XXIII, 502).

[104]   TEXAS

1. What number of slaves is there known or supposed to be in Texas, at the present time—how many from the United States—how many from Africa?

1. Not over 25,000, of which number about 23500 came from the U. States, and 1500 from Africa via Cuba.

2. The largest slave population is on the Brazos & Colorado rivers which is the western portion of Texas.

3. There are none.

4. They are chiefly employed in the cultivation of Cotton. Some corn & other produce for home consumption is grown. The time allowed for refreshment & repose varies on different plantations, but it is similar to that of the S. W. portion of the United States.

5. Food is abundant & cheap. Therefore the slaves are better fed than in most parts of the U. S. They are fed on pork, corn bread &c. Their clothing, shelter, medical attendance &c are about the same as they are in the U. S.

6. No, but on the contrary they have diminished in numbers. Few are going in while many are coming out. They take them into Arkansas & Louisiana contrary to the laws of the U. S, but these laws are not rigidly enforced.

7. They do & successfully. They go to Mexico—President Houston lost two slaves in this way.

8. Low of course. Similar to that of Alabama. The preachers at Houston & Gavelston (sic) preach every Sunday afternoon to the slaves.

9. It has never been enforced.

10. Not over 100 thousand people.

2. In what parts of Texas are they principally located?

3. What laws are in existence in Texas regulating their condition?

4. What are the labors to which they are generally appointed—what time is allowed them for refreshment and repose?

5. What is their actual condition in relation to punishment, food, clothing, shelter, medical attendance &c?

6. Have their numbers been latterly much increased by purchase or by the emigration of Southern planters with their slaves into Texas?

7. Do the Slaves make frequent attempts to escape—state whether successfully or otherwise and where they go?

8. What is the moral and religious condition of the Slave population of Texas?

9. What has been the effect of the law expelling the free people of color from Texas?

10. What is the estimated population of Texas at the present time?

11. Have any slaves been introduced into Texas from the French & Spanish or other West Indian Colonies?

12. What is the mortality among the slave population of Texas?

(*Memorials and Petitions*, 1840–1843, p. 120).

11. Not over 1,500. See 1.

12. They live longer than the same class of persons do in the U. S., owing partly to the salubrious climate, which is far better than it is in the extreme South of the U. S.

"Slavery is less profitable in Texas than was expected, owing chiefly to the low price of staples, & the difficulty of transporting cotton &c overland, and the Custom House regulations of the U. S. for transit.

"The above facts are given me by an intelligent citizen of Texas—a man of principle and may, I think, be relied upon.

"The slaves in Texas are held generally by small slave holders. There are not more than 20 or 30 who hold a hundred & upward. Nearly every slaveholder in Texas was originally from the United States, chiefly from Alabama & Tennessee. The slaves are sparsely scattered over the whole country.

"The white population of Texas is about one hundred thousand and the voters do not probably exceed 12000.

"Previous to this year the cotton grown in Texas went to England via New Orleans, but now, in consequence of being obliged to pay a duty to the U. S. (3 cts per lb which is however refunded when the cotton is cleared at N.O. for a foreign country) the cotton is shipt to England direct. The gentleman from Texas with whom I have conferred, says that the above tends to alienate the people of Texas from the U. S. and to increase their desire to cultivate friendship with England.

"☞ He states that the most intelligent & influential men in Texas are beginning to think that the country can never prosper while slavery continues there; that slave labor is unprofitable; and that the prosperity of the Republic depends greatly upon promoting emigration from the U. S. & elsewhere of white people. He informs me that already there is much conversation on the subject in Houston & Galveston the two principal towns in Texas. He himself is decidedly in favor of abolishing slavery. He remarks that many are in favor of calling a Convention to abolish the present Constitution & adopting a new one prohibiting slavery & making other beneficial changes. In two of the New Orleans daily commercial papers of this month I perceive two editorial articles in which the rising feeling in Texas in favor of making the Republic a free State is alluded to with reprobation. On conversing with some of the editors of our papers here to-day I found they had overlooked the matter entirely. Mr. Bryant of the Evening Post promised to copy the articles from the N. O. papers to-day. If it should prove true that the most virtuous & intelligent inhabitants of Texas are in favor of making it a free State, it will be a glorious event indeed! Then a barrier will be made against the progress of the accursed system, and slavery be left to die out in the U. States unless it shall cease by the action of law or popular commotion.

"My informant says that if ten thousand white persons should emigrate to Texas from our Northern States they might effect the change the virtuous have so much at heart. And that G. Britain might by a judicious interference influence the people to an abandonment of the system of slavery. A million of pounds sterling loaned on land securities, contingent upon the abolition of slavery, would he thinks effect the object.

"Truly your's
"LEWIS TAPPAN."

"Great Western.

"NEW YORK
"May 25/43.

"JOHN SCOBLE, ESQ.
London.

"My Dear Friend,

"Yours of 15 April by Mr Wm Bennett was duly received. He called a moment & I have not seen him since. He did not disclose the 'benevolent objects' he has in view. I rather imagine that the quaker friend who accompanied him is somewhat shy of abolitionists, and may have persuaded W. B. that it is not prudent to be too intimate with that class of persons. I know scarcely one *stiff* quaker but Joseph Sturge. Would there were a thousand such!

"Your other letter of 15 Apl is also at hand, enclosing a copy of a letter from M. Isambert.[105] You will see it in the *Journal of Commerce* of this day.[106] The editor struck out part of the preliminary remarks, recommending to the French nation the immediate abolition of slavery without compensation.

"I forwarded your letters immediately but the time is almost

[105] Monsieur M. Isambert was Secretary of the French Society for the Abolition of Slavery.

[106] The *Journal of Commerce* was generally pro-slavery in tone.

too short for replies to be prepared & sent in season to be laid before the Convention. Judge Jay has sent a reply which I have handed to our excellent brother Kellogg [107] who takes passage to-day in the Great Western. You will find him a warm hearted intelligent, amiable and uncompromising christian abolitionist.

"I will not take up more of your time just now to read my letters, as you will be fully & more advantageously engaged with matters pertaining to your Convention. I pray God to bless you, and all the members of the Convention & ardently hope that your deliberations & acts may be peaceful & efficient.

"Very cordially your's,

"LEWIS TAPPAN."

"ON BOARD THE HIBERNIA
"ATLANTIC OCEAN, Augt. 13. 1843. [108]

"Dear Scoble—

"In the face of a strong & constant head wind, we have been prospered so far on our voyage that we expect to reach Halifax tomorrow, & Boston on the 16th, or morning of the 17th, making the voyage in a little less than 13 days. The first part of the voyage was quite disagreeable, through the motion of the ship, but for the last five or six days, most of the passengers, including our 'three Friends,' have been quite cheerful. I have missed some of the contents of my trunks, so unluckily left in London, & have consequently failed of almost all the work for which I had made preparations for the voyage. But indeed, I do not think I should have accomplished much in the way of work, for one half the time has been spent in getting sick, & the other half in getting well again. Should my trunks come to hand by the next steamer, I shall lose no time in completing the paper on the financial evils of

---

[107] "Allow me to introduce to you the Rev. H. H. Kellogg of Illinois who goes to attend the London Convention. He is at the head of a literary Institution at the West, and is a most respectable & deserving man, besides being a true-hearted abolitionist" (Tappan to Scoble May 9, 1843).

[108] With Tappan and Leavitt at the Convention of 1843, letters were not to be expected from America. Tappan seems to have gone at the last moment at the request of John Quincy Adams. The work of the Convention, as it affected the United States, will be revealed little by little in the ensuing letters. The Garrison group did not attend this Convention, neither did their friends in Great Britain, the Hibernian Anti-Slavery Society. Both bodies took offence at the very wording of the call, which they interpreted as an insult. See *Twelfth Report of the Massachusetts Anti-Slavery Society*, p. 45.

slavery, & provided you go on with the proposed publication, shall probably be able to furnish the copy by the time you require it. Please let me know how soon you will require it. I also intend to prepare a letter from our Committee to the French Society [109]

[109] It would seem not to be out of place to insert at this juncture Clarkson's letter to Guizot regardless of the fact that it be of later date. It was sent on behalf of the B. & F. A-S. Society Committee.

"To M M GUIZOT
&c   &c Paris.

"PLAYFORD HALL NR IPSWICH
"Oct 27. 1843

"My much esteemed friend

"May I hope that you will excuse the liberty which I am once more taking of trespassing upon your valuable time.

"I have lately seen, at different times, several gentlemen from the United States of America who take an interest in the abolition of Slavery there. They are men not only of probity and honor, and incapable of disguising the truth, but men of solid intellect and sound judgment, and they give it as their decided opinion, that if France were to abolish Slavery in her Colonies, such a measure would have great influence, from motives of policy in producing the abolition of American Slavery. I received this opinion with feelings of Joy, because I thought that if you were to know it, as coming from such men, you might be encouraged not only to hasten to bring forward the great question of Slavery before your two Chambers, but that it would strengthen your influence there by announcing to them the probabilities of such an event.

"I cannot, Sir, doubt for a moment your anxiety to do every thing in your power to accelerate such a movement in the Chambers. You will probably recollect the words, which you used, when you did me the honor to write to me, 'We work' you said 'both of us under the same Master.' These words made so deep an impression upon me, that they will be always brought to my memory whenever your name is mentioned, they inspired me with hope and confidence as far as you was concerned in our Sacred cause, they implied that we could not have a higher motive to promote our cause than that of doing the will of God, and that this consideration ought to produce in us an energy of action, suitable to the supremacy of Him, whom we profess to serve. These sentiments are a full assurance to me of your hearty cooperation in this great work of philanthropy and Justice.

"Permit me now to inform you, that the enlightened and religious part of the English people are waiting with painful anxiety for the decision of France on this great question, could Louis Phillippe your Sovereign see the sufferings of the victims, and the many acts of injustice on the part of their oppressors, which take place only in one day in a Slave Colony, his benevolent heart would shudder at the sight, and he would think that even an hours delay in applying a remedy was criminal. Why then, when the project of a law for abolition is drawn up already, should any time be lost in presenting it to the French Chambers? Is it that slavery has been lately discovered to be just? No, Slavery is the parent of numerous crimes, all of which are punished in every civilized State. Is it because it has lately been discovered to be politic? No, emancipation in the British Colonies has been proved to be like a divine gift, the greatest blessing, that could have befallen them.

"I know, Sir, that you have many difficulties to encounter, perhaps you are not agreed as to the measure in your own Cabinet, the Cabinet of Ministers, and you will have many opponents elsewhere. The Party in the Chambers who are on the opposite side in Politics will be against you—

as soon as I can. Indeed I have made some progress towards it already. I shall trouble you with the forwarding of it when completed. The copy of the French Report, you know, was not procured. If it can be had, to cost not more than 30s., without putting you to too much trouble, I shall be glad to receive it before the sitting of Congress next winter. It can be sent through Wiley & Putnam, or direct to me at Boston. I will thank Joseph Soul to write me, if he has not, in regard to my luggage, on which I wrote him a hasty note from Liverpool on the 4th. It was quite a disappointment not to meet it, but I have not felt as if it would be lost. If it has not been recovered, I should like to know whether there is opportunity for me to recover an indemnity of Chaplin & Horne, for really there was more value than I can well afford to lose. J. S. must let me know what expence he is at, that I may reimburse it, & as for the trouble, I will do as much for him if there is opportunity, or if not, then for somebody else, which will keep the account balanced so far as the world at large is concerned. I remember with warm gratitude, the many kindnesses I have received from friends, old & new, in London, & cherish the hope that I have seen none of them for the last time in the flesh. It seems now to be such a trivial affair to cross the Atlantic, that occasions comparatively trifling might bring me again to London.

"You remember the subject was referred to us, of devising a mode of facilitating the interchange of pamphlets, &c &c. I made some inquiries on the subject, & the best mode I could learn was through Wiley & Putnam, & I have written a paragraph for my paper, which you will see. I trust we shall be able to reduce our present exorbitant duties, at least to the rate of those on your side; in fact, *pamphlets* ought to be duty free as they are rarely reprinted except for gratuitous circulation. It would be a good step towards peace, as well as to strengthen the hands of reform, to abolish all duties on books imported into either country—each party of course

you must expect enemies both in the Colonies and maritime Towns of France, men who view the question in the false light of expediency, and not in the moral light of right & wrong, will look upon abolition as a doubtful if not an injurious proposition. But you have already had many storms and tempests in the two Chambers to encounter and you have triumphed over them all. I hope this will be the case again and that you will be assisted by the omnipotent arm of a merciful providence.

'I am Sir with my best wishes for your health & happiness, and with regard and esteem.

"Yours very Sincerely
(Signed) "THOMAS CLARKSON"

(*Memorials and Petitions*, 1843–1853, pp. 35, 38–39).

protecting its own copy rights, by a prohibition of reprints of such works.   This would be better than any inter-national copy right— which never will be conceded in the United States.

"Lord Brougham's privilege to British subjects, giving them time to sell their slaves, assumes that an Englishman *may* buy slaves innocently, not knowing them to be stolen!   I hope his monstrous blunder or rottenness will be well exposed.

"Wishing you all needed wisdom to meet the various exigencies of our great cause, I am, as ever.

"Sincerely yours,
"JOSHUA LEAVITT."

"NEW YORK.
14 Aug. 1843.

"JOHN SCOBLE, ESQ

"My dear Friend,

"Here I am, at my own desk, safe & sound after an absence of 9 weeks.[110]   Very highly have I enjoyed the voyage.   Most advantageous has it been to me.   And I hope the cause in which we are engaged has received no detriment at my hands.   Have the goodness to present my kindest regards to Mrs Scoble & your dear children, to the gentlemen of the Committee, and to those in the office.   Mr Beaumont's kindness to me I shall never forget, & I felt grateful for Mr Soul's attention.   I will thank him to remember me to William & to Mrs Merrington who was very attentive to my comfort.   I wish I could sip a cup of tea in your room, with you & the other gentlemen, once in a while, but probably this pleasure will never again be granted me.   Please tell our friend Beaumont that the pictures arrived safe & give much pleasure to my friends.

"You may be gratified to read the annexed letter to our friend J. Sturge, & it will save me from repeating any of the items to you.

110 See letter of April 24, 1850, for Tappan's own explanation of how he came, after all, to attend the Anti-Slavery Convention of 1843.   Also, *Memoirs of John Quincy Adams*, XI, 380, "Mr. Tappan told me he had himself been urged to go to England and asked my advice what he should do.   I declined advising, but said I wished he would go, were it only for the possibility that he might contribute to advance the cause."   Adams distrusted the British government on the tenth article of the Webster-Ashburton treaty, on Texas, and accused it of being feeble in the cause of world emancipation, while Calhoun condemned it for too great zeal.   *Idem*, XI, 405 ff.

"On arriving at Boston I had the address in the Reporter—put in by mistake—crossed & the address by Mr. Bowley [111] pasted in instead of it. The editor of the J. of C. found a mare's nest. He conceived that the address in the Reporter was found too severe, & that the Convention had substituted a milder address in lieu of it! He therefore published the wrong one as 'The Rejected Address.' I have written the editor a note correcting the error & requesting him to publish Mr Bowley's address.

"I expect to address a large meeting to-morrow evening in Brooklyn for 2 hours giving an account of the proceedings in the Convention & also saying something about temperance &c. I am written to from various quarters for information. If the weather had allowed I would have written a Reporter Extra on the passage. When I shall get time I can not say. The accumulation of business in my office is great & I am here in the midst of the busy season

"With great regard
"Yours very truly,
"LEWIS TAPPAN

"A meeting is to be held in this city this evening with a view to call out public sentiment with respect to an alteration in the Constitution of this State. Mr. Young, Sec. of State, is expected to be one of the Speakers. I am told that one of the reforms he will recommend is abolishing the odious distinction now made between White & black citizens. He is, it is said, for allowing the coloured citizens to vote on the same terms whites are allowed, viz, to be 21 years of age, an inhabitant of the State one year preceding any election & for last 6ms. a resident of the county where he may offer his vote, except felons who have not been pardoned."

[111] Mr. Samuel Bowley, delegate from Gloucester in the Convention of 1843, read an address bearing the signature of Thomas Clarkson, June 20, 1843—"*To the Christian Professors of Every Denomination in America, and in all Other Countries where the Influence of Slavery Exists.*" It is to be found in *Proceedings of the General Anti-Slavery Convention*, which convention was called by the Committee of the B. & F. A-S. Society, London, June 13 to June 20, 1843. Josedes Castillo of Havana, who frequently furnished the B. & F. A-S. Society with items of Cuban news, made a touching reference to this address, which he had read in the B. & F. A-S. *Reporter* of July, 1843. "It appeared to me," he wrote to Scoble, October 5, 1843, that "I was reading a letter of St. Paul or of St. John to the first Christians. . . ."

"BOSTON, Sept. 1, 1843

"JOHN SCOBLE ESQ.

London

"My dear Sir,

   "The results of our Liberty Convention at Buffalo have not yet been received. Our prospects for votes are highly encouraging. One district in Illinois gave 1200 Liberty votes last month for Member of Congress. The vote in Indiana was upwards of 2000. We expect a large vote in Maine & New York. The subject of most general interest to the cause at this time is Cuba. Although many still believe that a desperate attempt will be made to annex Texas to our Union the coming winter, the more prevalent opinion seems to be, that the slaveholders already see that they must abandon that, as clearly impracticable, & that they will now attempt to transfer the same machinery to Cuba— I trust you will keep a vigilant look-out for their machinations. Pennington has just published a card fully setting at rest the story about his having a doctorate.[112]

     "...

    "JOSHUA LEAVITT

"P. S. I hope to receive the Reporter always by the *Steamer*. Since I came home, I have received as many as seven or eight papers, sent by sailing vessels *via* New York— Send by the Boston steamers—mail.

       J. L."

      "BOSTON, Oct. 16, 1843.

"My Dear Sir—

  "The movement by the British Government in favor of the abolition of slavery in Texas [113] is exciting the greatest agony among

112 The card, presumably, did not reach England; for the B. & F. A-S. *Reporter* August 1, 1851, found it worth its while to quote from the New York *Standard* the following facts relative to the colored preacher, the Reverend J. W. C. Pennington, reputed D. D. At the time of the passage of the Fugitive Slave Act, he happened to be in Great Britain and, being afraid to return to the United States, because a fugitive, knew not what to do until some friends abroad raised sufficient money for his purchase ($150). He was sold to a third party who liberated him. In the process "A Bill of Sale for a Doctor of Divinity" was made out.

113 Among the many subjects discussed by the Convention of 1843 and decisions appertaining thereto arrived at, that of Texas was one of the most

our slaveholders.   The New Orleans papers are out in full cry for

important. Just as in 1841, members of the B. & F. A-S. Society had felt
that any recognition of Texas was "confidence-destroying" (Letter of William Bale to Tredgold, dated Kendal, January 13, 1841), so now they felt
that annexation to the United States, augmenting the strength of its slave-
holding portion, would be simply disastrous. The sessions of the Convention
ended on the twentieth of June, having lasted exactly one week. Immediately,
thereafter, steps were taken to make its proceedings known *in toto* to all
parts of the world interested in or designed to be affected by them. In
the midst of very grave domestic affliction, George W. Alexander, bereaved
by the death of his wife, had yet thought for their publication in the next
Reporter, "the whole of the resolutions moved & passed . . . as well (as)
the addresses adopted during its sittings, including that to the American
nation which he understands to be rather a long one but very interesting and
important . . ." (W. Bell [for G. W. A.] to Scoble, dated Rochester, June
22, 1843).

The next step was to communicate the necessity for alertness or for
action to the Home Government. In early July, Clarkson addressed his long
letter on Texas to Lord Aberdeen (*Introduction*, pp. 18–20) at about the
same time that Scoble sent the following:

"I am requested by the Committee of the British & Foreign Anti-Slavery
Society to solicit for a deputation of that Body, the honor of an interview
with your Lordship to present to your Lordship certain resolutions relative to
the present critical position of Texas, passed by the late Anti-Slavery Convention and entrusted to them for that purpose, and to bring other matters
of importance relative thereto, under your Lordship's attention. The Committee would feel extremely obliged, if it met your Lordship's convenience
to be favored with an early interview."

At a special meeting of the B. & F. A-S. Society, August 21, 1843, the
progress of events, to date, was reported:

"The Secretary reported that, in company with George Stacey and
S. P. Andrews he had had an interview with Lord Brougham on the subject
of Texas in which it had been suggested to him to ask the Government for
information respecting negotiations with Mexico and Texas, which were understood to be pending, and to press upon them the importance of making the
Abolition of Slavery by the latter Country, a condition for the recognition
of its Independence by the former, and by every means in their power to
forward so important a result.

"The Secretary also reported that in compliance with the suggestions
made to him, Lord Brougham had brought the subject of Texas under the
attention of the House of Peers and had elicited from the Earl of Aberdeen,
on the part of the Government, a highly satisfactory declaration of their
determination to do all that could properly be done to secure the abolition
of slavery in Texas.

"The general question in reference to the Abolition of Slavery in Texas
having been thoroughly canvassed, it was concluded that, for the present,
nothing more could be done by the Committee, than carefully to watch the
events in connexion therewith, beyond addresses to the Presidents of Mexico
and Texas, urging such topics on their consideration as might be expedient
with a view to the promotion of that object.

"The Secretary was requested in conjunction with Mr. Andrews to prepare drafts of such addresses to be laid before the Committee at its next
sitting" (*Minute Books*, II, 103–105).

war with Great Britain at once. The Madisonian,[114] President
Tyler's mouthpiece, alleges that any interference of Great Britain
with Texas will be cause of war to us, & it says the fullest instructions have been given to our ambassadors in England, Mexico
& Texas. Mr. Henry A. Wise, who was nominated by President

At a meeting two days after, the Committee considered the drafts of the
addresses which Scoble and the American visitor, Stephen Pearl Andrews,
had, in the interval, prepared and then voted that George Stacey and Scoble,
assisted by Andrews, should revise them in readiness for final action at some
subsequent meeting (*idem*, p. 110). The addresses to Santa Anna and Houston
were finally approved, October 1, 1843 (*idem*, p. 119).

[114] Many articles, bearing upon British activities in and supposed designs
upon Texas, appeared in the *The Daily Madisonian* at about this time, Great
Britain feared republican France, ran one editorial, and "how much more reason
has she to fear the peaceful, rapid, and prosperous growth of Republican
institutions in our country? . . . She naturally looks upon the union of our
States as another Confederation of the Rhine, and doubtless entertains a
desire to detach some of them from the Confederacy. And hence we should
not be surprised at the efforts of the foreign *philanthropists*, who under the
guise of the best motives in the world, would hurl the brand of discord among
our citizens.

"The British Government has proclaimed to the world that, in negotiating
a treaty with Texas, the design is to procure the abolition of slavery in the
United States. How careful of our interests. A parent could not be more
so. . . .

"Should Great Britain pour into Mexico and Texas one half the amount
of the subsidies voted to Austria and Prussia (during the French Revolution
& Napoleonic Empire), there will be no want of bayonets to second the
operations of her *philanthropists*" (September 25, 1843, p. 2).

In this same issue appeared an article, taken from *The New Orleans
Daily Republican*, which stated that a claim for three million acres of land,
granted to Englishmen and Americans but since declared null and void was
to be pressed by the British Government and, if held valid by Texas, would
be but the precedent for others.

In the issue of September twenty-eight, the slavery question was again
reverted to. If Great Britain acquire Texas, it will be "*for the purpose*, not
of preaching abolition doctrines in the Southern States, but of *speedily re-
ducing the theory to practice*. Suppose a treaty should be effected by the
British Government with Texas, the former stipulating to relieve the latter of
its pecuniary embarrassments, and to *coerce* Mexico into an acknowledgment
of its independence. To enforce the latter stipulation, perhaps, Gt. Britain
would *lend* to Texas an army of 25,000 men . . ." (p. 2). The article concluded with the warning that, as the safety of the United States had hitherto
been dependent upon Anglo-French rivalry, so, without that in the future,
Great Britain would close in on the United States both in Texas and in Oregon.

Tyler as ambassador to France,[115] has recently published a letter on the subject, full of fury. He says 'The question of slavery has at length become a national one'—'I dread England's rapacity. She hates the United States. We alone stand in the way of her domination; she is wise, crafty & hypocritical, & has a party of fanatics among ourselves.' 'I would say now to England "You shall not interfere at all to the injury of or interference with our institutions in any way whatever; if you do, it shall be at your peril & cost. I will defend my own institutions, at least, against your intervention. How? Texas is bone of our bone & flesh of our flesh, *Verb sat. sap.*"' And he closes with the following toast —'England & America—Texas & the United States—Whatever we may have to do with slavery on this continent ourselves no European power shall intrude upon its domestic relations.'

"I do not think the toast quite clear but it evidently contemplates making common cause in defence of Slavery, with all the powers of 'this continent' including of course the Brazils. The editor of Hill's Patriot from which the enclosed extract is taken, is one of the ablest Democratic editors in New England, but for a year past has supported Mr. Tyler's administration. It is all evidence of the intentions of the present Executive administration. Fortunately, the Executive is the feeblest possible, having no favor with either of the two great parties, despised by all, & used by them for their own purposes as far as possible. The Northern Democracy which used to be wholly subservient to the slaveholders, but that day is over. I have no doubt a desperate effort will be made to secure the annexation of Texas to our Union at the coming session of Congress, but I trust the conspiracy will be defeated. I am sure no effort will be omitted on our part.

"Yours as ever

"JOSHUA LEAVITT"

115 Henry A. Wise's nomination was rejected by the Senate, but he was later confirmed as minister to Brazil, where he worked incessantly for the suppression of the slave trade. "The very lands in the Old and in the New World, where world conventions are held, and where abolition petitions flow, are the lands where there are manufacturers of 'goods fit for the coast,' and where the owners of vessels to be 'chartered and sold deliverable on the coast of Africa,' . . ." Wise, Barton H., *The Life of Henry A. Wise of Virginia*, pp. 113–114.

"NEW YORK,
"Oct. 19/43

"JOHN SCOBLE, ESQ.

"My dear Sir,

"I rec^d your letter by Mr Andrews, who arrived here safely a few days since. He is very gratefully impressed with the attention &c,. he rec^d on your side the water.

"As the session of the new Congress approaches the Texas question is more discussed in our newspapers. The Madisonian, the Government paper at Washington, openly advocates the admission of Texas into the Union,[116] and several papers of less importance echo the arguments used on behalf of that side of the question. On the other hand several leading gazettes that are opposed to the administration, and not tecnically anti-slavery papers, oppose the annexation with some zeal & ability. The storm is gathering. An attempt will be made to bring in Texas. The ancient jealous feeling towards Great Britain is appealed to by the friends of Slavery to excite the passions of the people so that they may favor the admission of Texas, if for no other reason, out of spite to England. G.B. say they proposes to prevent the annexation. She cares nothing for freedom, but wishes to extend her power, her commerce &c. She aims forsooth, to prevent the extension of Slavery on this continent, & pretends that if the system is abolished in Texas it will come to an end in the United States. Let us not be dictated to by her imperious statesmen—let us do as we please, &c &c. Such is the language uttered by these admirers of perpetual Slavery. If this question continues to be pressed here an opposition will be excited that will agitate the country as it never has been excited before on the slavery question.

"On this great question we look to the God of the oppressed for his interposition. We look also to England, and the world expects that she will do her duty.

"The elections are proceeding here with vigor, and the abolitionists, as well as the two great political parties, are quite ani-

116 Tappan, like Leavitt, was amply justified in saying this. For example, in the successive daily issues, September 21, 22, and 23, appeared editorials on the designs of British abolitionists on America, their project for the abolition of slavery in Texas with the resultant abolition in the republic to the northward. *The Daily Madisonian* ran from December 15, 1841 to June 30, 1845. There was also another paper of similar name and politics, *The Madisonian*.

mated on the occasion. There is to be a 'Liberty Party' meeting held at a large public Hall on friday evening of this week and I have resolved to attend it & do what I can to promote the election of good men to office. Hitherto, as you know, I have refrained from any active efforts with those who have been zealous in promoting the Anti-Slavery Liberty Party, but I deem it my duty now to aid in every way in which I can consistently.

"Not having time to add anything further at present I subscribe myself your friend & fellow-laborer,

"LEWIS TAPPAN.

"The *Reporter* is suspended for the present for want of an Editor."

"NEW YORK, Oct 25/43

"JOHN BEAUMONT, ESQ
    27 New Broad St
        London
"My dear Friend,
" . . .

"Your's very truly
"LEWIS TAPPAN

"P. S.

"I send some newspapers which will show you the state of things here in some measure.

"Newport Henry of this city wants a copy of the Proceedings &c. Will you send it to me for him, with my copy, & charge to me?—

"I send you by Mr Hunt several copies of an *excellent* pamphlet just published, entitled 'The Great Obstruction to the Conversion of souls.'[117] Please have them put into the hands of those to whom they are directed. Please ask them to *read* it. There is a great thought in it. . . ."

"BOSTON, Nov. 15. 1843.

"My Dear Friend,
"JOHN BEAUMONT—
    "Your kind letter of the 18th ult. was duly received, and afforded much gratification, as a revival of the in-

[117] Lafon, Thomas, *The great obstruction to the conversion of souls at home and abroad.* Union Missionary Society, N. Y., 1843.

teresting occasions in which I was privileged to participate with you, and the many kind attentions which I shall ever keep in memory in association with your name. The thought that I may never again see or mingle with those honored philanthropists—the London Anti-Slavery Committee, always gives me pain, & yet I know that having once enjoyed that high satisfaction is not only more than I deserve, but far more than I once would have had any reason to expect. It grieves me that our beloved Scoble [118] should be laid aside, even temporarily, from the post where he is so much needed, but on looking back I can see why it ought to have been expected, considering the indications given so early as the 1st of August. I trust that the next Steamer which is to arrive, & which left the port on the 7th, may bring accounts of his complete restoration to health. I have nothing definite to communicate respecting Cuba at this time, for, although I have no doubt the plot is going on, there are few outward movements as yet. No satisfactory explanation has been given of the quietness with which Valdes ceded his authority in Cuba, at the command of the new Government of Spain. Can you throw any light on it?

"The case of the seven negroes recently escaped from Florida to the Bahamas will probably become an important one, as I believe it will, by a curious fatality, be the first under the Ashburton

[118] Scoble, still "very poorly at times," was at this time at Hazelwood, near Kingsbridge, at the "quiet retreat of our friend Richard Peck" (Scoble to Beaumont, October 24, 1843), within reach of his aged parents at Dodbrook, Andrew Scoble and his wife (Same to Same, October 30, 1843). He had taken the papers of the "Appendix," a voluminous part of the Convention report, with him and was much chided by his colleagues for so doing, rest being absolutely necessary for his restoration to health. How weak he was can be gauged by the fact that he was quite unequal "to encounter the reading of Zulueta's trial. . . ." He did, however, manage to glance at the strictures in the *Times*, the articles in the *Globe* and *Patriot*, and the leader in the last *Reporter* and was fain to think that "the indecent conduct of the friends of Zulueta in Court, and the wretched articles in the *Times* and *Herald* . . ." could not be held as "any proof that the public mind is perverted on the subject of slave-trading." He begged that should another leader be prepared for the *Reporter*, it might be made to include what can be deduced from Zulueta's evidence or admissions that something like 132,000 slaves had been purchased. "This," wrote Scoble to Beaumont, November sixth, "is an appalling fact." Scoble was yet recuperating at Hazelwood in early December (Scoble to Beaumont, December 7, 1843).

Treaty, Art. 10.[119]   I have written somewhat at length on the
subject to Mr. Clarkson.

[119] During all this time, the B. & F. A.-S. Society Committee had not relaxed
its efforts in the direction of a modification or entire abrogation of this article.
At its meeting, the last of March, the Secretary had reported that

"the various matters referred to in Minutes Nos. 89, 90 and 93, relative
to the 10th Article of the Washington Treaty and so much of Minute No.
93, as respects calls on Lords Palmerston and Howick on the same subject
had been attended to" (*Minute Books*, II, 64).

Subsequent to the Convention, a further record was made. This was at a
meeting of the Committee, July 19, 1843, and it was to the effect that, the
Secretary,

"in company with Joshua Leavitt of Boston, U. S. . . . had waited on Chas.
Buller, and Vernon Smith, M. P.'s, and had had two interviews with each
of them on the tenth Article of the Washington treaty, and found both disposed to forward the object of the Committee—the former by getting a strict
definition of the Crimes inserted in the Bill (for carrying the treaty into
effect), and a declaration from the government that the first case of fraud,
should terminate the operation of the Article:—and the latter that he would
endeavor to obtain a recognition of the various checks laid down in the resolutions of the Committee to prevent fraud" (*idem*, p. 90).

On August 25,

"In reference to no. 71 relative to the 10th Article . . ., the Secretary
reported that the Bill for giving effect to it had become law, and specially
called the attention of the Committee to its 2nd Clause, by which it was
enacted—'That in every such case copies of the Depositions upon which the
original warrant was granted certified under the hand of the person or persons issuing such warrants, and attested upon the oath of the party producing
them to be true copies of the original depositions, may be received in evidence
of the criminality of the persons so apprehended" (idem. pp. 106–107).

On September 29, it was decided that the same matter should be a subject
of discussion for the next meeting (*idem*, p. 114); but, when that meeting,
came, October 6, Scoble was ill and "Beaumont was requested to ascertain
whether he has taken any steps in preparing the memorial to Lord Aberdeen,"
which had previously been authorized (*idem*, p. 119). At a special meeting,
October 11,

"An address to Lord Aberdeen on the subject of an Act for giving effect
to the 10th clause of the Treaty of Washington was brought in, and with
some alteration adopted, the same was directed to be signed by Thomas
Clarkson and forwarded to Lord Aberdeen" (*idem*, p. 121).

On October 27, Beaumont reported the acknowledgment by Canning of the
Address to Aberdeen and the same was read (*idem*, p. 125). The text of
the Address was as follows:

To the Right Honorable the Earl of Aberdeen &c &c
My Lord,

The Committee of the British & Foreign Anti Slavery Society beg to
draw your attention to the act recently passed "for giving effect to a treaty
between Her Majesty and the United States of America for the apprehension
of certain offenders" the second clause of which they cannot contemplate
without serious anxiety.

"The question of Texas is assuming its most portentous aspect. Lord Aberdeen's answer to Lord Brougham has, as I anticipated, waked up the slaveholders to an agony, which has been, if possible, aggravated still more by a report now rife in our papers, that

The act, having provided in the first instance that, upon certain "requisition by the United States, parties accused of certain crimes shall, upon certain evidence be apprehended, goes on to provide in the second clause "That in every such case copies of the depositions upon which the original warrant was granted certified under the hand of the person or persons issuing such warrants, and attested upon the oath of the party producing them, to be true Copies of the original depositions may be received in evidence of the criminality of the person so apprehended."

It must be very evident to your Lordship that depositions of the Class here referred to may be, not only erroneous in fact, and liable to satisfactory explanation, but deceptive in design, and the vehicle of a charge altogether unfounded. Nor is it at all impossible that papers presented as such depositions may be fabrication merely, fraudulently got up for a purpose.

That cases of this sort would be rare and highly improbable in the ordinary routine of judicial proceedings, the Committee would readily admit; but in the case of a fugitive slave, the eagerness of the pursuer to recover what he shamelessly calls his property and the infamous frauds to which slave owners notoriously have recourse with this view fully warrant the suspicion that either the one or the other of the courses adverted to might without scruple be pursued.

The Committee cannot disguise from your Lordship, that they regard the clause in question as offering an enormous bounty to perjury and forgery, and as subjecting fugitive slaves to a dreadful system of kidnapping under forms of law.

They are quite aware that some degree of weight must in the first instance be allowed to depositions presented, whatever their character, but they must strenuously contend for the institution of all possible checks on the mischiefs to which the second clause of the act, opens so wide a door. And in particular they beg to submit to your Lordship's consideration, whether instructions might not be sent out to the British functionaries in North America, directing them to send immediately home all depositions laid before them in order to the apprehension of any person under this Act. In this case the documents would be not only subjected to the scrutiny of the Government and its law officers in England, but would through the tables of parliament be accessible to the public also.

No duobt can exist but that the chances of exposure thus arising would operate as a salutary check on a system of deception which might otherwise be carried on with impunity to an unlimited extent.

I have the honor to be
My Lord
On behalf of the Committee
Yord Lordship's obedient Sv^t
(Signed) THOMAS CLARKSON

27 New Broad Street
    11th. Oct 1843.

(*Memorials and Petitions*, 1840–1843, pp. 234–235).

Additional Clarkson letters bearing upon the tenth clause, its interpretation and its application, might here, appropriately, find a place:—Clarkson wrote to Scoble, on the sixteenth of June, 1843, while the Convention was sitting,

begging him "to ask the Rev^d. J. Neavitt (Leavitt)? of Boston and all the Americans you see whether it is the *Opinion* of the Americans that the new *Treaty* will give *Power* to the *Planters* and others to go into Canada to claim their fugitives. Do the American Planters think that the Treaty extends

Gen. Houston, the President of Texas, is actually negotiating to make it a British colony, on condition that he shall be Governor

to criminals of the *black population* as well as the whites and is it believed by others in the United States that it will have such extension Please to let me know what their opinion is, as I mean to act upon it—and lastly I would trouble you to find out the Rev^d Mr. Blanchard, Delegate for Ohio, that is, his Lodgings and to send him the inclosed note.''

On December fifth, Clarkson wrote to 27, Broad Street,

''I send you . . . Joshua Leavitt's letter to me, from Boston— Be so good as to lay it immediately before the Committee and ask what they mean to do with it. My own opinion is, that this Committee ought to have it copied and a copy of it sent to Lord Aberdeen— Lord Aberdeen *ought* to *know the case* & I think he would take it as a compliment, if you were to send it to him—you will send it to him on the supposition that he will be immediately applied to on the subject, and you thought it *right* to send it to him, that he might have *more time* to consider what answer he ought to give to the application of the United States when such application arrived. This is only my opinion— do as you please about it. . . .

''P. S. Would you send the whole or Part of this letter only to Ld Aberdeen— You might omit the four or five first lines— He ought not to know that I have written Sir C. Metcalf.''

Two days later, Clarkson wrote,

''Today I have written a Letter to Sir C. Metcalf— I send it cpen to you, that you may read it before it be sent off. . . .'' and, in February, 1844, he wrote again and again about affairs and conditions in America. With regard to his forthcoming pamphlet-letter ''On the Ill-Treatment of the People of Colour in the United States,'' dated finally February 15, 1844 (B. & F. A-S. *Reporter*, March 20, 1844, pp. 43–46), he wrote to Soul, on the twenty-fourth,

''You will not fail to tell J. Leavitt and L. Tappan that if they should find some little errors about American statements they *will alter* them or correct them at their own discretion.''

He had earlier written, on the twentieth, that is, with regard to this particular work of his,

''I am convinced that they, who read it, if sensible people will see that their nation is hastening fast to *destruction* in consequence of the great Influx of Depravity, which the continuance of Slavery is pouring in upon them. . . .'' The debt repudiation in the United States was some evidence to him of a low morality. In a letter of the fourteenth, he had ascribed the ''present laxity of morals in the United States'' to Slavery.

The following documents have a bearing upon the Clarkson-Leavitt correspondence and to the case which it was its object to bring to the notice of the British and Foreign Anti-Slavery Society and through its agency to the British Government:—

(a) ''To the Right Hon: The Earl of Aberdeen,
     &c &c

''27 New Broad Street
''Decr. 6 1843

''My Lord

''I have the duty of transmitting to you an extract of a letter from the Rev. Joshua Leavitt, dated Boston Novr. 15 1843 relating to the case of the seven slaves who have recently arrived, from Florida at Nassau.

General for life. The Galveston papers declare peremptorily that Andrews is not in the confidence of Houston. Our 'Accidental President,' who has a national itch for notoriety, inflamed by his unlooked for elevation to power, & the indignity to which he is continually subjected, has, it is believed, seized upon this as a dernier resort, to force somebody to be his friends. Mr. Wise,

"Although it is probable that your Lordship may already be in possession of the facts through official channels, it scarcely seemed right to withhold from the Government the contents of Mr. Leavitt's letter, on a matter of such extreme & critical importance. A case of that class concerning which the British public have felt such intense anxiety & concerning which also the British Government have given such distinct & reiterated pledges, has now occurred, and the eyes of nations—it might almost be said, the eyes of the world—will be fixed on the proceedings which are taken with respect to it. That the Slaveholders will press the surrender of the parties with an unbridled impetuosity, cannot be doubted, & as little, I trust, may it be doubted that the attitude taken by the British Government will be discriminating & firm.

"I have the honor to be
My Lord
"Your obedient Servant
(Signed) "J. H. HINTON"

The following is a Copy of the Enclosure.

"The object of this letter is to call your attention to a new aspect of this business, occasioned by the case of seven runaway slaves, recently arrived at Nassau. It seems they 'stole,' as the slaveholders call it, or seized a small sloop, & put to sea from some port of Florida, and after hovering along the coast or tossing upon the ocean for two or three months, were fallen in with by a British Wrecker & carried into Nassau. The St. Augustine papers, declare that they are chargeable with murder, as well as theft, & that they will be demanded by our Government, & certainly delivered up, unless the treaty is a mockery. I hope, my dear Sir, that the Governor of the Bahamas is duly notified of the terms of the Act of Parliament, and also properly instructed in the details of the responsibility thrown upon him, so that he will not only delay acting in the case until the demand is made through the Government of the United States, but will deem it a case of sufficiently grave importance to be referred to his own Government for direction. There ought to be the most satisfactory proof in relation to the charge of murder— the charge of stealing of course will be of no account, as it does not come within the terms of the treaty. The alleged murder rests, I believe, on a mere vague rumour that they landed on a wild part of the Coast for supplies where there was a German family, and killed the man and put to sea. The question of the identity of the persons, & the question whether the killing, if done at all, was not in self defence, to avoid recapture, naturally suggest themselves.''

who is believed to have a magical influence over Mr. Tyler, has given forth the word, that it should be deemed by our Government good cause of war, if Great Britain in any way interferes with

(b)

"FOREIGN OFFICE
"Dec. 20 1843

"Sir,

"I am directed by the Earl of Aberdeen to acknowledge the receipt of your letter of the 6th Instant, and its enclosure, respecting seven slaves said to have recently arrived at Nassau from Florida, and to have been claimed by the Government of the United States as prisoners fugitive from Justice under the Treaty of Washington.

"I am to inform you in reply that Her Majestys Government, will not fail to give their attention to the proceedings which may be had with regard to these slaves, in order to secure the due execution of the Treaty stipulations under which they are claimed.

"I am Sir,
"Your most obedient
humble Servant
Signed   "CANNING

"J. H. Hinton Esq"
&c   &c   &c

"27 NEW BROAD STREET
"Decr. 14. 1843

(c)

"My Dear Brother,

"In the temporary absence of the Secretary (Mr Scoble) from this office, I have the duty of writing to you in relation to a matter of the deepest interest to the Anti-Slavery cause.

"Information has been received here via the United States, that seven slaves, escaped from Florida in a small vessel, have been brought in to Nassau; and that they will be claimed by the American Government under the tenth article of the treaty of Washington, as charged with the commission of murder. The ends which the Committee desire to effect by this letter to you are two: first to put you in possession of such matters as may be material in the case, in hope that you may be able to communicate them to official parties, if needful; & secondly to request that you will transmit to this office full & prompt information of all that transpires in relation to the proceedings. They can have no doubt of your willingness to co-operate with them in both these methods.

"Allow me in the first place to make you acquainted with the ground on which these poor fellows are liable to be claimed by the Americans.

"The treaty between Great Britain & the United States lately negotiated by Lord Ashburton, & called the treaty of Washington, contains the following clause known as the tenth article viz:—

(see Reporter Vol 4 page 154).

slavery on this continent. A letter from Maine, in the Mercury, Charleston, South Carolina, gives intimations of another branch of the plot—which is, to couple the question of the annexation of Texas with that of the possession of the Oregon country, & in that way secure sufficient strength to carry it through our Congress. I do trust & hope that all these machinations of the wicked

"An act of parliament was passed in the present year to give effect to this treaty; a copy of which you will find accompanying this letter. You will perceive that it requires the observance of some highly important particulars in the course of any proceedings which may be adopted; and particularly that the application for the surrender of alleged criminals must be made *by the Government of the United States,* and *not by that of the particular state* from which they have escaped.

"Should an application from the general Government of the United States be presented to the Governor of the Bahamas, it will of course be of the utmost importance that the character of the evidence by which it is sustained should be thoroughly sifted, both as to whether the alleged fact of killing took place, & whether it was not an act of self defence, or justifiable homicide.

"It may be suggested also that in so very critical & important a case, involving beyond all question the lives of seven human beings, & being the first of this class under the treaty, Sir F. Cockburn would not feel it his duty to send home the whole case, and suspend his ultimate step till he had received instructions from the home Government.

"Although it is not stated in the act, we have reason to believe—that the Government have sent out instructions to the Governor of Canada, perhaps also to Nassau—that all documents relating to cases of this class shall ultimately be sent to this country, in order that they may be laid on the tables of Parliament.

"In conclusion let me assure you that the most intense interest is felt in this country as to the fate of these poor fellows, and that the keenest scrutiny will be exercised towards all that may be done concerning them. At present of course, they are free. Can they in the mean time reach any spot where they would be safer than at Nassau?

"You will do the Committee a great favor by writing, if it be only a few lines per next mail, & indeed by every mail, if it be only to tell us that you have no information to communicate. Say especially whether any thing useful in the case may be done in this country.

"Assured of your kind interest in this affair.

"I am my dear brother
Most truly yours
(Signed) "J. H. HINTON

"To the Rev Henry Capern
      Nassau, New Providence
          Bahamas.

(Act of Parliament enclosed 6° & 7° Vict. Cap 76.)"

will be defeated, but undoubtedly the utmost energy and vigilance will be required on the part of the friends of Liberty. There remains no doubt that the annexation will be brought forward most prominently in the forthcoming Message [120] of the President to Congress, on the 1st Monday of next month. An exciting rumor that the cabinet was divided on the subject, has been contradicted *by authority*. It will be presented and pressed home by a strong appeal to the Anti-British passion, and urged as necessary to the national honor & to check the alleged designs of Great Britain against our republic. I had an article prepared for tomorrow's Emancipator, giving the documents in detail, but it is crowded out by the election. Our Liberty vote is highly encouraging everywhere. I do not hear anything about the published 'Proceedings,' nor the 'Papers' of the Convention. The incessant demands on my time, including lecturing, with no aid in my editorial labors, have prevented my preparing any additional papers. Please to give my kind regards to your family—also the most fraternal respect to the friends at 27, & believe me, truly your grateful friend.

"JOSHUA LEAVITT."

"P^r Mr Dean on the Siddons.

"NEW YORK,

"REV. J. H. HINTON   Dec. 26/43
27 New Broad Street
London.

"My dear Sir,

"Your letter of Oct 12th & December 4th were duly received. The letter to General Houston [121] President of Texas, was forwarded to a friend in New Orleans who w^d transmit it to Gen. H.

"The Barque Altorf, Capt Bogardus, arrived at this port several days before the reception of your letter of the 4th. I went to the consignees, Custom House, & on board. The crew had been all discharged, the black man among the rest after being paid off. Capt B. came to see me. He says the cook, called John in the papers you sent me, is a native of Boston, & of course a free man. He denies that he was cruel to him &c. He promised to find the man & bring him to me. Whether he will be able to find him is

120 Richardson, IV, 257–272.
121 See *Introduction*, pp. 147–149.

doubtful. Nothing can be done unless the man himself enters a complaint against the captain for ill treatment.[122]

"I thank you, and the other friends of liberty, sincerely for the interest you have taken in this matter.

"Mr. John Quincy Adams, after a vigorous defence[123] in Congress of the right of petition, succeeded in getting a set of Resolutions[124] referred to a Special Committee. These resolutions were from the Legislature of Massachusetts touching a proposed amendment of the constitution of the U. S. in relation to that clause in the Constitution authorizing an increased representation in Congress founded upon the slave population. Twenty-two representatives now hold their seats in the House of Reps. by virtue of the slave population. Massachusetts would do away with this practice. The most violent opposition was made to the reception & reference of the resolutions, but several of the slave-holding members at length declared that they gave up the contest, that henceforth they would make no opposition to the reception of petitions &c. We consider this result a great triumph.

"In haste
"Yours
"LEWIS TAPPAN"

THOMAS CLARKSON TO LEWIS TAPPAN

"PLAYFORD HALL Nʳ. IPSWICH[125]
"January 10 1844

"My dear friend

"A variety of occupations has prevented me from answering your letter so soon as I could have wished, and also the Blindness, increasing Blindness of my eyes, for I am obliged to look well to find the place, where I am to put down the pen to the paper before I can write a word, and this takes up so much time, that I am nearly a Day, before I can finish a single letter, so that I almost dread to make use of pen and Ink.

"I am glad that you have a Bible which *takes a part against Slavery*.[126] I am sure that one was wanted against the idle trash

122 The judicial procedure, which was adequate to protect the white man, often failed to help the black.

123 Abolition petitions were discussed repeatedly in December, 1843. See *The Congressional Globe*, 1st sess., 28th Cong., XIII, 56 ff., 60 ff., 66 ff.

124 *Congressional Globe*, 1st sess., 28th Cong., XIII, p. 65.

125 *Memorials and Petitions*, 1843–1853, pp. 44–47.

126 Reference is probably to Weld, Theodore D., *The Bible on Slavery*. See letter, Dec. 12, 1842.

which I have seen in American writings, about patriarchial slavery.
You promised to send me a Copy. I thank you equally as if you
had sent it, but I doubt whether I shall be alive to receive it when
it should come, and so therefore would not trouble you to send it.

"I am sorry that in your letter, you do not say how our cause
goes on in your part of the world. This would be more to me than
any other news. What real symptoms have you of its advancement? and how long do you think it will be from present appearances before any grand movement will be made in our favour?
Judge Jay in his letter to Gerrit Smith, says, that if Texas be *not
annexed* to America this Session of Congress, Slavery has not two
years to live. How does he make out this?

"I have received a most kind and affectionate letter [127] from S^{ir}.

[127] Evidently the answer to Clarkson's of December 7, 1843. On the
same subject, Clarkson had written also to Sir Charles Metcalfe on September
6, 1843. Both letters are here given in full:

"To His Excellency Sir Charles Metcalfe Bart Governor General of
Canada &c &c
"Sir

"I have taken the liberty to write to you on the subject of the Bill
lately passed through Parliament relative to Fugitive Slaves in Canada, and
knowing as I do, your judicious and humane Treatment of the *free peasantry*
while in Jamaica, and the interest you took in their welfare *I am sure* that
you will receive this letter—though I am personally unknown to you—with at
least your usual courtesy, and I may add as an apology for having taken this
liberty, that I consider myself as deeply interested in this Bill, having been
the *first person* in England who took up the great cause of Slavery and the
Slave Trade, and having followed it in its progress diligently and laboriously,
giving the greatest part of my time to it for now 59 years. I hope also that
the *information which* I shall give you on this subject *will be acceptable to
your excellency.*

"As soon as I was acquainted with the nature of the Treaty, which the
Bill now mentioned is designed to execute, I foresaw that the Masters of
Slaves in the Southern parts of the United States *would avail themselves*
of it to reclaim their Fugitives in Canada with *more* activity than ever.
I wrote therefore to Lord Ashburton immediately (as the framer of the
Treaty) to apprise him of *my fears*. He did me the honor to reply to me
in two very long and feeling letters, in which he said, that he did not think
that the American Masters would act as I had anticipated, and that if, when
he made the Treaty he had conceived that the words of it would be so interpreted as I had interpreted them, *he should ever regret that he had been employed in making it*, but desired me *to be comforted* by the consideration, that
if such practices as I had anticipated, should be resorted to with success
they might be stopped, for one of the articles of the Treaty expressly stated

C. Metcalf, Governor of Canada in behalf of fugitive slaves, who that if either of the Parties concerned *were dissatisfied* with it or with any part of it, *it might upon notice given be immediately dissolved.*

"After this I began to have other fears; that is, not only that the Slaveholders of the South would under the new Treaty pursue their Fugitives in greater numbers and with more activity than ever, but that they would probably *pervert one of its articles at least to a meaning which it was never intended to convey.* Thus for instance, one of the crimes specified in the Treaty for which a Slave may be given up is *Robbery.* Now might not these Slaveholders extend the meaning of this word to *petty thefts.* If so, a fugitive could *scarcely escape,* for your Excellency knows, that *Petty thefts* are the *common vices* of slaves, mostly beginning from hunger. I therefore signed a letter to Lord Aberdeen asking him to grant an interview with a Deputation of our Committee on the Subject of the Treaty. This interview was readily granted, the Deputation waited upon his Lordship accordingly, but I did not accompany them being very ill at the time, and at a considerable distance from London. The Deputation however was much gratified with their reception; and his Lordship endeavored to lessen their fears, by stating first, that mere *running away* from a Master was no crime; that if the Fugitive *stole* a *boat* to escape by water or a *horse* to escape by land, having no other means of escaping, this would not be robbery, neither would running away *with their masters clothes on their backs,* be considered *as any theft of the clothes.* They could only be delivered up *for one of those crimes which were named in the Treaty;* and that *Petty thefts could not be included in the word Robbery;* and that the crime must be *proved entirely to the satisfaction of the Magistrate.* When the Treaty came from the House of Lords into the House of Commons; there *was great opposition* to the Bill. *Lord Stanley and the Attorney General* were *very earnest* in expressing their opinion on two points. They insisted upon it, that as the *English Law by which alone the criminal was to be tried* in Canada made *a wide distinction* between *Robbery* and *Petty thefts;* the Canadian Magistrate would not do his duty, if he did *not make the same distinction* when he gave his judgment in the Case, and they both maintained that he (the Magistrate) would again not do his duty if he convicted a Fugitive Slave where there was *any doubt in his mind* about his criminality. For one of the articles of the Treaty was very strong in its language 'that the Magistrate *must be perfectly satisfied of the guilt* of the criminal.' Lord Stanley again observed (to make the matter more palatable to the House) as Lord Aberdeen had observed to me, what was true, 'that another of the articles in the Treaty was to the effect' that if the evils anticipated were realized, *the Treaty* upon notice given would be at an end—

"But another fear came into my mind and of which I cannot even now at this moment *divest myself that false or forged charges,* would be brought against the Fugitives to regain possession of their Persons, where self interest is concerned, a man will frequently *overstep the Bounds of truth* to gain his point, but where men have little or *no moral Principle,* or no fear of God before their eyes (for the Slaveholders of the South have given up Holy Scriptures as a *rule of faith and conduct*) what are we in the case of the poor friendless fugitive to expect from them? It is my *firm belief,* as well as that of *all my friends,* not only that the charges

are now settled, or who may fly there.   When he left his Govern-

brought against them *will be exaggerated*, but that some will be *even invented*
to get them into their power; ask a Canadian borderer as I have done what
he thinks *not believe one word they say.*   Now, Sir, how are you to provide
against *false accusations*, when the Fugitive has *no opportunity* of rebutting
them by any evidence he can bring forward.   I am of opinion, either that
counsel should be allowed to the criminal at the Government expense, to cross
examine the prosecutor severely, or that a *special court* should be established
to try such cases (called a court of protection) and that a Jury *should be
empannelled* I believe such a court will be found absolutely necessary.

"And now your excellency will permit me, as the case is actually *a case
of life and death* to the unhappy Fugitive's to make one or two observations
of my own.   The Law of England as interpreted by Lord Mansfield in the
case of Somerset, after a five days hearing says that 'if a slave once sets
his foot in British Territory, he is *from that moment free.'*   You cannot
therefore give up a Slave *merely because he has run away from oppression,*
and our Government *stick to this same principle,* at this moment.   But the
person running away is in this case *chargeable with crime.*   This entirely
alters the case.   God forbid that I should have a wish that any man guilty
of an atrocious crime should escape justice, but when we consider that an
innocent man may be convicted *under fabricated charges,* and how *mon-
strously disproportionate* the punishment by the Planter may be to the offence (for I have become acquainted with such instances of Punishments
merely for running away as *it would harrow* up your soul to relate, independently of being restored to a cruel slavery.)   I cannot but think that
the slaves now under our consideration, are entitled *to our commiseration,*
and that *every chance* should be given them in the course of the trials.   The
fugitives too, who are at present under our Government in the Canadas,
are People of a *sober and moral character,* so as to have gained the esteem
of their neighbours.   They consume our manufactures, and how great in
time would this consumption be, if they were let alone to increase and multiply: and moreover they are a *loyal people* and *to be depended upon* in a
crisis of which *you had* ample experience in the late insurrection.

"I shall close my letter by informing you that the people of England
take an *intense interest* in their welfare, and that they are now *watching with
anxiety* the issue of the Treaty when it comes into operation, and will assuredly go to Parliament if any of the outrages by the Americans should
occur which they anticipate.   I am sure the people of England will hold in
grateful remembrance any act of humanity shown on the part of your Excellency towards these unfortunate people, not that popular applause would
be any motive with you to the exercise of humanity and justice towards
them; but we have a pledge in *your own heart,* as made manifest to us
during your Government in Jamaica, that these estimable qualities will not
be wanting in you on the present occasion.

"With an *anxious desire* that you may enjoy your health (the greatest
earthly blessing) in your new Government, and all the happiness you can
wish for yourself; and with great esteem for your personal character.

"I am, Sir

"faithfully yours

(Signed) "THOMAS CLARKSON

"Playford Hall nr Ipswich Suffolk"
   Sep 6 1843.

(*Memorials and Petitions*, 1840–1843, pp. 220–221).

ment at Jamaica [Metcalfe had been appointed to the governorship

"To Sir Metcalfe &c   "Playford Hall
                                                  "Ipswich
                                        "Dec 7. 1843.

"Sir
    "Permit me to express to your Excellency my warmest thanks, though
I want words to represent the feelings of my heart for the letter which I
received from you some little time ago. This letter has made me a *happy
man.* You have relieved my mind from a *load of anxiety and uneasiness*
which I could not but feel for the fate of many of the poor Fugitives now
in Canada, and of many of those who might hereafter fly for refuge there.
May God shower down his blessing upon you, for your kind intentions towards
these poor Fugitives, and may they for ever retain a grateful sense of your
favours, so as to produce in them an affectionate attachment to your Person,
and also to the Government which you represent. I have long thought that
the kindly reception and treatment of such poor wretches as should hereafter
wish to escape from Slavery into your Colony/independently of its being an
act of Mercy which would draw down the divine approbation/might be productive of great good to the *mother Country.* If, for instance two acres of
land were granted to each male fugitive, these would be *speedily and well
cultivated.* No one knows better than your Excellency the *spirit of inde-
pendency,* the *industry* & the *prodigious exertion* of the *free negro* in Jamaica. The cultivator in a little time, say two years might become an *independent man,* after which he might become *comparatively rich.* In this
case he could afford to purchase our Manufactures. Suppose then the time
should come when the Colony should increase by means of the birth of Children and fresh fugitives to *fifty thousand souls,* what an addition would this
make to the demand for British Goods. You will know from your experience
in Jamaica, the innocent foible in the negro character which delights in a
love of finery and good clothes, and that in this way they are extravagant.
And what other advantages would you not have in the increase of an industrious population? Besides an *industrious* you would have a *religious population.* You know well that the negroes in Jamaica desire *no one thing more*
than religious instruction. Being then a religious, they would be a *quiet* and
orderly people and give no trouble to the Government; and let me add that
they would be a *loyal people,* attached to the Government which protected
them so as to be trusted on all occasions. Such a people if we look to the
recent history of Canada, would be very acceptable there. You tell me in
your letter that you have yet had no application for the restoration of fugitive Slaves. I do not know what power your Excellency may have from
Government of *allotting counsel* to cross-examine the owner or pursuer of
the fugitive slave, but such a power is absolutely necessary. If however, you
should not have *such a power permanently,* you might perhaps be permitted
to use it in the *first five or six cases* which occur. By a very strict Cross-
examination by counsel, the fugitive might escape; if so in the first five or
six cases, the fugitive should escape you would have but few applications
afterwards. If on the other hand, the fugitive for want of counsel should be
delivered up, you would be for *ever pestered with such applications.* It is
therefore of great importance that every thing that can be done justly, should

of Jamaica in 1839 but his health compelled him to surrender it in 1842. Not long after his return to England he was appointed to the governor-generalship of Canada] ten thousand emancipated

be done to procure an acquittal in these first instances. If the owners or pursuers should be defeated in their first attempts they would go home under the *impression* that it was not *worth while* to travel three or four hundred miles and back in search of a fugitive, while the *Treaty itself did not allow of his surrender*, Petty thefts not being included in the word Robbing.

"I have been greatly amused, I may say greatly delighted by a book lately published in London, called 'Phillipos Jamaica'—you know, I believe Mr Phillipo a Baptist Missionary personally, at least I have heard him speak of you/for he was in England lately) with great warmth and affection, as if he had known you well. His work is most comprehensive, omitting scarcely any subject worth mentioning, and is written in a style far from common. His accounts of the religious situation of the free Negroes would warm your heart. You yourself come in for almost an unbounded encomium, and I love the man because he seems to love you. His work is so pleasantly written, that it has had a wide circulation. The Second Edition of a thousand was advertized yesterday. If I were living in London & knew how to get a book safely conveyed to you I would send you this book of Phillipos, but your London Agent on receiving orders from you, could procure it & send it in the proper way.

"I send you enclosed the copy of my speech/cut out of a newspaper/to the great convention held in London lately, which consisted of Delegates from *various parts of the world.* You will see what progress we have made in the cause, though it has taken a long time—fifty-nine years—to do it.

"I cannot expect on account of your Excellencys numerous occupations that you can reply to this letter, but remember that as the *Protector of the fugitive slaves* in Canada, I am *deeply interested in your health;* I only wish to know what you have so far experienced, whether you think the climate in which you now live will agree with you for any length of time.

"I am, I cannot express with how much gratitude and esteem

"Yours truly

Signed "(THOMAS CLARKSON).

"(P.S. to a Dup: Copy sent Jany 4. 1844).

"I hope it may turn out that you will not resign your Government, of which intention there was a rumour some days ago. I fear our poor Fugitives would suffer greatly by such a determination, for who will take up their cause like yourself? who knows so much of their character or feels for them so much? Pray forgive me for suggesting to you what would be most desirable in case of such a melancholy event. If you were to chalk out on Paper the Plans, and leave it behind you, which you yourself intended to pursue relative to these poor people in case you should be applied to for the surrender of them—or make preparation for the appointment of Courts or of magistrates charged to carry the Treaty into Execution, or any other measures, Perhaps your successor—but God forbid such a change—might be induced to adopt them" (*idem*, 1843–1853, pp. 40–43).

slaves followed him to the water's edge with Tears, to take their leave of him.[128] He is the same benevolent man in Canada, as he was in Jamaica as far as the poor negro is concerned. I am sure from his language that he will go to the utmost length that the late Treaty will allow him to go to protect the unhappy Fugitive against the claims of an enraged master, and he is quite aware of all the Tricks & lies which will be made use of in trying to establish such claims.

"I am now employed for four or five days in taking up the cause of the free people of Colour in your Country in a little pamphlet [129] which will take no more in print than about 12 or 13 pages. I have limited it to this small size, because *few* people will read a *voluminous* essay, and because it will cost but little to print it, and will be easy of distribution as it may be sent in a letter.

"In handling the subject I show first that the free people of Colour are looked upon *and treated* in your country as an *inferior race* of Men, as *outcasts* of Society, not to be spoken to but with contempt, and this estimate prevails, *universally* in the *southern* and *more than generally* in the northern States, and find that *no one,* not *even one good reason* can be given for such Treatment.

"I then show, that by such Treatment, their Persecutors violate the *most ancient* law of Society as to right and wrong, and that consequently the American nation is below the Practice of *Heathens,* and by looking into the laws of *personal treatment,* both among the ancient and the modern America is not yet to be *ranked among* the civilized *nations of the Earth.*

"I then show that such conduct is *blasphemy* or finding fault with God for creating the first man of such materials as to make him (the posterity of Adam) turn to a black colour, and that the apostles were worthy of severe censure, if knowing that God had designed the black man to be treated as an inferior thing, then went *first* to Ethiopia and Abysinia, as they did, where *all were*

[128] Almost identically the same story was related of Sir Lionel Smith at the time of his departure from Jamaica. The version given in *The Emancipator,* November 7, 1839, was as follows:

"It is said . . . 'the road for six miles was lined with the emancipated population, who turned out *en masse,* as it were, to bid adieu to the good old governor, while tens of thousands, amidst cries and sobs, exclaimed, 'Massa governor, don't leave us, don't leave us, Massa Governor, for if you do, we be again sent to the dungeons!'"

[129] B. & F. A-S. *Reporter,* 1844, pp. 43–46 "On the Ill-Treatment of the People of Colour in the United States, on Account of the Colour of their Skin."

black, to establish the gospel *first* in that *part* of the *world,* that is before going into any other, for that purpose.

"I then show that this contempt of the free black men arises solely from the *Establishment of Slavery* in the United States, the colour of slaves, being black, and ask what would be a remedy for the evil, and answer, that *while Slavery lasts there,* no remedy can be found. This leads me to exhort the Americans, if they are wise, to abolish Slavery without delay by which Slavery and the contempt of its colour would fall together; and I urge this on the Principle, that if slavery be allowed to go on much longer, so that if new lands are opened to a new Slave population to the extent that America has the power of doing it, there will *be a laxity of morals,* so extensive and so frightful, that America will be driven out of the pale of civilized Society, among the nations of the Earth, and that other civilized countries will have *few or no dealings with them.* One crisis has therefore already arrived, the real offspring of the Immorality and Infidelity, which slave-holding has produced in the Southern states, and which *Slaveholding Connexions* with the northern has produced in part in the northern, and unless slavery is checked as soon as possible, a *second crisis* will follow infinitely more ruinous to both than the former namely the heavy judgments of God—on which a stress is laid.

"I shall contrive to send you this little piece of writing when it is finished and hope it will be printed and circulated throughout the United States. I think it will make some impression on the reader, as it puts the subject under a new point of view, and is very short, and has a tendency to produce *shame* for the illtreatment of the coloured race, when *not one argument* can be given for such treatment. If you remember, this subject was discussed when you and J Leavitt were at my house, and you approved of my taking it up, but I could never find time to follow up the design till two or three days ago. I hope you will be favoured with Health and strength to carry on your labour in behalf of our good cause.

"I remain with great regard
"Yours sincerely
(Signed) "THOMAS CLARKSON.

Do you know a young medical man of New York a member of the Society of friends, who is a warm abolitionist. His name is Thomas Clarkson Collins, and he lives at 4½ Willet [Willow?] Street."

"WASHINGTON CITY, Jan 12 1844.

"My Dear Friend—

"I was too much pressed by a variety of cares & labors here, to write you by the last steamer, though I suppose you received by it my letter written for the previous mail, but detained by some accident between this & Boston. You will be gratified to learn the result of the Florida application for the seven fugitive slaves that our republican navy chased & hunted so long. The Baltimore American of yesterday, gives the following statement from a captain of an American brig, the Fairfield, which was cast away Dec. 13. on the island of Samana,

'We learn from Capt. Wilson, that during his stay at Nassau, the U. S. revenue cutter, Nautilus arrived there to demand the slaves who fled from Florida some time since, committed a murder at Key Biscayne, & then took refuge at Nassau. His gun was found to have been discharged—a clear case of self-defence. The Nautilus was compelled, however, to sail again without accomplishing her object. The authorities at Nassau refused to give up the fugitives from justice, on the plea that the proofs were not sufficient.'

"I wish you to notice that no reference is made to the fact that the demand was not made through the Government of the United States, as I understand was required by the Act of Parliament. Will you look into that matter?

"I shall enclose to you a scrap from the N. Y. Courier & Enquirer, that you may see what the evidence was on which the demand is grounded. No notice has yet been taken of the subject in Congress, except a passing allusion by Mr. Giddings & response by Mr Levy, of Florida. But I shall be surprised if the return of the Nautilus does not produce some agitation. Perhaps we shall have a resolution of inquiry today in the Senate.

"One of the items of news this morning is the removal of Mr. Slocum, our Consul at Rio Janeiro, who is said to have been sincere & efficient in his efforts to prevent the prostitution of the American flag & papers to the uses of the slave trade. He was fool enough to suppose that our rulers meant as they said, when they professed to oppose the slave trade.

"Mr. Proffit, appointed by the President to be minister at Rio, has been deservedly rejected. He is a mere rowdy, & was appointed as a mercenary of Mr. Tyler. Yet it is possible a more adroit & therefore more dangerous man may take his place. *Gen-*

eral Duff Green has been rewarded, in part, for his labors & sufferings by having his son appointed Secretary of Legation to Mexico. As Gen. Thompson, our minister, is on his return, this young sprig will be acting minister. Green, the father, who is a bitter enemy of the Roman Catholics, & a devoted & perhaps paid agent of Texas, once interceded with Gen. Almante, the Mexican minister here to procure from the Roman Catholic bishops, such papers or certificates as would enable him to pass with security & secrecy through Mexico. The pretext was, to facilitate the construction of a rail road from Missouri to California!

"Mr. Adams has succeeded in getting a resolution of inquiry passed, calling on the President to communicate the instructions given to our African squadron under the Ashburton Treaty, & also the instructions of the British Government to their cruisers. The President has not yet responded. You will recollect the statement made in Parliament, last August, by Mr. Duncombe, that our cruisers were instructed that their principal business was to protect our commerce against the British aggressions.

"You will learn from the papers, what encouraging progress we are making in Congress. The Committee on the rules of the House have reported a new code, which leaves abolition petitions to take the ordinary course of business, & the House shows a determination quite favorable to the adoption of the report. A resolution of the Legislature of Massachusetts in favor of amending the U.S. Constitution, was to abolish the representation in Congress now allowed to the States for three-fifths of their slaves, has been received after a severe struggle, and referred to a select committee of which Mr. Adams is chairman. That Committee are now collecting materials for a report, and will take time for making a most important document. A poor negro was taken up in the city on suspicion of being a fugitive slave, imprisoned for a month, & as no one claimed him, advertised to be sold as a slave for life to pay the fees & expence of his imprisonment. He was aided to prepare a petition to Congress, and its presentation created a strong sensation indeed. After a short but desperate resistance by the slaveholders, his petition was referred to one of the regular committees and that Committee is about to report a bill for the repeal of the horrid law. The fact that the Liberty party which in 1840, numbered only one vote in 400, now numbers one in 40, is one which Congressmen can feel the force of, however insensible they may be to the motives of humanity & justice. In this change of the current, you will easily see that the slaveholders have more than they can do to maintain their present ground, and have no time to rally for the annexation of Texas. I hope we shall now keep them on the retreat. I fear the Senate, however, more than I have done heretofore. They are so far removed from the people by the tenure of their office, there are so many of the Northern members who have, politically, nothing to lose, & two or three whom the President has it now, probably, in his power to compensate for the loss of their integrity beyond anything they would look for politically in the paths of uprightness, that I tremble. Then, the *Triumviri*, Tyler, Upshur & Wise have now nothing to hope for at present & nothing to lose at present & may therefore well be the more desperate in trying to secure some future claim upon the South. We fear there is a treaty now in progress, & that Houston has pulled the cotton over the eyes of the British Government, so that the treaty will be made and ratified which annexes Texas to the United States, at the very moment that the managers on the part of Great Britain think they are just about to succeed in all their designs. A most insidious pamphlet is just published here, from a member of the Texian Congress, addressed to J. Q. Adams. If the slaveholders can be kept off until the 4th of March, 1845, I think we shall be safe on that score.

"Do let me hear from you by return of mail. It was a disappointment not to hear how it is with our dear Scoble. I pray that he may be at the post of love & labor again, with renovated strength. My own labors & responsibilities are now somewhat onerous, as I am here the sole representative & correspondent of the Liberty press & party, & the only working abolitionist in the city to watch & aid & encourage & inform the Members of Congress in regard to all the matters that are continually turning up.

"I wish very much to learn whether any representations have been made to the British Government within the last year, relative to the detention of a seaman or seamen in jail at Charleston, South Carolina, on account of color. Some allusions were made in a debate in the legislature of that State, & I have not been able to get at the whole truth. It alarmed the Carolinians considerably, & came very near producing a relaxation of their laws. Can you not ascertain whether such a case has been reported, & what steps have been taken by the British Government? Why do they not press that subject vigorously?

"Please to present my most fraternal regards to all the honored members of the Committee, & to other excellent friends whom I had the happiness to see during that grand event of life, my brief sojourn in London. And believe me,

"fraternally & faithfully
"Your friend & brother
"JOSHUA LEAVITT.

"Mr. Soule,
27, New Broad Street
London"

"*Pr Britannia*   "NEW YORK,
                                                                "January 30th 1844.
"JOHN BEAUMONT, ESQ.
London,
"My dear Friend,

"Your letter of 2d of 1st month reminds me of my neglect in not having addressed you or some other member of the Committee on subjects connected with the anti-slavery question in this country. I will now endeavour to fill up this sheet with brief notices of such matters as I think may be most interesting to the Committee.

"1. TEXAS.

"It is evident that a large part of the politicians in the slave-holding States are in favor of the annexation of this territory to the United States and that the most desperate among them (including several members of Congress) would do it at the risk of plunging this country into a war with England. These men have been very industrious in exciting the people to a belief that your country was insidiously attempting to obtain an undue & dangerous influence in Texas, and that it was for the interest and welfare of the whole people of this country that Texas should speedily become an integral part of our Union. Mr Tyler, the acting President, undoubtedly lent himself to this faction and conveyed to Congress, in his annual message,[130] intimations calculated

[130] As soon as the content of President Tyler's annual message for this year was known to the B. & F. A-S. Society, its Committee "considered the question of the abolition of slavery in Texas in the light" of it and decided to write to friends in the United States for more information. This decision

to persuade that body and their constituents that sound policy required prompt action to baffle the designs of England & secure to the United States the acquisition of Texas. But Providence so ordered it that a contradiction was soon given to the report of secret negotiations between England & Texas from Texian authority. This was most timely and beneficial, and cooled the ardent feelings that were rising on behalf of the measure so desireable to holders of slaves in both countries & all who aim to profit by extending & perpetuating the miseries of mankind. Still the friends of freedom are on the alert, lest during the present session of Congress the fiery spirits there, who know that upon the annexation of Texas depend the success of their speculations in Texian lands, and in the bodies of their fellowmen, should by some stratagem bring about the event so much feared by the enemies of oppression. On a former occasion Texas was recognized by our Government, just at the close of a session of Congress, to the astonishment of a majority of the People, and thousands & tens of thousands of our citizens are now watching lest Texas should, in a similar manner, be annexed to this country during the session of the present Congress. Mr Adams, now in his 76th year, is in his seat, in Congress, every day, vigilant as a sentinel, and is associated with a few other members who sympathise with him fully, and with a large number who will never consent to the extension of slavery on this continent. Under God the friends of freedom repose great confidence in the watchfulness, wisdom & fidelity of these men, and endeavor to stay up their hands in this moral conflict.

''Several leading newspapers, in different parts of the country, papers too that have never expressed approbation of anti-slavery measures, are discharging their duty in this matter & nobly contending for the integrity of the union. Even in the Slave States and among the Slave holders we have coadjutors. Cassius M. Clay,

was reached at a meeting held the twenty-ninth of December, 1843 (*Minute Books*, II, 144), and, at that held on the twelfth of January, 1844, Beaumont, acting as secretary in the continued absence of Scoble, reported that Lewis Tappan (of New York) and Joshua Leavitt, of Boston, had been applied to to furnish this (*idem*, p. 151). Letters from the two men were read February twenty-third and the ''minute discharged'' (*idem*, p. 162); but not the subject; for at the meeting of twenty-sixth of April, ''Extracts of letters from Lord Morpeth and L. Tappan, of New York, relative to Texas having been read, it was thought desirable that a question should be asked of Sir R. Peel in the House in conformity therewith and that the Secretary be requested to take steps accordingly'' (*idem*, p. 184).

Esq. of Kentucky, a young man of wealth and influence is exerting a wide-spread influence, not only against the admission of Texas, but against the system of slavery in the United States. His essays and speeches are characterised by fervid eloquence, forcible illustration, & powerful argument. In his last speech [131] Col°. Johnson, ex-vice President of the United States presiding, Mr Clay boldly asserted that the annexation of Texas would ensure the dissolution of the Union, & that in the event of a dissolution he would be found with the North! He also spoke of the great body of the abolitionists in this country with great respect, and unhesitatingly avowed that their principles were his principles, & the principles of the founders of the Republic both in the Slave and Free States. I send you a newspaper (by Mr Sturge) containing his speech at length. It will richly reward a perusal when your Committee is in Session, and I could almost take a voyage to London, were it necessary, to have the pleasure of reading that eloquent and soul-stirring speech to the brethren at one of their regular meetings. Thus you see that Divine Providence is awakening the patriotism of slaveholders themselves on behalf of the true interest of the nation, and of the poor slaves.

"Gen. Houston has refused laying before the Texian Congress the present state of the negotiation between his government and your's and evinces a becoming temper & spirit on the great subject of human rights. By the way I see in the Reporter that his name is considered Sam Houston, as he usually signs it, but it should be Sam. Houston, his first name being Samuel. Our friend S. P. Andrews is in Boston. He desires his best regards to yourself & the other members of the Committee. He has made up his mind, he informs me, not to return to Texas, but to remain in the Free States and do what he can for the promotion of emancipation.

"I should have mentioned that a large part of the newspapers at the North even do not insert the speeches &c of Mr C. M. Clay at length, nor such parts of them as mention with approbation the principles & measures of abolitionists. The time has not yet arrived for such editors to do justice to those they have for years libelled. Magnanimity it seems is no part of their nature. And

[131] Clay, Cassius Marcellus, *Speech of, against the annexation of Texas to the United States, in reply to Colonel R. M. Johnson and others, in a mass meeting of the citizens of the eighth Congressional district . . . on Saturday, December 30, 1843* (Lexington, 1844).

some of them are virtually advocating the admission of Texas. *The Journal of Commerce* of this very day has a short leader in which it is absurdly stated that the South is not bent on the extension of Slavery, that the question of the admission of Texas has nothing to do with Slavery, that it is merely a question of the extension of the Union, 'by which the chief benefits will always accrue to the commercial & manufacturing districts.' The editor forgets, or affects to, that the annexation of Texas would increase the demand for slave labor & thus tend to the increase of the number of slaves & lead to the exaction of greater toils & sufferings from the slaves. Alas! that 'commercial and manufacturing' interests should lead to the degradation & sufferings of our fellow-men! That it should induce men born in Free States to become, unwittingly sometimes, the abettors of a cruel & hellish system that grinds one portion of the human family to the earth to enrich their masters.

"II. Congress

"A friend of mine, now on a visit to Washington, writes that when he was there a few years since most Northern men hesitated about even speaking to a man of color, lest he should be taken for an abolitionist, and be 'lynched,' but now abolition is the topic of conversation in all the boarding-houses, hotels, parties &c., and that the House of Representatives appears to him like an Anti-Slavery Convention. This gentleman has not practical knowledge of what an anti-Slavery Convention is—at least not such Conventions as you have where there is general unity of sentiment & harmony of feelings, but he meant to say that Slavery was the great object of interest in Congress at the present time. The obnoxious 21st Rule alias Gag Law has not yet been repealed, but the subject is discussed, almost every day, & the opposers of the right of petition are evidently a majority in Congress. Mr Adams, it is said, is preparing an elaborate Report on the subject of the Resolutions of the Legislature of Massachusetts. Both political parties of that State have sanctioned these resolutions & nothing has been presented to Congress that has spread such alarm among slaveholders. These resolutions are in favor of such an alteration in the Constitution of the U. S. as will put an end to the representation in that body founded upon slave property. Twenty members of the H. of R. now hold their seats by virtue of the slaves in their Districts. The people of the South are so blind to their true permanent interests & welfare as not to see that if this provision of the Constitution was stricken out they could, of themselves, achieve a measure that would give them a much larger number of representatives, than they could lose, and the abolition of slavery & the extension of the elective franchise to the colored man.

"A southern member of Congress has announced that when the bill relating to the Oregon Territory comes up he will move as a rider, a resolution for the admission of Texas. In this, or in some other way, the question will probably come up for discussion during the session. There will be a fierce debate if it comes on, & one in which the whole people will take an interest. This Oregon question is used to increase the ill will that always rankles, in some breasts here, against England, with a view to obtain Texas in order to *spite* your country. Let England, however, pursue a magnanimous policy, doing as Lord Aberdeen said in my hearing, nothing in an underhaad manner; let her act out the policy that sent Lord Aberdeen to this country & which influenced that distinguished man in his negotiations here; and above all let her discard a warlike spirit, a spirit of aggression & monopoly, and do justice not only to her own subjects but to the family of man, and there can never be another war between England & America. The generous & elevated principles alluded to will find a response in the heart of a sufficient number of the people of this country to prevent a war. Oh that Great Britain which has so long wielded the sword would henceforth extend the olive branch to every other nation. Adopting the motto taken from one of her own poets 'Be just and fear not,' she would have the respect & confidence of every civilized nation, and soon under the smiles of Providence, bring about the day when wars should cease, & peaceful commerce encircle the globe.

"III. *The Fugitive Slaves at Nassau.* The British authorities have, it seems, refused to deliver up the seven men who sought a refuge there. The documents presented by the American agent were deemed insufficient.

"IV. *The Van Zandt case.* Mr Van Zandt, a farmer, in Ohio, undertook to befriend one or more fugitive slaves on their route to Canada, and was tried, convicted & fined about $1500 equivalent to £300 stg. Paying it would about strip him of his property. The friends of freedom induced him to take an appeal to the Sup. Court of the U. S. at Washington, & it is honorable to ex-governor Seward of this State that he has consented to act, gratuitously, as counsel in the case.

"V. *Emigrants to Canada*. Fugitive slaves are wending their way constantly to Canada. We hope that the good people of your country will supply them with schoolmasters and preachers—that the temporal & spiritual welfare of those much-wronged people will be regarded by the benevolent people of England & Canada.

"VI. *Anti-Slavery missions*. There is a growing feeling in this country that it is wrong to support missions of a pro-slavery character. Considerable sums have been contributed to support missionaries who are not connected with such associations. And foreign missionaries are considering whether it is proper for them to be connected with Boards that solicit funds from Slaveholders. Oppression they say, is the great obstruction to the conversion of the heathen at home & abroad & it is inconsistent to take money from men who are patronising heathenism here under the pretence of converting men from heathenism in foreign countries.

"VII. *Anti-Slavery Societies*. There is very little vigor in these associations at the present time. They seem to have performed the work for which they were organized. Now, special Conventions are held when business of importance is to be transacted. The great body of abolitionists in the land now belong to the 'Liberty Party' as it is called. They unite moral & political efforts for the abolition of slavery. The Garrison party is less numerous than it has been & is, I think, dwindling every day. It is so connected with other subjects that it has not the confidence of the moral & religious part of the community which abhors slavery. Were it not that many members of the Society of Friends are connected with it especially that part called Hicksites it would soon become insignificant. There is, in general, a more harmonious feeling among abolitionists than there has been for a few years past.

VIII. *Church Action*. The number of churches, of different denominations, that are passing resolutions to have no christian fellowship with slaveholders is rapidly increasing, and the resolutions are assuming a more decided character. I think too that many intelligent & influential writers, who belong to no Anti-Slavery Society, & who have been silent on the subject of slavery are taking an active part in discussing the great question.

"I rejoice to learn that our excellent friend Scoble is convalescent & again employing his talents in the advocacy of the righteous cause to which he has directed so much physical & intellectual strength.

"The venerable *Clarkson* still lives, we rejoice to learn, and employs his active pen in the good cause. He is held in grateful remembrance here by those who have seen his revered face & by the tens of thousands who have perused his works. May his last days be his best days!

"My sheet is full. There are some other topicks I should have been pleased to notice. With cordial sentiments of esteem towards yourself & every member of the committee. I remain, dear Sir,
"Your assured friend & hearty fellow-laborer,
"LEWIS TAPPAN."

"BOSTON, Feb. 2. 1844.
"My Dear Friend—

"My return to Boston, & the delay of the steamer on account of the ice, enable me to add to what I then wrote, the following paragraph which appeared in the Daily Advertiser, of this city, on Tuesday last. It shows that the insufficiency of the evidence was the alleged ground of refusal to give up the negroes. The American agents took the indictment, as I understand, and took witnesses to identify the negroes as the same persons who escaped from St. Augustine, but had no witnesses to identify them as the persons who killed the man down the coast, nor to show that the killing was not in necessary self defence. This shows that they were intent only on getting them back as slaves, not as criminals, & that they expected the authorities of Nassau to be as ready as themselves to employ the forms of the treaty as a colorable pretext for the return of those men to slavery. They were disappointed there, and will doubtless find themselves equally disappointed in the only remaining hope they can have, which is, to make the refusal the means of awakening [feelings (?) obliterated] of indignation against England. You remember that in the case of the Creole, the subject was introduced into Congress instantly, as soon as news arrived. But in the present case, not a single call has been made on the President for information, & not a single indignation speech has been made by the slaveholders, not a single allusion has been made to the affair by any of them, nor has it been named, except by Giddings, to complain that the U. S. Navy should be employed in hunting runaway slaves. The slaveholders are afraid to bring it up, so greatly has the temper of

Congress altered in two years. I am glad your Committee took such effective measures to inform the government, and hope the authorities at Nassau are now fully instructed in regard to the case. At present, it seems likely that we shall have more important cases arising at Nassau than in Canada. The excitement, the debates, the doings in parliament, have done so much to awaken public attention, that the slaveholders will not be likely to make application in that quarter, unless some extraordinary case should arise, & then I trust the present Governor is prepared for their tricks.

"With regard to Texas, I have nothing new to offer. No definite information has been received as to the final [action?] of the Texan Congress on the subject of annexation. Our own Congress are giving the slaveholders business enough at home, so that they seem to have little leisure or energy to expend for Texas. There is always danger, where so great an object is in the hands of such unprincipled men, but I trust that unceasing vigilance will defeat them.

"Faithfully your friend
"& fellow laborer
"JOSHUA LEAVITT"

"By E. Wright, Jr.

"NEW YORK, Feb. 27/44.[132]

"JOHN SCOBLE, ESQ
 London,

"My dear Friend,

"Hearing that you were ill I have forborne to trouble you with letters. I was not surprised at your illness after knowing something of your arduous labors. It has given me very great pleasure to hear that you were convalescent. I hope to hear that you are in the enjoyment, once more, of a sound mind in a vigorous body.

"As our excellent friend Elizur Wright Jr will hand you this there is no necessity for my saying anything respecting the Anti Slavery cause in this country. Mr. W. can tell you all. He has been, as you know, an active & unwavering friend of the cause.

"He goes to England on literary pursuits.

"Be so kind as to present my sincere regards to Mrs. Scoble

<hr>

[132] Doubtless the letter read at the meeting of the B. & F. A-S. Society Committee, March 29, 1844 (*Minute Books*, II, 172).

& your dear children. I do not forget my young friend, Ellen T. Scoble. Her little name sake here is well.

"With affectionate regards
ever your's
"LEWIS TAPPAN.

"Yours of Sept 7 (the day of my marriage!) was duly received.

"Mr. Andrews is at Boston. He desires his regards to you. He has abandoned all intention of returning to Texas or the S. States & has publicly identified himself with the abolitionists as a member of the Liberty Party."

"BOSTON, March 1. 1844.

"Dear Scoble

"A most astounding Providence has just occurred, which will probably defeat the Texas scheme for the present. By the bursting of the paixhan gun on board of the Princeton, two members of the Cabinet who were the champions of annexation were instantly killed, Gilmer,[133] Sec. of the Navy, and Upshur,[134] Sec. of State, both Virginians & both fierce for annexation, & the President narrowly escaped. The news arrived this morning. It cannot but produce serious embarrassment to the war party. Independently of this, a strange uncertainty was brooding over the public mind on the subject that I was at a loss what to write. The Advocates of Annexation were boastful of immediate success, & there was a dreadful apathy in the minds of the politicians who profess to be opposed to the scheme. I suppose something might be done and learned at Washington, but we have nobody there to attend to it.

"The House of Representatives on Monday adopted some abstract resolutions against abolition, and on Tuesday rejected finally, the old 21st rule.[135] The vote stood for its readoption yeas 85 nays 107. The rule was thus voted down by a majority of 22!

[133] T. W. Gilmer.
[134] Abel P. Upshur.
[135] *Memoirs of John Quincy Adams*, XI, 521, February 27, 1844, ". . . a direct question was taken on the gag-rule, which was rejected by a majority of twenty against the rule. But it was in vain. Barringer . . . moved a reconsideration. . . ." Also, *The Congressional Globe*, February 27, p. 341, gives the vote as 86 to 106.

"I am about establishing a daily paper,[136] as you will see. It is an arduous undertaking, but I was put up to it. I intended to have written on several topics, but have been too much hurried. Benton's motion to abrogate the 10th Article is extraordinary, but it has not yet passed, nor has the information yet been communicated.

"In haste
"Your brother
"Joshua Leavitt

"I rejoice greatly, more than I have now time to tell, at your recovery."

"Naples 23rd March 1844.

"My dear Sir

"I avail myself of a leisure moment to render you an account of the disposition I have made of the Anti-Slavery tracts in Arabic which the Committee of the British & Foreign Anti-Slavery Society through you did me the honor to entrust to my care on my departure from London for Egypt.

"On receiving these tracts it immediately occurred to me that I could not do better with them than place them in the hands of a gentleman whose opportunities for making a good use of them would be greater than my own. Hence I left one hundred with the agent of the Malta Anti-Slavery Soc[y]. The constant intercourse between Malta & the Mahomedan countries on the Mediterranean will enable the Society to dispose of the Tracts to the best advantage. On my arrival at Syra which is in the direct route between Constantinople & Alexandria, I called on your Consul Mr. Wilkinson for whom I had a letter of introduction, & requested him to accept of fifty of the tracts. He received them very cheerfully & promised to embrace the facilities his position afforded for making a judicious use of them.

"At Cairo I had the pleasure of making the acquaintance of the Rev[d]. Mr. Leider. He very readily accepted one hundred tracts, saying that his familiarity with Egypt would enable him to place them where they would be most likely to do good.

"The Rev[d]. Mr. Kruse was on the eve of his departure on a visit to various villages in Upper Egypt. He also very cordially took another hundred to distribute on his journey.

[136] *The Boston Chronicle.*

"Not having the honor of an introduction to H.M's Consul General in Cairo, Col. Bartlett, I addressed a note to him, stating that your committee had entrusted these tracts to me, but that being an entire stranger in Egypt, & intending shortly to leave it, I was at a loss how to forward the benevolent views of the committee more effectually than by taking the liberty of sending him a portion of the tracts, feeling confident that he participated in the desire for the abolition of human bondage which so honorably distinguished his government & Nation. This note, together with a bundle of one hundred tracts I personally delivered to his servant, who promised to give them to his master. Having received no reply from the Consul general to my note I am unable to predict what disposition he will make of the Tracts.

"During the short time I was in Egypt I distributed your Tracts in the Slave Market, in the Bazaars, in a public Coffee house, in the Hotels & to persons in the Streets.

"A gentleman long resident in Egypt & in whose piety & information I have full confidence, or reading one of the Tracts, expressed to me his regret that it was addressed exclusively to Mahomedans & not to Slaveholders generally, remarking that the Coptic *Christians* were great Slave holders, & far more cruel Masters than the Turks, & that their Clergy justified Slavery from the Bible. I confess, however, that these reasons for changing the address of your Tracts are in my opinion far from being conclusive. I have seen too much in my own country of the fatal influence exercised by Bishops & Clergy in vindicating Slavery, & paralyzing the consciences of Slaveholders, not to be convinced that the disciples of the false Prophet will be more accessible to your arguments & remonstrances, than a people who are taught to believe that our blessed Redeemer authorises the abolition of the conjugal & parental relations, & the conversion into beasts of burden of those for whom He died. The late conduct of the Bey of Tunis forms a strong although mortifying contrast with that of Slaveholding Christians generally.

"It may not be improper to mention, that on embarking at Syra (Ist Jan.) for Alexandria in the French government Steamer 'Scamandre' I found on board a number of Turks, & 4 females in turkish costume, 3 white, & 1 black. It was soon whispered among the passengers that these females were slaves, going from Constantinople to a Market in Egypt, their owner was pointed out, & even the price mentioned, which he demanded for one of them— On speaking to an Officer of the Ship, he acknowledged that these females were slaves, & when I remonstrated with him on the impropriety of receiving them on board, he treated the subject with levity. It should be recollected that these Steamers are armed vessels commanded by officers wearing the royal uniform.

"It can scarcely be doubted that on proper representations being made to the Govt. orders would be issued prohibiting this portion of the French Navy from affording in future any facilities to the detestable commerce in human beings—I remain my dear Sir

"Your friend & Obd^t. Servt.

"WILLIAM JAY

"John Beaumont Esqr."

"NEW YORK,

"JOHN SCOBLE, ESQ.   "March 28/44.
London.

"My dear Friend,

"I was very much rejoiced to receive a few days since, your letter dated Paris, 27th Feb. 'Sweet are the uses of adversity.' 'It is good for me that I have been afflicted.' Often have I had occasion to think of these sayings, one of them from the inspired volume. I am happy to learn that sickness is felt by you to be a blessing. 'Thy *rod* and Thy *staff* they comfort me,' said Richard Baxter, tho' perhaps he mistook in his interpretation of the original as to the word rod.

"Your suggestions will be attended to.

"Mr Alexander's letter, annexed to your's, gave me much pleasure.

"The infamous gag rule of the H. of R. in Congress was well-nigh repealed, but the whole subject at length laid upon the table.

"What an awful lesson has been taught our pro-slavery men at Washington by the explosion aboard the *Princeton*. Upsher & Gilmer thus cut down at a blow, were the chief actors in the nefarious scheme of introducing Texas into this Union. Mr Tyler is no better. He will do all he can to bring about the annexation. I do not believe it can be accomplished. But there is no knowing what the Satanic designs of wicked men may achieve. The great act among certain of our politicians is—and always has been—to carry measures by arousing jealousy & hatred of England. It is now trumpeted forth by this class of politicians that General Henderson, the special envoy from Texas, who is daily expected at Washington, is charged to inform this Government that if they do not agree to annex Texas he is to proceed to England & offer Texas to the British Govt! If the people can be made to believe this the effect will be great & pernicious. It is said that Texian script is distributed very freely. The truth is a most desperate game is playing. The *Journal of Commerce* of this city is advocating the annexation provided some restrictions can be made with regard to Slavery! Other papers, from the editors of which better things might be expected, are urging for annexation. All the stratagems that can be employed by unprincipled men are at work. Still I do not think they can succeed. I cannot think the God of the Oppressed will permit it.

"C. M. Clay, it is said, has emancipated his slaves—over 100. Noble man! It would be well if his uncle, H. Clay, would follow his example.

"Please remember me affectionately to your dear wife & children not forgetting little Ellen Tappan Scoble.

"When you see Mr. Alexander please tell him I have recᵈ his letter & will write to him very soon.

"Mr G. Thompson has, I perceive, returned from India. My kind salutations to him.

"Let us not be weary nor overwork ourselves, but work while the day lasts, in full faith that our labor will not be in vain.

"Affecʸ your's
"LEWIS TAPPAN"

"'Pr Shakespeare.

"NEW YORK,
"April 10/44

"JOHN SCOBLE, ESQʳ
27 New Broad St.
London.

"'My dear Sir,

"I recᵈ your letter, annexed to Mr. Alexander's from Paris, & thank you for the same. By & by I will reply at more length to both of you.

"The present is barely to inform you that by this vessel I have sent about 50 copies of the *Commercial Advertiser*, containing a Letter from the Ex Com. of the Amer. & For. Anti-S. Society to the Commissioners of the Free Ch^h of Scotland,[136] now in this country, solemnly remonstrating with them against soliciting money from the slaveholders of this country. They have visited several slave states & taken up contributions & solicited donations, and two of them are now at Charlestown S.C. for this purpose. We consider this a monstrous error, & tending to paralize the efforts of Christian abolitionists in this country.

"We hope the letter will be speedily republished in England, & sent freely over G.B. especially over Scotland. Should the Free Ch^h refuse to receive the money collected of the Slave holders here it will strengthen our hands greatly. We earnestly hope they will. Pray do all you can to arouse them on the subject.

"I have directed one of these papers to Judge Jay. Please call his attention to the subject.

"Judge Jay will I hope also address the French Com. on the subject of slavery in the West Indies.

"The whole country is now discussing the subject of Texas annexation. It is probably true that the new Sec. of State Mr. Calhoun, has signed the treaty and that it will very soon be laid before the Senate.[137] The partisans of Texas confidently assert that 2/3 ds of the Senate (the constitutional number necessary) will ratify the treaty. Our hope, under God, is in the divided counsels of the Southern Senators.

"The J. of Commerce here & one of the Boston papers openly advocate the annexation. On the contray some editors in the slaveholding States are directly opposed to it. We earnestly hope & pray that the Almighty will avert from this nation such a direful calamity. "L. TAPPAN."

Copy.
"JOHN SCOBLE, ESQ.
        London.

"NEW YORK,
        "June 29/44.

"My dear Friend,

                "The account of your anniversary was read here with much interest, but we regretted the 'untoward events' connected with it.

[136] B. & F. A-S. *Reporter*, 1844, p. 228 ff.

[137] Tappan was correct in his prognostications. The treaty was transmitted to the Senate by President Tyler, April 22, 1844 (Richardson, IV, 307–313).

"Congress has adjourned. By a decisive vote in the Senate the Treaty for the annexation of Texas was not ratified. And the Com. on Foreign relations in the House of Representatives declined making any report on the President's message, received after the vote in the Senate, recommending 'action' in the matter. Thus the project has its quietus-for the present. It is said the Cabinet are now discussing the subject of the President's issuing his proclamation for an extra Session of Congress to consider & act upon the subject of Texas. Many members of Congress left Washington with the expectation that they would be recalled within sixty days. From the best information gained I do not believe there will be an extra session of Congress, or that Texas will be annexed to the Union under Mr. Tyler's administration. Still the slaveholders will play a desperate game, and violent efforts will be made to effect their object as speedily as possible. They will not scruple at any measure that seems likely to accomplish it.

"Mr. Polk, the democratic candidate for the Presidency, is for the annexation, nolens volens, but all who will vote for him have not taken this ground. These will vote for him because he is the candidate of their party, though they disapprove of his avowed desire to have Texas annexed in any event.[138] They hope probably to exert an influence, should he be elected, to prevent the annexation in the manner projected by Mr. Tyler & approved by Mr. Polk. Should Mexico consent to the annexation the party would be nearly or quite unanimous in favor of it. Mr. Clay, the Whig candidate, although a slaveholder, professes to be opposed to annexation under present circumstances, though there is not much doubt but he—the man who carried through the Missouri compromise, by which slavery was extended nearly a quarter of a century since, over so large a territory out of the original limits of the United States—would readily acquiesce in the annexation of Texas if the measure should prove popular with his party. It is probable, from present appearances, that Mr. Clay will be elected to the Presidency next November, & be inducted into office March

[138] Students of American history are deeply indebted to Professor Eugene I. McCormac for his excellent *James K. Polk, A Political Biography*. In speaking of Polk, McCormac says (p. 612), "Like Jackson, he desired to extend the boundaries of the United States and to increase its power and prestige, but neither man was interested in promoting the spread of slavery. In supporting the annexation of Texas and in planning the acquisition of other Mexican territory Polk acted as an expansionist, and not as a slaveholder."

4, 1845. The abolitionists generally prefer him to Mr. Polk, not on account of his general character, but because he is more committed against the annexation of Texas. Still, in order to bear their testimony against the election of a slaveholder and a man who, though eminently gifted by nature & well qualified by education & experience to fill with ability, grace & dignity the office of Chief Magistrate, and to increase the Liberal Party, the abolitionists generally will cast their votes for Birney, the uncompromising advocate of immediate emancipation.

"The American & Foreign Anti-Slavery Society had a good, though quiet anniversary this year. The Executive Committee was enlarged, & I hope they will act more efficiently than their predecessors. We shall be glad to maintain a correspondence with your Committee, and to co-operate with them in their noble efforts for the abolition of slavery and the slave trade, by moral, political & peaceful means, throughout the world.

"We do not learn that the Free Church of Scotland have taken any measures with respect to the solicitation of funds from American slaveholders by the Scotch Commissioners who were recently in this country. Surely the christian abolitionists of Scotland and England will not suffer this matter to rest. There was far less cause for excitement in Great Britain in consequence of the atrocious conviction & sentencing of John L. Brown [139] to death in

[139] The excitement in Britain over the notorious John L. Brown case lasted for some time and was not easily allayed. In the A. & F. A-S. *Reporter* for September, 1844, is a reflection of Tappan's thought that it was, perhaps, in excess of the need, considering how many things there were that called for an outburst of indignation. An account is given in the A. & F. A-S. *Reporter* of the fact that at a late meeting of the B. & F. A-S. Society some severe remarks had been made against the United States. Among those who spoke on the occasion was Daniel O'Connell who introduced a resolution expressing horror at the death sentence pronounced against John L. Brown by Judge John Belton O'Neall of South Carolina. The resolution was carried by acclamation. Elizur Wright, Jr. was present and being touchy at the reflection cast upon his country or, as the A. & F. A-S. *Reporter* would have it, apprehensive lest O'Connell's resolution might work mischief there, rose to speak. His concluding remarks are indicative of his resentment:

". . . This man was condemned; how? Under republican law? No. I beg to state, it was under a law enacted in 1754, when America was a colony of George III. . . ."

Loud cheers greeted him, the British present being too good-natured to retort that it was, nevertheless, under republican institutions that it had been retained and applied. To soothe still further Wright's ruffled feelings,

an attempt to aid a female slave to escape from slavery than in the case referred to. Those Scotch ministers, however good may have been their intentions, did the anti Slavery cause irreparable injury by their proceedings here. Public attention was awakened to the letter of the Ex-Com expostulating with them. If then, their constituents, take no notice of the matter, if they retain the money, a blow has been inflicted upon the anti Slavery cause here that will be felt for years to come. Will our friends in your country suffer it to be thus?

"At the request of a member of our Committee Theodore Sedgwick Esq. a talented young lawyer of this city & who was of counsel for the Amistad Africans, wrote a pamphlet [140] against the annexation of Texas, under the signature of *Veto*, which has been widely distributed. We hope another edition will speedily be put to press. He is of the Democratic (Van Buren-anti Polk) party. I send you a copy, and a few copies for other friends, through Wiley & Putnam of London, which please forward as directed.

"Rev. H. H. Kellogg had a quick and safe passage home.

"Rev. Charles T. Torrey, an active abolitionist, is in jail in Baltimore, awaiting a requisition from the Governor of Virginia, under a charge of aiding fugitive slaves.

"Judge O'Neall has addressed a letter to me, covering a report of the trial of John L. Brown, who it appears escaped without any punishment. He attempts to justify himself & is very severe against the abolitionists. No doubt he feels very sore in consequence of the judgment passed upon his conduct by so many respectable persons at home & abroad.

"Be pleased to present my best regards to the members of the Committee & believe me to be very truly & affec⁷ yours

"LEWIS TAPPAN"

O'Connell explained that he had been misunderstood. He had made no reference to republican institutions in his resolution and had had no intention of condemning them.

[140] Sedgwick, Theodore, *Thoughts on the proposed annexation of Texas to the United States.* First published in the *New York Evening Post* under the signature of VETO . . . (New York, 1844).

"NEW YORK, July 31/44. [141]

Copy.

"JOHN SCOBLE, ESQ.
London.

"My dear Friend,

"I was very glad to see in yr Ann[l]. Report & in a subsequent Reporter honorable mention of the Liberty Party in the U. S. Though I stood aloof from this movement awhile, believing I could labor more efficiently in the cause if disconnected from it, yet I always voted for their candidates. And I have been for sometime persuaded that all the abolitionists in this country (thorough-going abolitionists) will either unite with the Garrison party or be out and out Liberty party men. A day or two since a Liberty Association was formed in the city of Brooklyn, where I reside. We took 'for our motto a sentiment of Washington, as follows—'There is but one proper and effectual mode, by which the overthrow of slavery can be accomplished, and that is by legislative authority; and this, so far as my suffrage can go, shall not be wanting.' The object of the association, as stated in the Constitution shall be 'to elect to office honest and capable Liberty men; to rescue our country from the oppressive domination of the Slaveholding Oligarchy; to deliver the Nation and State from all responsibility for slavery; and to carry out the principles of Impartial Justice and Equal Rights into practical application, by the instrumentality of the ballot box.' An association had existed in Brooklyn previously & several abolitionists here, good men and true, have done good service to the cause, but the new Association includes the other & is proceeding more formally and efficiently. Similar associations exist in many parts of the country, and are battling for liberty with energy & increased success.

"Recently at Detroit, a public discussion has been held in the Town Hall, before the elite of that city, respecting the principles of the Liberty party. Our friend Mr. Birney, who was there on a visit, was invited to engage in the discussion, and acquitted himself with unusual ability.[142] In that city, where a mere handful of

141 This letter, practically in its entirety, was printed in the B. & F. A-S. *Reporter*, September 18, 1844, p. 183, except that the uncomplimentary reference to Phillippo's work was omitted and, as was invariably the usage, the postscript was moved up into the body of the letter.

142 For Birney's part in the anti-slavery contest, see Birney, William, *James G. Birney and His Times.* The Genesis of the Republican Party with

abolitionists met in some obscure hall, a few years since, the principal people now assembled in the largest hall in the place, to hear a discussion of the principles they had so lately contemned. Surely this indicates progress. The District Judge of the U.S. for Michigan, a distinguished jurist, came forward recently & avowed himself a Liberty man & has joined the association.

"M[r]. Leavitt's new daily paper, the Boston Chronicle, meets with much encouragement. It is acknowledged to be one of the best, if not the best, commercial paper in that city, and it discusses with freedom & ability the principles of the anti-slavery cause, & especially the distinguishing principles of the Liberty party. Dr. Bailey of Cincinnati, Ohio, also edits a daily anti-slavery & commercial paper,[143] which is highly esteemed. The other anti-slavery papers in this country, chiefly weekly publications, are too numerous to be mentioned here. The largest part of them advocate the principles of the Liberty party. As soon as we can procure a suitable editor our Committee intend to resume the publication of the Reporter, & hope to issue it regularly.

"The Union Missionary Society (an anti-slavery Asso[n].) publish a paper called the 'Union Missionary,' & have issued large editions of the first two numbers. The leading men in the northern states, both clerical and laical, belong to the great Religious institutions of this country, viz. the 'American Board of Commissioners for Foreign Missions,' the 'American Home Missionary Society,' the 'American Bible Society,' &c. &c.; and these Institutions have done little or nothing to oppose American Slavery, while some of them are favoring it by many indirect means. To the honor of the Home Missionary Society it should be said that in their Annual Report, of May last, they spoke in decided terms against the cruel system, and it is the first time that either of the Societies above named have ever uttered condemnatory language against it. The language referred to is as follows—'*Another* obstacle' (to the moral renovation of the country)—'and one of increasing magnitude—which may well fill the heart of philanthropy with deep concern, is the existence of that horrible anomaly in American institutions, *slavery*—covering so large a portion of our territory, and enthralling more than two and a half millions of souls, made in the image of God, in a bondage worse than Egyptian—that prevents

Some Account of the Abolition Movements in the South before 1828 (1890).

[143] Bailey, Gamaliel, *The Philanthropist*, beginning April 15, 1836.

the most direct and effectual efforts for their salvation.' The
Union Miss. Soc. hope, by the blessing of God, to convince the
leading religious men at the North, who at the best are only *abstract* abolitionists, that Slavery is the greatest obstruction to the
progress of the gospel and the conversion of men, and to induce
them, as individuals, and as Associations, to oppose Slavery directly, as THE OBSTRUCTION to the spread of the gospel so far as the
American Churches are concerned.   The great obstacle to the prevalence of anti-Slavery doctrines in this country from the beginning
of the contest has been the apathy of the great Religious institutions above named, and the countenance they have given to Slaveholders, and to Slavery.   In this connexion I would say that Dr.
Lafon's address showing that oppression is the great obstruction
to the conversion of souls at home and abroad has made a powerful
impression in this country.   He was a slaveholder, was several
years a missionary at the Sandwich Islands, and is now here laboring with his pen & tongue to convince clergymen and laymen that
American slavery is the great obstruction to the progress & success
of the gospel here and in foreign lands where American missionaries labor.

"There is no just cause of apprehension that Texas will be
admitted into the Union under the present administration.   If
Mr. Polk should succeed he will exert his influence to bring about
annexation, but already there is a schism in his party on this very
subject.   The general opinion is that he will not be elected President.   Mr. Clay's prospect is more favorable.   He & his party, the
Whigs, are apparently committed against annexation, but if you
read attentively his letters & declarations you will perceive that this
wary politician, this great Compromiser, no where asserts that
he is opposed to the annexation of Texas.   He is opposed to the
violation of treaties, he is opposed to admitting Texas unless a
considerable portion of the people are in favor of it.   But if he
is elected President, and popular feeling is manifested in favor of
annexation, Mr. Clay can easily, without violating any of his
declarations favor the object & use his powerful influence in consummating the deed.   What need then of Liberty Associations,
of untiring vigilance on the part of American abolitionists, of
the watchfulness of our transatlantic brethren, of wise & firm action on the part of European governments, of untiring supplications
to the Almighty Disposer of human affairs!

"I am in correspondence with Judge O'Neall, of South Carolina, the judge who sentenced Brown [144] to death. He is, it seems, a deacon of the Baptist church. He seems to think that Slavery is a Bible institution, that the wickedness of it consists in the ill treatment, physically, of the Slaves. I am trying to convince him of the moral turpitude of Slavery—that Chattelism is the great iniquity of the system—and that sound policy as well as enlightened Christianity require immediate emancipation.

"Rev. Charles T. Torrey, of Massachusetts, long known as an active abolitionist, is now in the common jail at Baltimore having been indicted both in Maryland and Virginia for aiding slaves in attempts to escape. He has able counsel, & collections are making in different parts of the country to aid him in his defence. Should he be convicted the punishment is 20 years imprisonment in the State Prison. Mr. J. Q. Adams who honored me with a call on his journey from Washington to Quincy thinks that Mr. T. should be taken before the Chief Justice of the United States, Mr. Taney (pron. Tawney) who resides in Baltimore by a writ of Habeas Corpus, that the question as to the constitutionality of the law may be argued.[144] Mr. Adams thinks that Judge Taney, who once liberated all his slaves and is not now a slave holder, would be inclined to pronounce the law unconstitutional, but if he should not he advises that an appeal be taken to the Sup. Court at Washington, & the first talents in the country be engaged to argue the various important points connected with the case.

"Mr. Adams has now entered his seventy eighth year. Though he appears more hale than men usually do at that advanced age, yet he is evidently becoming weaker & more infirm. His powerful mind, like a steam engine, is too strong for the fragile house in which it operates, & bids fair ere long to break it down.

"Rev. John Cross, of Illinois, long laboring in the anti-slavery cause in this State and in the state of Illinois where he now resides, was arrested some months since on a charge of aiding slaves in their flight through Illinois from a Slave State, the 'Free' State

---

[144] "By the laws of those States," said he also, "a person who is indicted at the same time in both States can not be admitted to give bail—thus the great constitutional right of bail is denied; & whenever persons residing in different States enter into a conspiracy & get a man indicted there is, under existing laws, no relief."

of Illinois having, to please a slave-holding sister, passed laws inflicting punishment upon her own citizens who should act against the policy of the Slave States. When Mr. Cross was brought into court for trial, and it was found that instead of feeing pro-slavery lawyers to defend him he was prepared to defend himself, rather than suffer the anti-slavery harangue in open court a nole prosequi was entered & Mr. Cross was set at liberty.

"We are sorry to learn from undoubted sources that the work of Mr. Phillippo, on West India Emancipation [145] more like a fable than a narration of facts. Mr. Clarkson told me at Playford Hall that he thought the work might be relied on. He has been imposed upon. The religious, nay the moral state of the emancipated negroes in Jamaica has undoubtedly been greatly exaggerated. The absurdities & impieties of the leadership system and the use of intoxicating drinks have prevented Christianity having its legitimate influence among the coloured population, and there is more of heathenism still in the island than the friends of the negro race have supposed. Until the missionaries there set an example of rigid temperance, and discountenance every species of fanaticism, religion can not flourish nor the emancipated become an example, worthy of imitation. The work of Phillippo, refuted as it must be, will prove a curse rather than a blessing & the real facts of the case in Jamaica prove another obstacle to emancipation in this country.

"We are exceedingly mortified that the Free church of Scotland has treated our remonstrances with such neglect. They have, by the virtual sanction of the conduct of their Commissioners to this country, rebuked the abolitionists & encouraged the slaveholders. If the religious people of Scotland cease to aid us in our responsible work let them not throw obstacles in our way. The £9000 sterling solicited here is dearly acquired at the expense of disheartening American abolitionists and cheering on the upholders of American slavery.

[145] Phillippo, James M(ursell), *Jamaica: Its Past and Present State* by . . . of Spanish Town, Jamaica, Twenty Years a Baptist Missionary in That Island (London, 1842 and 1843; Philadelphia, 1843).

In the B. & F. A-S. *Reporter* for November 14, 1842, pp. 202–203, was published a letter written by Mr. Phillippo, giving a favorable account of the results of emancipation in Jamaica.

"With affectionate attachment to you and to the members of the committee I remain, dear Sir,

"very truly your's
"LEWIS TAPPAN.

"I rejoice at the stand you & your coadjutors have taken on the Sugar question.[146]

"J. Scoble, Esq."

Copy.

"G. Western.

"NEW YORK, Nov. 9/44.[147]

"JOHN SCOBLE, ESQ.
London.

"My dear Friend,

"I received yours of Oct 11th & immediately forwarded to Mr. Torrey the official letter[148] to him. He has

[146] The sugar question is discussed in the B. & F. A-S. *Reporter,* 1844, p. 53 ff. Sugar duties naturally arose as part of the free trade agitation. Joseph Sturge wrote for the B. & F. A-S. Society Committee against slave grown sugar. He was vigorously supported by Daniel O'Connell, one of the most ardent anti-slavery men in the world, who wrote: "It is no answer to say, 'That we use slave grown tobacco, and slave grown cotton.' My reply is—that I would prevent both if I possibly could; and it is no reason at all, that, because I cannot prevent two existing crimes, therefore I should consent to the commission of a third crime." Sturge, in his letter, said: ". . . the recent trial of Zulueta has proved that the slave-trade is mainly sustained by British capital."

[147] For the printed form of this letter, see B. & F. A-S. *Reporter,* November 27, 1844, pp. 223–224. The only omission of importance from the letter as sent was the reference to French emancipation.

"Oct. 10, 1844

[148] "REV. C. T. TORREY,

"Dear Sir,

"The enclosed resolution, signed by the venerable Thomas Clarkson, on behalf of the Committee of the B. & F. A.-S. Society, will show you the estimate which the abolitionists of Great Britain and Ireland have formed of the infamous prosecution to which you have been subjected on the alleged charge of having aided some of your Countrymen to escape from slavery; and the deep sympathy they feel for yourself under the extraordinary circumstances in which you are placed.

"The noble letter which you have addressed to the people of Maryland, and through them to the world, forbid the friends of human freedom here to doubt that the dignity of the great cause for which you are in bonds will

received it. A correspondent of the Boston Chronicle, who visited Mr. Torrey in prison writes, 'He had just received a letter signed by Thomas Clarkson and John Scoble, on behalf of the British & Foreign Anti-Slavery Society, that cheered his drooping spirits. It was affecting to see him reading that letter, clad in his night clothes, with a prisoner's towell tied around his breast, as he stood where the light of an American October sun streamed faintly through his iron grates. Oh slavery! When shall thy tyrant dominion have an end?' Mr. T's attempt to break jail is consid-

be injured by you, or that you will fail to meet with Christian courage and constancy the issue of the trial which awaits you.

"The next mail from the United States will be looked for with intense interest and anxiety, as it will no doubt bring intelligence of the primary steps taken in your case, and whether the law of righteousness or the law of iniquity has prevailed.

"Trusting that Wisdom & Grace equal to every exigency may be granted you & that the wrongs of the oppressed may be fully vindicated in your person

"I am . . .
"JOHN SCOBLE"

(Enclosure)

At a Meeting of the Committee held at the B & F Anti-Slavery Society on Friday Oct 10th. 1844—

Geo: Stacey Esq in the Chair.

It was unanimously resolved:

That considering the enormous wickedness of American Slavery, whether viewed in relation to the iniquity of its principle which deprives nearly three millions of human beings of their personal rights, or to the atrocity of its practice which subjects them to the deepest degradation and misery, this Committee feel it to be their duty publicly and warmly to express their sympathy with those devoted friends of humanity *Messrs. Work, Burr and Thompson, who are now suffering a lengthened imprisonment among felons, in one of the Jails of the State of Missouri, for having attempted to aid some of their enslaved Countrymen in their escape from bondage; and to assure these christian philanthropists that they † consider the cause for which they are now incarcerated as honorable to them as men, and as christians; and the Laws under which they have been condemned ‡ as utterly disgraceful to a civilized community, and in the highest degree repugnant to the spirit and precepts of the Gospel.

(Signed) THOMAS CLARKSON
President

*to the Revd. C T Torrey & Capt Jonathan Walker who are now incarcerated in the Prisons of Maryland & West Florida for having aided or attempted to aid &c

† may hereafter be called to suffer &c   ‡ are to be arraigned.

ered a most unfortunate affair. It will prevent his procuring bail. The trial is set down for the February term of the court. He will be ably defended. The letter [149] for Capt. Walker was sent to Florida by a legal gentleman who has proceeded thither to defend him in the courts. The Boston committee advanced $750, which I handed over to this attorney, who has strong expectations of obtaining Capt. Walker's release or acquittal. Though a Southern lawyer he will argue the unconstitutionality of slavery in a Territory of the United States. Walker was also piratically seized upon the high seas, and by persons acting without legal authority. The letters [150] for the excellent young men in the Missouri Penitentiary will be forwarded the first opportunity. I doubt not that they, as well as the other men who are suffering for 'righteousness' sake'

[149] TO CAPT J WALKER   "Oct 10 1844

"Dear Sir

"The painful circumstances in which you have been placed by your humane and christian attempt to deliver some of your fellowmen from the sufferings and degradation of Slavery, are not, as you will perceive by the accompanying resolution unknown to the abolitionists in Great Britain. They truly sympathise with you in your affliction; and they trust that the efforts which are to be made for your deliverance from the power of evil men and evil laws will be succeeded by the divine blessing.

"Your faith and patience may be greatly tried, but I trust you will be divinely sustained through the conflict, and that you will have a large share in the prayers, as well as in the sympathies and assistance of your friends.

"Trusting that you will meet with becoming fortitude, your approaching trial, and, that whatever may be its issue, you may find the Joy of the Lord to be your strength.

"I am Dear Sir
"With great respect & esteem
"Yours very truly
"JNO SCOBLE"

[150] "To Messrs. Work Burr and Thompson the following letter was addressed—

"Oct 10 1844

"Dear Sir,

"I have great pleasure in transmitting you herewith Copy of a resolution passed unanimously at a General Meeting of the Committtee of the B & F Anti Slavery Society, holden at its offices on the 4th. Instant. It will show you, not only that British Abolitionists warmly sympathise with you in your present circumstances, but that so far from regarding the act for which you are now imprisoned as a crime, they consider it worthy of being followed by every christian philanthropist, and the laws, under which you have been condemned, as meriting the indignant reprobation of all good men.

"You, my dear Sir, and your Companions in affliction, will remember who hath said 'if when ye do well, and suffer, ye take it patiently, this is acceptable with God,' and again, 'But and if ye suffer for righteousness'

will be cheered by this manifestation of sympathy on the part of the venerable Clarkson and the Committee of your Society.

"Copies of the letters were immediately forwarded to Mr. Leavitt.

"Our committee will open a correspondence with the French committee, and urge upon them the importance of doing all they can to bring about immediate emancipation in the French colonies.

"The Presidential contest is over, and it is supposed that James K. Polk of Tennessee is elected President of the United States for four years from March 4/45. He is 49 years of age, a slaveholder & has been speaker of the House of Representatives & Governor of Tennessee. He is a man of fair talents & character. He is, as well as his competitor, Mr. Clay, a slaveholder. The contest has been conducted very acrimoniously. Knowing that the Liberty Party was strongly united in Mr. Birney & fearing that the withdrawal of many whigs from the support of Mr. Clay would endanger his election the whig party bore down very hardly upon Mr. Birney in hopes of ruining his reputation & inducing the Liberty Party men to withhold their votes from him. To this end a letter purporting to be written by him, with an accompanying affidavit, was published far and near, in which Mr. B. was made to declare that he was secretly acting for Polk. This nefarious artifice did turn many from Mr. Birney, but his true-hearted friends were inspired with more determination in consequence of this base forgery. The Liberty Party vote is greater than ever,

sake, happy are ye.' This is your position, you have done well in seeking to deliver your oppressed brethren from the horrors of Slavery—you are suffering for righteousness' sake as a consequence of that act. I doubt not that you bear with Christian patience the punishment that has been inflicted upon you; and, that the privilege of being truly happy is yours, notwithstanding the seclusion, restraint and privations of your Prison-house.

"I cannot but doubt that in reference to yourselves, some wise purpose will be answered by your imprisonment, and that it will materially tend to hasten the downfall of that atrocious system of Slavery, under which nearly three millions of human beings groan, and from which they sigh to be delivered.

"Trusting that you may be enabled to bear this trial of your faith and patience, with Christian Magnanimity and that it may please Divine providence, in a way honorable to yourselves and to the great cause for which you suffer, speedily to deliver you.

"I am Dear Sir
"With great respect & esteem
"Yours very truly
"JOHN SCOBLE"

"a Copy to Each of them"

The above letters & resolutions were sent pr the Great Western, addressed to Lewis Tappan Esq for him to forward (*Memorials and Petitions*, 1843–1853, pp. 129–132; *Minute Books*, II, 251).

& the whigs impute to this party the defeat of their candidate. The probability is that the whig party will be broken up, & be merged in a new party called the American Republican Party,[151] which has been formed to withstand the influence of foreigners who are supposed unduly to influence our elections. This party expect to have the naturalization laws amended so that much longer residence shall be required of foreigners before they are permitted to vote. The time is now 5 years, & efforts will be made to extend it to 21 years. The origin of this party was the influence exerted by the Papists in the elections with reference to the exclusion of the Bible from our common schools.

"Mr. Clarkson's Letter 'to the Christian and the well disposed Citizens of the Northern States of America'[152] has been extensively published in this country. The writings of such a man have power, are circulated, and do immense good.

"By this opportunity I send you our new Reporter No 2. Yours are regularly received & do much good here.

"There was never more zeal and liberality among the abolitionists of this country than at the present time. A wonderful impulse has been given to the cause within a few months. We look upon the present moment as highly auspicious to a dissemination of anti-slavery principles. We hope & pray that He who ruleth among the nations will give great efficacy to these principles & great success to our labours.　　　"Very affec' yours

"LEWIS TAPPAN.

"P. S. You will naturally desire to know what effect the election of Mr. Polk will have upon the cause of freedom in this country. He is in favor of the annexation of Texas, many of the most influential men in the democratic party are also, and attempts will doubtless be made & persisted in to accomplish this object. But the Senate will be whig—the new President of Texas is said to be opposed to annexation—many of the democratic party in the United States are opposed to it—a strong opposition will be made from other quarters. We therefore, in view of these facts, and of that great fact, *The Lord God Omnipotent reigneth,* feel a calm belief

---

[151] See Birney's *Birney, passim.* As pointed out elsewhere the recent immigrants were regarded as hostile to the freedom of the slave and as somewhat dangerous to American institutions. Eventually, the Republican party won the election by winning over many immigrants, particularly from among the Germans, led by such men as Carl Schurz.

[152] Dated August 30, 1844, and published originally in B. & F. A-S. *Reporter,* September 4, 1844, pp. 169–170.

that Texas will not be annexed to this country—that anti slavery principles will prevail—and that we shall yet be a *free* and happy, and respected nation.''

Copy.

"Josʰ. Sturge   "New York, Novʳ. 15. 44.

"My dear Friend,

''Your note of Oct 22nd was duly recᵈ. & the 'Pilot' also. It is an elegant paper & I hope will do much good. If ever I get time I will address a letter now & then to the Editor, but I am driven every day and all day—but why do I say that to you?

''I enclose a letter said to be written by Thoˢ. Chalmers, D.D. of Glasgow to Thoˢ. Smyth D.D. of Charleston, S.C.[153] All the newspapers throughout this country are circulating it. It will be universally read— The effects will be similar to the conduct of the commissioners of the Free Church of Scotland in soliciting money from the Slaveholders of the United States. I hasten to send you a copy of the letter & beg you to have such a course taken as will bring public sentiment to bear upon the Author— In this country

[153] ''Dr. Chalmers & Slavery— We have, says the Presbyterian, been favored for publication with the following letter from the Rev. Dr. Chalmers of Scotland, to the Rev. Dr. Thos, Smyth, of *Charleston*, South Carolina.

'My dear Sir,

'I do not need to assure you how little I sympathize with those who, because slavery happens to prevail in the Southern States of America, would unchristianize that whole region, & who even carry their extravagance so far as to affirm that so long as it subsists, no fellowship or interchange of good offices should take place with its churches or its ministers.

'As a friend to the universal virtue & liberty of mankind, I rejoice in the prospect of those days when Slavery shall be banished from the face of the Earth; but most assuredly the wholesale style of excommunication contended for by some is not the way to hasten forward this blissful consummation.

'Few things would afford me greater satisfaction than to hear of a commencement in your country of that process by which the labor of freemen might be substituted for that of Slaves. As I mentioned to you in conversation, I was exceedingly struck so far back as 25 years ago, by a description of such a process in Humboldt's Travels through South America. This was long anterior to the abolition of Slavery in the British Colonies, & such was the confidence I then felt in its efficacy that I ventured to draw out a sketch of the Spanish plan, which if adopted at the time, might have ensured a far safer & even earlier emancipation than took place afterwards. You will find my account of it in the 12th vol of my works, from page 395 & onward. I have not been able to engage in any sort of public business since I had the pleasure of meeting with you, but I observe that in our Assembly's commission of a few weeks back, the subject of American Slavery was entertained. I do hope that the resolutions which they have adopted will prove satisfactory.

as probably in yours, his reputation stands high.   I cannot convey
to you an adequate idea of the immense mischief such a letter will
do in this country.   Such a letter written by any distinguished
Slave holding preacher in this country, would be of slight injury,
comparatively, to the Anti-Slavery cause.   Nay, if one of our Northern preachers should have written a letter of similar import the
injury would not have been one tenth so great as such a letter
from a distinguished Minister of Great Britain.   Its tendency is
to put down what we have been attempting for 10 years to build up
— It is taking sides with religious professors who hold slaves,
whose consciences have been reached by anti-slavery discussions.
It is administering an opiate to Northern pro-slavery ministers
who have been placed in an awkward position by Anti-Slavery arguments & entreaties.   Such a letter as this proceeding from the
pen of one whose writings are exerting a great influence in this
country, will do more injury than all the good that will be done by
his publications in past years—   Why will your ministers of the
gospel launch such missiles against the sacred cause of abolition?
Why do they so dishearten us when we are toiling day & night at
such sacrifices, to change public sentiment & win over the consciences of our countrymen—& bring about the overthrow of the
cruel system of slavery?   I have not words to express the grief

'I feel it a great acquisition that I have made your acquaintance.   We
owe you much, & I trust the Ministers of the Free Church of Scotland will
ever retain a grateful sense of your able and disinterested services—   Do
believe me my dear Sir,
'Yours most respectfully & truly,
(sgd)   'THOS. CHALMERS.
'Edinburgh Sep. 25th 1844.' ''

Dr. Chalmers' letter, given wide circulation in the United States, was
also printed in the B. & F. A-S. Reporter, December 11, 1844, p. 229, and
some British reaction to it in the Reporter, December 25, 1844, pp. 236–237.
This reaction took the shape of a correspondence between him and E. Cruick-
shank and John Dunlop, secretaries of the Edinburgh Emancipation Society,
who cited ''American Slavery as it is'' and ''The American Churches the
Bulwarks of American Slavery,'' which the reverend doctor agreed to read
in his own good leisure.   In this latter issue of the Reporter was likewise published a long letter to the Witness, written by the Reverend Henry Grey,
Moderator of the Free Church, from which the following is an extract:

''. . . . No plausible presentation of their case as slave-holders—no
flattering consideration of ours, as Free-Churchmen, can bring us a hair's
breadth nearer to each other.   We must necessarily condemn their position,
and must proffer them the help of our strong conviction and urgent representation of what religion demands in their situation . . . They (the Northern
people) are bearing obloquy and scorn in the righteous cause, and have the
bitter array of wordly selfishness banded against them. . . . Is our cause
of the kind that should seek its support among the most disreputable and re-
provable classes of the Christian community?''

& astonishment I feel at such strange conduct— It will not put a
stop to anti-slavery effort but it will prolong the contest; it will induce slave holders to go down to the grave & to judgment, without
repentance & reformation; & it will sooth the consciences & blind
the eyes of many in the free States who would otherwise have
speedily united with us in our great struggle for human rights—
Dr. Chalmers ought to know better than to speak of American
slavery or American abolitionists as he has done, & he should be
made to feel the injury he has done the cause of truth & humanity—
In addition to the general character of the letter let me point your
attention to some of the expressions in it, that are in themselves very
reprehensible, & unworthy the character of Dr. Chalmers as a man
& a theologian— 'Because Slavery *happens* to prevail in the
Southern States of America' Happens! Is this proper language
for a doctor of divinity to use in speaking of a moral offence? Or
does Dr. C think slaveholding consistent with morality & religion?
From the expressions quoted, it would seem that he does, & that he
scarcely thinks it even an offence against humanity & common
justice—Slavery prevails in our Southern States, be it known to
Dr. C. because 250,000 slave holders will that it shall prevail. They
hold their fellow-men in bondage, keep them in ignorance; stop their
ears at the cry of the oppressed; & at the remonstrances of the
friends of the slave, because, having the power, they will not relinquish it. 'Happens' indeed. The abolitionists of the United
States, Dr. C intimates would 'unchristianize' the whole South
because slavery 'happens' to prevail there. Where did he learn
this? Not from any Anti-Slavery publications or anti-slavery acts
— He goes on to assert that we affirm, that so long as it (Slavery)
subsists, no fellowship or interchange of good offices should take
place with its Church (the Southern region) or its ministers. This
also is not founded in fact— We do say that no intercourse should
prevail between Northern Christians & Slaveholding preachers or
laymen that implies approbation of their conduct, or a recognition
of their Xian character— But refusing to fellowship a man as a
Christian does not necessarily imply that we pronounce that he
is not a Christian— Has Dr. C noticed this distinction? If a professor of religion is guilty of a disgraceful practice he should not
be recognised as a Christian until he has repented, & exhibited the
evidences of it— Is it not correct that we should say to a minister
of the gospel, or layman who holds slaves, who buys & sells his
fellow men, we will not recognise you as a Xian while you do thus?
If this be contrary to Christian charity, to the gospel of the blessed

Saviour, and it can be made so to appear, we shall be glad to be instructed in the matter by expounders of Christianity on your side the water. But if we are right, let not English or Scotch doctors of divinity assail us, & tell Southern despots that we do not understand the religion of Christ— Dr. C proceeds to say, in effect, that he is opposed to immediate emancipation—He prefers gradualism — He would be glad to hear of a *commencement* of a process by which Slaves would ultimately become freemen, or rather by which freemen would take the place of Slaves. He does not say where the freemen should come from, or where the Slaves should go— And do your eminent theologians hold this doctrine? Will public opinion in your country sanction it?

"Dr. C, in his letter to Dr. Smyth, who is, I presume, a Slave holding minister, says, 'We owe you much'—For what? He goes on to unfold the origin of the debt. The Ministers of the Free church of Scotland will ever retain a grateful sense &c—Aye the debt of gratitude arises from the services of Dr. Smyth in promoting the interests of the Free Church in the Southern States— 'We owe you much'—how much? Your proportion of 9000£ sterling, the sum contributed in the United States for the Free church of Scotland—

"Dear Friend, I doubt not you will feel indignant at the letter of Dr. C & do all you can to have him placed before the British Community in a proper manner,

"Well, the Presidential Election is over. Mr. Polk, the democratic Candidate is elected by an unexpected majority. He is young compared with his competitor Mr. Clay, the former being 49 & the latter 67. Mr. Polk is a new man. Both are slaveholders—Polk decidedly for the annexation of Texas & Clay ostensibly against it. The Abolitionists have generally voted for Mr. Birney. The Clay party, the Whigs, assailed him violently, & spread abroad the most fraudulent misrepresentations respecting him & the Liberty party.[154] Thus they overawed & seduced many. We preferred Polk to Clay because the whole course of the latter evinced that he was a determined friend of Slavery—the opponent of Abolition—and had no objection to the admission of Texas provided the admission could be brought about in a way that would render his administration popular. We could not trust him. Polk is a man less to be feared, because he is an inferior man, has a better private

[154] For the correspondence in which John Scoble rose to the defence of Birney and the Liberty Party as against the scribbler in the London *Patriot*, see B. & F. A-S. *Reporter*, December 11, 1844, p. 230.

character, will not be sustained by all of his own party. Besides, there is a prospect that the Senate will be Whig, & thus a check will be put on the new President's pro-slavery propensities. Congress will meet early in Dec^r.—The new President will not be inaugurated till the 4th of March next. Mr. Polk will doubtless do all he can to have Texas admitted into the Union, & we are not without our fears. It is time however we ceased from man & put more confidence in the Almighty Ruler of Nations—

"The Anti-Slavery cause has had a wonderful impetus given to it during the Presidential Canvass. The Whigs professed to be anti-slavery men, in order to gain abolitionists, & published Anti-Slavery matter far & wide. They are now exceedingly exasperated against us & attribute to the Anti-Slavery party their defeat. This is undoubtedly true—So many more Whigs withdrew from *their* party, than democrats did from their's that Polk was elected. We hope for the best—The Policy of the new administration will soon be developed. We think that a slaveholder will never again be elected to the Chief Magistracy of this country. The Elections were conducted, generally, in a very pacific manner.

"With kind regards to your Sister & our friends near you
"I remain as ever,
"very truly & affec^y yours
"LEWIS TAPPAN.

"P. S.

E. Wright jr. finds employment in the office of the *Boston Chronicle* at a salary sufficient to support his family economically. I offered him a situation in my office, but he has done better.

"Mr. Torry (Torrey?) is still in jail & is to be tried next Feb^y: A legal gentleman has gone to Florida to defend Capt. Walker at an expense of $750, raised by the friends of the cause chiefly in Massachusetts.

"A Mr. Fairbank & his wife are in jail in Kentucky charged with the crime of aiding their fellow creatures to obtain liberty."

Copy.

"Pr Acadia

"JOSEPH SOUL, ESQ.   "NEW YORK, December 31/44.
          London.

"My dear Sir,

"I now transmit to you a letter for Mr. W. Owen with such answers as have been received. I hope they will not be too late.

They were kept back in hopes that others would be received to accompany them. They are in a parcel to be delivered to you for $2.62 at your office. Let me know if you receive them.

"Mr. Clarkson's letters—through your hands—have been received. Dr. Marsh's letter to Judge O'Neall . . . . . to be forwarded. Mr. Lewis Weld sent it to me a few days since. He had a stormy passage, but arrived safely.

"Mr. Clarkson's letter is well done & it will be published here. Indeed it has been already in one paper.

"Will you be so kind as to forward the letter for Rev. W. Raymond by the first opportunity? The Mission House in London may forward it. He is greatly obliged for the Reporter sent from your office. Anything useful, in the reading way, will always be acceptable to him. Do you forward the Reporter to Rev. Thomas Raston and Rev. William Dove, Wesleyan Missionaries, Sierra Leone? They would be very glad to receive it?

"Mr. Torrey is sentenced to the State Prison for 6 years & 3 w^s. & Miss Webster, at Lexington, Ken. to two years!

"Very truly yours
"LEWIS TAPPAN"

"If you send via Boston or if others do from your office let them direct to

"Lewis Tappan

"care E.E. Dunbar [155] & Co.

Boston"

Is the portrait [156] of Jos. Sturge completed & is there an engraving? I want also the engraving of the picture in the Anti-S. Convention of 1843. Will you send them to me?

. . .

"L.T."

[155] In February, 1843, Edward E. Dunbar had become the partner of Lewis Tappan in the Mercantile Agency that the latter had founded in June, 1841.

[156] In 1842, Joseph Soul had seemingly got himself into trouble for putting the portrait of Joseph Sturge on sale. See the following:

"To the Committee of the British & Foreign Anti-Slavery Society—

"An artist has executed an engraving of a likeness of me from a picture not in my possession & I am surprised & not a little annoyed to see that it is advertised in the Non Conformist (& probably in other papers) in a way that you may suppose is painful to me to be had of Joseph Soul 27 New Broad

"CINCINNATI
"Jan 19 1845

"REV. J. SCOBLE:—

"Dear Sir,—

"You must not smile at my *late* acknowledgement of your letter, brought me by Mr. Blanchard [157] on his return from England. There have been times when many things of interest might have been communicated to you in reply to your request, but here, amid the new life of the 'backwoods,' we are always in a hurry. We live too fast. Action, too much action, leaves little time for letter-writing.

"You are aware that Cincinnati is located in the South Western part of Ohio, immediately on the Ohio river, overlooking the land of Slavery. The constitution of our State contains a noble prohibition of slavery within its limits; but we have not escaped the depressing influence of this dark system. Trade and social intercourse have especially subjected Cincinnati to such influences, so that it has been no easy task to kindle and keep alive the fire of Liberty in this place. The paper which I edit (the Philanthropist) is now in its ninth volume. Three times has the Mob risen against it, destroying four presses, and a large amount of other property but it has survived all assaults, and is now more firmly established, and more widely circulated than ever. And this is not all:—public sentiment has become so changed, that no mob could now be mustered to disturb it.

"Our sister State, Kentucky, (a slave state) is at this time an object of great interest to the philanthropist. The people there generally regard slavery as hostile to the best interests of the state. The proportion of slaveholders cannot be more than one in six of the whole white population. It is the only slave state, I believe, in which emancipation is allowed, without coupling it with transportation. Perhaps Maryland is in the same category. A law was

Street. I must respectfully request that you will please not only to put a stop to this in future but as far as you deem it proper correct the impression that Jos. Soul was authorized by the Committee to make their office a place of sale for this portrait.

"Very sincerely & respectfully
"Jos. Sturge
"B—ham 2/24, 1842."

157 Rev. Jonathan Blanchard, of Cincinnati, Ohio, was a delegate to the London Convention of 1843.

passed in Kentucky in 1833 prohibiting the importation of slaves into the State, the object being to keep down the slave population, and keep open the way for emancipation. Year after year since then has the Slaveholding Interest labored to effect a repeal of that law; and last winter it succeeded in one branch of the Legislature, but failed in the other. This year the usual effort was made but in both houses it has failed most signally. The project of calling a Convention of the People of the State is now becoming a favorite idea:—the purpose being to amend the Constitution in various particulars, but especially so as to secure the ultimate abolition of slavery. In four years' time I have little doubt, that such a Convention will be held. Were Kentucky to abolish slavery, other states would soon follow her example.

"But, light is needed. We want correct information as to (the) condition of things in the British West Indies.[158] Mr. Calhoun in his letter [159] to Mr King, our Minister to France, has ventured upon

[158] Bailey made this request for more nearly correct and exact information about the British West Indies at a most opportune moment; inasmuch as the B. & F. A-S. Society Committee had been engaged in collecting such for some months past. Other countries besides the United States were interested in the British experiment. At the close of the previous year, a request very much akin to that of Bailey's had come from Holland (Alexander Jay to Scoble, dated Rotterdam, December 19, 1843) and men who had visited or had resided in any of the islands of the West Indies or countries of the Caribbean were constantly being called upon to supply the lack of knowledge or voice their own opinions. To be prepared for all emergencies, the B. & F. A-S. Society Committee drafted a set of queries—too many for our space—that, if rightly answered, would leave no possible aspect of emancipation unexamined. A letter intended to accompany them was explanatory of their two great objects; viz., to counteract misrepresentations and to prevent the introduction, under pretense of supplying a pressing economic demand, of Orientals or other cheap laborers (Memorials and Petitions, 1843–1853). Many a like measure the B. & F. A-S. Society had opposed; e.g., emigration from Sierra Leone (Address to Lord Russell, February 11, 1841, idem, 1840–1843, pp. 31–32), and another, championed by Sir George Stephen, that had very objectionable compulsory features attached to it (Minute Books, II, 35, 39). The misrepresentation of West Indian affairs was widespread and probably as bad in character as when Lewis Tappan came back from attendance upon the Convention of 1843 and announced that Clarkson had told him that he possessed "full proof that the United States Consul, at Kingston, Jamaica, was in the habit of sending to the United States fabricated and false information concerning the working of emancipation in the British West Indies . . ." (Anti-Slavery Almanac, 1844, p. 18).

[159] "She [Great Britain] has failed in all her objects. The labor of her negroes has proved far less productive, without affording the consolation of

certain bold assumptions in relation to these Islands; asserting that
the productions have greatly fallen off, and charging this alleged
fact upon the indisposition of the negroes to labor. The debates [160]
growing out of your sugar-question are referred to, in proof, &c &c
—these statements are repeated in Kentucky by the pro-slavery men,
and have much weight. How such averments and statements have
been met, you may have seen in the Philanthropist: still, we wish to
be better furnished with facts. Is it in your power to transmit to
me statistics, official, or if unofficial, accurate, of the exports and
imports of the British West Indies from 1830 up to the present
time,—also some data by which the amount or value of the productions can be at least tolerably estimated. I can easily believe that
the production of one or two great staples may have fallen off—but
has labor been directed in other channels? Has the totality of
production increased? Ample information upon these points
would be of vast, of incalculable benefit just at this time, in the
present state of the question in Kentucky and other parts of the
South.

"Will you, my dear Sir, please say to the editor [161] of the Non
Conformist, that his paper, received formerly in exchange for mine
has ceased coming to me for more than a half year past. I miss it
much. It would greatly gratify me if he would continue the exchange. I should be pleased also to receive the Reporter more
regularly than I now do. I do not know that my own paper is
regular in its visitations to London, but it is regularly mailed both
to the Reporter and to the Non-Conformist. I hope Mr. Miall will
not forget that we have quite a world in these Western States, and
feel no small interest in all the great movements of Reform in the
'Mother Country.'

"Permit me in conclusion, my dear Sir, to express to you my

having improved their condition. . . . While this costly scheme has had such
ruinous effects on the tropical productions of Great Britain, it has given a
powerful stimulus, followed by a corresponding increase of products, to those
countries which have had the good sense to shun her example . . . the freed
negro, after the experience of sixty years, is in a far worse condition than in
the other States, where he has been left in his former condition.'' John C.
Calhoun to William R. King, August 12, 1844, *The Works of John C. Calhoun*,
ed. by Richard K. Crallé (1888), VI, 385–386, 390–391.

[160] The sugar duties, West Indian distress, the possibility of producing
sugar and other tropical products more largely in the East Indies fill many
pages of *Parliamentary Papers and Debates*.

[161] Edward Miall.

high admiration of the wisdom and energy which you and your
associates in London have displayed in the management of the
great cause entrusted in your hands.   May Providence long preserve you and make your efforts still more fruitful of good to your
country and to the Human Race.

"Yours very Respectfully,

"G. Bailey jr."

"Pr Cambria. "New York,
"Jan. 30/45 [162]

"John Scoble, Esq.
"My dear friend,

"Your letter with the resolution [163] of your Ex-
Com relating to Texas were received a few days since.   The Ex.

[162] From this time on, the American letters recovered are few and far
between, one for 1845, one for 1846, five for 1847, one for 1848, and so on;
but there must, originally, have been others since, in the B. & F. A.-S. Society
Minute Book for any specific date, are to be found entries like the following:

January 3, 1845—"A letter from Jos. Leavitt, Boston, requesting the
return of certain documents laid by him before the late anti-slavery Convention, the Secretary was instructed to forward to him copies of the
same, and to request in return the originals of those taken away by him
and Amos A. Phelps as soon as possible" (II, 275);
February 21, 1845—Extracts of letters from Lewis Tappan and J. G.
Whittier respecting the annexation of Texas and other anti-slavery matters
were read to the Committee by Joseph Sturge (*idem*, p. 290);
October, 1845-, at the earlier of two meetings in this month, letters from
various people, including Lewis Tappan, were read (*idem*, p. 353);
April 24, 1846—Letters from various persons reported—"A. A. Phelps,
relating to A.-S. triumph in N. Hampshire, the Revd. C. T. Torrey &c. J. G.
Whittier, the same . . . and L. Tappan respecting C. T. Torrey" (*idem*,
pp. 403–404);
April 15, 1847—Letter read from L. Tappan relating to A.-S. affairs
(*idem*, p. 498).

One available Scoble letter for 1845 is of interest, not only because of its
bearing upon this point, as indicating an irregularity or resumption of letter-
writing, but also because it communicated intelligence of the completion of
British emancipation.   It was written December 2, 1845, and published in the
A. & F. A.-S. *Reporter* for the following January, pp. 94–95.

"My Dear Friend:—
"I shall be most happy to reciprocate your kind offer, and
to furnish you monthly with such anti-slavery information as may serve to
mark the progress of the cause on this side the Atlantic.
"You are by this time aware of my recent tour in the South of
France. . . .
"The Law recently passed by the Chambers will either be a dead
letter or provoke such hostility in the French Colonies. . . .
"At length the British abolitionists can say, that no human being
. . . can be legally held as a slave in any part of the wide dominions of

Com will duly appreciate the expression of sympathy and the proffer of aid. Resolutions [164] for the admission of Texas have passed the H. of Rep. by a vote of 118 to 102! The successful proposition is from a Tennessee *Whig*. The scribbler in the London Patriot should know this & furthermore that if the proposition passes the Senate the deed will be done not because the Liberty Party did not vote for Mr Clay but because the Tyler administration achieved the iniquitous act. Nearly all the democrats in this State voted against the proposition. This is the effect of the strong Lib-party vote in the State of New York. I verily believe that if all the abolitionists in the country had voted the Lib. party ticket an impression would have been made that might have defeated annexation. We have hopes that the Senate will reject the proposition but the result is doubtful. The vote will be a very close one probably. Oh my country! [165]

"Truly your's

"LEWIS TAPPAN.

his country. The last corner of the empire in which it found refuge was Ceylon, and there it received its death-blow in December, 1844. . . .
"I am delighted that a grand effort will be made in the Free States to prevent Texas being received as a Slave State into the Union. . . .
"I am, my dear friend, yours faithfully
"JNO. SCOBLE"

[163] This resolution of the B. & F. A-S. Society Committee, relative to the annexation of Texas, was transmitted to Lewis Tappan in accordance with *Minute 572*, thus reported the Secretary at the meeting, January 17, 1845 (*Minute Books*, II, 277). Considered as urgent, it had been given the right of way at the preceding meeting of the Committee, on January 3, taking precedence over an *Address to the Abolitionists of the United States* (*idem*, p. 270), which had been decided upon in December "with particular reference to the proceedings of the Liberty Party, and the annexation of Texas" (*idem*, pp. 306–307). A sub-committee, composed of Alexander, Hinton, and Scoble, had prepared the address (*idem*, p. 273) and, on January 31, 1845, it was declared ready for forwarding to Lewis Tappan to be distributed at his discretion (*idem*, p. 280).

[164] *Congressional Globe*, XIV, 193, Jan. 28, 1845. Vote given as 118 to 101.

[165] An almost equally intense feeling with regard to the matter had already manifested itself within the ranks of the B. & F. A-S. Society Committee. At its meeting of January 31, the following minute was recorded:

Minute 611, "In consequence of the recent decision of the House of Representatives of the United States in favor of the annexation of Texas to that Country, it was ordered that a Letter be drafted by the Secretary for transmission to Lord Aberdeen expressive of the unabated interest which the Committee take in the question; and urging upon him the use of the peaceful influence of the Governments of the United States and Texas to prevent such a catastrophe" (*Minute Books*, II, 287).

"I have written to J. Sturge more at length on this subject. Complaint is made that the Reporters arrive here with old dates. Suppose you send a few parcels directed to 'Lewis Tappan, Care E. E. Dunbar & Co. Boston,' by the steamers, with a letter to them to forward the same to me. Thus we can see what the expense is. L. T."

(a)   TEXAS

"To THE RIGHT HON THE EARL OF ABERDEEN
"My Lord
   "Among the events which have recently occasioned the friends of human freedom in the United States as well as in this Country, much anxiety and alarm, has been the fixed determination of a portion of its citizens deeply implicated in the continuance of Slavery and unfortunately, having the power of the executive Government, at present in their hands, to annex the Republic of Texas to their own. Already has the House of Representatives by an unlooked for majority passed resolutions in favour of the project, and it is said to be extremely doubtful whether the Senate may not be induced to affirm them. In that event the consent of Texas alone will be required to consummate the Act.
   "It is, however, satisfactory to remark that many, the Committee believe, most, of the eminent men of the United States are decidedly opposed to annexation on constitutional grounds; whilst it admits not of a doubt that the more intelligent and religious part of the community are strenuously opposed to it on those of humanity and morals. They dread, in common with the Committee,

Between this meeting and that of the twenty-fifth of February, when the matter was finally acted upon, letters from Whittier and Lewis Tappan arrived, giving supplementary information to Joseph Sturge about the Texan status and to the Committee, in time for it to act upon it at its next meeting, that of the twenty-first (idem, p. 290), and the one subsequent (idem, p. 291), with the result that, in addition to the letter to Lord Aberdeen, the Committee adopted a series of resolutions condemnatory of American Slavery. The two documents are here inserted. They were worthy of a happier issue than that decreed by Fate. Events moved swiftly and all in a direction the opposite of that wished for by the abolitionists, yet, notwithstanding a consciousness of the futility of their every effort, they had the courage, on the great anniversary of British emancipation, the recent decision "of the Republic of Texas to be annexed to the United States" having been brought to their notice, to announce that "it was deemed necessary in the event of its final consummation to enter a solemn protest against it" (Minute Books, II, 338).

the indefinite extension of Slavery on the American Continent, to which such an event would probably lead; and would hail in common with the Committee, the legitimate and prompt exertion of the great moral influence of the British Government with their own to prevent so fearful a catastrophe.

"The free States are already moving against annexation. By the last Mail the Committee received information of a great meeting held at Fa . . . al Hall Boston, at which fifteen hundred delegates from the Cities and towns of the State of Massachusetts, attended to enter their solemn and united protest against a scheme which, if realized, would cover their Country with dishonour. Other States no doubt will follow the example set them by Massachusetts.

"But the Committee not only look with confidence to your Lordship to exert a wise and peaceful influence over the counsels of the United States; but also with the Government of Texas. Unless her consent be given annexation cannot take place; and it is hoped, that if strongly encouraged by the British Government to maintain her independence the base designs of bad men may be averted. Under a wise Government with free institutions, and a free people, there can be little doubt that Texas would ultimately become a great and powerful nation.

"The unabated interest felt by the Committee in this important subject will they trust be their apology for again directing your Lordships attention to it. But persuaded that they speak not only the sentiments of the abolitionists of this Kingdom but of the United States also they have felt it to be a duty arising out of recent events, of respectfully renewing their request that the exertion of the British Government may be continued to prevent the annexation of Texas to the United States.

"I have the honor to be
"on behalf of the Committee
"Your Lordships most obᵗ Servt
Signed "JOHN SCOBLE

"27 New broad Sᵗ
March 1 1845"

(b)   *Reply*

"FOR: OFFICE March 6 1845
"Sir
"I am directed by the Earl of Aberdeen to acknᵉ. the receipt of your letter of the 1ˢᵗ Inst, in which on behalf of the Comᵉ. of the

B & F A S Society, you request the peaceful interposition of Her
Majesty's Gov'. both with the United States Gov'. & with that of
Texas, in order to prevent the contemplated incorporation of Texas
with the United States.

"I am to thank you for your communication, and to assure you
that Her Majesty's Government will not fail to take such measures
as may be practicable and as they may deem best suited to meet
whatever circumstances may arise with reference to the object in
question both in the United States and in Texas.

"I am Sir
"Your most obedient
humble St
(Signed) "H. M. ADDINGTON

"To John Scoble Esq"
&c   &c

(c)   AMERICAN SLAVERY.

At a meeting of the Committee of the British and Foreign Anti-
Slavery Society, held at No. 27, New Broad-street, on Wednesday
the 26th day of February, 1845.   George William Alexander, Esq.,
in the Chair.   The following resolutions were passed unanimously.

That this Committee feel it to be their duty publicly to express
their deep sympathy for those estimable individuals now incarcerated in the jails and penitentiaries of Virginia, Maryland, Kentucky, Missouri, and Florida, on the charge of having counselled,
or aided and abetted certain slaves to escape from Southern
bondage.

That so far from regarding as crimes, the alleged acts for which
they have been condemned to various cruel and degrading punishments by the slave courts of the United States, they esteem them to
be deeds of Christian benevolence.

That, in the view of this Committee, the law of American
slavery, which condemns nearly three millions of innocent beings,
and their posterity after them, to perpetual bondage, with all its
revolting and cruel incidents, is, and should be considered by all
good men, as morally null and void, inasmuch as it is a manifest
violation of the natural rights of man, and an impious invasion of
the prerogatives of Almighty God.

That the wickedness of this law becomes the more apparent, in
that it requires other laws equally iniquitous in principle to sustain

it, laws which denounce acts of humanity as crimes, and punish deeds of mercy with chains and imprisonment, branding and the pillory; thus reversing the great Christian law of equity and benevolence which requires that we should do unto others as we would they should do unto us.

That this Committee therefore respectfully, yet urgently, call on the friends of humanity and religion in this and other countries to enter their emphatic and united protest against the system of American slavery, as founded in iniquity and upheld by oppression, and especially to urge on the Christian philanthropists of the United States the solemn duty of seeking by every constitutional and Christian means its immediate and entire abolition, and the universal application of the sublime truth contained in their Declaration of Independence, that "God hath created all men equal, and endowed them with certain inalienable rights, among which are life, liberty, and the pursuit of happiness."

Finally,—That this Committee tender their warm and heartfelt sympathy to the wives and children, and other near relations of their imprisoned friends, and affectionately commend them in their affliction, to the protection of Him who is the "God of the oppressed," and to the Christian regard and care of their fellow labourers in the cause of injured and oppressed humanity.

(Signed) JOHN SCOBLE, Secretary.

"NEW YORK,
"Nov. 30/46

"JOHN SCOBLE, ESQ,
London.
"My dear Friend,

"Yours of the 3d was duly received. It gave me sincere pleasure to hear from you. Whenever I take up the B. & F. Anti-S Reporter I feel that I have a communication from you, but a letter is dearer still.

"We have not heard from our dear friend Phelps [166] since his departure. He intended staying a while at Port au Prince & then to go to Jamaica. How glad would he be to be joined by Messrs Alexander and Wiffin.[167] If possible I hope they will go. The united labors of such men would act powerfully upon the general

166 The Reverend Amos A. Phelps.
167 George W. Alexander and Benjamin B. Wiffin.

cause. Do urge their going immediately. They could hardly do a better service to the cause in this country.

"I will convey your message to Mr Phelps.

"Wm. Goodell wrote the largest part of the Address on "Bible Missions."[168] I am pleased to know that Mrs Scoble approves it, as well as yourself. Professor Whipple [169] of Ohio has accepted the appointment of Cor. Sec. of the Amer. Miss. Asso[n]. & is here engaged in the duties of the office. We may suspend the publication of the Reporter while Mr Phelps is away, as I cannot devote the necessary time to editing it. The labor attending the Washington paper &c, takes up half my time. We are going on well with that plan. Dr Bailey intends to move immediately to Washington & issue his first number in Jan[y].[170] The name is to be the *National Era*.

"How unfortunate that T. Clarkson [171] should have lent his name to the project of Garrison! How strange that Geo. T. should

[168] William Goodell was one of the ablest and most prolific writers against slavery.

[169] Charles King Whipple.

[170] The first issue of *The National Era* was made in January of 1847, with Gamaliel Bailey, Jr., as Editor, Amos A. Phelps and John G. Whittier as Corresponding Editors, and George W. Alexander as one of the foreign correspondents. The introductory statement of policy gave notice that it would not be a one-subject paper and that it would be moderate in tone, although anti-slavery. It was regarded "as the metropolitan organ of the Third Political Party, and of the *American and Foreign Anti-Slavery Society*, in Washington . . ." (*Fifteenth Annual Report* of the Massachusetts Anti-Slavery Society, p. 30) and, at the time of its first appearance, the city government of Georgetown had it under consideration whether or no such a paper should be tolerated (*idem*). The Garrisonians, however, were of the opinion that nobody need fear the *National Era* because of the character of the man who was behind it. Bailey's attitude toward the Mexican War had made many dubious as to whether he were a genuine abolitionist (*idem*, pp. 30–31).

[171] Clarkson had died in September. Garrison was with him towards the last and the two men had come to a fuller understanding of each other than had been possible for a long time. The comment of Garrison's friends of the Massachusetts Anti-Slavery Society shows what it was supposed to signify. Clarkson's "native capacity," said they,

"made more keen by long experience, enabled him to discern who were the genuine friends of the Slave in the New World and what the true method of carrying forward his cause. And in spite of the sectarian *surveillance* under which *soi disant* abolitionists of the school of the British and Foreign Society attempted to keep him, he lost no opportunity of extending to us in this country his words of counsel and of cheer. At this last interview with Mr. Garrison he placed in his hands one of the latest productions of his mind,—his latest offering to Liberty,—entitled 'Hints to the American People in the event of a Dissolution of the Union' . . ." (*Fifteenth Annual Report*, p. 36).

enlist in such a crusade against this country & the principal part of the best abolitionists in England and the U.S.[172] Messrs Garrison, Thompson & Wright utter much truth, to be sure, but of what consequence is it when the spirit they manifest is so bad.[173]

"Mr Phelps wrote a long letter to Mr John Dunlop just before his departure, about the Garrison clique. I hoped it would have

[172] This was the year of the formation of the Evangelical Alliance and of the Anti-Slavery League, designed by its radical founders to be of antipathetic tendencies. Garrison, invited by resolution of the Glasgow Emancipation Society, had gone over to Britain once more and had gathered around himself, in closest bonds of sympathy, a great many ardent souls, among whom this latter organization had developed. "We are satisfied," reported the New England friends already referred to,

> "That there was never a time when the character of American slavery, the relations of the inhabitants of the Free and Slave States, the constitutional bulwarks of the institution, the position and difficulties of abolitionists in this country—in short the actual nature of Slavery and Pro-Slavery,—were so well understood and intelligently considered, in England, as at the present time. And we believe that we could never boast of a larger and more devoted band of faithful friends, in the mother-country, than we now possess. They have been well winnowed by the agitation that has passed over the land, but it was the chaff only that was scattered by its breath" (*idem*, p. 34).

J. B. Estlin, of Bristol, had brought out his timely *Brief Notice of American Slavery and of the Abolition Movement*, and Henry Clarke Wright, an American of all too fiery spirit, two or three of his many pamphlets dealing with the great topic of the day, the church controversy. On this subject, the Darlington Anti-Slavery Society and the Glasgow Emancipation Society were only two of the many organizations that had come out forcibly, and, at their meetings, men like Wright, George Thompson, James N. Buffum and Frederick Douglass were constant and popular speakers.

[173] What Wright's spirit was—and Thompson's was like unto it—may be surmised from the titles of some of his publications:

1. Manstealers: will the Free Church of Scotland hold Christian Fellowship with them? (Glasgow, 1845).
2. Christian communion with slaveholders: Will the Alliance sanction it? Letters to Rev. John Angell James, D. D. and Rev. Ralph Wardlaw, D. D., shewing their position in the Alliance (1846).
3. Free Church alliance with manstealers. Send back the money. Great anti-slavery meeting in the City Hall, Glasgow, containing speeches delivered by Messrs Wright, Douglas, and Buffum, from America, and George Thompson, esq. of London; with a summary account of a series of meetings held in Edinburgh by the above named Gentlemen (Glasgow, 1846).
4. The Dissolution of the American Union demanded by Justice and Humanity, as the incurable enemy of Liberty—Letters to the Glasgow *Argus* (1846).
5. On Christian Fellowship with Slaveholders—Letter to Drs. Chalmers, Candlish and Cunningham (1846).
6. Slaveholders or Play Actors, Which are the Greater Sinners? (Dublin, 1847).

been published before G. left the country. Is it too late now?
Mr Sturge had a duplicate I believe.

"Our Com. will, I think, address a letter to 'Sir Culling'[174]
about the Alliance.

"With kind regards to your dear wife & children not forgetting
little 'Ellen Tappan'

"I am,

"Yours affec[r]

"LEWIS TAPPAN.

"I have disabled one of my fingers, so that I find it rather difficult
to write."

Copy.

"NEW YORK, Feb 1/47.[175]

"JOHN SCOBLE, ESQ.

"My dear friend,

"Capt. Knight, of the packet ship Switzerland, has in
charge a parcel containing 350 copies of the Ex-Com's 'Protest
and Remonstrance against the course pursued by the Evangelical
Alliance on the subject of American Slavery.' It is just from
the press. We expect it will appear in the *National Era*,[176] but
we have printed an edition in pamphlet form for distribution.

"We hope you will have them directed to influential persons
and sent away immediately. Please inform me respecting the distribution. If the Remonstrance could be reprinted & widely dis-
persed we shall be glad.[177]

[174] Sir Culling Eardley Smith.

[175] A Lewis Tappan letter, January 27, 1847, published in *The National
Era*, February 4, 1847, contained a summary of British and American news
and called particular attention to a powerful memorial and remonstrance on
slavery addressed to the churches of the U. S. A. by the Synod of the United
Secession Church.

[176] "To the Christian Abolitionists of Great Britain and Ireland who met
at Freemason's Hall, London, August 19, 1846, to form an Evangelical alliance,

"Protest and Remonstrance of the Executive Committee of the A. & F.
A-S. Society against the course pursued on the question of American slavery.

"'We entreat you . . . to stand by the declared position of British
Christians, that the sin of slaveholding ought not to receive any countenance in the name of the Christian religion; and that . . . you can
acknowledge no union, and hold no intercourse with any branch of the
Alliance which shall swerve from this high and holy ground'" (*The National Era*, February 11, 1847, p. 4).

[177] At about this time the year before, the B. & F. A-S. Society Committee
was making its own plea to the Alliance for what it regarded as right conduct:

"A few days since I recd a letter from our dear friend Phelps. It was dated the last of Dec. at Kingston. He was better than he had been, but not so well as when he left this country.

To THE LONDON DIVISION OF THE PROVISIONAL COMMITTEE OF THE PROPOSED EVANGELICAL ALLIANCE.

"Gent:

"The Co. of the B. & F A S Socy. trust that no apology will be deemed necessary on their part for introducing to your serious attention a subject of great practical importance in connexion with the object you have for some time past been endeavoring to realize.

"You are probably aware Gent: that at this moment there exist in 13 of the States of the U S of North America nearly 3 millions of our fellow creatures of both sexes and all ages, in the dreadful condition of Slavery. The liberty of these unhappy persons was never forfeited by crime. They are innocent human beings who have been deprived of their freedom by the most inquitous laws to minister to the insatiable cupidity, the base passions or the pride of their Owners; and they are retained in their hard state of bondage by means the most revolting and cruel. They are the descendants, for the most part of Africans who were formerly removed by fraud or violence from their native homes by the Slave dealers; and whether viewed in relation to their physical sufferings or their moral condition—the outrage has been committed on their nature & their rights, or the helplessness & the hopelessness of their condition, should be the objects of the deepest sympathy to all Xtian Men, & of earnest prayer & zealous effort for their speedy deliverance.

"You are also aware, Gent, that these Slaves are Merchantable Commodities. In the eye of the Law they are regarded as mere property except when they commit crime, and can therefore, be bought & sold given away or bequeathed to meet the necessities or gratify the caprice of their Masters. They have no social or civil rights, and therefore no regard whatever is paid to the relationships they may sustain and they not only can be but are constantly subjected to the most heart rending separations. From 60 to 80,000 & sometimes considerably more, pass from one hand to another by sale every year; whilst the mode in which many thousands of them are raised from the Southern markets is too revolting to be described.

"The Law which regulates the condition of these Slaves does not sanction their marriage. If they enter into arrangements to live together as Man & Wife it knows nothing of the relation and consequently does not protect it. It may be sundered in a moment. The result is that not only is the divine ordinance of Matrimony set aside; but a disgraceful system of concubinage is established in its place, & a state of licentious indulgence generated which is frightful to contemplate. Neither do those laws recognize the parental relation. In this respect the Children of Slaves are placed on the same level with the offspring of Brutes; Both are property. The father cannot protect his Son from injustice—the Mother her Daughter from dishonor. The tears the lamentations, the intreaties of Parents are no more regarded than the lowing of Cattle; and should they become troublesome are punished with severity.

"The Committee dwell not on the continual injustice inflicted on the Slave by depriving him of the legitimate fruits of his labor, or the liberty of choice in respect of his employment and employer; nor of the cruel modes which are resorted to for the purpose of coercing labor, and of enforcing obedience. These are too well known to need description. It is quite natural that a system which violates all the essential rights of humanity and outrages the laws of God, should lead to the practice of every enormity which Wicked Men, could invent or human nature endure.

"The laws of the Slave states moreover rigidly exclude from the poor Slaves all instruction whether secular or moral. In some of the States the

"The great question of the day is, if new territory is taken from Mexico shall it be forever free? A warm discussion is going on in Congress on the subject, & the State Legislatures are expressing their opinions in the form of resolutions. We hope for the best, but fear that slavery will be triumphant now as heretofore. But none of these things move—duties are ours—events belong to God.

"Faithfully your's

"LEWIS TAPPAN."

heaviest penalties may be inflicted for teaching them the use of letters, and in one state death itself is the punishment for a second offence. The consequence is that in a land which boasts of its enlightened christianity & republican institutions there is a heathen & enslaved population from whose minds is systematically excluded not only the sacred verities of Religion but commonest rudiments of knowledge. If, in some instance light penetrates their minds it only serves to make the surrounding darkness the more palpable and hideous.

"And this deplorable state of things, not only exists with the connivance, but is sustained unhappily by the direct participation of several sections of the professedly Christian Church. Episcopalians Presbyters & Pastors, and Ministers, Elders and Deacons & Members are found among Slave holders and Sellers; and it is to be feared are in many instances, not less exacting and cruel than are the men who profess not to be actuated by their religious principles but who nevertheless urge in their defence their pernicious example.

"Now Gent: it appears to the Comᵉ. to be a sacred duty on the part of all who are sincere in their profession of obedience to the righteous precepts of the Gospel, and are influenced by its benign spirit, to plead the cause of the oppressed and to judge between them and their oppressors.

"In placing the foregoing statement before you the Comᵉ. venture respfˡʸ. to press on your attention the painful fact that a large body of Men in the U.S. who profess & call themselves Christians & would feel no difficulty in subscribing your confession of faith are the oppressors of their brethren or the apologists of the system of Slavery which exists in their Country at the present time and to implore you to pause before you invite them to your associatⁿ; nay, rather to urge you, in the spirit of christian fidelity and courtesy, to refuse to receive into your fellowship, all men, be their pretensions what they may who either directly participate or acquiese in upholding or advocating the enslavement of their fellow Men.

"It is due however to the purer branches of the Ecclesiastical organizations before noticed to say, that many of them are bearing a noble testimony against Slavery, that many of them have and all are rapidly separating themselves from official connexion with those who violate by their conduct, the fundamental principles of that Religion they profess to exalt.

"Composed as the Anti slavery body is of every class of Christian professors in this Country, they cannot but feel deeply interested in the course you propose to adopt in this particular case, and will be highly gratified to learn that your decision is to exclude the parties referred to from the proposed Alliance

"I have the honor to be Gent

"On behalf of the C. Your ob. Servᵗ.

"JNO. SCOBLE Secʸ.

"Anti Slavery Off. 27 New Broad St ⎱
    27 Febʸ. 1846 ⎰ delᵈ. 6. Mar 46"

(*Memorials and Petitions*, 1843–1853, pp. 307–310).

Copy.

"Per Steamer *Sarah Sands.*

"NEW YORK, Feb 23/47.[178]

"GEO. W. ALEXANDER, ESQ.
         London.
               "My dear friend,
                     "Today I recd. yours of Jan 18th. You will have noticed, by a recent letter in wh I speak of having drawn on you for £80 that I drew by mistake for £100. Being in Boston on the eve of the Steamer's sailing I drew a bill for £100, forgetting that I had already drawn for £20—but it will all stand right in my a/c. Mrs. Torrey will have her heart gladdened by the generous gift you and the other friends have made her.[179] I will draw for the sum authorized, and transmit the proceeds to Mrs. T. for herself and her little ones.

"The *Era* shall be sent to Mr. Reed (!) (indeed it has been already) and to Prof. David—and 8 instead of 10 will be sent to you hereafter. You can have as many as you choose, to be sent to any part of the world, without any additional charge.

"It will I fear be a long time before a Wilberforce will be raised up in this country to plead the cause of the slave. A man of his religious principles, devoted philanthropy & varied gifts is rare. Where in England is there another such man? With regard to the late Mr. Buxton,[180] however gifted & good he might be, no

[178] Read at B. & F. A-S. Society Committee meeting, April 15, 1847 (*Minute Books*, II, 498).

[179] The sympathy of the B. & F. A-S. Society for the Reverend C. T. Torrey, promoter of the Underground Railway (B. & F. A-S. *Reporter*, 1853, pp. 74 *et seq.*), and, subsequently, for his bereaved family was, on various occasions and in various ways, exhibited. The resolution, moved by George Thompson and seconded by George W. Alexander at the anniversary meeting in Freemasons' Hall, June, 1846, was but an earnest of the more material help rendered later.

[180] Sir Thomas Fowell Buxton had been now dead two full years. For some time anterior to his decease his health had been exceedingly poor. In June, 1843, he wrote to Scoble, regretting his inability, on account of it, to attend the great Convention then assembling. He was anticipating that much would be said about American slavery and the African slave trade; but, said he, "I am afraid I no longer can personally unite with you in fighting against these iniquities—but my prayer to God is . . . ." In August, 1844, Scoble visited him at North Repps Hall and wrote of him thus to Joseph Soul:

"I arrived here on Saturday Evening last, and had a most kind reception from Sir Fowell Buxton and his family. I am sorry that he

eminent man who is concerned in a distillery or brewery would have any influence as a religious man or philanthropist in this country, bad as the nation is.[181] We have had and now have men in this country who occupy the foremost station in the land, & who plead the cause of the slave—John Quincy Adams, our Ex-President, Governor Slade of Vermont, Dr. Channing of Boston, Judge Jay, Gerrit Smith, Governor Seward of this State &c &c. They are & were not all out and out abolitionists, but they are or were bold in denunciation of slavery. Our Everetts, Websters &c love popularity too well, and seek preferment too eagerly to take an unpopular side.

"I lament to hear of the death of the excellent J.J. Gurney.[182] He did not, it is true, help us any or but little, on the slavery question when he was in this country, but we reverenced his character & philanthropic labors as exerted in other countries. How many excellent men & women whom I saw when in England in 1843 are now among the dead! The sweet babe from whom you have parted I remember well. But it is rather a joyous circumstance than the contrary, I think, that she has gone to join her mother. Is it not so? I can not mourn over the decease of little children, for 'of such is the Kingdom of heaven.' I fervently hope

bears on his person the evident traces of infirmity; but he is as cheerful as ever, and equally interested, as ever, in the Anti-Slavery cause, though unable to give it any active assistance— At present N. Repps Hall is free from company, except a few visitors in the evenings, which suits me well, as I am by no means ambitious of a large acquaintance. Today the weather is very unpropitious—wind in the S.W. with heavy rain, or I should have been on the sand at Cromer, instead of writing you.
      "..."

At its meeting, February 21, 1845, the B. & F. A-S. Society Committee had cause to lament the passing out of its distinguished and highly esteemed member (*Minute Books*, II, 287), and, four days later, it adopted resolutions expressive of its own and the country's loss (*idem*, pp. 296–297).

181 Tappan was allied with the prohibitionists and his reference to Buxton must be regarded in that light. The anti-slavery struggle in America was contemporaneous with a prohibition wave which swept over the Union and made numbers of states dry until the Civil War caused a relapse. In England, on the other hand, the liquor business was regarded as legal and eminently respectable and generally the temperance forces of the country stood for moderation in drink. But the Americans lined up on the two extremes of wet or dry. A man eminent for the universality of his reformatory zeal was Lord Shaftesbury, 1801–1885, who is referred to in this study. For Garrison's opinion of the London World's [Temperance] Convention of 1846, see *William Lloyd Garrison*, III, 157 ff.

182 *Minute Books*, II, 479.

that both you & our friend J. Sturge will long be blessed in your domestic relations.

"I had a letter from A.A. Phelps dated Kingston, 14 Jan'. His health, tho' better than when he was in Hayti was not so good as when he left this country. He found the climate variable & damp on the mountains in Jamaica. He has given us much valuable information about the American mission on that island & made various suggestions with regard to their being strengthened & sustained. I will communicate to him your generous proposition. By & by you will probably see some letters in the Era from Mr. Phelps that are daily expected.

"The Tribune shall be sent to you. I will pay your Emancipator Bill.

"I thank you for the hints you give about the money market &c. Money is not scarce here, nor is it thought it will be. Such immense quantities of breadstuffs have gone and are going to England that exchange is very low, & specie will be brought here, it is tho't, in considerable quantities. Still the best notes are discounted by the Wall St. Bankers at 7 per ct & those of the 2d grade, where there is but one name, at 9 & 10 pr ct per annum.

"Seven numbers of the Era have been printed. Subscribers are increasing rapidly. The paper gives general satisfaction. Some wish there was more anti-slavery matter in the paper, but such must be patient. The editors sift in all they think it prudent to do for the present. A large number of persons, both in the free States as well as in the Slave States are reading the paper who never before perused an anti s. paper. The editor manages his difficult post with admirable tact. Calls are now made for the anti-slavery books & tracts promised if the funds would admit, and I think the Ex-Com will take early measures to supply this demand. The publication of the Era has infused a new spirit into the abolitionists of this country & inspired them with new hopes.

"Contemporaneous with the establishment of the paper are the discussions that have taken place in Congress with regard to the use to which any new territory gained from Mexico shall be put. A bill was proposed to grant three millions of dollars to the President, as secret service money, to enable him to 'conquer peace' as the military expression now is. A Mr. Wilmot a democratic member of the H of R moved a Proviso that slavery should not exist in any new territory. This produced a long & animated discussion.

Meantime several State Legislatures in the free States that were in session passed, almost unanimously, resolutions deprecating, in strong language, the extension of slavery over any part of the territory conquered from Mexico. Men of all parties united in passing these resolutions. Many of the administration presses also were either mute or expressed the popular desire in strong language. The Proviso passed the H of R. by 9 majority, the house being very full. The Bill is now before the Senate. The majority in this Body, at present (for the Senators from the new free States have not yet taken their seats) are from Slave States. It is hardly to be expected that they will vote for the Bill with the Proviso. If the Senate should strike out the Proviso & the House refuse to recede the money will be withheld. The slaveholding members all at once are clamorous for peace. They do not want to prosecute the war if they are to be deprived of the *privilege* of sending their Slaves into newly acquired territory! In this state of things it is not unlikely that peace may not be far distant, and yet it is very difficult for the administration to extricate themselves from the embarrassing position in which they are placed by their own foolish & wicked act.

"You will be gratified to learn that Delaware, the Slave State joining Pennsylvania shows a disposition to rid herself of slavery. A Bill for the gradual abolition of slavery has passed the lower house of her Legislature by a decided majority & is now before the upper house.

"There is a prospect that the Free American or a paper with some other name will be established in Kentucky by the gentleman (a South Carolinian) who was the editor de facto during a considerable part of the time the Free American was ostensibly edited by Mr. Clay. He has raised about 2/3ds the amount wanted & I have promised him £25 from 'a Friend' when he shall have, with this, secured the whole sum or $5000.

"I will ask the favor of your paying the Publisher of the *Non Conformist*—for the paper for William Goodell, of Honeoye, Ontario County, New York, what may be due for a year's subscription, and sending me a receipt for W.G.

"A great deal is doing in this country for the famishing Irish. My native town, Northampton, Ms. containing 4000 inhabitants, have given $5000. There must be sub-divisions of landed property, the cultivation of small farms on the best agricultural principles,

more equality of property, or G.B. will suffer immensely. It will
not do to *depend* upon foreign supplies for bread-stuffs. Every
nation should be able to feed & clothe its population. What occasioned great pain to me when in England was the inequality of the
condition of men. The rich would be better off if half or two
thirds their wealth were distributed among their poor fellow men.[183]
Happiness does not consist so much in widening the difference that
separates the affluent from the poor, but in lessening it. But the
unprincipled & the selfish have the management of the affairs of
this world. It is a consolation to know however that the disinterested & good have a moral influence that keeps in check the
numerical force guided by unprincipled politicians & ecclesiastics.
And especially that God rules over all, causing the wrath of man to
praise Him.

"The Mexican war is, as you say, detestable. It is not popular
in this country. The administration continues it with great difficulty. It is a political war for self aggrandisement. Horrible
that men clothed with brief authority, and panting for political
elevation, should plunge two nations into a state of war from selfish
considerations! But what an example has been set us by the old
governments of the world, and what apt scholars we have been!

"Why does the British Friend take such open ground for W.L.
Garrison? Do not the good people of England understand this
man?

"Truly yours

"LEWIS TAPPAN.

"You authorized me to draw for £25 towards the establishment of
the Free American or the establishment [184] of a similar paper by its

---

[183] Lewis Tappan held very positive ideas respecting the rightfulness or
wrongfulness of amassing wealth. In his *Is it Right to be Rich?*, he argued
that there was no moral objection to the making of money, but there decidedly
was to the hoarding of it.

[184] The B. & F. A.-S. Society Committee had not always been so generous
as this towards similar British enterprises. In evidence, note the following:

"REV J. M. PHILLIPPO   "LONDON, 2nd. Nov. 1844—
"My Dear Brother,
"In consequence of my having been a sort of acting Secretary through
Mr Scoble's illness to the Anti Slavery Committee in November last, I am
requested to write to you in relation to the expected grant of £100 towards
the first operations of your new liberation paper, concerning which you wrote
to Mr Sturge. The Committee met yesterday evening, and your letter to
Mr S. was read, he being in the Chair. The general—I may say the universal
impression created by it was one of mingled gratification and surprise; grati-

late Editor. The late editor, C.M. Clay [185]— . . . —is in the army that has gone to invade Mexico. Inconsistent man! I trust

fication that a journal deserving such high encomiums had at length been established in Jamaica, & surprise that any expectation should exist of a grant from the Committee. The Two interviews which you had with the Committee in October, & November last year, are clearly in the recollection of the members who were present, myself being one of them; & the Minutes made of them also are clear and distinct: but, as, on the one hand, the minutes contain no reference to such a grant, so neither does the memory of a single member supply any materials of a conversational kind out of which an expectation of it could have arisen. Under these circumstances the Committee feel themselves under no obligation from any thing that may have passed. And, looking on your letter as an application *de novo*, I am obliged to say, that, with all their kindness towards the West Indies too often & too expensively shown, to be called into question they feel considerable difficulty. There is in their proceedings, no precedent for any such grant; on the contrary, applications similar to yours have repeatedly been declined. Their feeling is that what they support by their money, they become to a certain extent responsible for; & as no question of control can arise with respect to the Jamaica Patriot, they feel that they must content themselves with very sincere good wishes. Should you or any of your friends think the Committee too scrupulous, I am sure that you will neither, on the one hand, suspect their unfeigned attachment to your cause, nor on the other, treat their integrity with contempt.

"On behalf of the Committee, I am,
"Dear brother, faithfully yours
(Signed) "J H HINTON"

[185] Upon the receipt of this news from America, it would not have been surprising had the B. & F. A-S. Society Committee regretted its approval of Clay's conduct three years before:

"To CASSIUS M CLAY ESQ.
"Sir
"It affords me much gratification to forward you copy of a resolution passed unanimously at a recent meeting of the Committee of the British & Foreign Anti Slavery Society expressive of the high sense they entertain of the eminent services you have rendered to the great cause of human liberty and happiness, and of the hope they cherish that your talents and influence may continue to be devoted to the promotion of the same noble object.
"The Society, of which the Committee is the Executive Organ, has for its object the universal extinction of Slavery and the Slave trade, by means which are strictly of a moral, religious and pacific nature; and may be regarded as a continuance of that great series of efforts by which the people of this Country have, under the divine blessing, successively and successfully secured the abolition of the African Slave Trade, and the termination of Slavery in the British West India Colonies, British Guiana, at the Cape of Good Hope, and the Mauritius; in British India and the Settlements at Malacca, Penang and Province Wellesley; in Scinde and at Hong Kong; and, by the operation of a registration law, in Ceylon also, with the exception of the district of Kandy, where there yet appears to be a few hundred of the natives in a state of bondage. To this statement I may add, that debtor bondage in the Tenasserim Provinces, and the Pawn System at the British Settlements on the Western Coast of Africa have been abolished.
"By the measures which have led to these important results not only has an extensive and execrable commerce in the human species been put down, but millions of human beings delivered from a system of Slavery more or less

you will give nothing to revive any paper to be edited by him while he is in such a disposition of mind. . . .

"...

"L. T."

"NEW YORK,
"May 15/47.

"JOHN SCOBLE, ESQ.
"My dear Friend,

"It is a long time since I have heard from you, and I have hardly fulfilled my obligations to you as acting Cor. Sec. of the A & F Anti-S. Society during Mr Phelps's absence. We had a good anniversary on the 11th & a Public Breakfast the next morning. The proceedings will be published at length in the *National Era*. The Breakfast was a novelty here. It succeeded

atrocious and degrading; and a foundation, broad and deep laid for the future elevation and prosperity of a large portion of the human race.

"The Friends of Justice and Humanity in this Country regard with intense interest the struggle which is going on in the United States for the freedom of the slave. That struggle they trust will soon terminate in a glorious triumph, and the great truth contained in its declaration of Independence be vindicated thereby in the eyes of the world.
"I have the honor to be
"Sir
"Yours respectfully
(signed) "JOHN SCOBLE
"27 New Broad St London
June 28 1844."

RESOLUTION

At a Special Meeting of the Committee of the British & Foreign Anti Slavery Society, held at No 27 New Broad Street, on Friday June 28 1844.
George William Alexander Esq in the Chair.
It was resolved unanimously

That the thanks of this Committee are eminently due and are hereby respectfully tendered to Cassius M Clay Esq of Kentucky, for his noble conduct in emancipating his late slaves, from a high sense of Public duty, and in proof of the sincerity of his convictions that the system of Slavery is incompatable with the prosperity and stability of States, the social and moral welfare of mankind, and, above all, the development and progress of religious truth.

That this Committee would cherish the hope that the worthy example set his fellow citizens by Mr Clay, may be extensively followed; and that swayed by his counsels and animated by his acts, his native state may speedily and completely abolish the system of Slavery which obtains there, and thus secure for itself a distinguished place among the free states of the Union, and an honorable position in the estimation of the devoted friends of human freedom throughout the world.

That this Committee sincerely trust the great talents for public usefulness possessed by Mr Clay, may henceforth be devoted not only to the extinction of Slavery in every part of his own Country, but to its abolition generally wherever it is found to exist.

very well. Rev. Ebenezer Davies, of British Guiana, was present
& made some interesting statements. Mr F. Douglas was invited
to attend but felt himself under the necessity of declining. I sent
you a newspaper, *The Tribune,* containing a brief account of the
anniversaries &c. F.D. made a good speech & it was well received. We had at our meeting *Henry Bibb,*[186] a fugitive slave
from Kentucky, a man, I am told of talents equal to Frederic
Douglas. He made some thrilling statements. It is an era in the
Anti-slavery cause in this city that we could have a Public Breakfast in the centre of the city in one of the most eligible Halls, of
white and colored persons, of both sexes, without any disturbance.
Another evidence of the progress of public opinion is that the
daily press, with one or two exceptions, made respectful reports of
the Anti-slavery Society's proceedings. The cause *is* advancing;
there is no doubt of it. Still there is great prejudice, ignorance &
wilfulness on the subject and a cruel war is carried on with Mexico
for the purpose of enlarging the slave territory on this continent.
God, in his providence may intend in this to break down the slave
power of this country. He can not be against us as we labor &
pray for the downfall of slavery; and therefore it becomes us to
exercise faith that events seemingly averse to emancipation will be
overulled in furtherance of that great object.

                                "Very truly your's
                                        "LEWIS TAPPAN.

"Mr Phelps has arrived in this country from Jamaica & went up
the Mississippi river to Cincinnati where he will remain a few
weeks before he comes to this city. We fear that his health has
not materially improved."

                                "NEW YORK, June 30/47.
"JOHN SCOBLE, ESQ.
                "My dear Sir,
                                "You will have seen an account
of our anniversary in the 'National Era,' but I send you a pamphlet containing the same with additions. By a Packet to sail tomorrow I shall send 10 to 12 copies of the pamphlet edition of the
annual Report &c. to your address for several individuals. The

---

186 For an account of Bibb, see *Narrative of the Life and Adventures of
Henry Bibb, an American Slave, Written by Himself, with an Introduction by
Lucius C. Natlack* (New York, 1849).

expense is paid here & I will be obliged to you to inform me if the
packet is delivered at your office free of charge. Will you be so
kind as to forward the pamphlets agreeably to the direction? I
make experiments of this kind in order to ascertain the best and
cheapest modes of transmitting pamphlets and letters.

"Mr. Phelps arrived here early this month, very feeble. After
remaining about a week he proceeded to his family at Castine,
Maine. He was not able to converse above a whisper, but he
communicated much valuable information respecting the American
mission at Jamaica. I do not think Mr. P. will live till fall. He is
quite resigned & feels that the Saviour is very gracious to him.

"Mr Vaughan has issued the first number of his anti-slavery
paper. It is printed at Louisville, Kentucky, weekly. The paper appears well as to selections and original matter. Mr V. assisted C.M.Clay & wrote many of the best articles in the 'True
American.' He is a man every way superior to Clay, & is by
birth a South Carolinean. This is an important step in the anti
Slavery cause.

"We do not think it worth while to form an anti Slavery
Evangelical Alliance [187] in this country. The Alliance stands but
little better here than the Colonization Society. Mess. Cox, Patton, Kirk,[188] &c found it very difficult to form any Alliance whatever, and the course pursued by them disgusted many who would,
under other circumstances, have united with them.

"Can you send me an authentic account of what Dr Cox [189] said

[187] The Evangelical Alliance in the United Kingdom had something in
common with the Know-Nothing Party in the United States. The conference
which formed it, in 1846, was first suggested by a conference held at Liverpool
in October, 1845. The real object of the Alliance was undoubtedly to check
the onward movement of Romanism and of Liberalism. In its preliminary
work there was some indication that it might be strongly anti-slavery and a
suggestion was made that slaveholders ought not to be invited to take part
in its discussions, but some, including the Reverend Thomas Smyth of South
Carolina, had already appeared and were admitted by virtue of the original
invitation. Dr. Wardlaw would have liked the Alliance to refrain from putting a ban upon the individual while condemning—and that strongly—the
institution (*Fifteenth Annual Report* of the Massachusetts Anti-Slavery Society, pp. 46–47).

[188] Rev. E. N. Kirk, an American delegate to the World's Temperance
Convention of 1846 and to the Evangelical Alliance.

[189] Dr. Samuel H. Cox and Abraham L. Cox were Americans. The former
abandoned abolition after being mobbed and burned in effigy. Dr. Francis A.
Cox, an English abolitionist at home, was silent in America. With him and

at an anti Slavery meeting at Liverpool about his practice of administering the Lord's Supper to whites & blacks indiscriminately
in his Church. He does not so administer it. I have been written
to for information respecting Dr Cox's sayings & doings here on
the anti Slavery subject and am collecting information. I am
fearful he did not act an ingenuous part in England.[190]
> "Truly your's
> "LEWIS TAPPAN."

"JOHN SCOBLE, ESQ.   "NEW YORK, July 31/47.
     Secretary &c.
"Dear Sir,
   "I have the melancholy task of informing you that the Rev.
Amos A. Phelps died on the 29th. near Roxbury, near Boston of
pulmonary consumption. He was in his 43d year. His end was
peaceful and happy. His voyage to the West Indies did him no
good. For the last thirteen years Mr. Phelps has been an active
and devoted friend of the anti-slavery cause, a friend of temperance, of missions, and of every good work. He had a discriminating
and vigorous mind, and was both a ready speaker and writer,
though his forte lay in writing. He has been an exceedingly useful man. I do not think any survivor in our ranks excelled him.
*Help Lord, for the godly man ceaseth; for the fruitful fail from
among the children of men.*[191]
   "The prospects of the Liberty party are very favourable. Independent persons lately belonging to the two great political parties
are leaving their old associates & coming out on the side of Liberty
—some of them being new members of Congress.
   "There is no present prospect of peace. This Mexican war
will probably overthrow the existing administration, & introduce
a new state of things.
   "Very truly your's
> "LEWIS TAPPAN.

others like him in mind, Garrison said, "We have had to say, 'Save us from
our English friends, and we will take care of our enemies. There have been
those who have gone over to America, and who have nobly stood their ground.
. . . That man (pointing to the chairman, Mr. Thompson) has gone through
it.' " *William Lloyd Garrison*, III, 163.

   [190] He was described as very venomous in his attacks upon Garrison (*Fifteenth Annual Report* of the Massachusetts Anti-Slavery Society, p. 46).

   [191] For a British appreciation of Phelps, see B. & F. A-S. *Reporter*, September 1, 1847, pp. 134–136.

"P.S.

"Judge Jay informs me that he has not received any intelligence from your side of the Bishop of Oxford's Work,[192] with a Preface by Judge Jay. And our Executive Committee have not learned anything respecting the Protest and Remonstrance sent to your office. Will you inform me whether the above were received— whether they were deemed worthy of republication &c. We have seen no notice of either in your Reporter.''

"BROOKLYN, NEAR NEW YORK, Nov. 14/47.

"JOHN SCOBLE, ESQ.

"My dear friend,

"Yours of [193] 10/4 was received during my absence to the National Liberty Convention at Buffalo. Mr Sam¹ Lewis, late candidate for Governor of Ohio accompanied me. We held anti-slavery meetings at Albany, Utica & Syracuse, on our way. At Albany we applied for the City Hall, & offered to pay the expense of lighting &c. The Mayor said, if the inhabitants wished to hear anti-slavery addresses the City Hall should be opened & the city would be at the expense. He directed the City Marshal to see that the Hall was duly prepared. Mr. Wood [194] late member of Congress, called on us & promised to attend the meeting. He belongs to that portion of the democratic

[192] Judge William Jay, ''Introductory Remarks to the Reproof of the American Church contained in the recent *History of the Protestant Episcopal Church in America*,'' by the Bishop of Oxford (Samuel Wilberforce).

[193] This was undoubtedly the result of Scoble's acquiescence in the wish of Joseph Sturge,

"My dear Friend
"I hope thou wilt not fail to write to Lewis Tappan pretty fully by the *Packet* which leaves London on Monday night also to Judge Jay who from the formers letter appears also hurt at our want of attention— I enclose an extract from the letter of a gentleman at Galatz— Doest thee know enough of it to notice it in the next Reporter? Please to request P. J. Bolton to direct in future H. H. Kellogg's Anti-Slavery Reporter to Clinton New York State.

"affectionately
"thy friend

"Birmingham 10/2, 1847.   "JOS. STURGE
"John Scoble
    27 New Broad Street
"London."

Tappan had written to Sturge, August 29, 1847 (B. & F. A-S. *Reporter*, October 1, 1847, p. 156), recounting the progress of the anti-slavery cause in the States. Men advocating the cause were being elected to Congress but there was a movement on foot to establish an opposition paper to the *National Era.*

[194] B. R. Wood, a representative from New York.

party called Wilmot Proviso men, because they have adopted the Proviso moved in Congress by Mr. Wilmot of the State of Pennsylvania, that if any territory shall be taken from Mexico & added to the U. S. slavery shall not be extended over it. This portion of the demoċracy is increasing.

"In this state it has produced a break in the Party—irreconcilable we hope. In fact independent men, in both the democratic & whig parties, are taking ground against Slavery. That is, they are pledging themselves to go against the *extension* of slavery, and in argument use much the same reasoning abolitionists do against the system itself & its encroachment. These politicians would be very glad to have the Liberty party go with them, but we tell them, you must go with us—we are not only against the *extension* but the *existence* of slavery. But, say they, we are more numerous than you, and the smaller body should unite with the larger. We reply, our principle is the correct one, & you should sacrifice your pride on the altar of principle & your Country. The Wilmot Proviso men have been desirous that the Liberty party should postpone its nomination of a President until next May or June in the hope that some coalition might take place to unite all who are opposed to the extension of slavery in the same presidential candidate. We had a good meeting.

"At Utica, where twelve years since, the abolitionists were mobbed by all the loafers of the place led on by twenty five of the most distinguished citizens of both political parties, we held a meeting in the same street, and near the same place, where we were routed in 1835,[195] which was largely attended. And it is worthy of remark that most of the 25 leaders of the mob, who opposed the anti-slavery movement from political & selfish considerations, have failed of the success they anticipated. The community frowned upon them, & they now feel rebuked by public sentiment. At Syracuse we had a large meeting. At all the places mentioned Mr Lewis delivered powerful addresses, & was listened to with much attention.

"At Buffalo we met about 500 true hearted abolitionists from nearly every free State in the Union. We held six sessions in all & animated discussions were conducted in a good spirit. Although efforts were made by Mr Gerrit Smith [196] & those especially sym-

[195] Garrison, W. P. and F. J., *William Lloyd Garrison*, II, 42. Gerrit Smith joined the abolitionists at this time (1835) in his Peterboro speech.

[196] Another illustration of the difficulty of organizing an Anti-Slavery party.

pathising with him & his peculiar views, to engraft upon the
Liberty party other branches of political & moral reform yet a
very large majority decided to adhere to the original principle of
the Association, and adopt no new test although there is a general
disposition to examine all questions relating to the best interests of
the country & of mankind. The final proceedings were unanimous
as well as harmonious. Hon. John P. Hale, of the democratic
party, but who voted against the annexation of Texas & has taken
independent grounds in opposition to the existence as well as the
extension of slavery, and who is now a member of the Senate of
the U.S., was nominated a candidate for President. Judge King,[197]
of Ohio, a well-tried abolitionist, was nominated for the office of
Vice President. You will see the official proceedings of the Convention in the anti-slavery newspapers. The resolutions adopted
embrace the cardinal principles of the Liberty men of this country.
We have had a grand Convention, & the members separated with
high hopes & resolute determinations. By efficient action, and the
blessing of God, we trust that the vote of 1848 will be greater than
ever, and that the principles of the Liberty party will be extended
far and wide. You will perceive that I have thus fully replied to
your question 'Can you give us any account of the Liberty party?'

"I thank you for the various information contained in your
letter. Your requests have been attended to.

"The *Reporter* is read here with new interest, and the volume
containing your annual Report is extremely valuable. Long may
you continue your labors in the cause! Your journey to the Continent will I trust, be attended with beneficial results.

"The *National Era* continues to be a popular & useful paper.
It exchanges with upwards of sixty newspapers in the Slave States,
and is probably read by a much larger number of persons, North
and South, than any anti-Slavery paper that has ever been established in this country. Eleven thousand papers are printed weekly,
but many of them are given away. The paper is conducted at a
large expense, but we hope that in a year or two, the subscriptions
will be sufficient to pay the whole.

"The Executive Committee have published a large edition of
the 'Liberty Almanac for 1848' prepared by our statistical & laborious friend Leavitt; 'Slavery examined in the light of the Holy

197 Leicester King.

Scriptures' by Dr Brisbane,[198] formerly of South Carolina, a re-

[198] Dr. Wm. H. Brisbane had shared with Cassius M. Clay the marked approval of the B. & F. A-S. Society Committee. Note the following documentary evidence:

June 14, 1844—''The noble conduct of Dr. Brisbane of South Carolina and Cassius M. Clay of Kentucky, evinced in the Emancipation of their Slaves, having come under the consideration of the Committee, a sub-committee composed of J. H. Hinton and Mr. Scoble was appointed to draw up resolutions to be transmitted to them expressive of the sentiments and feelings of the Committee relative thereto'' (*Minute Books*, II, 211);
June 28, 1844—After the resolutions, presented in rough draft, had been read, subjected to verbal alteration, and adopted, it was ordered that they should be forwarded ''with a suitable letter to each (of the gentlemen) from the Secretary'' (*idem*, p. 219);
July 12, 1844—The individual letters designed to accompany the congratulatory resolutions were approved (*idem*, p. 221).

''To the Revᵈ. Dr Brisbane,

''27 New Broad Street,
June 28 1844
''Dear Sir,
''I have great pleasure in forwarding to you Copy of a resolution passed unanimously at a recent meeting of the Committee of the British & Foreign Anti Slavery Society. This tribute of respect should have been paid before but I trust it will not be declined on that account.
''You will be glad to learn that in every part of the British Dominions Slavery may now be said to have received its death blow. As you are aware, it disappeared from the British West India Colonies—British Guiana—the Cape of Good Hope and Mauritius in 1834; from British India, Scinde, and the settlements of Malacca, Penang & Province Wellesley in 1843; and from Hong Kong in the early part of this year. Debtor Slavery in the Tenasserim Provinces, and the Pawn System, its equivalent at the British Settlements on the Coast of Africa, have also disappeared by the operation of Law. Ceylon is now the only exception to the general rule. In the Interior of that Island, a few natives are still held in bondage, but these we trust will be soon liberated.
''Trusting that Slavery may soon disappear from every state in your Great Republic; and that your example may be speedily followed by all who profess and call themselves Christians
''I am Dear Sir
''Yours respectfully & truly
(Signed) ''John Scoble
Secretary.''

Resolution

At a Special Meeting of the Committee of the British & Foreign Anti Slavery Society, held at No 27, New Broad Street, London, on Friday the 28th June 1844
George William Alexander Esq in the Chair
It was Unanimously Resolved
That the best thanks of this Committee are due, and are hereby tendered to the Revᵈ. Dr Brisbane late of South Carolina for the truly Christian conduct manifested by him in the emancipation of his late slaves; and for the generous sacrifices of home, and property he has subsequently made in giving full effect to his conviction of duty, whereby a noble testimony has been borne by him against the sin of Slave-holding, and a fine example set all persons, especially christian professors, unhappily found in similar circumstances, to go & do likewise.

nouncing and penitent slave holder; and we have in press Rev.
A.A.Phelps's letters to Dr Stowe [199] exculpating the Bible from all
sanction of Slavery & other kindred sins, which was prepared for
the press by our deceased friend a few days before his decease. I
hope you will see these works and recommend them to the attention
of our friend on your side the Atlantic.

"The 'unnatural' war with Mexico, as it has been styled by the
commanding general of the American forces, still continues, and the
administration see no way of getting out of it, not having magnanimity enough to confess & retrace their errors and crimes. The
people, however, are seeing that they have been bamboozled, as
O'Connell used to say, & will hold this administration to a strict account. Although the people of this country are infected with the
war virus, glory in military achievements, and are blinded by the
god of this world, yet there is a conservative power here, as there is
in your country, that will, sooner or later, with God's blessing, wipe
away our national reproach & redeem the native honor. The labors
of my devoted countryman, Burritt,[200] do much to bring the custom
of war into deserved condemnation, and it is to be hoped that they

[199] Phelps, Amos A., *Letters to Professor Stowe and Dr. Bacon, on God's
Real Method with Great Social Wrongs, in which the Bible is Vindicated from
Grossly Erroneous Interpretations* (New York, 1848). "After the return of
Mr. Phelps from the West Indies," says the editor, "he was requested by a
friend to revise his Letters to Professor Stowe, with a view to their republication (they had originally appeared in 1845) in a permanent form. At Castine,
Maine, a week or two before his death he performed this labor" and had completed the work four days before his death. At that time he had not revised
those to Bacon but said he saw no reason why they should not be included.
The contention of Phelps in the letters was that the individual practice, in
the case of slave-holding, is a sin. Dr. Stowe, like the American Board, had
condemned the system, sanctioned by the Calhoun-Hammond school, but had
exempted from condemnation the individual practice.

[200] Elihu Burritt and Gerrit Smith called a Convention at Cleveland in
August, 1857, and formed the National Compensation Society to free the slaves
from funds derived from the sale of public lands, a plan favored by Dr. Channing in 1828 and apparently by Daniel Webster. *William Lloyd Garrison*,
III, 461–462.

Burritt (1810–1879) was chiefly interested in international peace and co-
operated with the English and continental peoples in calling international con-
gresses in 1848, 1849, 1850, 1851, 1852, and 1853. He also took a prominent
part in the agitation for penny ocean postage and in the anti-slavery cause
when the Crimean War seemed to mock his peace efforts. He had been much
interested in the settlement of the Oregon Question.

will tend to make men on both sides the ocean, ashamed and afraid of shedding human blood.

> "With affectionate regard
> "Your friend & fellow-laborer,
> "LEWIS TAPPAN.

"How is your dear family? Little Ellen? My wife unites with me in friendly remembrance.

"I took the liberty to publish a copious extract of your letter in the National Era."

"NEW YORK, May 15/48.

"JOHN SCOBLE, ESQ.,

"Dear Sir,

"We had a good anniversary on the 9th. inst. The Tabernacle (our *Exeter Hall*) was well filled. Mr Stanton made an argumentative speech in explanation and defence of the 'Wilmot Proviso,' that is, in opposition to the extension of slavery over territory to be acquired of Mexico. He argued that the laws of a conquered country must prevail until new laws are enacted by the conquering power, and as the Congress of the U.S. have no constitutional authority to create Slavery freedom must continue in those portions of Mexico to be annexed to this country. Dr Vionis from Lyons, France, lately arrived here, made a short speech in broken English, expressing his hatred of slavery & his hope that it would speedily be done away not only in the Colonies & Dependencies of France but in this country & throughout the world. Nothing, said he will save the United States but the emancipation of the Slaves. The Hon. John P. Hale made a capital speech [201] in favor of continued agitation, especially at the North, pp. 106–107.

until Slavery is abolished. We had excellent singing by four brothers, black boys, named Luca from ten to fifteen years of age, natives of New Haven, Conn. The youngest is a remarkable proficient on the Piano Forte. It has been customary for some time for us to have Liberty songs sung at our anniversaries & public meetings. It adds greatly to the interest of these meetings.

"A sketch of the Annual Report was read. The report itself is

[201] John P. Hale had by this time become one of the most active anti-slavery men. He later was a member of the Republican party and a supporter of Lincoln in the United States Senate. B. & F. A-S. *Reporter*, June 1, 1848,

more voluminous than usual. When published I will send you some copies.

"A copy of the Resolutions [202] offered at the meeting are enclosed. They were enthusiastically adopted, though a few 'sons of Beliol' hissed when they were read.

"On the 10th we had a public Breakfast at the Coliseum, Broadway, at which about 400 ladies & gentlemen sat down. Several colored gentlemen & ladies were present. After the repast we had addresses from Mess[rs] Hale, Stanton, Dr Bailey of the National Era, Vionis, Hawkins,[203] Gonsalves, Gardner [204] &c. and several Liberty songs by the 'Hutchinson Family' and the Luca boys. Mr Hawkins is the pioneer of the Washingtonian temperance movement in this country. He has delivered upwards of 1500 temperance lectures in different parts of the country. He said this was the first speech he had ever made in an anti Slavery meeting, but it would not be the last. He had never known a thorough anti Slavery man who was not also a teetotaler. Mr Gonsalves is a native of Madeira. He has traveled at the South & in the British Islands among the emancipated & related what he had seen.[205]

"L TAPPAN"

[202] B. & F. A-S. *Reporter*, June 1, 1848, p. 106.

[203] John Allen Krout, *The Origins of Prohibition*, 1925, p. 184, ". . . the chief characteristics of the [Washingtonian] movement became the reformation of drunkards by reformed drunkards." John H. W. Hawkins, born of English parents in Baltimore, in 1797, was the ablest platform man of this particular type of prohibition agitation: "His ability to tell a story well, his judicious mingling of anecdote and argument and his understanding of the psychology of a crowd gave him an unusual mastery over large audiences," pp. 191–192. Krout, pp. 298–300, says that prohibition was regarded as distinctively American and a product of American evangelicalism as it was not in Europe. D. Leigh Colvin, *Prohibition in the United States*, p. 37, "There is no doubt that up to 1855 the prohibition movement was much more popular than the abolition movement."

[204] Henry J. Gardner, governor of Massachusetts during the Personal Liberty Law agitation.

[205] For a rebuttal of the charge that British emancipation had been a failure, see A. & F. A-S. Society *Annual Report* (1848), pp. 18–21.

Copy.

"OFFICE OF THE AM. & FOR. ANTI S. SOC.
61, JOHN ST.
"NEW YORK, July 20/49.[206]

"JOHN SCOBLE ESQ.
"London.

"My dear friend,

"It is a long time since I have had a letter from you.

"Did you receive a copy of our Annual Report? A copy was addressed to each Cor. member of the Society. Last year a copy was sent to each & also a letter requesting correspondence, but scarcely one of them replied. Why is this?

"I have relinquished my Mercantile business & am now devoting my time to the affairs of the A. & F. Anti S. Soc. Whatever papers, pamphlets &c you can send, from time to time, will be very gratefully received. Please let them be directed to the Society at this Office.

"I send a copy of the Tribune of this date. You will see by this what an advance has been made here, that a daily paper contains so much Anti S. matter.

"Dr. Bailey is getting along very well with the Era at Washington.

"I give Mr. Durkee,[207] a newly elected M.C. from Wisconsin a

[206] An interesting letter from Lewis Tappan himself, dated April 26, 1848, is to be found in the B. & F. A-S. *Reporter*, June 1, 1848, p. 107. The contents may be summarized thus:

General progress—in the anti-slavery cause shown by greater freedom of discussion. A mob failed to destroy the press of the *National Era.*

Ecclesiastical progress—A certain Englishman, a Dr. Burns, has had remarkable influence with the Free-will Baptist Connexion. The Unitarian, Methodist, Baptist, and other denominations, have borne decided testimony against American slavery. Missionary societies and Sunday School unions are becoming anti-slavery.

Political progress—Parties are divided, politicians puzzled. Great alarm felt in the Slave States over the possibility of French emancipation, but slaveholders rejoice over the establishment of the French Republic.

"We are not, and shall not be, a *model* republic, until slavery is abolished, and the spirit of war and conquest is put down. What a beacon-light the United States might be to the whole world! How dimly does the nation shine, and what a baneful glare is thrown around and afar. . . . We are strengthened by the sympathy and example of the abolitionists of Great Britain."

[207] Charles Durkee, originally a Free Soiler, later a Republican, served in both houses of Congress. Many of the anti-slavery leaders were also interested in Peace, as well as in prohibition.

letter to you. He goes to attend the Peace Convention, & is a devoted moral reformer. With love to your dear family, about whom I shall be glad to hear,

"your's very truly,

"L. TAPPAN."

Copy.

AMERICAN & FOREIGN
ANTI-SLAVERY SOCIETY
OFFICE 61, JOHN ST.
NEW YORK.

"NEW YORK, 19th Sept. 1849.

"JOHN SCOBLE, ESQ.
       "Secy. & c.
           "My dear Sir,
                       "Enclosed is a pamphlet respecting Cuba, being a translation of a Spanish publication, & published here at the instance of an American gentleman, who has resided at Havana some years. He has called at this office several times, and though in favor of the annexation of Cuba to the U. States is very anxious that it should be a free State. He entreated me to send the pamphlet to some friend in England so that the subject could come before the anti-slavery friends of England, and they be induced to make a representation to the Gov^t. immediately to influence it to take measures for the freedom of the slaves in Cuba. He says there are many of the inhabitants of that island who desire emancipation & would lament annexation with Slavery; and they believe that the British Gov^t. has it in its power to influence Spain to grant freedom to the blacks or to ensure their freedom in case of a change in the political relations of the islanders.[208]

"I request you to submit this publication to your Committee without delay.

"There are bodies of adventurers assembling at certain rendevous on the American coast in league probably with Spaniards preparing to make a descent upon Cuba. The Proclamation[209] of the Pres. of the U.S. has disconcerted them somewhat, but affairs seem ripening for a revolution at Cuba; and the slaveholders of

[208] The B. & F. A-S. Society Committee relied for their information on Cuba on Dr. R. R. Madden, *The Island of Cuba.* B. & F. A-S. *Reporter,* Nov. 1, 1849, pp. 171–172.

[209] Richardson, V, 7–8.

this country will strenuously aid in attempts to bring about annexation with slavery.

"Very truly your's,
"LEWIS TAPPAN."

"NEW YORK, October 13th. 1849.
"TO THE EXECUTIVE COMMITTEE
"OF THE BRITISH AND FOREIGN ANTI SLAVERY SOC:
"A communication from your Treasurer to the Cor. Sec. of the Amer. and For. Anti Slavery Society on the subject of a world's Anti Slavery Convention, to be held in this country, having been read in the Ex. Com. we have been appointed a committee of correspondence on the subject. Our committee are in favor of holding such a convention provided the friends of the cause in Great Britain, continental Europe & the West Indies will give satisfactory assurances that a sufficient number of delegates from abroad will attend the Convention. Without the attendance of a considerable number from England, the Continent, and the West Indies, we think such a Convention would not possess adequate influence as a World's Convention. We shall be happy to learn from you the number of persons whose attendance (D.V.) can be relied upon, say on the 4th. July next, and would respectfully request you to correspond with brethren residing in the Continent and give us as early intelligence as may be convenient.[210]

"Very respectfully & truly yours
"LEWIS TAPPAN
W. E. WHITING   }Committee."
SIMEON S. JOCELYN

[210] At its meeting, October 29, 1849, the B. & F. A-S. Society Committee authorized Scoble, George Stacey, and Josiah Forster, as a sub-committee, to communicate with the A. & F. A-S. Society Executive Committee on this matter, the holding of the next anti-slavery convention in the United States, but, upon the communication from that committee being read, further consideration of the subject was deferred (*Minute Books,* III, minute 318). The project was probably not received with much favor in England, where questions like free labour, the expediency of continuing the armed cruiser system, and the violation of treaties by Spain and Brazil were absorbing much of the attention of the B. & F. A-S. Society Committee. Sturge, writing to Scoble, the first of December, said,

". . . I hope thou wilt please not fail to write to the U. States—though I cannot see my way at all to a convention there next year. I am sorry the letter is not gone."

"NEW YORK

"Jan. 16/50

"My dear Sir,

"Your esteemed letter of Dec. 21st is just rec^d. It is addressed to me as a *merchant*. In my note of July 20th I informed you that having relinquished the mercantile business to enable me to devote my time chiefly to the anti-slavery causes I invited a renewal of correspondence as Sec. of the A. & F. Anti-S Society. For the committee I asked you whether you had rec^d. a copy of our Annual Report & if you could explain why copies, with letters, sent to each corresponding member, remained unnoticed. Would it be asking too much to request that when we send parcels of this kind to your office that the receipt be acknowledged, and that information be given whether they are forwarded?

"Sept. 19th I sent you a pamphlet on Cuba, requesting you to lay it before your Committee.

"Oct. 17th I sent you a letter from a sub. com. of our Ex-Com. on the subject of the World's Convention.

"Nov. 28th. A letter [211] was sent to you from this office for

[211] There was much controversy between the B. & F. A.-S. Society Committee and Lord Grey on the condition of the Negroes in the West Indies and on the subject of Coolie immigration. B. & F. A.-S. *Reporter*, March 1, 1850, p. 36 ff.; April 1, 1850, p. 49 ff.; Oct. 1, 1850, p. 149 ff.; Nov. 1, 1850, p. 165 ff.

[212] G. W. Alexander and John Candler were returning from a visit to the West Indies, a visit of investigation, undertaken at the request of the B. & F. A.-S. Society Committee. Because of the use made, forensically, of British West Indian experience, it was periodically incumbent upon that Committee to find out for itself exactly how things stood and it was continually issuing new pamphlets on the basis of new facts discovered. For instance, in the autumn of 1845, when a delegation of Quakers, including George Stacey and Josiah Forster, was about to proceed to the United States, John Scoble prepared a twelve-page tract containing the most authoritative information to date of the results of emancipation in the British colonies (*Minute Books*, II, 342–343), also a four-page tract, that Josiah Forster personally asked for, on the duty of immediate and entire emancipation (*idem*, p. 330).

What came to be the Alexander-Candler visit had been talked about at the time of the anniversary meeting and, at a meeting of the Committee, July 13, "the further consideration of the mission to the West Indies was gone into and the opinion formerly recorded was strengthened as to the propriety and necessity of its being undertaken, provided suitable persons can be found for the purpose. It was hoped that the Treasurer of the Society might feel disposed to be one of a deputation, and that Jno. Candler should also be invited to consider the subject" (*idem*, III, minute 263). On July 28, the Treasurer "stated he had seen Jno. Candler . . . who without committing

Lord Grey from our Ex-Com. with a request that you would properly direct & forward it.

"The object in mentioning the dates &c of these letters is to
enquire whether they have all been received. We fear that the
last mentioned one has not or you would have mentioned it more
particularly.

"The letter just rec^d. will be laid before the Ex-Com. at its next
meeting. The circumstances mentioned by you seem to render it
expedient to postpone any arrangements for a World's Anti-S.
Convention the present year. Probably our com. will so view it.

"We are looking forward with great pleasure to the arrival of
Messrs Alexander & Candler.[212]   Will you give me Mr Alexander's
address in Jamaica?

"Mr Bolton of your office is very obliging in writing to Mr
Harned our office agent, and in sending to him anti-slavery and
other publications. Does he succeed Mr Soul as y^r assistant?
Will you request him to send what he intends for the Anti-S. Society or Com. to be forwarded to me, 61 John Street?

"Do you continue to edit the Reporter?

"You have doubtless rejoiced that the Constitution [213] adopted

himself finally on the point, was inclined to undertake the mission with him in
case he should conclude it to be his duty to prosecute the same. The Committee
gave every encouragement to their friends to undertake the mission'' (*idem*,
minute 270). The upshot of the matter was that the two Friends selected
agreed to go, the one offering to pay the whole of his personal expenses and the
other very much the larger part of his (see minutes 296, 305, and 313), suggestions that the Committee gratefully accepted. Their route, as sketched before
they embarked at Southampton, the first of November, 1849, was as follows:
''Barbados, Surinam, *via* Guiana, return to that Colony, and proceed to Trinidad, thence to Grenada, St. Lucia, Antigua, Martinique and Guadeloupe, St.
Bart., St. Martin, St. Thomas, & St. Croix, Jamaica & thence to the United
States. . . .'' A modification of the itinerary was made necessary by the
unwillingness of the Dutch to have their colonies visited lest the visit might
impede a movement for emancipation then in prospect (*idem*, minute 335).

The chief contribution of the Alexander-Candler investigation to existing
knowledge was the sad neglect of what were designated *auxiliary measures*.
After doing a little itself, in the first years, and in collaboration with the
Trustees of the Mico Charity, the Government had left the education ''to the
caprice of colonial legislation, actuated by prejudice against the negroes''
(Hancock, W. Neilson, *The Abolition of Slavery considered with Reference to
the State of the West Indies since Emancipation*, p. 6) and it had neglected to
take precautionary measures against economic dislocations.

[213] Concerning this particular thing, Sturge had written to Scoble, December 5, 1849, and it is interesting to observe, by comparing his comment
with that of Tappan's, how much broader his sympathies were,

by the Californians forbids slavery. They will undoubtedly have a free State. The influential slaveholders in this country are more audacious than ever, but the northern politicians do not succumb as heretofore to their threats. Still *interest* renders the former more united & persevering than patriotism does the public men in the free States. The progress of anti-slavery sentiment is sure & encouraging. 'A better time is coming.' [213a]

"Your's faithfully

"John Scoble, Esq "LEWIS TAPPAN.
  Cor. Sec.

AMERICAN & FOREIGN "NEW YORK, April 17/50.
ANTI-SLAVERY SOCIETY.
Office 61 John St.
    New York.   "MR P.J. BOLTON
           "Dear Sir,
              "For two years

past I have sent to your office copies of our Annual Report directed to the Cor. Members, but have never been particularly informed whether they were ever forwarded to the parties to whom they were directed. With one exception no reply has ever been made by a Cor. member, except Mr Scoble & Mr Sturge. Will you be so kind as to inform me about them? Hereafter we will forward to those on the Continent of Europe directly from this city, and will be obliged to you to forward to those in your country what may be sent to your office. We shall always aim to pay the expense to your office & should any be incurred by you please charge it to the A & F Anti S. Soc. & acquaint me with the same.

    "Will you forward the note for Mr Soul to him.

"Truly your's
"LEWIS TAPPAN

"I do not write to Mr Pennington because I am told he is soon expected home. Will you tell him so?"

> ". . . Thou hast probably heard through the American papers what a mess of it the Free Soil Party or many of them appear to have made in New York, & though they have totally excluded slavery in the New Constitution of California I see the(y) exclude Indians & Negroes & their descendants from political rights."

[213a] From far distant Sierra Leone, John Carr echoed these sentiments.

> "I am glad," said he, writing to Scoble, January 21, 1850, "to observe the steady progress the good cause is making in the United States of America. When Slavery ceases in that Country we may hope to see its total abolition in all other civilized countries. . . ."

"New York,
"April 24, 1850.[214]

"John Scoble, Esq
Secretary &c &c.
"My dear friend,
            "Within a day or two I have received your favor
of the 4th instant for which I heartily thank you. Surrounded as
I am with my books and papers, preparing the Annual Report,
there is *material* enough to give you all the anti-slavery information
you desire, and the only difficulty in making a suitable reply consists in my want of time. If, therefore you will be satisfied, for
the present, with the rapid sketch I propose to give of the anti-
slavery cause in this country the past year up to the present time,
I will soon send you in printed form a more complete retrospect.
I now send by the first steamer that sails after the receipt of your
letter.

    "Slavery exists in this country, as you know, in despite of the
principles and intentions of the sages who framed the written
Constitution under which we live. They never intended that it
should extend beyond the limits of the original 13 states composing
the Union, nor that the General Government should have anything
to do with it. In fact, as has been said, one of their designs in
rebelling against Great Britain was to prevent the extension of
slavery.[215] They expected it would die out soon. But the inven-
tion of the cotton gin by Whitney so stimulated the growth of
cotton, and the demand made for it by your country was so great,
that the avarice of the South and its love of power together with
the dough-facedness of the North, combined to extend the system
of slavery over new States created out of the territories originally
belonging to the 13 States, and large provinces acquired by purchase and conquest. The number of slaves has increased from
half a million to three millions and besides there are as many free
people of color here as there were slaves at the commencement of
this Government, sixty years ago.

    "When I went to England with Mr Andrews, in 1843, at the

    [214] This letter was reported at the B. & F. A-S. Society Committee meet-
ing, May 17, 1850 (*Minute Books*, III).

    [215] Some of the colonies were opposed to the slave trade, Virginia, for
example; others favored it, South Carolina was one. For a discussion of the
question, see Carl Becker, *The Declaration of Independence*. Tappan is inaccurate in his statement.

suggestion of the late John Quincey Adams,[216] to lay before the British Government facts in relation to Texas, with a view to persuade her to interpose in a legitimate way to prevent the annexation of Texas to this country, and the consequent war with Mexico, and the extension of slavery over vast tracts of country, slavery in our Southern States was about to die of apoplexy. The suggestion made to your Government was that if a million and a half pounds sterling were loaned to Texas on security of her public lands with the condition that she would take measures to amend her Constitution so that slavery should be abolished by her, it was believed that her situation was such that she would accede to such a proposition. In making this suggestion the remark of Mr Adam's accompanied it, which he authorized me to mention that considering the steps taken by England for the emancipation of the negro race he thought she was bound to interpose and prevent the Annexation of Texas to this country with slavery. Lord Aberdeen, you will recollect, after consulting his colleagues, declined doing anything more than advise Mexico to consent to the independence of Texas on condition that she would abolish slavery. He gave two reasons. 1. England had acknowledged the independence of Texas, and could therefore treat with her only as she could with Portugal or any other independent Power, and 2. Parliament, he thought, would not sanction such a loan. Money could then have been had in London by Government at I think 2 per ct as I was assured by Mr Samuel Gurney, at very short notice.

"Some Americans then in London misrepresented this matter to the late Mr Calhoun, who has stated in the Senate more than once that he exerted himself to have Texas annexed to this country because Great Britain was about to take possession of it, or something to that effect. Never was there a greater mistake. Your Government acted in the most open and honourable manner on the subject, & though its refusal to interfere in the legitimate way suggested greatly disappointed the friends of the slave both in England & in the United States no one had a right to impute to her anything clandestine or unfair. But had she proposed the loan as suggested and had it been accepted what a noble & blessed achieve-

[216] Adams' statement is, "Mr. Tappan told me he had himself been urged to go to England, and asked my advice what he should do. I declined advising, but said I wished he would go, were it only for the possibility that he might contribute to advance the cause." Tappan sailed next day, June 1, 1843. *Memoirs of John Quincy Adams*, XI, 380, 405 ff.

ment it would have been in a moral point of view! This country
would have been prevented probably from waging the wicked war
on Mexico, and slavery would not have been extended beyond the
limits of the United States as then existing. All the gold found in
California, and all the glory (!) acquired by the wonderful achievements of the army in Mexico do not afford an equivalent for the
loss of lives and the loss of honor suffered by this country in that
unnecessary and wicked war.

"Well, California has adopted a Constitution prohibiting Slavery, has sent her Senators and Representatives to Washington, and
solicited admission into the Union on a footing with the other
States. A majority of both Houses of Congress are favorable to
her admission, and she will be admitted; but the Slave Power is
unwilling to admit her without connecting other questions with
the question of her admission. The whole session of the present
Congress from the 1st Monday in December until the present time
has been chiefly occupied with exciting discussions on this subject;
and it is not settled yet. The South has threatened disunion if
slavery is prohibited in New-Mexico as well as California; Texas
claims a large part of New Mexico; and the Mormons who have
settled a part of New Mexico claim that part be set off as a territory
named Deseret. The arrogance of the South was rebuked by able
speeches among the Northern members, & she somewhat lowered
her crest. Mr Clay then stept forward in the character he wore
in the Missouri compromise of 1820, with a project to *compromise*
the great question at issue by giving to the South nearly all she
claimed! His plausible scheme met with undeserved favor in various quarters, though the ultra slave-holding interest opposed it,
as well as the anti-slavery part of the community. The Southern
members began to be disunited themselves, and there was a fair
prospect that the South would be defeated in this grand attempt to
fasten slavery upon the immense territories recently annexed to
this country.

"To the astonishment of the country Daniel Webster now came
forward in the Senate as the advocate of Southern interests, in
total disregard of the declarations made by him for a series of
years. Calhoun gave him the right hand of fellowship as a half
converted political brother, while the whole South hailed him as
an ally. The title of 'Expounder and Defender of the Constitution' which had been awarded him for his eloquent defence of that

instrument against the aggressions and treasonable designs of South Carolina was superseded by the title of Defender of Southern institutions. Mr Calhoun soon after deceased, but his mantle fell upon Webster.

"The merchants, brokers and Whig politicians of this city applauded Mr Clay for introducing into the Senate his compromising resolutions; and the monied men, the owners of Bank, Rail road & manufacturing stocks, and admirers of Webster congratulated him on his Speech the ostensible object of which was to preserve the Union on what are called the compromises of the Constitution. It was mortifying to see among the signers of the letter to Webster, approving his course, the names of several men— clergymen, lawyers, literary men, physicians &c—who have been considered true to principle hitherto & above temptation to flatter even so distinguished a man in what was wrong. But a large number—a large majority—both here and at Boston, refused to bow the knee to men who seem ready to sacrifice humanity and conscience under the pretence of harmony & the common good of the country.

"The Senate of Massachusetts have most emphatically rebuked Mr Webster, by passing the following resolutions, which are couched in his own language employed on a former occasion.

> *Resolved.* That the opposition of the people of Massachusetts to the extension of slavery in this country and to the increase of slave representation in Congress, is general and universal. It has no reference to the lines of latitude or points of the compass. They will oppose all such extension, and all such increase, in all places at all times, under all circumstances, against all inducements, against all supposed limitations of great interests, against all combinations, against all compromises.

> *Resolved.* That the people of Massachusetts expect their Senators and representatives in Congress to conform to the sentiment expressed in the preceding resolve, whenever acting in their official capacity, in all places, under all circumstances, against all inducements, against all combinations, against all compromises.

"To show still further the healthy feeling still prevailing in Massachusetts on the slavery question I add that a friend has written that a member of the Legislature of that State recently said that so greatly offended were they with Webster that if he were now a candidate for the office he holds he could not get thirty votes in a body of two to three hundred.

"What will be done in Congress is uncertain. In the Senate a Committee of 13 members has been chosen to whom are committed the various schemes presented in that body. The Committee was elected by a bare majority and the election was considered a triumph over the non-extentionists. This Committee it is expected, will propose a compromise that will be acceptable to a majority in both houses of Congress. It is rumored that the substance of their report will be as follows:

> 1. The admission of California as a State.

> 2. The organization of New Mexico as a Territory (and perhaps Utah as another) with entire silence on the subject of slavery.

> 3. The satisfaction of Texas, by cash from Uncle Sam's strong box, for her pretense of claim to New Mexico this side of the Rio Grande.

> 4. The organization of a new State from western Texas, intended to be a slave State.

"I have just received letters from a member of the House and from a member of the Senate. The former says, 'The Senate is clearly enough, with the South, and I begin to doubt whether a majority even in the House will be found to stand up firmly for the North & for freedom on the great test questions.' 'We shall see,' the latter remarks, 'I do not despair of a favorable issue out of present embarrassments. We shall have an earnest debate on the coming in of the Compromise Report and if the North will but half sustain us we shall establish the Right.'

"It seems to be beyond a question that California will be admitted with her present immense boundaries as a free State & I fear that slavery will *not* be prohibited in the territories of New Mexico & Utah, but that it will be left to the people of those rapidly increasing territories to decide the question for themselves. If Texas is brought to relinquish her claim to a large part of New Mexico she will, I fear, in addition to receiving ten to fifteen millions of dollars have a new slave State made from her western portion, to satisfy the cravings of the Slave Power. It is probable also that some strong declarations will be made in the Compromise Report on the right of the South to recover fugitive slaves, but it will be inoperative. The moral sense of the free States will not allow inhuman provisions to be carried out.

"I am in the midst of preparation for the Annual Report. I have not prepared an abstract of it as yet. Our anniversary is appointed for May 7th. We were in hopes Messrs Alexander & Candler would have been here, but a letter from the former leads me to suppose they will not arrive here before 1st June.

"Yours faithfully,
"LEWIS TAPPAN.

"P.S. I learn that several respectable & influential persons are preparing to go to attend the Peace Convention."

AMERICAN & FOREIGN
ANTI-SLAVERY SOCIETY
Office 61 John St.
New York.

"May 8th 1850

"JOHN SCOBLE,
"Dear Sir,
"Mr. L. Tappan duly received your last letter, and carried with him to the Anniversary yesterday. He is engaged in an adjourned meeting this morning, or he would write to you personally. He sends herewith a series of resolutions presented yesterday and an abstract of the Report, which was presented by him, also a copy of the N.Y. Tribune of to day

"Yours &c
"EDW C. MILES."

"NEW YORK,
"May 25/50

"JOHN SCOBLE ESQ,
"My dear Sir,
"We had a good anniversary on the 7th. There were 2,500 persons present. The old Society had their meeting during the forenoon of that day & were much disturbed. The Police seemed willing that they should be. You will see the accounts in the newspapers. A few evenings after Mr Wendell

Phillips [217] was invited to Brooklyn (opposite New York) to deliver
an anti-Slavery address, by those who sympathise with our Society,
& there was a good meeting—a large church being filled. Mr P.
made a good impression. Still his *destructive* scheme is not liked.
He purposes to destroy the Government & the Churches, but proposes nothing to take their place.

"Mr H.W.Beecher, a popular & talented young clergyman made
the principal speech at our Anniversary. He is son of Rev Dr
Beecher of Cincinnati, O. With his voice & pen he is doing a
great deal for the furtherance of the Anti-Slavery cause. He
writes for the Independent, a copy of which I send you with this.
You will see in it an admirable defence of clergymen's introducing
the subject of Slavery into their pulpits, and a vindication of New
England with regard to the emancipation of Slaves.[218]

"There was some little disturbance at our anniversary. The
rowdies that had disturbed Mr Garrison's meeting had their appe-
tites whetted, and wanted a pretext for breaking up the meeting,
but no serious interruption took place. While I was reading the
resolution [219] relating to D.Webster there was a considerable outbreak, but the applauses of the large majority soon quelled it.
The whole went off very happily and to our entire satisfaction.

"I sent you soon after a printed abstract of the report with
the Resolutions. The Report itself is in the press, and will soon
be out. You will see that it is rather a voluminous document, but
I trust you will find the information contained in it of sufficient
value to reward one for the perusal. Very soon I hope to send
you some copies; meantime I send to Mr Bolton [220] twenty-five
copies of the abstract and resolutions in pamphlet form. Please
hand them to friends of the cause. I send to Mr Bolton also several
directed to different individuals.

"Nothing decisive has been done in Congress as yet. Mr Clay's
Compromise Bill, or as it is termed the Omnibus Bill is still under
discussion in the Senate and its fate is uncertain.

[217] Wendell Phillips, 1811–1884, was the greatest orator of the Garrison
party and his part in the anti-slavery conflict is told in Garrison, Wendell
Phillips and Francis Jackson, *William Lloyd Garrison, passim.*

[218] "Politics and the Pulpit," in *The Independent*, May 23, 1850, pp.
86–87.

[219] B. & F. A-S. *Reporter*, June 1, 1850, p. 99.

[220] Peter Jones Bolton, one of the many members of the Society of Friends
interested in various philanthropic causes, especially the anti-slavery and the
aborigines' protection. He was now of the staff at 27 Broad Street.

"There is a black man in this city by the name of Gottlieb Bordeaux. He is a young man, about twenty-seven, and was the leader of the insurrectionary party of negroes at St. Ciera,[221] July 3d 1848. He came to our office introduced by a colored man from the same island, who commanded troops in opposition to him during the revolt. Bordeaux and the other speak very highly of General Von Scholten. Bordeaux is represented to have been averse to the shedding of blood and says that during the whole of the difficulties he acted under the advice of General Von. S. It seems that B. was sent away from the island almost destitute, and he seems now quite poor. His *quondam* enemy however is befriending him.

"We are about sending a special agent to New Mexico to destribute [*sic*] the 'Address of our Committee to the Inhabitants of New Mexico & California'[222] in English and Spanish, three copies of which I send herewith.

"I send you a copy of the Independent, a new weekly paper printed here. The editors[223] assume pretty decided anti-Slavery ground. The long article[224] by Mr Beecher, excites considerable attention. The favorable reception of the article is one indication of an improved state of public feeling with regard to this question in this City & vicinity. It has been copied at length into the *Courier & Enquirer* a paper that took very decided ground against the abolitionists at the commencement of the conflict, & for several years afterwards.

"Never before were there so many anti-Slavery publications scattered over the land. 97,000 copies of Mr Seward's speech have been sent into different States. The anti-Slavery members of Congress now have their speeches printed, & distributed at Washington

221 The island is the Danish island of St. Croix. For an authoritative study of the Danish islands, see Waldemar Westergaard, *The Danish West Indies under Company Rule* (1671–1754), *with a Supplementary Chapter*, 1755–1917 (1917).

222 *Address to the Inhabitants of New Mexico and California on the Omission by Congress to Provide Them with Territorial Governments and on the Social and Political Evils of Slavery.* Signed by Arthur and Lewis Tappan, William Jay, Simeon S. Jocelyn, Joshua Leavitt, S. W. Benedict, George Whipple, J. W. C. Pennington and thirteen others. Published by the A. & F. A-S. Society (1848, 1849).

223 From 1848 to 1861, the editors were Leonard Bacon, J. P. Thompson, and R. S. Storrs with Joshua Leavitt as assistant editor.

224 "Politics and the Pulpit," in *The Independent*, May 23, 1850, pp. 86–87.

very widely. All the newspapers at Washington also publish the speeches made in Congress, & their Anti-Slavery sentiment is diffused throughout the country, South & North. This seed, so abundantly sown, will produce an abundant harvest—nay it is producing one. We feel greatly encouraged. The arrogance of the South has become intolerable to large numbers of Northern men who, hitherto, have neglected the subject.

"The descent made upon Cuba by General Lopez, a Spanish general who has been sometime in this country, with some hundreds of fellows late of the army of Mexico, has, it seems, proved abortive. Lopez has returned to the United States. He may make another attempt perhaps.

"Very truly yours,
"LEWIS TAPPAN."

"June 11/50.[225]

AMERICAN & FOREIGN
ANTI-SLAVERY SOCIETY.
Office 61 John St.
NEW YORK

"My dear Sir,

"Your letter of May 24th. was very acceptable. I thank you for the valuable information. The Reports from yr Office last year were received with much thankfulness, and the number was sufficient. I wish you had given the *dates* of my letters which you acknowledge.

"By Mr Edwards [226] I wrote you May 27th. and sent a few copies of the Annual Report, of the ordinary edition. I hope they have arrived ere this. The best edition, 8vo. is now in this office & I would have a number of them sent but the postage on your side is too high. However, I send one copy by this Steamer, directed to you. Please hand it to Mr Scoble. More will be sent by

---

[225] On June 7, 1850, Scoble called the attention of the B. & F. A.-S. Society Committee "to the proceedings of the New York State Vigilance Committee, during the past year, from which it appears that they have aided in their flight 151 Slaves to places of safety, and have rescued several persons from Slavery who were illegally held in bondage; and have several cases of this kind now on hand" (*Minute Books*, III, minute 413).

[226] A nephew of Lewis Tappan's. A letter of May 27, 1850, having more particular reference to him has been omitted because of no historical importance.

Capt. Knight, of the Packet *New World,* whose time of sailing is 6 July. He willingly takes parcels to & from England gratuitously, & is very friendly to our Societies & the cause. I will thank you to inform me the day the above copy arrives & the postage you pay on it. I fear you will have to pay 18ᵈ or 20ᵈ. if I understand your postage law. We pay 10 cents on the pamphlet here.

"I have a letter from G. W. Alexander dated Jamaica. He expects to leave on the 18ᵗʰ. for this port. Several letters from England await his arrival. He and his party will be joyfully received.

"The Compromise Bill is still before Congress. We fear it will pass the Senate. Its fate in the House is more uncertain.

"Do you know the fate of the Memorial respecting the Slave Trade, sent by our Ex.Com. to Earl Grey?

"Tell Mr Scoble that the Old School Gen. Assembly have met & adjourned—doing nothing on the subject of Slavery; and that the New School Gen. Ass. have passed Resolutions ostensibly more opposed to Slavery than any previous resolutions—but still they fall short of pronouncing Slavery a sin *per se.*[227] I shall look for your Ann. Report with much interest.

"I hope to receive, once in a while, similar letters from you, to the one dated May 24ᵗʰ.

"Very truly your's
"LEWIS TAPPAN

"Mr Peter J. Bolton."

"NEW YORK, June 28/50

"Mᴿ. SCOBLE

"My dear friend,

"I have just recᵈ yours of the 14th. Your letter to G. W. Alexander will be forwarded to him. He is at Washington & expects to be here in 2 or 3 weeks. Your Reporter of June 25 recᵈ & contains your valuable Report. You generously allow a large space to our proceedings.

"Copies of our Annual Report will be sent by Capᵗ. Knight of the New World, who is to sail July 6th. Until the receipt of your letter I thought proof sheets stitched had been sent by Mr. Edwards, but as you do not mention recᵍ them I conclude he did not take them.

---

227 "Resolutions of the New School Presbyterian General Assembly on Slavery," B. & F. A-S. *Reporter*, August 1, 1850, pp. 130–131.

"It is natural for us to think well of our Reports, after devoting so much time to preparing them, & even to consider them more interesting than reports of other Societies. In truth I think with you that they are.

"The Omnibus Bill remains *statu quo*. It is amended & discussed, but no decided advance made respecting it. Very unexpectedly to everybody intelligence has just arrived that the inhabitants of New Mexico, impatient at the non-reception of their Delegate in Congress & the establishment of a Territorial Gov.̇ have met in Convention and formed a State Gov.̇ the same as California —prohibiting Slavery! This will greatly embarrass Mr. Clay & the friends of the Compromise Bill, as by jugglery & rhetoric it is called. The Slaveholding members of Congress are at variance also. The administration is unfriendly to Clay's Compromise & will not oppose the admission of California & New Mexico as States, it is believed.

"Your's very truly
"LEWIS TAPPAN

"P. S.   I put into the envelope a note for Mr. Sturge which, after reading please seal & forward.   You will be amused on reading the Speech of T. Stevens of June 10 in the N. Era.[228] Dan.̇ Webster, Prof. Stuart [229] & Dr. Woods [230] are superannuated men, with their physical powers if not their moral sense, greatly impaired.
"John Scoble, Esq.
    London"

"WASHINGTON 7mo 3.1850.

"My dear friend,

"We [231] left New York after a tarriance there of two days for Philadelphia where we lodged & proceeded on the next day (the 27th of last mo) to Washington where we have comfortable

---

[228] *The National Era,* June 27, 1850, p. 101. The speech dealt largely, in connection with its consideration of the California question, with the power of Congress to legislate for the Territories. It is to be found in full in the *Appendix to the Congressional Globe,* 21st Congress, 1st sess., XXII, Pt. I, pp. 765–769.

[229] Moses Stuart, 1780–1852, an American scholar and writer.

[230] Leonard Woods, 1774–1854, an American Congregational theologian, active in the American Tract Society, the American Board of Commissioners for Foreign Missions, and other organizations.

[231] G. W. Alexander and John Candler.

accommodation close to the Capitol. There are in the same boarding house with us several members of Congress & members of their families. Two of these members of Cong. are Southern men & slave holders, one a free soiler & the other four Northern men more or less opposed to slavery. I understand that the house where we are is the only one in which there is such a mixture of members of Congress holding conflicting opinions. I am not sorry that we are thus situated although it allows of little freedom of speech when we are together. It has given me at least a better opportunity of knowing all the difficulty that exists in social intercourse in this slave holding country & partially slave-holding Legislature than I might otherwise have had. It is not I believe either wise or expedient to give utterance here to the feelings of a full heart on the subject of slavery except it be done in such a manner as may have some tendency to inform the judgment & quicken the conscience without giving any needless offence & I confess that I scarcely possess or do not possess the wisdom that is needful for this difficult task. There will not however I believe be any mistake with regard to our strong & invincible repugnance to slavery on the part of those into whose society we are principally thrown. I should add that one of the boarders (Walter Underhill) with his wife are members of the Society of Friends, a Representative for the city of New York. He does not come up to our mark but will I hope vote against the compromise bill should it pass the Senate (which is not generally expected) & be carried to the House of Representatives. W.U's wife is a superior & truly estimable woman whose heart & judgment are with us but who as I think very wisely rarely speaks on the subject of slavery. On one occasion I grievously offended one of our boarders who is a Representative from North Carolina & I am therefore perhaps the more careful now although I fear that I am scarcely sufficiently so. Do not fear that we shall become trimmers & I hope that we shall not fail to speak wherever duty requires us to do so. We have need indeed to be wise as serpents & harmless as doves. Whilst at New York we were delighted in visiting the colored asylum for Orphans in which I think there are from 170 to 180 children. I felt however greatly grieved & disappointed at the extent of the cruel prejudice that prevails in New York & as we are told still more strongly at Philadelphia against color. During our stay at Washington we have generally attended the Senate during the very interesting debate that is carried on there. I have scarcely ever been absent although the weather is very oppressive & long sitting fatiguing. Yesterday I heard a capital speech [232] from Senator Seward but most of the speeches on the great topic are intolerably & unreasonably long, occupying several hours in the delivery. We have made the acquaintance of some of the most distinguished free soilers or abolitionists—Hale, & Chase in the Senate & Giddings, Horace Mann, & some others in the House of Representatives. We spent part of an evening with those I have mentioned a few days since at Dr Bailey's. His paper has now a circulation of 15,000 nearly the whole of which are paid for & the payment of two dollars is made in advance. I saw yesterday a colored school at which were 50 or 60 children including one slave who appeared to be a lighter color than any of his companions. Slaves may be taught if the consent of the owner be obtained. What an intolerable restriction at the seat of government on the right of intellectual culture & what a specimen of the extent to which slaves are taught in day schools! I am not sure whether I have requested thee to send the A.S. Reporter to David Winton, [. . . sic] Grange Hill Post Office Jamaica, Jas. Niven, Friendship Savanna [. . . sic] P.O. Jam[a], & John Aird Green Island P.O. Jam[a] also to all the other Presbyterian Baptist, Wesleyan & London S[y]'s Miss[s]. We shall I believe be well paid for the Reporters thus to be sent. With kind regards to thyself, wife & family, to all members of the Com[ee].

"G.W. ALEXANDER.

"You may be pleased to learn that the offence taken by the North Car[n] was soon terminated as far as this could be done as the occasion was quite unintentional.

"L. Tappan has not forwarded thy last letter wh. I expect to receive at Baltimore. We intend to make a short stay at that city & at Wilmington & a longer one at Phil[a], New York & Boston.

"PHILADELPHIA 7mo 9.1850.

"I add a few lines to those already written. We left Washington early on the morning of the 6th & reached Baltimore to breakfast. In the course of the day we visited the Penitentiary where poor Torrey terminated his earthly existence. There is now in the same prison a person confined for 14 or 15 years for giving a slave a free pass. We were informed by an individual who is likely to be acquainted with the facts of the case that it is his belief that the

[232] *Appendix to the Congressional Globe*, 31st Congress, 1st sess., p. 1021 ff.

prisoner on whom this hard & cruel sentence has been passed was
not aware that the man whose freedom he had asserted was a slave.
The offender against the slave code of Maryland has a wife & several
children. We learn that an atrocious law has been passed in the
same state within about two years by which colored persons who are
sentenced for a second time to imprisonment are sold as slaves out
of the state for the period during which they would otherwise be
confined & there appears to be no security for their restoration to
freedom. A white man may be imprisoned for an indefinite number of times—so unequal is the law as respects men who boast a
white skin & those who have a colored complexion. I learned from
a fellow passenger in the steam boat from Baltimore that the Di-
rectory published there contains a list of white & colored persons
arranged separately the latter as might be supposed in such case
being placed at the end. When & where shall this odious distinction terminate in this part of the world of which I sometimes feel
quite sick in contemplating the cruel injustice & degradation to
which our sable & colored brethren are subjected. J. Candler & I
have talked over the manner in which it may be best to present to
our friends the result of the information we have obtained in the
West Indies. We had at one time thought of making a joint report
in as condensed a form as we could to do justice to the subject but
I rather lean to the opinion on further consideration that the letters
written by J. C. to J. Forster either in their original state or thrown
into that of ordinary narration would be a preferable mode. In
either case it would be desirable that they should undergo a careful
revision & that omissions or additions should be made where either
is needful. Within the last few days my wife & I have received a
very unfavorable account of the state of health of Catharine's
brother. It is quite possible that the circumstance may hasten our
return home. Should this be the case I shall the less regret it as
there appears to be little opportunity for us to do good here & I
think that if any good can be effected by our instrumentality this
will be much more effectively accomplished by a judicious publication than in any other manner. If the information we have obtained be presented to the American public in an interesting form
I believe it will find many readers although we might not find a
large number disposed to listen to oral statements. I wish that we
could present a second Winter in the West Indies as interesting as
was that of our late dear & valued frᵈ J. J. Gurney. We hear today

that there are accounts of the alarming illness of the President. In some of the towns in the west there have been very serious reports of the prevalence of cholera.

"Farewell."

(G. W. ALEXANDER)

"Boston, August 21/50.

"Dear Sir,

"I thank you for your note of July 5th.[233] We did

[233] Scoble must have written to Tappan immediately after the adjournment of the B. & F. A-S. Society Committee, July 5. At that meeting Joseph Sturge had "intimated the probability of Henry Garnett, of the U. S., coming to this country to plead the free-labor produce question, and (had) enquired how far the Committee would feel disposed to recognize him—the matter to stand over for further consideration" (*Minute Books*, III, minute 425). The Committee did not act upon the matter until the second of August and it then resolved that it would be prepared to recognize Garnett, officially, and to cooperate with him as opportunities might offer but not to be "held responsible for any expenses his visit to this Country may involve" (*idem*, minute 439). At this meeting, be it remarked, letters were read from various people, including Alexander, Candler, and Lewis Tappan, and it was to receive Alexander, "Treas. . . . on his return from the B. Colonies and the United States . . ." that the next meeting, that of August tenth, was called (*idem*, minute 445). A more formal reception of the travellers was made the occasion for a large public meeting late in the autumn, although the real reason, perhaps, for its being held was to express indignation at recent United States enactments.

(*a*) "My Dear Friend

"I understood from Peter Bolton yesterday that thou wert expected in town today and I suggested that the subject of promptly holding a Public Meeting should be considered. I am very jealous in the present state of Public feeling in America of improperly interfering with the Anti-Slavery question there but I think we could have a good public Meeting for the purpose of expressing our Sympathy with the Abolitionists & People of Colour in America & also to receive G. W. Alexander & John Candler on their return with propriety & the attention of the world is now so turned to this subject in America that it would tell well— I write to G. W. Alexander to ask him to come up to the Committee— I have been in Town twice within 5 days & cannot comfortably come again on 6th but if any thing further strikes me to suggest I will write tomorrow again.

"affectionately thy friend

"B-ham, 10/30 1850.   "JOS. STURGE.
"John Scoble"

(*b*) "My Dear Friend

"I wrote thee a few lines yesterday respecting the propriety of a Meeting which I see by the note I had to-day is to come under the consideration of the Committee tomorrow. Although I believe there is cause to be increasingly cautious how we as Englishmen meddle with the Anti-Slavery question in the United States yet I think on this extraordinary occasion a Meeting might be held with advantage— It might be advertized perhaps somewhat in this manner—'A Meeting to consider the Pro-

not look for a *reply* to the letter to Lord Palmerston, but supposed
you might receive an acknowledgment of its receipt &c.

"... "Your's truly,
"L. TAPPAN

"Mr Bolton"

> priety of an address to the Abolitionists and people of colour of the
> United States on the position in which they are placed by the atrocious
> provision of the Fugitive Slave bill recently passed' at which John
> Candler & G. W. Alexander recently returned from the British West In-
> dies & the U. States will be present. Or you might make the welcoming
> of our friends' return the more prominent object of the Meeting but I am
> inclined to think that if the Meeting is to tell well upon America it should
> be kept out of sight as much as may be that it is called by the Anti-
> Slavery Society— Probably a good day Meeting at the City of London
> Tavern would have the best moral effect & I think a good one could be
> had if S. Gurney wd. take the chair—Or perhaps Dr. Lushington would.
> The latter end of next week would probably be a good time say 6th or 7th
> Day— I should like to be one of the audience if I can be there but the
> beginning of the following week I go to (?) to a Peace Meeting to meet
> Rich⁴. Cobden at the particular request of some of my relatives the Dar-
> leys—
>
> "Affectionately thy friend
> "JOS. STURGE.
>
> "Birmingham 10/31, 1850
> "John Scoble"

At its meeting, October 24, 1850, the B. & F. A-S. Society Committee had
empowered its Secretary to prepare a resolution expressive of the views entertained relative to recent legislation of the United States Congress (*Minute
Books*, III, minute 446) and, on November 1, it had laid before it a preliminary
draft of several resolutions on the subject of the extension of slavery, "but
more particularly with respect to the Fugitive Slave Bill." These—revision
and adoption concluded—were entrusted to the Secretary for insertion in such
daily and weekly papers as would receive them and for transmission to New
York where Lewis Tappan was to use them at his discretion (*idem*, minute
459).

The further business of this meeting had, likewise, a bearing upon American affairs, Scoble being

> "requested to draft a Memorial to Lord Palmerston relative to the laws
> of the Slave States of the U. S. affecting B. colored subjects resorting
> thither; and in relation to the bearing of the Ashburton Treaty on Fugi-
> tive Slaves, charged with crimes, for the purpose of being recovered by
> their masters (*idem*, minute 460).
> "The propriety of holding a public meeting on the Fugitive Slave
> Bill, having been discussed by the Committee, it was agreed that it should
> not be an Anti-Slavery Meeting, called by the Committee, but that if a
> respectable platform of City men could be obtained, such meeting should
> be called. C. Gilpin and Jno. Scoble to make enquiries, and Jos. Forster
> requested to ask Sam¹ Gurney to take the Chair, and in case of failure Dr.
> Lushington to be applied to (*idem*, minute 462).
> "Letters were read from L. Tappan, respecting the Fugitive Slave
> law, from Jas. Ketley, Demerara, relative to the Licence law; and from
> Jos. Sturge and G. W. Alexander, on the subject of a public meeting, the
> former rather opposed to it, and the latter suggesting it should be de-
> ferred until near the assembling of Parliament" (*idem*, minute 463).

AMERICAN & FOREIGN
ANTI-SLAVERY SOCIETY   "BOSTON, August 21/50.
  etc.,

   "My dear friend,

     "I received your letter of July 8th. after Mr Alexander had sailed. His visit to this country gave much satisfaction to all the friends of the anti-slavery cause who had the pleasure of seeing & conversing with him. We regretted that he could not stay with us longer.

  "The Compromise bill, as you will have learned, was defeated in the Senate by the united exertions of the free soil and ultra Southern members! This defeat was considered a victory by the friends of freedom, not with standing it was brought about by the aid of the Propagandists. Since the defeat, several bills have passed the Senate, embracing portions of the defeated bill, but generally it is considered that they are not so objectionable as the Compromise bill would have been. The Fugitive bill remains to be definitely acted upon in the Senate; & meantime the bills that have passed the Senate are before the House, where they meet with much opposition. ¡What will be the final result no one can tell, but we can not but hope that slavery will be shorn of its brains in the present Congress.

  "I thank you for the volume you have sent. I could use another copy advantageously.

  "The Reporter is read with undiminished interest. Ex-governor Hammond of S.C. wrote me that he had dropt all the Abolition U.S. newspapers, but he wished to continue to take the B. & F. Anti-S. Reporter! I gave Mr. Alexander a copy of his note to me, which will amuse you. It should not however find its way into any print.

  "In Prof. Cleveland [234] you must have found an intelligent & warm hearted friend of the cause.

  "D. Webster made himself very unpopular with the great body of the people by his conduct in the Senate, and his retreat into the office of the Sec. of State was a lucky affair for him. In this office he will, I think, endeavor to act more worthily & to build up anew the reputation he suffered to be so much damaged in the Senate. The rebukes he has received will naturally induce him to make the effort.

[234] C. D. Cleveland.

"The new Cabinet is a more able one than the last & I think more inclined to the cause of freedom. Still it is conservative.
"With unabated regard,
"Very truly your's,
"LEWIS TAPPAN.
"John Scoble, Esq."

"NEW YORK, September 17/50

"My dear friend,
"The different subjects included in Mr. Clay's Compromise Bill have been put into separate Bills, and after a brief discussion passed by both Houses of Congress. You will be surprised at this —as vast numbers were in this country—and will wish to know the reason. Not half of either branch of the National Legislature would have voted for the Bill as it originally stood, and yet decisive majorities promptly voted for the measures separately. But the same individuals did not vote on all the Bills alike. Votes were changed on all subjects, except those of a determined minority of the South which went against all the Bills, and a resolute band of Northerners who voted against all except that for the admission of California.

"Some of the reasons for the swift passage of these Bills, after nine months legislation respecting them, are the following: 1. Influential members of the Senate exerted an influence over the members of the lower House. 2. Webster's position as Secretary of State, and 'Prime minister' of the new administration, enabled him to work efficiently in favor of the passage of the Bills. 3. The influence of the administration, in the way of reward, may have had an effect upon several members. 4. The ten millions of dollars, to be given to Texas, was to be distributed among needy & persevering bond-holders who thronged the avenues to the halls of Congress exerting the influence desperate men thus circumstanced, can exert over unprincipled legislators. 5. The influence of the manufacturing & commercial interests. 6. The threats of the South, fears of a collision with Texas, nullification in other States, &c.

"Strange as it may appear, General Taylor, a Southerner by birth & a slaveholder, had he lived, would have taken decided ground against Texas, and probably prevented the passage of the worst of these Bills. A State paper was nearly prepared, and would soon have been issued, it is confidently stated, that would have placed President Taylor in the commanding position, relative to Southern arrogance, that General Jackson secured when he issued the celebrated Proclamation [235] respecting nullification in South Carolina.

"The commercial, trading, manufacturing interests of the country are exulting over the victory that has been achieved, while the free people of color are greatly alarmed at the passage of the bill for the reclamation of fugitive slaves,[236] and the ultra slave-factionists of the South are exasperated at the admission of a new free State on the Pacific. So far from stopping agitation, by the passage of these Bills, it will doubtless be increased. But I have not leisure to enlarge at the present time. The interests of a gold-loving & war-making people are opposed to human rights & to the republican principles of the founders of this Republic, as the interests of all other nations, of similar aspirations, are to the progress of freedom & a recognition of the equality of man. [Do not think the abolitionists of this country are disheartened by the flagitious proceedings of Congress. You know of what materials majorities of legislative bodies are often composed—selfish, ambitious, time-serving, reckless men. Measures will be taken to obtain a repeal of all unconstitutional & oppressive sections of the acts recently passed, & a future Congress may undo, to a great extent, what the present Congress has done. Be this as it may, the abolitionists here have never lost their faith, under previous trials and disappointments, in the ultimate success of their labors, nor their determination to prosecute the moral warfare in which they are engaged until complete success shall, by the help of God, crown their efforts.]

"Very truly yours
"LEWIS TAPPAN.

"Mrs Pringle & her sister arrived here about a fortnight since. They have gone to Phil[a]. to meet their brother & expect soon to return here. It has given me pleasure to attend to these worthy ladies."

[235] Richardson, II, 640–656.

[236] *The Congressional Globe,* 31st Congress, 1st sess., XXI, Pt. II, 1806, 1807, 1812.

"NEW YORK, Nov. 25/50

"JOHN SCOBLE, ESQ.

"My dear friend,

"I have rec[d] your two letters of the 8th with the Resolutions & the communication for Mr. Chaplin.[237] The sum of $19,000 is required for bail. His friends are trying to raise the sum. If they do the bail will be forfeited. There is no chance for him if he stands trial. He used no fire arms & did not know that the slaves had any until they used them. If convicted he will probably be sentenced to the Penitentiary for at least 12 years. He has [sic] numerous friends & is an intelligent & benevolent man. Great prejudice exists against him in Maryland. So much exasperation prevails throughout the country on the Fug. Slave Bill, pro & con, that a man who gets into the power of the Slave-holders now stands a poor chance of escape. The large cities that trade so much with the South are favorable to acquiescence in the law, but the country generally is opposed to it. It will, notwithstanding the alarm & distress it occasions, do great good in opening the eyes of the people.

"Very truly your's
"LEWIS TAPPAN"

"NEW YORK,
"April 3rd 1851.

"JOHN SCOBLE, ESQ.

"Dear Sir,

"With this I send you a new pamphlet of *Hancock*.[238]

"Will you put the following question to Dr Lushington and

---

[237] The following minutes have reference to this man:

Minute 445. At the meeting on October 24, 1850, the Secretary was instructed to draft resolutions "expressive of sympathy felt by this Com. with W. L. Chaplin now in prison for aiding fugitive slaves to escape from bondage. . . ."

Minute 458, November 1, 1850. "In relation to Minute 445, the Secretary reported that the Resolutions respecting W. L. Chaplin, had been forwarded to him, through Lewis Tappan of New York."

Minute 475, January 3, 1851. "In relation to the two sets of resolutions relating to W. L. Chaplin and the Fugitive Slave Law, the Sec[y] laid before the Com. acknowledgment of their receipt by Lewis Tappan, New York."

[238] Hancock (pseud.), "A letter to the Hon. Samuel A. Eliot, representative in Congress from the City of Boston, in reply to his apology for voting for the fugitive slave bill" (Boston, 1851). The authorship of this pamphlet was ascribed to both Judge Jay and Franklin Dexter.

communicate his answer? If an American slave flees to Canada, and takes the oath of allegiance to the British Government will he be claimed as a British subject, should he on visiting the U.S. be seized as a fugitive slave? If Dr Pennington should take the oath to the British Government, return to the U.S. and be seized as a slave, would the British Government claim him?

"I feel almost ashamed that I have not acknowledged your letter of 15th November more particularly, although you intimated in it that you would write again on the same subject.

"We made as strong an effort as we could to prevent Henry Long being remanded to Slavery. For 17 days we maintained the contest in the courts. If the Judge of the State Court had done his duty Long would have been liberated. While the question of the legality of the person claiming to be an U.S. Commissioner was under consideration the Judge, instead of appointing an officer to take the custody of Long, allowed the U.S. Marshal to retain him. Had an officer of the State court held him & the Judge proceeded to decide the case Long would probably have escaped. He had no opportunity to do so when a new process was commenced because he was held by the U.S. officer.

"I do not think the persons indicted at Boston on the charge of aiding Shadrach to escape can be convicted.

"The Fugitive Slave Bill is not popular anywhere. Interested politicians, manufacturers, merchants & subservient preachers pretend to justify or excuse it, but it is distasteful to the great body of the people, especially those who reside in the country towns. It may remain on the statute book but if so it will become a dead letter. Some good effects have followed the enactment of the bill. The people are discussing the nature of their obligations, the meaning of the Constitution, their rights &c. They are beginning to find that when a man takes an oath or affirmation to support the Constitution he is bound by his oath or affirmation to oppose every unconstitutional enactment.

"I continue to read the Reporter with interest. The consistent and untiring efforts of your Committee act beneficially upon the Anti-slavery body in this country.

"The passage of a cheap Postage Bill,[239] by the late Congress will aid the Anti-slavery cause as well as every other valuable

[239] *United States Statutes at Large*, IX, c. XX, 587–591.

interest of the country.[240] For some years I have been Treasurer
of the N.Y. Cheap Postage Association & have reason to be thankful
for the opportunity of contributing to bring about the important
change. We hope that Ocean postage will be reduced. What a
blessing it would be to the inhabitants of both England & the U.S.
if a penny or three cent postage existed on letters sent across the
ocean.

"We expect to hold our anniversary on the 13th May as usual.
To human view the system of Slavery seems to be in the ascendant.
Our profligate politicians & their no less profligate supporters
seem disposed to yield everything to the Slave Power, but the
leaven of Anti-slavery is working among the masses. It will leaven
the whole lump. This belief encourages us to go forward, relying
upon the promises of Him who has declared He will break the rod
of the oppressor.

"Very truly yours,
"LEWIS TAPPAN."

OFFICE OF THE AMER: & FOR.
ANTI-SLAVERY SOCIETY.
No 48 BEEKMAN STREET,
"NEW YORK.
"May 15/51.

"JOHN SCOBLE, ESQ.
Secretary &c.
"My dear Sir,
"We had a better anniversary than usual. The
meeting was held on the 6th in the spacious Broadway Tabernacle,
which was filled by a highly respectable audience who seemed delighted with the proceedings during the three hours they remained
together. I sent you a small pamphlet containing the Abstract of

240 The "tremendous boon" that cheap postage had been, for eight years,
to Great Britain, the "great moral power," was set forth in a pamphlet, entitled, *Cheap Postage, Remarks on the Subject of Cheap Postage & Postal Reform in Great Britain and the United States* (Boston, 1848). The author of it
was Joshua Leavitt, Corresponding Secretary of the Cheap Postage Association. Rowland Hill had argued that a money gain would result from a lower-
ing of the postage rates; but Leavitt was of the opinion that no proof was
wanting that the British system had been adopted, in 1840, with sole reference
to general benefits and the will of the people, no regard being paid to the
probable loss of revenue or to a possible gain.

the Annual Report and the set of Resolutions that were presented
to the meeting. Our practice has been, for a few years past, to
make a statement on paper of some of the principal topicks of the
Annual Report which occupies 12 to 15 minutes, as an audience
would not listen patiently 35 or 40 minutes to hear the Abstract
read; and to follow it by reading a set of Resolutions. The Abstract of the Abstract & the Resolutions were received with much
applause, a few persons only expressing their disapprobation by
hissing. The gentlemen who addressed the meeting did not offer
any Resolutions. Rev. Henry Ward Beecher one of our most
popular preachers (he is a Congregational minister at Brooklyn,
near this City) made the principal speech.[241] He spoke in a very
animated manner for an hour & a half. His speech was taken down
by several Reporters & has been published in several of the City
papers. I send you a copy of the N.Y.Sun, which contains the best
report I have seen. This paper has a daily circulation of forty
thousand copies. You will be pleased to learn that the editors &
proprietors of this paper—who not long since were decidedly opposed to the anti-slavery movement, offered to print 65,000 copies
of their weekly (the one I send you) containing Mr Beecher's
speech & send a copy to every clergyman in the U.S. of every denomination.

"Rev. Dr Willis [242] of Toronto, Canada West, favored us with
his presence, & made a short speech. He also made a more extended address at the adjourned meeting May 7th. Rev C.G. Finney our countryman, who has lately returned from London,
addressed the meeting also. Their speeches will be published with
the Annual Report [243] which is now in the press. It will be a
document about as large as the 8vo edition of last year. I regret
that I have not time to write farther at present.

"Very truly your's

"LEWIS TAPPAN"

[241] For Beecher's speech, see *Report of the American and Foreign Anti-
Slavery Society*, 1851, pp. 5–15, and Henry Ward Beecher, *Patriotic Addresses*,
ed. by John R. Howard (1887), pp. 178–195.

[242] President of the Anti-Slavery Society of Canada.

[243] The *Report*, although Tappan made no reference to the fact in this
letter, contained many pages about fugitive slaves, a subject of transcendant
importance to his British correspondents. It also borrowed from the B. & F.
A-S. *Reporter* Alexander-Candler remarks about their recent experiences, particularly in the West Indies.

"NEW YORK,

"JOHN SCOBLE, ESQ.   "June 6/51 [244]

"My dear Sir,

"Yours of May 23d was rec^d on the 4th. May 15th I sent you a small pamphlet containing the Abstract of our Annual Report, and the Resolutions adopted at the Annual meeting. Thus I have anticipated your request in part. The A.R. is not yet out of the press. It is voluminous with a copious Index. The printers have so much to do immediately after the Anniversaries that it is difficult to get a Report printed & bound very soon. I shall send you a copy as soon as I can procure one, even if it is in sheets. The Report instead of giving a particular account of what the Ex. Com, have done, (too little it must be confessed!) gives a year's history of the Anti-Slavery cause.

"You speak of having received the N.Y. Evangelist & Observer, that give some account of the Annual Meeting. The former paper always speaks of the Society in a friendly manner, but the latter sneers at all our efforts.[245] The Independent—do you not receive it? It published the Abstract of the Report & Resolutions at length.

"It is pleasant to see the doings of the non-established churches [246] in your country & the Evan. Alliance with respect

[244] Published in the B. & F. A-S. *Reporter*, July 1, 1851, pp. 114–115. The reference to English drinking habits and brewery-owning philanthropists was, however, omitted without indication and a comment from the *Observer* added.

[245] In the issue of May 8, 1851, appeared an account of the A. & F. A-S. Society Annual Meeting (see p. 150), not exactly an inaccurate account, but an unfriendly one, the tone creating a contempt for the thing it described. The Reverend Samuel Irenaeus Prime had returned but recently to the editorial staff.

[246] At a meeting of fifty-one Baptist ministers in London, May 1, 1851, a resolution was passed,

"'That they unite in expressing their abhorrence of the American Fugitive Slave-law, as opposed alike to every feeling of humanity and to the principles of religion; and that they deem it right to avow their detestation of this enactment, and of the support which it has received from many of the ministers of the Gospel in America, & by declaring their resolution not to receive into their pulpits any minister from America who is known to support this most cruel and iniquitous measure'' (*The Patriot*, May 12, 1851).

The following Sturge letter must have had reference, anticipatory, to this same matter,

"My Dear Friend
"I wrote thee a line yesterday in haste without making any remark upon thy suggestions— I quite approve of thy proposition to insert

to Amer.-slaveholding ministers & their allies.[247] But our pro-slavery ministers and others will evade the resolutions. The Patriot [248] of May 19th, now before me, says your ch[hs] 'will make themselves partakers of the sin of slave-holders, if they admit to their occasional fellow-ship any Americans who are favorable to the continuance of Negro Slavery.' True enough, but no one who goes from this country to England will acknowledge that he is favorable to the continuance of Slavery. Oh no!—They all consider Slavery an 'evil'—wish the country was rid of it—the gospel will effect it in due time—sorry the abolitionists are so rabid &c &c &c. I see by the N.Y. Observer [249] that the right hand of fellowship has been given to Rev. Mr Chickering of Portland, Maine, as a true Anti-Slavery man. The Observer claims that he is just such an abolitionist as he is, and as are all Northern ministers!

"Dr Cox,[250] who, in England was an abolitionist *par excellence* now abuses abolitionists—not the Garrison school merely, but *all* abolitionists—makes addresses at Colonization meetings—speaks

a resolution in the religious periodicals but as we shall have to pay for it as an advertisement please condense it as much as thou canst—and also that some communication sh[d]. be made with the religious bodies thou name[st].— I need not say that no time sh[d]. be lost if this is acted upon as I believe the Baptist meet next week. . . . I am glad to see Dr. Campbell is taking up the matter so warmly— I have just got a letter from S. Bowley. I fear he will hardly have is (*sic*) address ready and that it will be too long— It should be as short as possible consistently with the object in view. "Affect[ly]. thy friend
"Jos. STURGE
"Birm[ham] 4/20, 1851
"Jno. Scoble.''

[247] "Resolved, therefore, that slaveholders shall not be admissible as visitors to the proposed Conference'' (B. & F. A-S. *Reporter*, June 2, 1851, p. 94).

[248] Editorial, a suggestion to British churches:

"The rights of hospitality will be desecrated if extended to slave-holders, or to the apologists for Slavery. The sanctity of the Christian pulpit will be seriously compromised, if any ministers of pro-Slavery principles be admitted to address any of our congregations. Christian Churches will also, in our opinion, make themselves partakers of the sin of slave-holders, if they admit to their occasional fellowship any Americans who are favourable to the continuance of Negro Slavery'' (*The Patriot*, May 19, 1851, p. 321).

[249] Despite the fact that the Reverend Dr. Chickering of Portland and the Reverend Dr. Murray of Elizabethtown were not outspoken Abolitionists when in America, when in England the one had attended the Congregational Union meeting and the other had spoken at the Bible and Tract Society anniversary (*New York Observer*, June 5, 1851, p. 178).

[250] Note, in *New York Observer*, May 29, 1851, p. 174, an allusion to the change in opinions on slavery of the Reverend Dr. Cox of Brooklyn.

of John Bull and his calves—and defends Daniel Webster [251] in his apostacy & measures.

"Again, our pro-slavery men say 'Reprovers should have clean hands. How much beer the English drink. Their eminent philanthropists own Breweries. This is as bad as Slavery!'

"It makes one heart-sick to hear all the objections & accusations made. Let us meekly and patiently do our duty, and leave the result to God.   "Truly yours,

                                         "L. TAPPAN.

"The best Report of Mr Beecher's speech was published in the *Sun*. A better report, however, will be published with the Report."

                                         "NEW YORK,
                                            "June 25/51.

"My dear Sir,

            "After a long delay, we this day sent off nearly the whole edition of the Annual Report—4500 copies. Nineteen or 20 copies are sent by the steamer that will sail—per enclosed list.

"Mr. Harned, the office agent, will forward 30 copies more, directed to the B.&F. Anti. S. Office to be sent to such individuals as will be glad to receive a copy. Can you send a copy to David Turnbull [252] Esq—to Dr Madden.

"Can you forward copies to the Cor. members of the Com. if I send them to you free of expense!

[251] Tappan's own opinion of that apostacy can probably be derived from the following:

"... There was a juncture when he might by his personal influence have arrested the iniquitous measures for giving slavery a chance of extension over the new Territories, checked the arrogance of the slaveholders in Congress, and given a mighty impetus to the anti-slavery cause. Instead of this—at the exigency, when the eyes of the nation were upon him, and in full recollection of his former declarations on the side of freedom—he astonished the nation by giving in his adherence to the Slave Power!" (A. & F. A.-S. Society *Annual Report* (1851), p. 94).

[252] Turnbull had but recently returned to England and on his way thither had tarried awhile in New York, where he had given the Abolitionists his very positive opinion that the depression in Jamaica was due to other causes than Negro emancipation (A. & F. A.-S. Society *Annual Report* (1850), p. 144). This was in contradiction to what had been asserted in letters from Jamaica, published in the New York *Evening Post*. Turnbull's reliability as a witness was not, however, wholly unquestioned. Years before this, when he was holding the Cuban Consulate, a certain man, named Cocking, resident at Havana, had frequently communicated to the B. & F. A.-S. Society Committee in London facts that reflected very unfavorably upon him.

"I shall be glad to know the *postage* on the copy this day sent to you & if it arrived in good order in the style sent.

"I am sorry to see by the Reporter that the Abstract of the Report failed to reach you. It was sent in a newspaper and also in a pamphlet.

"Mr Beecher's speech in the Report is quite different from the speech published in the newspaper, having been taken down verbatim & carefully revised by him.

"If you want more copies please inform me.

"The Southern Slaveholders are compassing sea & land to divide California and thus make a new slave state; and also to introduce slavery into New Mexico & California. See Amer Miss: [253] (a copy of which is sent you herewith) see also our agent Mr Keppars (?) letters [254] in National Era, &c. "In haste Your's truly,

"LEWIS TAPPAN.

[Enclosure]

"Copies of the Annual Report of the A.&F. Anti. S. Soc. sent from New York. June 25/51 to the following:

Alexander G.W.
Buxton Sir E.N.Bart
Brougham Lord
Beckwith Gen.C. (U.S.A.)
Cropper John
Cobden Richard
Carlisle Earl
Eardley Sir C.E.
Gurney Sam¹
Garnett H.H.
Opie Amelia
Pennington J.W.C.
Oxford Bishop
Russell Lord John
Stanley Lord
Scoble John
Sturge Jos
Thompson Geo
Webb Richard, Belfast."
19.

[253] *The American Missionary* was the publication of the American Missionary Association. It was founded in 1846.

[254] These letters have not been located. The writer was possibly John Kephart.

"New York, August 2/51

"Peter J. Bolton, Esq.

"Dear Sir,

"If I have not acknowledged the receipt of your esteemed letter [255] of 6th May (written on the day of our anniver-

[255] Bolton in this or in other letters must have had a great deal to communicate. The *Minute Books* testify to how much the B. & F. A.-S. Society Committee had been occupying itself with American affairs. On December 6, 1850, it had adopted a *memorial*, submitted in rough draft by Scoble, to Lord Palmerston on the "treatment of British colored subjects in the U. S.; and in relation to the Fugitive Slaves escaped into Canada . . ." (*Minute* 466½).

TREATMENT OF BRITISH COLORED SUBJECTS IN THE UNITED STATES—
FUGITIVES IN CANADA.

"TO THE RIGHT HON: LORD PALMERSTON &c &c
"My Lord,
"The Co. of the B. & F. A. S. Society have felt it to be their duty on several important occasions to direct Yr. Ldship's attention to the Laws which exist in the Southern or Slave States of the U.S. affecting colored Subjects of this Kingdom, who may occasion to resort thither for business or other lawful purposes. These particular Laws & the police regulations founded upon them in Southern ports, infringe the just liberties of a large body of mariners, & independently of the wrong which they inflict on them, they seriously interfere with the commercial pursuits of British Merchants & Ship Owners.
"Every colored person, as Yr. Ldship is aware, is seized the moment he reaches these ports, as if he were a felon, taken to the Common jail, and there kept until the departure of the vessel on board which he had been engaged as a Seaman; and what adds indignity to this monstrous proceeding is, that they are taken from on board British vessels, covered by the British flag, in defiance of treaties which exist between this Country & the U. States, which guarantee protection & security to the subjects & citizens of the two Countries within their respective dominions, when pursuing their lawful business.
"The plea set up, that the Southern States are Slave States, and therefore require laws of this kind to protect the institution of Slavery, cannot, the Ce. conceive be admitted to be of any value as against British subjects of any class. But in addition to this the Ce. would observe that the treaties of Amity & Commerce which this Country has had with the U.S. are not made with the Several States, but with the Federal Govt. representing the entire Union; this Country, therefore, cannot recognize a local legislation, which infringes the stipulations of such general treaties. They would therefore respectfully urge upon Yr. Ldship the necessity of applying a sure remedy to this monstrous grievance by urging upon the Federal Govt. of the U. S., either to call upon the Several States, in which such exceptional Laws exist, so to modify or repeal them, as to bring them into harmony with the just claims of this Country, or by an Act of the U.S. Congress to set aside such Laws as conflict with existing treaties, & the rights of British Subjects without distinction of Color.
"Another point which the Ce. are anxious to bring under Yr. Ldships attention, is, the liability of Fugitive Slaves who seek refuge from the oppression of their Masters in Canada, under the plea that they have committed crimes which bring them within the scope of the Extradition Clause of the Ashburton treaty. Yr. Ldship is aware of a recent Law passed by the Congress of the U.S. of a most cruel and unchristian character, for the capture of fugitive Slaves who have fled into the Free States. In consequence of the terror occasioned by this inhuman piece of legislation, large numbers of colored persons, who were usefully engaged in the Free States, have been compelled to fly from their homes & to seek refuge within the Queen's dominions. There can be no

sary) it has not been from indifference to it. Far from it. Your letters always give me much information, & are perused with pleasure.

"I wrote immediately to Mr. Hammond & enclosed the bill. He has not replied. Why, I cannot say. It may be that as he is a dis-

doubt that great efforts will be made by unprincipled men from the South to get up charges against some of these unhappy persons with a view of dragging them back to Slavery. By the law of Nature & of Nations, a slave is undoubtedly intitled to effect his escape from bondage & to use or take such things as he may require to accomplish his object. It is therefore not improbable that applicat^n. may be made to the Authorities in Canada, for the delivery of colored persons on all sorts of charges; & inasmuch as they cannot be demanded as fugitive Slaves, but as criminals the greatest care must be taken by the Magistracy in Canada, or else the most grievous injustice & wrong may be done to persons whose sole crime has been their escape from Slavery. The C^e. would therefore earnestly ask of Y^r. Ldship to forward such instructions as shall effectually protect the fugitive Slaves, who may seek an asylum under the British Crown, from re-capture; and thus vindicate the great principle of the right of every human being to his personal liberty, and this Country from the dishonor of aiding & abetting the Slaveholders of the United States in the accomplishment of their nefarious designs.

"I have &c
"JOHN SCOBLE SEC^y.
"London 20 Decr. 1850"

Reply.

"FOREIGN OFFICE 31st Dec.1850
"Sir
"I am directed by Viscount Palmerston to acknowledge the receipt of your letter of the 13th. inst. complaining of the hardship & injustice of the Laws of the Southern or Slaveholding States of the American Union, with respect to colored persons arriving in the ports of these States, & I am to state to you for the information of the B & F. A. S. Soc^y., that the matter treated of in your Letter is involved in considerable difficulty, but that it has attracted & will continue to engage the attention of Her Majestys Govt.

"I am &c
"STANLEY OF ALD^y.
"John Scoble Esq"

At its meeting on January 3, 1851, it learned that these matters had been duly attended to and itself received additional enlightenment on some of them from Lewis Tappan (*idem*, Minutes 476, 481). Then, at its seventh of March meeting, it considered (*idem*, Minute 500) the correspondence that had taken place meanwhile between the United States and Great Britain relative to the imprisonment of British colored seamen, the most material evidence in the complaint having been received from Matthews, the British consul at Charleston (see B. & F. A-S. *Reporter*, Jan. 1, 1851, p. 4). It is exceedingly interesting to note that both British and northern American newspapers took, in this connection, identically the same view: viz., that Clayton's argument in defence of the South Carolina law was absurd (*The Patriot*, February 20, 1851, p. 116). He, as Secretary of State having the matter in hand, had replied to the remonstrance of the British Government that the law complained of had been passed in the normal exercise of the power of state sovereignty.

The highly important subject of Negro emigration from the United States

unionist he does not wish to continue correspondence, or he may be absent from here. Expecting to hear from him I put your letter where it could be taken up when his answer should be received. I am sorry for it, for it has given an appearance of intended neglect to your requests. Having now ordered the Independent, Commonwealth, & Tribune to be forwarded to you, I must ask pardon for the delay with a hope that the papers will be received punctually.

and from Canada to the West Indies, principally Jamaica, had also been considered and acted upon by the B. & F. A-S. Society Committee and the Secretary, at the early March meeting, reported the particulars of an interview he had had, on the matter, with Lord Grey (Minute 501). This was not the first time that the B. & F. A-S. Society Committee had had reason to object to Earl Grey's policy touching the labor situation in the West Indies (*Minute Books*, II, 488, 499, Minutes 1023, 1034; *The British Banner*, January 26, 1848, pp. 62–63, February 2, 1848, p. 78). Of British newspapers, *The Patriot* was the most emphatic in opposition (see issue of January 6, 1851, and of September 15, 1851).

Yet another phase of the anti-slavery cause came before the B. & F. A-S. Society Committee in the winter of 1850 and 1851 and the spring of the latter year. The Great Exhibition was being prepared for and it was expected that it would prove an attraction to American tourists and an opportunity for the British to do some proselyting and propaganda work.

> Minute 508—April 4, 1851—"The subject of an Address to the British people on American Slavery, in view of the great Exhibition was considered, when it was resolved that Samuel Bowley of Gloucester, should be invited to prepare it, and that the one drafted by the Secʸ to the Americans should be forwarded to him."

The address was published in pamphlet form and ten thousand copies ordered for distribution (Minute 515). It carried an announcement of its own object,

> "To arouse and deepen in the mind of every American this moral sentiment, is the imperative duty of Englishmen whilst performing the rites of hospitality, or extending the hand of fellowship to their transatlantic brethren. Let us not forget that on our faithfulness in this matter much may depend, as to whether the influence of each individual, when he returns to his native shores, shall be exercised for good or for evil, on this great question. And permit us especially to warn those who have the control of British pulpits, to be careful how they allow them to be occupied by those ministers of religion, who are not prepared most unequivocally to denounce the condition of slavery as utterly repugnant to the spirit of the Gospel; and its sanction, even by silence, as a dereliction of Christian duty. They can be no fit teachers of the doctrines of Christianity, who are swayed, by the mere colour of the skin, from the practical exercise of its blessed precepts."

A special address "to the various religious associations of this country on the conduct to be observed towards American professors of religion who may come during the great exhibition" was adopted by the Committee, April 21, 1851 (Minute 511).

We shall pay for these papers here & not subject yr Society to any charge.

"I am surprised to learn that only *one* copy of last year's Report was rec^d. at your office. This year I hope they will not miscarry. Please inform us in your next how many you have rec^d. I am anxious to send them to Corresponding members on the Continent, & suppose we must do it, if at all, thro' England. I wait to be advised by you on this point. Mr. Harned sent proof-sheets, at 2 or 3 different periods. Were they received? Nothing was said in the July Reporter, & therefore I inferred they did not come to hand.

"Recently I rec^d a letter & Ms from Dr. Carove [256] of Heildelbergh via London & your office I presume. Very few reclamations under the Fug. Slave Bill are made. It costs more than the slaves are worth. The Act will, I think, be a dead letter. To repeal it would offend the pride of the South & the Northern parties would lose their votes.

"Truly yours
"LEWIS TAPPAN"

"NEW YORK, August 18/51.
"MR. PETER J. BOLTON,
"My dear Sir,

"A few days since I received Mr. Scoble's note of the 1st. giving the agreeable information that he expected to embark on the 9th. for Boston.[257] We shall be very glad to see him.

[256] From the B. & F. A-S. Society records is gathered,

"The manuscript copy of Dr. Carove's address on Slavery ordered to be forwarded to Jos. Leavitt, Boston, to be subject to such revision as may be required to secure accuracy, and that Lewis Tappan of New York be informed of the fact, that, if needful, he may communicate with Jos. Leavitt, relative to its being printed and circulated among the German population of the United States" (*Minute Books*, II, p. 219).

"At meeting, July 12, 1844, The Secretary reported that Dr. Carove's German manuscript had been forwarded to Lewis Tappan, of New York by the hands of Judge Jay accompanied by a letter from the Treasurer" (*idem*, p. 222).

[257] The purpose of this visit is thus intimated:

Minute 544—August 1, 1851—

"The Secretary having brought under the attention of the Committee his desire to visit Upper Canada to enquire into the number, condition, and prospects of the colored population, particularly the fugitive slaves, with a view to suggest plans for their benefit, and generally to promote the Anti-Slavery Cause, the Sec^y proposal was unanimously concurred in, it being, at the same time, understood, agreeably to the wishes of the secretary, that the proposed visit should be regarded as personal and not official."

"Enclosed is a communication for the Reporter. Who the editor pro tem. is I do not know. I have no objection to my name being published with the letter. I have to-day written a long letter [258] to Rev. Jas. Sherman respecting Rev. Mr. Chickering, with leave to publish it in the . . .
or other paper. If you do not see it in that paper or elsewhere, after the lapse of 2 weeks from the receipt of this you may drop a line to him asking him if he means to publish it & if he does not it can be offered for publication to the Reporter.

"My last to you was dated.

"With much regard
"Truly your's
"LEWIS TAPPAN.

"I have read, with much satisfaction, the account of your Anniversary [259] in the paper sent me."

"NEW YORK, August 18, 1851.

"TO THE EDITOR OF THE B. & F. ANTI SLAVERY REPORTER:

"The firm and decided action taken by so many ecclesiastical bodies in England in relation to American slave-holders, pro-slavery ministers, etc. has given great satisfaction to the abolitionists of this country.[260] It is bearing a faithful testimony on behalf of the righteous cause in which we are laboring, and affording essential aid. We lament to see that notwithstanding your precautions and faithfulness some of our preachers and laymen evade your scrutiny, and appear on your platforms as *pro tem.* abolitionists. No American minister probably would hesitate to say in England that he

[258] For this letter in published form, see B. & F. A-S. *Reporter*, September 1, 1851, p. 149.

[259] It had been held somewhat later than usual because the great Soirée had appropriated a May date, May nineteenth, and it had aimed to stress the American situation,

> *Minute 519*—May 23, 1851—"The question of the propriety of holding the Annual Meeting of the Society in Exeter Hall with a view of giving prominence to the subject of American Slavery and the Fugitive Slave Law, having been considered, it was resolved that such meeting should be held on the evening of the 21st of July next, if the Hall can be secured for the purpose.
> *Minute 520*—"The draft of a series of Resolutions on Amer. Slav. and the Fug. Slave-Law having been read, it was agreed to consider them as a basis of those to be proposed at the intended public meeting."

Two Americans, at least, had been present at the annual meeting, Elihu Burritt and the Reverend Amos Dresser, the latter from Oberlin, Ohio.

[260] Published in B. & F. A-S. *Reporter*, September 1, 1851, p. 149.

was anti-slavery in his principles, and most of them would there
speak and pray for the downfal [sic] of the unrighteous system.
It is easy to do so there. But a large portion of such men act here
as if they were indifferent or hostile to the cause of freedom. They
do nothing for the abolition of caste or the downfal [sic] of slavery,
but much the other way. Their ecclesiastical connections with
southern ministers, their deference to political men high in office,
their aversion to the Garrison school of abolitionists, their unwillingness to offend rich parishioners in trade with the south or associated in political parties with southern men, are the reasons why
many are silent, equivocal or opposed to the cause of abolition.
Christians on your side the Atlantic can aid us essentially if they
continue to bear decided testimony against slavery, slave-holders,
their apologists, and those who are not out-spoken, *at home*, against
the giant sin of this country.

"To-day I have addressed a letter to Rev. James Sherman
respecting the *abolitionism* of Rev. Mr. Chickering, who lately
appeared at public meetings in London as an American clerical
abolitionist, when he was wholly undeserving of the character.
Judge Darling, also, who was recently received among you as an
anti-slavery man, does nothing in his own country, so far as I can
learn, in aid of the cause.

"I am advised that Rev. John O. Fiske, of Bath, Maine, is now
on his passage to England. A sermon of his has been sent to me
'On the Duty of Obedience to Government,' entitled 'A Thanksgiving Sermon,' preached on the day when so many of our ministers,
with one consent, took the side of Government against the poor
slave, after the passage of the Fugitive Slave Bill; and I have
been urged by friends of the anti slavery cause in the State of
Maine to furnish British abolitionists extracts in proof of the extreme pro-slavery character of the author. The text is, *Let every
soul be subject unto the higher powers*, &c.—a favorite text with
this class of preachers. In allusion to the infamous Bill above-
mentioned he confounds disobedience to it with open resistance,
and argues that men have no right to disobey even such a law as
that. Conscience he avers is not man's final tribunal (guide) 'unless the individual is so enlightened that his conscience teaches him
to obey the law of the land.' But otherwise, 'however conscientious
any one may imagine himself to be, if he resists (or disobeys) government, he is deceived—he resists the ordinance of God, and sins.'

"He says, 'the agitators of the present day, who would break the Constitution and resist the laws of our country, can have no such defence,' as had Daniel and his companions, and Paul & Peter. With respect to the constitutionality of the Fugitive Slave Bill he says, 'there seems to be no more good reason to doubt, than the constitutionality of any law which we have.' He says, 'when called upon to aid in their escape (the fugitive slaves) . . . we ought to refuse.' And further:

" 'It is the law of the land, that upon requisition of the master, on a prescribed form, the fugitive slave *shall be restored,* and that law ought to be obeyed, unless some express, written divine statute to the contrary can be produced. There is no such written statute, to my knowledge in all the word of God. . . . *No written command of God forbidding us to return that slave can be adduced.* The state into which we are called upon to aid in his being returned, is not a state positively and *expressly forbidden any where in the word of God.* . . . Abraham, Isaac and Jacob, and many of the holiest men of old, were owners of slaves, as thousands of sincere Christians at the South are at the present day. . . . The command to 'let the oppressed go free &c.' . . . and others of a similar nature, found in the writings of the prophets, and also of the New Testament, can refer only to such cases of oppression and bondage, and fraud, as were contrary to the laws of the land.'

"He calls abolitionists 'agitators,' 'fanatics'; and moral reformers. He says:

" 'The extreme doctrines of the agitating party of the present day *have been* destructive of order and peace in every age & country where they have obtained currency, and have invariably led to bloodshed and the most barbarous war. The men who have professed to have such a peculiar love of liberty and such a deep hatred of oppression as to lead them to break the laws of their land, have often been found afterwards the most savage, unrelenting butchers and tyrants, under whose crimes the world has ever groaned.'

"He speaks of the evils that would result from a dissolution of the Union, of the wars that would ensue, & adds:

" 'Oh! compared with these evils, slavery, as bad as it is . . . is *a most trifling affair.*' The italics throughout are the author's. He concludes the sermon by eulogizing the politicians & merchants who have held meetings denouncing abolitionists.

"It is consoling to know that a large number of American ministers, of different denominations—and the number is increasing—take high ground against slavery & the abominable Fugitive Slave Bill; and that several eminent jurists allow that, under certain circumstances a citizen may disobey an unconstitutional act. Chief Justice Shepley of the same State with Mr. Fiske, in a recent charge to the Grand Jury, says:

" 'A person may believe that an act of the Legislature is unauthorized by the Constitution of the State, or of the United States; and the inquiry is presented whether he should obey it. . . . After obtaining the best information within his power . . . he may assume the responsibility, disregard the enactment, and abide the consequences.' . . . 'A person may believe that an act of a legislative body, legally passed in accordance with the provisions of the constitution, by which it is governed, is contrary to the laws of God. The inquiry is then presented respecting his duty to obey it. When this has been ascertained clearly . . . the human law is to be disobeyed, and the divine law obeyed. The person is not at liberty to obey the human law.'

"Mr. Justice McLean, also, of the Supreme Court of the United States, in a recent letter, goes further and says:

" 'An unconstitutional act of Congress imposes no obligation on a State or the people of a State, and may be resisted by an individual or a community. No one, I believe, will controvert this.'

"Respectfully your's,

"LEWIS TAPPAN.

"P.S. Rev. Dr. Spring, of this city, has called my attention to the following passage, quoted from *his* Thanksgiving discourse, on the recent Annual Report of the American & Foreign Anti Slavery Report—'If by one prayer I could liberate every slave in the world, I would not dare to offer it.' He says *in the world* should be *in the United States*. The quotation was taken from the newspapers of the day. To a note of inquiry, whether the newspaper report of the sermon was not correct as it was delivered, the reverend gentleman has made no reply. He is welcome to the correction."

"NEW YORK
Nov. 6/51.

"Dear Sir,

"Mr Scoble after a very pleasant visit to us & a profitable one to the Anti-Slavery cause, left yesterday p.m. for Philadelphia, to embark from that port in the Steamer 'The City of Glasgow.' We should have been very glad to have detained him longer.

"The elections are taking place in the different States. So far the success has been on the part of the Democrats and of course against the Whig administration (Mr Fillmore's). The Democrats in *principle* are more friendly to the Anti-Slavery cause than the Whigs, but policy has hitherto restrained them from taking a decided Anti-Slavery part. The leaders of this party have deceived them, and for the sake of obtaining the aid of the Democrats in the Slave States at National elections, have not only betrayed the mass of their party but the interests of the country also. It is hoped that if they obtain a decided ascendancy throughout the country they will be more true to the instincts of freedom than they have hitherto been. But, after all, but little can be expected from political parties, rivaling each other in attempts to strengthen themselves, obtain power & disburse the patronage & money of Government.   "Yours truly,

"Mr Bolton."   "L. TAPPAN.

                              "NEW YORK Nov. 26/51
"My dear friend
                 "I suppose you see the *Liberator* & *Standard* regularly. The latter paper attacks the *Rev. J. S.* accusing him of favoring the expatriation of the col^d. people. Did you throw out anything leaning towards Colonization [261] in your Buffalo [262]

[261] There is one presumably unpublished letter at Denison House that was written by Scoble while he was away bearing upon this. It was written from Buffalo to Bolton and contains a summary of what he has, to date, been able to ascertain about the colored folk in Canada.

Their number, he wrote, "has been variously estimated at from 25,000 to 35,000, the greater portion of whom are fugitive slaves. Of course the male sex greatly preponderate, the wives and sisters of many of them being still in bondage. . . . Since the pressure occasioned by the atrocious fugitive slave law it is said from 10,000 to 12,000 fugitives have entered Canada, driven thither by their fears, or to escape threatened capture, but many of these have returned to the States for various reasons, and have thus exposed themselves anew to the operation of the law. . . ."

He wrote, moreover, in criticism of a sort of dole system, or relief from the United States and of the prejudice in Canada against mixed schools, of the existence of separate churches, and continued,

"At Toronto I fell in with Mr. Weyman Anderson of Jamaica. He has come here as an Agent from the Jamaica Planters, to enquire whether the colored people are willing to emigrate to that Island. He has laid his

Speech? [263] In Mr. Anderson's Speech in this City he is reported to have said, 'It is evident to me that the United States is no proper home for the colᵈ men.' This was an unfortunate expression— being rank Colonization. And in your speech at the Scotch Church you are reported to have said, 'What then is your duty to yourselves & to your children? I say, go where God has evidently placed an open door before you &c.'

"This I wish you had not said, but it does not justify the abuse of the Standard. Knowing your sentiments on Emigration I can not but think you are greatly misrepresented.

"You will perceive that I wrote a short note [264] to the Standard, to correct their base allusion to you & myself in one or two particulars, not caring to undertake your vindication against their other charges, because I supposed you would, if you thot it necessary, attend to the matter yourself.

"I refer you to the Liberator of 21 Nov. p. 1 to an article taken from the *National Era.* How would it do to publish this article, omitting the closing remark of the editor, in the Reporter, with a short Preface to this effect— We take the following excellent article, originally published in the *National Era,* a paper established our readers will recollect, by the Committee of the Amer. & For. Anti-S. Soc. from Mr. Garrison's *Liberator,* who commends it, as well he may, and it is not, by any means, the only terse and strong article that has proceeded from the same source, though we

views upon this subject before them, and so have I mine. . . . Besides Mr. Anderson I find there is another Agent in this country from Trinidad, Mr. N. W. Pollard, but I am satisfied that our colored friends will not move until they know that we are satisfied in England that their condition would be benefitted by removal. . . .''

[262] We assume from the following that Gerrit Smith was instrumental in getting Scoble to visit Buffalo. He had heard at what time Scoble was expected to be in Toronto and wrote,

". . . Can you not my dear Sir, be in Buffalo the week after? The National Liberty Party Convention is to be held in Buffalo 17th & 18th inst. The Convention would be very glad to see your face & hear your voice.

"I scarcely need add, that it would afford me great happiness to see you under my roof
"With great regard,
"Your friend,
"GERRIT SMITH''

(Gerrit Smith to John Scoble, dated Peterboro, September 7, 1851).
[263] For Scoble's Buffalo Speech, see B. & F. A-S. *Reporter,* November 1, 1851, pp. 176–177.
[264] See *The New York Standard,* November 20, 1851, p. 102, for Tappan's letter of defense in favor of Scoble.

have not often seen them transferred, as in this case, to the columns of the Liberator.

"I began this sheet merely as a memo. but I am compelled to send it as a letter.

"I send you a slip from the Standard of Nov. 20th. I have not seen fit to answer it, altho' an invitation, as you will see, is held out to me to do so, thinking that my letter to the Editor is a sufficient answer. If you read it carefully you will see that it cuts in various ways, some of which the sapient editor did not perceive.

"The editorials in the *Standard* about you, from time to time, will do you no injury in this country. Still if you choose to reply to any of them I will, if you desire it, see that the editor has your articles.

"What noble sentiments Kossuth has uttered in England! I fear, however, that Mr. Walker of this country, 'the candidate for Prest of the U.S.' has poisoned his ear, as I perceive the great Exile talks about not meddling with the 'domestic institutions' of any nation. Where could he have got this phrase but from an American Slaveholder!

"Mr. Harned has had Mr. Anderson's Address in the Cold Ch. in this City & yours in Dr. Pennington's Ch. printed in a pamphlet. As they contain the extracts made above I told him it would compromit the A & F Anti-S. Soc. & Am. Miss. Asso. if the pamphlet goes out under a supposition that it has been published by either Society or that they or he are responsible for the sentiments. The free people of Color are very sensitive as well they may be, about anything savoring of Colonization. And anything from you that can be made to look in that direction will be eagerly seized hold of by the Standard, etc.

"Very cordially your's

"John Scoble Esq."   "LEWIS TAPPAN

"NEW YORK,   January 5/52 ²⁶⁵

"JNO SCOBLE ESQ.

    "My dear Friend,

       "I am rejoiced to hear from you. Your letter of Dec. 12th, although it gives me some pain, is gratifying on

---

265 Of the discovered Tappan letters this is the first of a date posterior to the foregoing. Scoble's movements and activities in the interval are best

other accounts. I rejoice to hear of the peaceful and triumphant death of your venerable father. May it be your prayer & mine, 'Let me die the death of the righteous, and let my last end be like his!' Joseph [266] will, I hope, return soon or at least give you evidence that he has come to his right mind. I can imagine how afflictive such conduct must be to affectionate parents. Put your trust in God, my dear friend. Assure Mrs Scoble that I deeply sympathise with her in all her trials. Whom the Lord loveth he

ascertained from the B. & F. A-S. Society *Minute Books* and from some of his own miscellaneous letters. From New York, on the twenty-first of October, he wrote to Peter Bolton about various matters, about the Christian Anti-Slavery Convention that had been held in Chicago, the previous July, about E. Mathews and his letter, about George Thompson and his attacks, about the mutual admiration society which he and Garrison seem to have formed, and, finally, about his own tour through Canada, and his programme while in New York City,

"I may just mention that I have in my tour thro' Canada held a series of meetings exclusively for the people of color. . . . On Monday evening I addressed one of the largest colored meetings ever held in New York. . . . On Thursday evening a meeting has been prepared for me in the City of Brooklyn to address the *elite* of New York society. . . . The meeting will be held in Mr. Beecher's Church. This will be my last effort in this direction. Lewis Tappan arrived yesterday & a meeting of the Executive Comee of the American & Foreign Anti-Slavery Society will be summoned to meet me on Tuesday next—it could not be done earlier—and on the following day (D. V.) I shall embark for Europe."

At the B. & F. A S. Society Committee Meeting, November 29, 1851, he reported on his visit to America and it became matter of record that

"In reference to the free people of Color and fugitive Slaves in Canada, the Secretary gave a variety of details, which he proposes to embody in a Report, and which will be inserted in the Anti-Slavery Reporter for January in the next year, together with suggestions for their social and moral elevation" (*Minute* 562).

At the meeting in early December, December 5, Scoble furnished additional material on Canada and announced, incidentally, that the "present offices, 27 New Broad Street," had, from Christmas day on, been let to the Alta Californian Gold Company (*Minutes* 560, 566). Some American matters were discussed and

"The Committee having considered the proposition of Wm. Lillie of Kelso, relating to the liberation of Messrs Drayton & Sayres now imprisoned in Washington Jail for aiding fugitive slaves to escape felt it would be improper to place an application for their freedom on the grounds proposed" (*Minute* 572).

[266] ". . . very glad to hear you have found poor Joseph & trust he may be in a proper state of mind & that what he has gone through may be of real service to him. . . . I go from home tomorrow & mean to read Lewis Tappan's letter &c. on the road" (Sturge to Scoble, dated Birmingham, January 25, 1852).

chasteneth & scourgeth every son & daughter whom he receiveth. I am happy to learn that both you and your dear wife are disposed to confide implicitly in your Heavenly Father. Joseph may be greatly benefited by contrasting the rough usage he may receive with the kindness of a mother & the faithfulness of a father, and return, an altered person, to cheer & to bless your declining days.

"Should my letter to the *Examiner* be printed I trust that you will clear it of every expression that you think I would do on a more deliberate preparation of it for the press.

"Dr. Campbell's article was coarse & passionate. It is republished here in the religious newspaper where Mr. Chickering resides, & will probably go into the U. S. Observer & kindred papers. How many will be glad to see L. T. humbled, 'his influence destroyed,' &c. Dr. C. should have waited until Mr. C. denied the statements & until I had opportunity to prove their truth. Mr. Sherman has written to me for such evidence. Dr. C. should also have considered that I had made myself responsible for the statements of my informant, & therefore he could not with propriety accuse any one of attacking Mr. Chickering behind a *mask*. Mr. C. wrote to me to know who my informant was. I replied that if he denied the statements he should have a satisfactory answer. He has written again that he has found out who my informant was, and asserts that he is anti-slavery &c &c.[267] The Rev. Austin Willey, editor of the

[267] To the several things mentioned in respect to this unpleasant personal dispute there seems little necessity for individual reference. The general content and the whereabouts of the chief of them are here set forth,

(a)   Letter, May 20, 1851, of the Reverend James Sherman re (to?) Reverend James White Chickering, growing out of certain remarks made by Chickering at a meeting of the Congregational Union, in May, 1851 (*The Patriot*, May 26, 1851, p. 343; B. & F. A.-S. *Reporter*, June 2, 1851, pp. 91–92). Sherman complained that explanations attempted by Chickering were unsatisfactory and went on to say that if the American ministers were as hostile to slavery as they are to intoxicating liquors slavery would disappear. "As a nation, America ranks amongst the most sober and temperate; and on the question of abolition, they would conquer too, if their efforts and example were combined in one contest."

(b) Letter from Lewis Tappan to James Sherman, August 18, 1851. Sherman sent it to *The Patriot* and it was published, occupying over a column of fine print, September 25, 1851, p. 622. Tappan submitted evidence and argument that Chickering "was not and is not" an anti-slavery man, that his prejudice against the African race was conceded, colored people not being welcome in his church. To Sherman himself, he said,
"We thank you and others for taking such a consistent stand, and for your endeavours to discountenance American slaveholders, their apologists, and all who do not cordially advocate the emancipation of the coloured people."

Portland Inquirer, my 'informant,' writes that he will prove **every-**
thing he wrote to me to be true. Mr. Willey is a thorough-going
abolitionist & has long been esteemed as a very reliable man.

(c) *The Patriot,* January 22, 1852, p. 50— Mr. Chickering's defence. A
letter from Lewis Tappan to James Sherman had appeared in *The Patriot*
and *The British Banner,* of which Dr. Campbell was the editor, printed a
reply by Chickering and *The Patriot* inserted it in its January twenty-
second issue. Chickering had asserted that he and nearly all New Eng-
landers are good anti-slavery men, although most of them belong to
neither one of the two American anti-slavery societies.

(d) *The Puritan Recorder,* February 12, 1852, p. 26—Editorial on ''The Banner on Abolition.''
    ''Our readers have been previously informed of an attack, made in
the *British Banner,* by Lewis Tappan, Esq., on Rev. Mr. Chickering, of
Portland, accusing him of many pro-slavery misdemeanors. *The Banner*
of *Jan. 21st,* contains Mr. Chickering's self defence. It is enough to
say of this, that it is perfectly satisfactory to the editor of *The Banner,*
who has been sufficiently predisposed to make us all pro-slavery, with the
exception of a few of the most distinguished abolitionists, he, like most
of our brethren in England, having failed to make just discrimination in
the case.'' The writer of the editorial goes on to say of Tappan, ''Even
with truth on his side he would not make a distinguished figure; but as
an advocate of error, the hope is forlorn.''

(e) *The Christian Mirror* of Portland, Maine, February 17, 1852, pp. 114–115.
A resumé of the case, republishing the whole article from *The British
Banner,* including in it, Lewis Tappan's letter to the editor, December
18, 1851 and Chickering's letter of the same date, also a letter from
Amos N. Freeman, Pastor of the Colored Congregational Church in Portland, also a separate note from Chickering on the evidence collected by
Tappan from thirteen people that Tappan looked up in Maine. In this
note, Chickering said (p. 115),
    ''. . . I accept the main point to which they tend, as truth; and I
might easily have spared my indefatigable friend, Mr. Tappan, the trouble
of his explorations, by admitting it, if called upon, in advance. It is
simply, that I am not found *in their ranks* in supposed furtherance of the
cause of emancipation; do not appear at politico-religious anti-slavery
conventions; and am in short a 'pro-slavery' man, in Mr. Tappan's sense
of the term, agreed to by himself as such, and claimed to be an allowable
use of the English tongue; viz., one opposed at heart to slavery and expressing that opposition, but not in the way judged by certain others to be
suitable and consistent.''
    Dr. Campbell's comment upon Tappan's refusal to give the name of
his informant or of Chickering's accusers comprised his characterization
of Tappan's methods as Star Chamber procedure and his dissent (p. 114).
    ''We disapprove of the uncourteous, the ungenerous, the unfair, the
unjust, the false, the base, the cruel, under any circumstances. Uttered
by a masked mouth, they are abominable; and when with open face by an
otherwise reputable citizen, still the matter is but slightly mended, since
what is gained to courage is lost to decency. As night is the appropriate
element of the bat and the owl, of every foul and hateful bird, so is darkness of calumny, slander, and falsehood.''

(f) *The Puritan Recorder,* March 11, 1852, pp. 41–42—Tappan's defence
against Dr. Campbell and Mr. Chickering. The *Recorder* printed this
letter of Lewis Tappan's, despite its objectionable tone,
    ''We are somewhat amused by Mr. Tappan's assurance, in **saying**

"I presume you see the *Standard* regularly. If so, you will have noticed the Note I addressed to the editor respecting the notices of the Brooklyn meeting. No one, not even the editor, probably believes now that you had anything to do with the notices. As to the other accusations of the Standard respecting you, I have not thought it worth while to write anything, altho' the editor of that paper threw out an invitation to me to do so.

"You will have seen our Address to Kossuth & his Reply. The Standard abused me, for the Letter that accompanied the Address, and a few persons—some of the Garrison School & some friendly to our Society, have objected to the tenor of the Address. Like your

that it would be no attack upon us, to say that we never favored the cause of emancipation, and expecting us to feel bound to publish the slander.'' In his letter, Tappan reviewed the entire controversy, saying that Dr. Campbell was now in possession of the full case against Mr. Chickering, with all of the accumulated evidence, but that nothing had been published to date.

(*g*)   *The Christian Mirror*, April 20, 1852, pp. 149–150—a long Tappan letter, a defence by Chickering, and an editorial. The editorial is plainly on Chickering's side,
     ''. . . from his (Tappan's) method of presenting his 'argument,' we saw no prospect of the controversy ever reaching a termination. He spreads himself out so far on every side to obtain data for his deductions; the amount of argument being so lamentably disproportionate to the words employed, . . . that we shrunk from the task imposed on us.
     ''Moreover, his object appeared to us most odious— . . . to convict a Christian minister of acting a double part, when the contrary had already been demonstrated; . . . .''

(*h*)   *The Christian Mirror*, April 27, 1852, pp. 153–154—
     ''He (Mr. Chickering while in England) was obviously understood to mean, that the churches and ministers of New England, aside from Mr. Garrison and his friends, were zealously engaged in anti-slavery labors— preaching, praying, talking, voting, and earnestly prosecuting the enterprise with the same zeal and devotedness that the majority of them enlist in the cause of temperance and missions. He was also understood to intimate that *he*, though not a member of any anti-slavery or abolition society, was so faithful and out-spoken in the glorious work that the reproof of the English minister, however applicable to many of his clerical countrymen, had no application to him!'' (*Letter of Lewis Tappan*, April 27, 1852.)

(*i*)   *The Christian Mirror*, May 4, 1852, pp. 157–158—A long Tappan summary, also a final statement from Chickering.
     ''If my friends wonder that I deemed any reply or explanation necessary, I can only say that it is my first personal experience of the operations of that 'philanthropy' which has stabbed at so many better men; and I may in time learn to bear such blows in silence.'' Chickering was examined, so he affirmed, by a committee of the Congregational Union to see whether the body from which he came had ever favored slavery or sustained the Fugitive Slave Act. An editorial, p. 158, ended the matter by deciding for Chickering and against Tappan.

James Haughton [268] they wished we should endeavor to attach Kossuth to us, even if it defeated him in the great objects of his visit to this Country. We cannot please everybody.[269] Men look at things thro' different mediums. But I am happy to say that a very large portion of the anti-slavery people of this Country approve both the Address & Letter. I enclose a more correct version of Kossuth's reply than you have seen. How blind is any one not to see that such an Address, with such a Reply, will not do great good to the Anti-Slavery cause!

"Mr. Chickering rather taunted me about a suit that has been on trial here against me since you left. It was a suit for a Libel, brought by a trader in Ohio, in consequence of what he called defamatory statements respecting him & his mercantile business on the books of my Mercantile Agency. When I sold my establishment, nearly three years since, I took a Bond of Indemnity from my successor, against such claims & liabilities. The suit in question therefore, altho' against me in form was virtually against my suc-

---

[268] How Sturge tried to reason with the Irishman, James Haughton, is to be, in a measure, inferred from the following:

"I have been corresponding with James Haughton about his letter he is not willing to withdraw it but as thou wilt see by the enclosed . . . he thanks me for my suggestions & has altered it in respect to any personal imputations—he wishes that it should be inserted as he now sends it—I hope thou wilt therefore let it go in—and at the same time I think I should insert the address itself and after that the extract which I sent thee of Lewis Tappans letter . . . except the first line which alludes to Jas Haughtons previous letter (to?) Kossuth. It might be headed somewhat in this way—We do not offer any remarks ourselves either upon the address itself or Jas. Haughtons letter upon it which James Haughton has felt it his duty to send us for publication but we think it right to insert the following extract which as (*sic*) been furnished us by Jos. Sturge from a letter he has recently recᵈ from Lewis Tappan in reference to the views which induced the Committee of the A. & F. Anti-Slavery Society to take the course they did.

"... ."

(P. S.) "Please let the Paragraph of Lewis Tappan's letter begin at 'If Kossuth were visiting different countries etc.' "

(Sturge to Scoble(?), January 23, 1852.)

[269] Some critics, *e.g.*, a Baltimore newspaper, attributed to the A. & F. A-S. Society a peculiar motive for favoring Kossuth, the wish to establish a precedent for interference in the internal affairs of other countries. Tappan himself had said (letter to the Editor of the *Commonwealth*, December 20, 1851, printed in *The National Era*, January 1, 1852, p. 2), in explanation of the Kossuth "Address" and "Letter," that what had been done had been done without any idea of evasion but at the request of the Hungarian patriot himself that he might not be involved in the anti-slavery controversy in any way whatsoever.

cessor. The counsel on the side of the Plaintiff were 'Union Safety' men, and did all they could to inflame the minds of the Jury, so that a large verdict was rendered—£2000. An appeal is taken to a higher court. The Plaintiff, during the trial made, thro' his counsel, an overture for a settlement & would gladly have taken £200, in addition to his Counsel's fees & the costs. I might have avoided the suit by disclosing the name of my correspondent in Ohio, but this I would not do. The mercantile community here are indignant at such a verdict & the extraordinary verdict is a matter of amusement to all. No doubt my abolition sentiments had a good deal to do with the matter.

"Receive, my dear friend, assurances of my continued friendship & best wishes, & offer to Mrs Scoble on behalf of my family & myself the kindest regards.

"Affec". yours
"L. TAPPAN

"It is not improbable that some persons in England may publish the result of the Libel suit to prejudice the British public against me. If so I leave it to you to make needful explanations.

"I thank you for the Kossuth [270] pamphlet & for Baird's [271] also."

"NEW YORK, Feb. 7/52.

"My dear friend Scoble,

"Since my letter to you of Jan' 5th I have nothing from you except a slip containing our Address to Kossuth & his Reply. The Standard, Liberator, etc. complimented Judge Jay as the author of the Address & abused me as the author of the Letter, when the fact was I wrote the Address & Judge Jay the Letter. But this *inter nous*. (*sic*)

[270] Kossuth landed in New York, Dec. 5, 1851. Before leaving England the Edinburgh Emancipation Society and the B. & F. A.-S. Society had supplied him with materials on American slavery. The former body had adopted an address asking him, as the friend of *universal liberty*, to help the cause of the slave. B. & F. A.-S. *Reporter*, Dec. 1, 1851, pp. 197–198.

[271] Possibly one of these, more probably the second of them, the third being seemingly out of the question.

Baird, Robert, *Impressions and Experiences of the West Indies and North America in 1849* (Philadelphia, 1850).

——, *The Progress and Prospects of Christianity in the United States of America; with remarks on the subject of slavery in America; and on the intercourse between British and American Churches* (London, 1851).

——, *State and Prospects of Religion in America* (1855).

"I have been interested in your account of your Visit to Canada. I notice that at the head of the 2^d Col. page 1st you say 'no white American would sit with them,' & that in the same paragraph you say, you except 'a large number of Americans &c.' In the Reporter of Decr. I think you copy from Douglass' papers in which he speaks of the prejudice abating on the public roads &c. Everywhere now in New England Colored men & women can travel on the Cars without molestation.

"About the middle of January I went to Augusta, Maine, about 400 miles from here, with a view to inquire into the facts in relation to Rev. J.W. Chickering at Portland and to attend a Religious Anti Slavery Convention at Augusta, the capital of the State. The result of inquiries respecting Mr. Chickering confirmed substantially what I wrote last August to Rev. Jas. Sherman respecting him. By this opportunity I have put both Dr. Campbell & Mr Sherman in possession of the facts in the case.

"I shall send you a copy of the *Portland Inquirer* of the 5th containing a report of the doings of the Convention at Augusta if I can. Should you not receive it by this vessel Mr Sherman will have a copy. I hope you will copy the Resolutions &c into the Reporter.

"The *Tribune* published the other day a notice of the death of James G. Birney with a statement that he had lately published an Address [272] to the Colored People advising them to emigrate to Liberia! Mr B. is in usual health I am assured, but he has written such an Address which many of his old friends much regret. He is stedfast with respect to his anti slavery sentiments & his estimate of the Amer. Colonization Society, but considering the hostility to free col^d people, & the condition of Jamaica, Canada & Liberia he prefers the latter for the col^d people & advises them to go there. Colonizationists will make a great deal of this Address & it will add to the weight that is well nigh crushing the poor blacks. If we give up the contest for the free col^d people, if they give it up, the cause of the slave is hopeless. The great battle for Freedom can

---

[272] *The New York Daily Tribune*, February 2, 1852, p. 4, published, in an editorial, an announcement of J. G. Birney's death at Saginaw, Michigan; of a Colonization pamphlet, then in press at Cincinnati; also of the distressing fact—distressing, that is, to the abolitionists—that, in 1844, Birney and Henry B. Stanton had assured the election of Polk by working for the Liberty Party, thus dealing anti-slavery a blow from which it could not recover—traitors to their own cause.

not, it would seem, be successfully waged unless the colored people
'abide in the ship.' If the wicked prejudice that weighs them
down is invincible, if they are to be driven out of the country, if
the nation is to continue impenitent on this great subject, what
can we expect from the Almighty but his frown & indignation.
His retributive justice is more to be feared that (sic) all the injury
that can arise to the country from the continuance of the blacks here
& the continued struggle for the emancipation of the slaves.

"Very truly your
"L. TAPPAN.

"P.S. Have you any intelligence respecting your Son?
What has become of my letter to the Bristol Examiner?
You have learned ere this that the letter from the Austrian
Minister to Webster was a jeu d'esprit. It was by a corre-
spondent of Wright's *Commonwealth*.
I send you a *Tribune* containing extracts from Mr Birney's
address."

For the B. and F. Anti Slavery Reporter.
Kossuth and the A. and F. Anti Slavery Society.

"To JAMES HAUGHTON, ESQ. Dublin—
"Dear Sir:—Your note in the *Reporter* expressing
'disapprobation of the course pursued by the American and Foreign
Anti-Slavery Society, in their communication with M. Kossuth,'
has been published in several of the anti-slavery papers in this
country. It is evident that you, as well as others, are under some
misapprehension on the subject. There are professed abolitionists
who seem to take satisfaction in misrepresenting the matter; and
when their error is pointed out they persist in it. Not so with you,
however, for I feel assured that your candour and good sense are
such that the truth will not be shut from your eyes if it can be
fairly presented.
"The Executive Committee adopted an Address to Kossuth,
and a Delegation presented it with a Letter, both of which have
been published in the Reporter. You do not intimate whether you
disapprove the Address or the Letter, or both; but I presume it is
the latter, because I have not seen a word of censure with reference
to the former. You ask, 'Why, then, should an Anti-Slavery Society volunteer to relieve him from the necessity of taking a part,

either for or against the colored man?' And you intimate that
the Delegation, in their Letter (if you, as I suppose, alluded only
to the Letter) did volunteer to relieve Kossuth from taking such
part, and that the course was 'an unjustifiable one.' BUT THE
DELEGATION HAD NO INTENTION OF SAYING ANYTHING TO RELIEVE
KOSSUTH IN THE PREMISES, NOR DID THEY SAY ANYTHING TO HIM TO
THAT EFFECT. They simply told him, they did not expect *any reply
to the Address,* and the reason given was, that in the opinion of
some it might seem to involve him with one of the parties in this
country. Though thus relieved, if he saw fit, from making *a reply
to the Address,* he was left quite free to express his opinions, in
other ways, on the subject of American Slavery.

"The anti-slavery sentiments expressed by the distinguished
Hungarian in his own country, and in England, were so excellent
that the Committee, while paying their tribute to the Exile, thought
it a fit occasion to give wide circulation to them in that way, and
at the same time observe proper courtesy in view of the errand that
had brought him to this land. We may have erred, but these are
the FACTS, and though, misunderstood by some, and misrepresented
by others, have been appreciated by large numbers of the uncompromising friends of liberty. Thanking you for the kind construction you have given to the motion of the Delegation, and assuring
you that they are not behind any others in sincerely aiming to
'promote the cause of emancipation,' at home and abroad, I remain
dear Sir

"Very respectfully your's
"LEWIS TAPPAN
"One of the Delegation."

"NEW YORK, 7 feb. 1852

"My dear Sir,

"Your note of 12/12/51 was duly recᵈ. I am glad
to learn that you made so good a use of the Reports.

"I thank you for the English papers you have sent from time
to time. Hereafter please direct them to me instead of Mr. Harned,
except the Reporters for distribution here.

"I have not seen British Banner since Nov. 26. If anything
has appeared, or will appear, relating to Mr. Chickering or myself
will you send me the papers? Also anything of importance relat-

ing to the Anti-S. cause either in pamphlets or newspapers; and please keep a memo of the expense, which I shall be glad to pay.

"Very truly yours
"LEWIS TAPPAN

"P. J. Bolton, Esq.
London"

"NEW YORK, March 2/52.

"John Scoble, Esq
"My dear friend,

"On the 28 feb. I rec'd a copy of my letter to the Editor of the British (Bristol?) Examiner, in pamphlet form, with your neat & appropriate introduction. I feel under great obligation to you for what you have done in the matter. Probably you will send some copies to me for distribution here. Should not [MS. damaged] Committee be at the expense of printing the pamphlet? I have . . . .

"But I turn to a matter of more importance. On the 7th Feb. I sent Dr Campbell, editor of the British Banner, a reply to his articles of Nov. 26th. On the 11th, after reading the Banner of January 21st. I wrote a joint letter to Messrs Sturge [273] & Sherman & yourself, enclosing copies of my printed letter &c., requesting you three gentlemen to do the needful, as, after such reiterated abuse from Dr. C. I could not address him again. Feb. 20th. I wrote again to Mr. Sturge, intending the letter for your & Mr Sherman's perusal also.

"Nothing has ever tried my feelings so much, during the last nine years, as the extraordinary, unjustifiable and injurious conduct of Dr. Campbell; and no blow has ever been inflicted on the anti slavery cause in this country equal to this brutal attack by a professed friend. Personally I feel it as an unprovoked & wanton insult, one calculated to injure me not only in England but in this country, to cause not only the Garrison party to exult, but also

[273] Extracts from Sturge letters—

"I am obliged by thine of yesterday and am glad thou hast succeeded so well or art likely to succeed with Dr. C—it is more than I expected but mind as he does not yet give it the slip— I conclude thou wilt write L. Tappan the particulars by Friday's Mail— I fear I shall hardly have time to write him . . ." (Joseph Sturge to John Scoble, March 10, 1852).

". . . I have a letter from Lewis Tappan in which he expresses himself well satisfied with the steps taken in Dr. Campbells matter which I am glad of— He wishes to have a copy of Webb & Quincys pamphlett . . ." (same to same, July 17, 1852).

every pro-slavery press and minister in this country. Mr Chickering, a man who has been an opponent of the anti-slavery enterprise
in this country from his settlement in the ministry, is shielded &
upheld by Dr. C. while those who told the truth about him are
abused & vilified by this British editor & abolitionist! And abused
in language as coarse as the N.Y. Herald has ever employed against
the abolitionists of this country.

"Then look at the almost ludicrous position Dr. C. has placed
himself in without seeming to know it. He holds me up to ridicule
and contempt, while he eulogises the Society of which I am Secretary, and the officers & members of it who agree with me in sentiment; and after his tirade against me he turns to Mr. Garrison &
his party, pourtraying them as infidels &c. in concurrence with my
letter to the British Examiner!! What effect has all this upon the
pro-slavery editors & ministers of this country? Why simply this
—Dr. C. comes out against both the Garrison party and the A. &
For. Anti S. Soc.—vituperating both—and vindicates Mr. Chickering and those who agree with him, as the Simon Pure abolitionists
of the U.S. After this, from 'the Coryphœus of the Congregational
Body in England,' as one of our religious newspapers has recently
called him, what are we to expect, in the way of Co-operation,
henceforth, from the ministers of England. And after such in-
discriminate articles in the Banner, what influence will Dr C's
editorials on American Slavery have here with either the Garrison
party or the members of the A & F. Anti S. Society?

"I might have written thus to Dr. C.; I might have reasoned
with him; have endeavored to show him the wrong position he has
taken—but of what use—cui bono? So wrong-headed & ill-tem-
pered has he seemed to be that it would probably have only re-
kindled his wrath, and provoked him to pour forth another stream
of abuse. One of our anti-slavery brethren here says, perhaps Dr
C. will see his error, magnanimously confess it, and come out
against Mr. Chickering in a way he deserves. Perhaps he may,
but I confess I have little expectation of it. A man who can view
the subject as he has done with the evidence before him, has not, I
fear, magnanimity & Christian principle enough to make the
amende honorable, acknowledge that he has been deceived by his
friend Chickering and that he has injured the anti slavery cause
by his hasty & violent defence and attack. If, however, he should
view the matter in its true light, and as Mr. Finney predicted of

him, 'turn right about,' he will entitle himself to the thanks of Christian abolitionists in this country.

"Placed in the awkward situation I was, and precluded by self-respect from writing again to Dr C. all I could do was to write to you, Mr Sturge & Mr Sherman to confer together & do, in the premises, what truth and justice required, not merely or chiefly for my sake, but for the sake of the cause of which in this matter I have been made the representative. I wait impatiently to hear from you what Dr C. decided to do on receiving my letter to him with the documents, and what the trio, my approved good friends & the consistent & long-tried friends of the slave, resolved to do in case Dr C. persevered in the wrong course he had pursued.

"Think of Dr C. publishing Jan. 21st the note from me, intended for a private note, and then blaming me in such opprobrious terms because I made such a meagre apology for myself!

"Mr. Willey has been extremely anxious that I should write for his paper respecting Mr. C and Dr C., but I have kept back & kept him back until we heard from you. I have written one letter to the editor of the Portland *Christian Mirror* who copied Dr. C's article of Jan 21st. & a letter to the editor of the Boston Puritan Recorder, who published an abstract of it. Neither, as yet, have published my letter. They may refuse to do it. They will be glad to co-operate with Dr C. in abusing us. Dr C. and the pro-slavery editors here united to crush the Christian abolitionists of the U.S. and uphold the pro-slavery ministers!!!

"But my time is out.

"Dont publish this letter. You can make what use you please, otherwise, of its contents.

"Let me hear from you soon & fully.

"Ever & truly your's
"LEWIS TAPPAN

"Dont be discouraged in reading this because in my hurry it is so imperfect."

"NEW YORK, April 10th 1852

"My dear Friend, Scoble,

"Day before yesterday I rec^d yours of the 26th March, with the *Banner*. I feel under obligations to you, Mr. Sherman & Mr. Sturge for all you have done respecting this Chickering controversy. Had it not been for public considerations I could not have

spent so much time upon him or Dr. C.   If Chickering triumphs in
the matter all our dough-faced ministers will find access to your
Anti-Slavery Platforms.   You ask who Ray Palmer is?   He is just
such a man as Mr. Chickering.   No one ever dreamt that he was
Anti-Slavery in any proper sense.   He was predecessor to Mr.
Fiske of Bath of whom I wrote you last year.—the man who [274]

"Dr. C. is aiming to make it appear that Chickering & those
(who) agree with him, are the conservative & reliable anti-slavery
men of the U. S.!   Well, they will laugh in their sleeves at the
gullibility of John Bull.

"I felt ashamed of Dr. C's praise, in such a connection.   It is
more mortifying than his censure.   I hope & trust you will oblige
him to make a manly & full acknowledgement, and a fair presentation of the facts, or act independently of his paper & publish the
facts far and wide.

"I have availed myself of your hint & by this opportunity
forward my no. 1 to the Ed. of the London Patriot.   It gives a
history of the Anti-Slavery parties in this country & their present
position & principles, arranging Dr Spring &c where they belong,
and Chickering, Palmer &c where they belong.   In my next number I shall examine Mr. Chickering's pretensions &c.

"Then you have determined on emigration! [275]   Well, my dear
friend, I hope & pray that the step may be for the welfare of your

[274] Sentence unfinished in the original.

[275] Scoble would seem not to have communicated his plans to his colleagues
in England until the meeting of the B. & F. A-S. Society Committee, June 4,
1852, when he announced his intention to emigrate to Canada and settle "in
some central position among the colored refugees in Canada West."—A sub-
committee was appointed "to confer with him with a view of ascertaining
whether his conclusion be final, and if they find that to be the case, further to
confer with him" (*Minute Books*, III, minute 626).   That Scoble was serious
in the matter his friends soon discovered.   Several letters passed between him
and Sturge about it, the subjoined being one of them,

"I sent the sketch which thou rewrote in reference to thy removal to
Canada to Robt. Forster (as I understand Josiah was from home) for his
remarks or approval and asked him to apply to S. Gurney & Dr. Lushington
to be on the Committee but have not yet any reply from him & I write him
again by this post— I have a note from Josiah Forster from Tindal in
which he says he had enccuraged thee to write a full statement of the
reasons which had induced thee to conclude to remove to Canada— I
quite approve of this suggestion and hope thou wilt do so.   A good deal
of our pecuniary success depends upon S. G. & his family circle cordially
approving the step— I conclude that thou art still looking to the latter
end of next month as the time for you to leave" (Sturge to Scoble, July
17, 1852).

little family. It will be exceedingly pleasant to have you on this continent & yet I feel that you will be a great loss to the Anti-Slavery & Peace associations. My family are well & desire kind regards to you, Mrs Scoble & all your children. We rejoice with you in your domestic affairs.

"Ver[y] truly your's
"L. Tappan

"How ready Dr. C. is to publish R. Palmer's letter—giving it full credence—while he abuses me for writing to Mr. Sherman—R. P. must be believed of course!

We are preparing for the anniversary—Shall not write a long Report—We expect a good meeting.

It was thought best, on the whole, that Mr. Goodell [276] should take his History & [277] . . . & publish it on his own account. He was on the whole desirous of doing this. Please remember me cordially to Mr. Sherman.

We have in the press an Address,[278] written by Judge Jay, to circulate among anti-slavery men & I will send you a copy, if I can by this opportunity."

For the B. and F. Anti-Slavery Reporter.

AMERICAN SLAVERY AND AMERICAN MINISTERS.

To the Editor of the Reporter:

In your paper of October 1st. 1851 was published my letter to Rev. James Sherman, respecting Rev. J. W. Chickering of this country, a "pro-slavery" minister, who, at the meeting of the Congregational Union, last June, assumed the character of an American abolitionist, in fact if not in name. The Editor of *The British Banner,* published the letter November 26th., with upwards of two columns of editorial strictures upon myself and the individual who had given me the facts respecting Mr. Chickering. You will recollect that I informed Mr. Sherman that Mr. Chickering

---

[276] William Goodell had already published various things connected with the anti-slavery cause; *e.g., Views of American Constitutional Law, in Its Bearing upon American Slavery* (New York, 1844). *Come-outerism: The Duty of Secession from a Corrupt Church* (Boston, 1845).

[277] Goodell, William, *Slavery and Anti-Slavery, a History of the Great Struggle in Both Hemispheres; with a View of the Slavery Question in the United States* (New York, 1852).

[278] Judge William Jay, *An Address to the Antislavery Christians of the United States.*

was "not an Abolitionist, has never favoured the cause of emancipation, and has been considered a conservative and pro-Slavery man." The *Banner* took exceptions to this, and said, "We, then, pin Mr. Tappan down to this description, since it involves the integrity of a man eminent among the churches of New England." *In opposition to this, we now place the declaration of Mr. Chickering, his written, spoken declaration, made in our hearing, both in public and in private, in Great Britain!* The *Banner* complains that I had quoted the testimony of persons without giving their names, rung the changes upon "men in the *mask*," and called upon me to give the names of my Correspondents. To stimulate my zeal, the editor doubted "the propriety of the compliment implied in the language of Mr. Sherman towards Mr. Tappan," when he called him his "honoured friend"; stated that I had opened "the vials of vituperation, that he (I) may pour them out on the hapless head of Mr. Chickering"; that I had armed myself "with the testimony of the anonymous skulker"; that "mask whispers into the ear of mask, and mask supplies a missile to Mr. Tappan, who hurls it across the Atlantic into the character (reputation) of Mr. Chickering!" Also, "Mr. Tappan has a wonderful taste for the mask," and "deep, indeed, will be our disappointment if he (Mr. Chickering) be not in a position to read Mr. Tappan a lesson which will be long remembered."

On receipt of this extraordinary editorial—I will not call it "vials of vituperation"—it seemed to me rather odd that the erudite editor should be so excited at my omitting to give the name of a Correspondent, whose letter I had quoted in my letter to Mr. Sherman, since I had, by giving my own name, made myself responsible, and thus wore no "mask." It was of no consequence to English readers who my informant was, since I had used his language as my own. But I went deliberately and calmly to work to ascertain the truth of the statements, since they had been denied so authoritatively by the editor of the *Banner*. December 8th Mr. Chickering wrote to me for the name of my informant. I replied that if he *denied* the truth of his statements he should be promptly satisfied on that point. The editor of the *Banner* has called this "absolute trifling—a discreditable evasion." December 30th Mr. Chickering wrote that he had learned that Rev. Austin Willey was the individual, and he, at the same time denied the truth of his statements to me. Determined on making personal investigation I went to the State of Maine, saw Mr. Chickering, attended a State Religious Convention, and made thorough inquiries respecting the course Mr. C. had pursued, as to the Slavery question, the past sixteen years. Eleven gentlemen, some of them of high standing, gave their written testimony. Prefaced by a letter I sent the whole, for convenience, in printed form, to the editor of the *Banner*, presuming that, as an act of justice and fair-dealing, he would lay my letter and the evidence, or the substance of them, at once, before his readers.

Within two or three days after I had transmitted my letter the *Banner* of January 21ˢᵗ. arrived. In it appeared Mr. Chickering's DEFENCE, with a short letter of mine to the editor, not written for publication, and another editorial blast. Mr. Chickering is pronounced by the editor "a much better Anti-Slavery man than we thought him." The course I had pursued is styled "extraordinary, and every-way indefensible," and it is said, "the case of Mr. Chickering is complete, and will give intense satisfaction to the bulk of the British people into whose hands it may come." As for myself the editor says, "he is certainly not a very good reasoner," and of my private letter, published by him as my defence, it is said, "a letter more meagre, more unmanly, more ungenerous, more unjust, and, on all points, more pitiful or contemptible, it was never our lot to receive or read." And the editor says, "did we not dare Mr. Tappan to the proof?" Well satisfied that, after such outpourings, there was no probability that the editor would, on the receipt of the evidence which he had *dared* me to produce, publish it promptly and fairly in his paper, I immediately transmitted to three friends of truth and freedom, in England, copies of my letter & the accompanying testimony, requesting them to see the editor of the *Banner*, and if he would not publish the evidence he had challenged me to produce, publish it themselves, so extensively that the readers of the *Banner*, and all persons concerned, would see it.

My letter to the editor of the *Banner* must have reached him about the 18ᵗʰ February, but not a word was said about it by him until March 24ᵗʰ., when, instead of publishing my letter and the evidence accompanying it the editor published a long letter from Rev. Ray Palmer, of Albany, in the State of New York, formerly of Bath, Maine, and a personal friend of Mr. Chickering, in defence of that gentleman. In that letter the editor is complimented for his "exceeding thorough and caustic, but certainly just, castigation of Mr. Lewis Tappan,'' and he publishes this from a pro-slavery friend of Mr. Chickering, personally unknown to him, while he suppresses testimony from me that had been in his possession upwards of a month, demonstrating that what I had said of Mr. C. was true, and that he was wholly undeserving of the reputation of an abolitionist, nay of an anti-slavery man in any proper sense of the term! Neither Mr. Chickering nor Mr. Palmer have ever been recognised as practical friends or advocates of the anti-slavery cause, and yet the editor of the *Banner,* a professed abolitionist, allows them to rebuke me and through me, virtually the American and Foreign Anti-Slavery Society, and the associated anti-slavery men of this country, who all sympathise with me in the representations made respecting the position of Mr. Chickering, and those who think & act with him on the subject of American Slavery. Is this British justice? Is this affording help to the abolitionists in the United States who are engaged in the death-struggle for the overthrow of Slavery? Is it fair treatment in any point of view?

The editor of the *Banner,* in introducing Mr. Palmer's letter, so full of sophistry and misrepresentation, adopts a somewhat milder tone, almost mortifies me by mixing up his compliments with censure, and suggests that he may publish, some time or other, an abstract or extract from the ''enormous epistle to ourselves,'' notwithstanding ''the blunders with which he (myself) has been chargeable.'' He intimates, at the same time, that if he does this, he is prepared to say more ''hard things'' of me. He, also, thinks he now understands the question, so far as it relates to this country; that ''there are three parties—the Garrison on the one hand, and the Tappan, or American Anti-Slavery Society on the other, and between both, Mr. Chickering, and the men of moderation, but of principle.'' Mr. Garrison ''with a band of infuriated adversaries to the Gospel''; Mr. Lewis Tappan and his friends, who are a somewhat motley multitude of men of divers creeds, but all professing a regard for religion''; and Messrs. Chickering and Palmer, and men of like stamp, who compose the great, conservative, reliable anti-slavery host of the United States! The editor should be informed that it is not ''Mr. Lewis Tappan and his friends'' who belong to the American Anti-Slavery Society, but Mr. Garrison and his party, while the great body of Christian abolitionists in this country belong to the American & Foreign Anti-Slavery Society, of which I have the honor to be Corresponding Secretary. The "motley multitude of men of divers creeds, but all *professing* a regard for religion" are Judge Jay, Arthur Tappan, Samuel Fessenden, S. S. Jocelyn, F. Julius Le Moyne, Abraham Pennock etc. —Episcopalians, Presbyterians, Congregationalists, and Friends— evangelical Christians sympathising with the Gurneys, Forsters, Hintons, Staceys, Sturges, Carliles, Burnets and Buxtons of England.

Thus much I have thought it my duty to say to the readers of the *Reporter,* whether the editor of the *Banner* has, or may see fit, to publish a *digest* of the evidence sent him or not. They ought to know the facts in the case, and to be assured that injury is done by English abolitionists to the cause of freedom in this country, rather than aid extended, by blind, undiscriminating censure of American abolitionists and undeserved approbation bestowed upon men among us who have no heart in the cause.

LEWIS TAPPAN.

"MR. SCOBLE

"In great haste I have prepared this article for your paper. Correct any error.   "Yours affec^{ly}

"New York, April 21/52."   "L. TAPPAN.

"NEW YORK, 8th May, 1852.

"JOHN SCOBLE, ESQ.

"My dear friend,

"Yours of April 23d. was rec^d. yesterday; you see therefore that, should I send you soon an Abstract of our Annual Report, it could not reach you by the 17th. Besides, although I finished the Report yesterday an abstract of it is not yet made. I would enclose you a copy of the Resolutions to be offered, but they have not yet had the concluding emendations of the Committee.

"Our anniversary is to be held (D. V.) on Tuesday next, May 11th. at the Broadway Tabernacle, at 3pm. Judge Jay is expected to preside. The Speakers will be Rev. Henry Ward Beecher, Rev. John S. Raymond (an estimable col^d. Baptist preacher in this City) and Hon. E. D. Culver, late member of Congress from Washington Co. N.Y., who is also a member of our Ex. Com. We expect a large audience & an interesting anniversary.

"Dr. Campbell's 'Digest' is exceedingly unfair, & the whole article adds insult to injury, & shows a recklessness that is truly astonishing. It omits much, in the testimony, that shows Mr. Chickering's pro-slavery character.

"I send you the *Christian Mirror* of April 20 & 27 and May 4th. in which you will see 3 of my articles on Mr. Chickering's Anti-Slavery, with his comments & the strictures of the editor, who is a man like the editor of the *N. Y. Observer*. He is J. W. C's intimate friend, Par nobile fratrum. The paper containing my no. 1 is not at hand. It contained a copy of my letter to Mr. Sherman, the origin of this controversy, & some introductory remarks. I shall be glad to have Messᵣˢ Sherman & Sturge see these papers, after you have read them. Both the *Mirror* & J. W. C. seem to take it for granted that if it can be proved that J. W. C. is acceptable to Dr. C., and an anti-slavery man, in *his* estimation, the case is decided in his favor! But Dr. C. has shown that he is no more anti-slavery than is J. W. C., while his manners are far inferior.

"Mr. Sturge writes, April 23d that he had advised that the whole of my little pamphlet shd be published in London, with a suitable introduction. If you & Mr. Sherman concurred it has probably been done ere this, & therefore it is unnecessary for me to make farther suggestions. Your Preface will, I hope, supply the deficiences of the bastard 'Digest,' and present both Dr. C. & J. W. C. in a true aspect. I hope this publication will be made, for other reasons because in my printed letters to the *Mirror* I intimate that it has been done. If it be not done J. W. C. & the Mirror will exult more than they now do. If, on receipt of this, your Introduction or Preface is not completed, I beg you to be faithful, bold and thorough. The copies of the *Mirror* I now send you will help somewhat & the materials you will have are sufficient to enable you to place the matter in a right point of view. J. W. C. affect to exult very much, sustained as they are by Dr. C. I have not words to express my abhorrence of his shuffling, evasive, illogical & inexcusable course.

"The remarks you make about your family &c interest me very much. May the Lord guide & bless you all.

"Truly & affec^y your's

"Lewis Tappan

"I am writing a few off-hand letters in the *National Era,* signed *Manhattan* ²⁷⁹—*inter nous.*"

---

²⁷⁹ In the *National Era* there are a number of letters that would seem, judged by internal evidence, to be of Tappan authorship. Some are not signed

"NEW YORK, June 15/52.

"PETER J. BOLTON, ESQ.,

"My dear Sir,

"I am indebted to you for sundry London newspapers. The *Patriot* of May 20ᵗʰ was recᵈ. containing my first letter to the Editor. If he publishes the other two letters I hope to receive copies.

"By Rev. Dr. Willis, of Canada, who sails for England tomorrow, I send you a copy of a most interesting work by Mrs. Stowe, entitled 'Uncle Tom's Cabin &c.' It has met with an unprecedented sale & richly deserves it.

"May 29th. I sent, by Miss Clark, whose *non de plume* is *Grace Greenwood*,[280] & by Mr. Gould [281] several copies of our Annual Report in pamphlet form. I hope to hear that they were recᵈ. at the office. Miss Clark intended visiting Mr. Jos. Sturge before going to London.

"Dr. Willis will take a few more copies & also some copies of an Address [282] to Anti Slavery Christians just published. These you

at all and some are signed under an obviously false name, such as *John Smith, the Younger*. The frequency of Tappan's "Manhattan" letters can be determined from this list:

April 22, 1852, Letter of April 17, 1852, *re Uncle Tom's Cabin* and the lethargy of members of the United States Congress in contrast with British leaders.

April 29, 1852, Letter of April 24, 1852, *re* Kossuth, General Cass, Mrs. Stowe, etc.

May 6, 1852, Letter of May 1, 1852, *re* New York local affairs, Senator Seward, imprisonment of colored seamen at Charleston, S. C., Slavery and the Methodist Church, Mrs. Stowe, a new volume of Bancroft's *History of the United States*, and annual meeting of the A. & F. and the Amer. A-S. S.

May 27, 1852, Letter of May 15, 1852, *re* anniversary meetings, chiefly.

June 3, 1852, Letter of May 28, 1852, *re* Postage, Colonization, Jenny Lind, Kossuth, etc.

June 10, 1852, Letter of June 4, 1852, *re* affairs in Great Britain taken from British papers.

June 17, 1852, Letter of June 11, 1852, *re* Tammany Hall, the Whigs, Irish patriots, Kossuth, the Slave Trade, Grace Greenwood.

June 24, 1852, Letter of June 17, 1852, *re* Kossuth, Judge John B. O'Neal of South Carolina, Cheap Postage, Henry Ward Beecher, *Uncle Tom's Cabin* in the South, etc.

July 1, 1852, Letter of June 25, 1852, *re* Politics, local and national, Kossuth, M. Rothschild, the Emperor Soulouque of St. Domingo, the Whigs, Horace Greeley, etc.

280 In *The National Era* for 1852 are to be found many letters by "Grace Greenwood," written from London.

281 What Gould this was is not clear.

282 *National Era*, June 24, 1852, pp. 101 and 104. The headings indicate the comprehensive nature of this A. & F. A-S. Society *Address to Anti-Slavery*

will I hope, direct to influential persons. Please let me know if all the above come to hand in good time.

"Can you send me a pamphlet recently published by R. D. Webb [283] in reply to my letter in defence of the A & F Anti S. Soc. against the aspersions of G. T. &c? Everything of this kind I shall be glad to receive & you must make a charge of them.

"Very truly your's

"LEWIS TAPPAN.

"As it is published in London I will not trouble Dr. W. to take it, especially as I do not know that he goes to London."

"NEW YORK, October 26th 1852.

"Dear Sir,

"Your letter was duly received. Mr. Scoble arrived on the 21st,[284] after a tolerably pleasant passage. His numerous friends in this country are happy to greet him once more.

"Since July 1st I have travelled nearly 4000 miles for the purpose of attending Conventions and other anti-slavery meetings.

Christians,—Extension of Slavery and Panic about the Union; Slavery Anti-Scriptural and Sinful; Government Implicated with Slavery; The Churches Implicated with the Sin of Slavery; The Wickedness and Inhumanity of Caste; Atrocity of the Fugitive Slave Act; The Christians' Affair; Coercing People of Color; Delinquency and Duty of the Church; Objects of the Society; It Aims to Rectify Public Opinion; Wants of the Society; Appeal for Funds.

[283] Webb, Richard D., *The National Anti-Slavery Societies in England and the United States; or Strictures on "A Reply to Certain Charges Brought Against the American & Foreign Anti-Slavery Society . . ."* by Lewis Tappan . . . with an Introduction by John Scoble (Dublin, 1852).

[284] Scoble made his own report of the voyage and arrival,

"We have had foul weather down the channel, and we are now at anchor windbound— All have been very sick, especially Mary Ann and Maria, and I may add our little Nelly . . . . We have a large number of steerage passengers on board—principally German and English . . . .

"If we stay here a day or two, and I get sufficiently well, I shall send you some matter for the next '*Reporter*'—otherwise I must get you to fill up the last two columns as well as you can— My son Richard will probably give you a little help—

"...

"It has struck me—that the Memorial to Mr. J. Pakington might be put in the place of a leader, if you do not hear again from me . . ." (Scoble to Bolton, dated Portsmouth Road, Monday, September 21, 1852).

". . . arrived today with my family, after a four weeks voyage. . . .

"My dear wife has suffered most. . . .

"Please let all my friends, particularly the members of the C[ee]. know of my safe arrival— You may let Dr. Campbell, Mr. Conder, and Mr. Miall know of my safe arrival

". . ." (same to same, dated New York, October 22, 1852).

The Convention of the Free Democracy at Pittsburgh, Penn. in August, has had a most happy effect. The excellent principles there promulgated contrasted with the 'Platforms' of the Whig and Democratic parties, both of which denounce anti-slavery agitation, and uphold the infamous Fugitive Slave Act. Our Platform commends itself to every true-hearted man, and gains his *respect* even if it will not secure his *vote*. Messrs *Hale* and *Julian,* the nominees of the new party, with a large number of able and eloquent supporters, have been lecturing in the different States, and I am greatly mistaken if the Presidential Candidates whom the Free Democratic party supports do not receive a vote, on the first tuesday of November, that will astonish the partisans of generals *Pierce* and *Scott.* This vote would be greatly increased if numerous electors, who agree with us in our principles, were not anxious to cast their votes for one whom they think will be elected, although such candidate impugns these principles. They do not realize the importance of voting for a *principle* instead of a *candidate.*

"*Daniel Webster,* the great lawyer, scholar and Statesman and Secretary of State, died on the 24th in his 71st year. While England mourns the decease of the renouned *Wellington* the United States mourns the decease of her greatest citizen. Had it not been for Webster's advocacy of the odious and inhuman Fugitive Slave Bill and had he been free from the bad habits to which he was notoriously addicted, his fame would have suffered no eclipse. The eminent services he performed for Freedom and Constitutional rights, in his palmiest days will ever be held in grateful remembrance, while his advocacy of the wrong will be an everlasting reproach to him, as has been the great defect in the character of *Bacon* to that eminent man, of whom, in other respects, your nation is justly proud.

"Mr. Webster said, a few days before his death, as I am credibly informed, 'General Pierce will be the next President, and then the Whig party will cease to exist.' A short time will determine whether this prophecy proves correct. It deserves extinction as does the other party, with its sham *Democracy.*

"The Annual Meeting of the anti-slavery Society called the *American Missionary Association,* of which I am Treasurer, was held at Bangor, Maine, September 29th. This Society sustains 138 missionaries and teachers in Jamaica, in the interior of West Africa, in Siam, the Sandwich Islands, Canada, among the Indians west of Lake Superior, in two of the Slave States, and in several of the new free States. This Society was founded by abolitionists, has been sustained by them, and has been greatly blessed by the great Head of the Church. The missionaries & teachers are all anti-slavery men and women, and inculcate right principles, denouncing slavery and caste, and asserting the equality of all men before the law, and in the sight of God.

"On the 5th October a Convention of 500 Congregational ministers and laymen met at Albany, N. Y. to consult upon the matters pertaining to the denomination, and the interests of Christ's Kingdom. It was nearly 150 years since a similar convention had been held in this country. The Convention sat two days, and various matters of interest were discussed and amicably disposed of. Among other matters that underwent discussion, was the relation the *American Home Missionary Society* sustains to slaveholding churches. About 50 of the missionaries of this influential Society preach to churches in Slave States, and it has been believed that they exclude no one because he is a Slave-holder, that Slaveholders are not disciplined, and that the missionaries have not preached very faithfully on the sinfulness of slave-holding. The subject was referred to a committee of fifteen, who reported, 9 to 6, in favor of some action different from the course so long pursued. The minority made a report in favor of continuing essentially the present system. An animated debate arose, and the whole subject was re-committed to the same committee, who subsequently unanimously reported a resolution, that took higher ground than the report of the majority, and it was adopted by the Convention with great unanimity. This marks such a pleasing advance in this country, on the subject of American Slavery, that I send you a copy of the resolution, for the gratification of your readers, as follows:

Resolved, That in the opinion of this Convention, it is the tendency of the gospel wherever it is preached in its purity, to correct all social evils, and to destroy sin in all its forms, and that it is the duty of Missionary Societies to grant aid to churches in slaveholding States, in the support of such ministers only as shall so preach the gospel, and inculcate the principles and application of gospel discipline, that with the blessing of God, it shall have its full effect in awakening and enlightening the moral sense in regard to slavery, and in bringing to pass the speedy abolition of that stupendous wrong; and that wherever a minister is not permitted so to preach, he should in accordance with the directions of Christ in such cases, 'depart out of that city.'

"Be assured that the Anti-Slavery sentiment in this country is rapidly increasing. The people, when their eyes are opened to see the course taken by the demagogues who have deceived them, will embrace anti-slavery doctrines with avidity. The fact that *Uncle Tom's Cabin* is so generally read, and its representation of slavery so extensively approved, indicates the state of feeling in the country. The seed thus sown will surely spring up and bear fruit. I rejoice to see, by your newspapers, that this admirable work is received with so much favor among your intelligent and philanthropic people. The exemplification of Christian character, in this work, will do as much good as its portrait of American Slavery. The author is a Christian woman, and wrote the book not to gain fame or money, but to do good. A few of our newspapers join with the London *Times*[285] in decrying the work. They bite against a file. Fair minded Slaveholders accept the book as a fair delineation of the system of which they are ashamed.

"Very truly your's

"LEWIS TAPPAN

"Editor of the Reporter."

(On outside is this address:

Peter J. Bolton, Esq.
27, New Broad St.
London

B. & F. A.S. Society).

"NEW YORK, November 20th. 1852.[286]

"TO THE EDITOR OF THE REPORTER:

"The extraordinary political excitement into which the whole country has been thrown, with regard to the Presidential election, has nearly subsided. The Democratic party, of which General

[285] *The Times* (London), in reviewing *Uncle Tom's Cabin*, September 3, 1852, charged that its picture of slavery is overdrawn, that its Negro is painted too white, its white man too black, that the book would harden the heart of the slave-owner and, consequently, do more harm than good.

"The gravest fault of the book has, however, to be mentioned. Its object is to abolish slavery. Its effect will be to render slavery more difficult than ever of abolishment. Its very popularity constitutes its greatest difficulty. It will keep ill-blood at boiling point, and irritate instead of pacifying those whose proceedings Mrs Stowe is anxious to influence on behalf of humanity."

Without the consent of Southern white men, argued the reviewer, slavery could never be abolished or the Negro protected.

[286] This letter minus certain important passages, the first two paragraphs and "The newspapers have blazoned . . . to lament his decease," was published in the B. & F. A-S. *Reporter*, January 1, 1853, pp. 6–7.

Pierce was the selected candidate, succeeded by an unexpectedly triumphant vote. Electors favorable to him have been chosen in nearly every State. They will soon meet in the respective States, agreeably to the Constitution, and cast their votes. The Whig party, of which General *Scott* was the chosen candidate, has been signally and as is believed irretrievably overthrown. While the Democratic party was united, North and South, the Whig party was disunited. Besides, in imitation of the Democrats, the Whigs had adopted a pro-slavery platform, contrary to their reiterated professions, and the people saw through the hypocritical pretence. Many whigs voted the democratic ticket, either because they were offended that General Scott was selected by their party instead of *Daniel Webster,* or because they preferred the younger to the older general. Mr Hale, the candidate of the Free Democracy, received a large vote, though not so large a one as Mr. Van Buren received in 1848. Many who voted for him were not true-hearted anti-slavery men, and at the recent election voted for Pierce, and a large number of persons, of anti-slavery tendencies, including many professed abolitionists voted for Scott because, for seeing that either he or Pierce would be elected they preferred Mr Scott. They now see that they lost their votes, and realize what they seemed blinded to before the election, that had they voted for Hale they would not have lost their votes because they would have voted for a principle. A conscientious man who, on some occasion, was in a minority of one, said that as he voted right, while all the rest voted wrong, he had God on his side, and therefore was virtually in the majority. In the excitement of an election it is difficult to induce even some good men to forego a seemingly temporary advantage for a real and permanent good.

"Just before the election Mr. Webster was called to yeild (*sic*) up his breath. A portion of the Whigs had persisted in holding him up as a Presidential candidate, and after his decease many of them voted for General Pierce.

"It is impossible to predict the course that will be taken by the new administration that will come into power on the 4th March next. The triumphant success of the party should inspire them with magnanimity and forbearance. If General Pierce, who is a man in middle life, of good person and address, and of competent abilities should pursue a wise course he will be popular with all parties. There are those who think it is more probable he will thus act in consequence of his having received the suffrages of men of different political opinions, and of having such an immense majority than if he had barely succeeded. Had the two great parties cast about an equal vote, their rivalry would have been prolonged, and while the defeated party would have kept up a vigorous and heated opposition the victorious party would have been tempted to use desperate measures to retain power. Now, the Whigs acknowledge themselves to be defeated and powerless, and the Democrats, secure in their success, feel good natured and can afford to be generous, considerate and just. Let us hope for the best.

"It is believed that the defeat of the Whig party will prove advantageous to the anti-slavery cause; that the conscientious Whigs will unite with the friends of Freedom; and that even many democrats will perceive that the *true* democracy of the country is in the Free Democracy. It is quite evident that the asperity of party has subsided, that a more genial feeling prevails throughout the country, and that men of all parties are in a way to act more independently than they have done. God grant that they may acknowledge that Righteousness exalteth a nation while sin is a reproach to any people.

"Mr. Webster, I doubt not, died of a broken heart. His habits for many years, had probably enfeebled his moral sense. He was induced to believe that by throwing his influence on the side of the South he could be elevated (as if political preferment could in truth elevate such a man!) to the presidency. The tempter seduced him. At an exigency when, if he had gone for Freedom, he might have saved the nation from the deep iniquity of the Fugitive Slave Act, and perhaps have brought the slavery question to a crisis, he apostatised. Instead of supporting him for the highest office the Southerners abandoned him. He deeply felt their ingratitude. Latent tendencies to disease were developed and were aggravated by his state of mind, until, suddenly, they assumed an alarming form & ended speedily in his death. The newspapers have blazoned his remarks on his death bed, and represented him almost as a saint. Even the religious press with a few exceptions, have attempted to make it appear that he died in the faith of the Gospel; & I am sorry to add that many clergymen, in their Lord's day discourses, have extoled the deceased as a man who lived and died a Christian. No doubt Mr. Webster had an intellectual conviction of the truth and excellence of Christianity. His earlier emotions were undoubtedly revived as he drew near to the grave. But if we are to judge of a man's religion by its fruits it seems criminal to represent such a man as Mr. Webster to be a follower of Christ. What exercises of mind and heart he had on his death-bed it is not for mortals to decide. If he has been accepted through the atoneing sacrifice of the Redeemer angels and good men will forever rejoice, but it does no service to Christianity to represent such a man as a saint. He was great, preeminently great as a law-yer, a statesman, an orator, and a man, according to human stand-ards, and had he died previous to his speech in the Senate, March 7, 1850, when he advocated the Fugitive Slave Act, his fame would have been less sullied, and a nation would have had more cause to lament his decease. It is remarkable that on his death bed he made no allusion to the course he pursued on that memorable and sad occasion. He expressed no repentance of the deed, *nor did he allude to it with approbation.*[287]

"You will be surprised to hear that the world-wide renowned philanthropist, GERRIT SMITH, has been elected to the Congress that commences its term next March, and by the suffrages of all parties in his district. It is a significant sign of the times when an ultra abolitionist has been thus elected. The time is approach-ing when the great body of the people will, in like manner, overleap the divisions of party, and elect men of principle, lovers of their fellow-men, and friends of Humanity and Freedom.

"An important judicial case has recently been determined in this city. A Virginian Slaveholder, named LEMMON, recently ar-rived at this port *en route* for Texas, with eight slaves—one of them a woman with three children who had been torn from her husband. As they were about being transferred from the steamer to a vessel for New Orleans the free colored people obtained a writ of *Habeas Corpus,* and had the Slave holder & his wife (who was the legal holder) with the slaves brought before a Judge of the Su-perior Court of this State, Judge Paine, who, after full argument of counsel, decided that the persons claimed as slaves were *free.* There is a law of this State that provides that if slaves are brought into the State by their owners they shall be free. The counsel for

---

[287] Accounts of Daniel Webster's death and religious views (November 4, 1852, p. 354) show no sign of his having had any regrets for his political past. His religious views were apparently orthodox. Note reference to them in the funeral speeches, including that delivered by Edward Everett (p. 358).

the slave-holder contended that the law was intended to apply only to such as were brought here to reside, & that it could not apply to slaves brought merely to send to a slave State. The judge decided otherwise. A great clamor has been made by the pro-slavery press and merchants & professional men interested in the Southern trade. It is called 'persecution,' 'robbery,' 'violation of rights,' 'trampling upon the Constitution,' etc. and strange as it may appear to you a subscription has been set on foot by our *Cotton* editors and merchants to raise £1000 to indemnify the slave holder for his loss! These gentry think that such a judicial act, if not counteracted, will drive away Southern customers from this market, and thus result in a loss of trade!!

"UNCLE TOM'S CABIN" continues to be sold in large quantities throughout the whole country. Some attempts have been made to suppress it at the South, but in vain. The book-sellers there now advertise it. A splendid edition, with numerous illustrations, is in the press, to be brought out by Christmas. Mrs. Stowe is preparing an Appendix [288] to the work, containing recent facts demonstrating that slave parents are separated from their children, and that her work is in no respect an exaggerated statement of the enormities of American Slavery. The Rev. Dr. Stone of this vicinity recently told me that a highly respectable Southerner recently said, in his hearing, 'I feel bound to accept the work as, on the whole, a fair representation of Southern manners and usages.' A brother of Mrs. Stowe has been engaged in a controversy with Rev. Joel Parker,[289] a Presbyterian minister of this city, who on former

---

[288] Stowe, Harriett Beecher, *A Key to Uncle Tom's Cabin, Presenting etc.*

[289] Parker, Joel, and Rood, Anson, *The Discussion between . . . on the question, "What are the Evils Inseparable from Slavery?" which was referred to by Mrs Stowe in "Uncle Tom's Cabin"* (New York, 1852). The foregoing discussion was reprinted from the Philadelphia *Christian Observer*, 1846. It would seem that the Reverend Mr. Rood, in his weekly contribution to the New York *Evangelist* referred to the action of the Synod of Virginia in animadverting with some severity upon resolutions, passed by the General Assembly at their session in Philadelphia, reprobating the system of slavery. Mr. Rood, "in a kind and temperate article," defended the General Assembly. Dr. Parker took exception and, among various things, said, "What, then, are the evils inseparable from Slavery? There is not one that is not equally inseparable from depraved human nature in other lawful relations." Mrs. Stowe, in "Uncle Tom's Cabin," paraphrased this to "Slavery has no evils but such as are inseparable from any other relation in social and domestic life," and Parker rightly claimed that she had changed the meaning.

occasions has been proved to be a man of frail memory, with regard
to an allusion made to him by Mrs. Stowe in the earlier editions of
her work. This doctor of divinity undertook, for sooth, to threaten
Mrs. Stowe, the wife of another doctor of divinity, with a law suit,
in consequence of the allusion to him as an apologist of slavery.
It is thought by many that he was not misrepresented at all, and a
large number of those who think he was consider the misrepresentation unintended, of small importance, and that the damages claimed,
(£4000 stg.) involved the reverend precentor in an absurdity, to
say the least. My friend, Rev. Mr. *Thompson*, of this city, in one
of his speeches before the CONGREGATIONAL UNION made a mistake
in saying the matter had been satisfactorily arranged, & that Dr.
Parker had denied & repudiated the statement imputed to him,
withdrawn the suit, &c. He has not denied it nor withdrawn it,
nor made the *amende honorable*, but there is no probability he will
persist in a suit against the judgment of most of the community,
lay & clerical, and the advice of his judicious friends. He called
upon Mrs. Stowe to retract what she had innocently imputed to
him without stating what he did mean. There is reason to believe
that the pro-slavery interest here (perhaps aided by individuals in
England) entered into a conspiracy to use the small matter of
which Dr. Parker complained to defame and injure Mrs. Stowe and
her admirable work, in order to uphold the institution of Slavery
or to suppress, if possible, the increasing anti-slavery sentiment of
the country. They have been sadly disappointed.

"Respectfully your's

"LEWIS TAPPAN."

"New York, Dec. 10th 1852 [290]

"My dear Sir,

"Yours of the 19th Nov. was duly rec^d. I hope you
will hereafter receive the *American Missionary*, regularly. The
Independent also. If either fails please let me know it immediately.
You speak of the *Commonwealth* as the organ of the Free Soil
party. It is their organ in the State of Massachusetts & not for
the whole country, as there are several other similar papers in other
States.

[290] Published, with the exception of the first four paragraphs, in the B. &
F. A-S. *Reporter*, January 1, 1853, pp. 7–8.

"I will endeavour to keep you advised of the best anti-slavery works, as they issue from the press.

"The Chart sent to Mr. Harned is very beautiful, but I do not think any of our Booksellers would take it in hand, especially at this late day.

"I thank you for the information given respecting Mr. Scoble. He is here at present & will probably remain until June. Before rec⁸ your letter I made a private arrangement with him to stay here 6 mˢ. from Dec. 1st to aid me. What you have written or may write respecting him will be considered private & confidential. He leaves today for a short visit to Toronto.

"I send you a newspaper that contains an analysis of the Report of the Superintendent of our Census of 1850, recently published. It unfolds some curious facts, and is worthy of study. It shows, among other matters, that there are much fewer immigrants in this country than was supposed. It reveals also the large number of emigrations of white men going on from some of the slave States. This document will be read with interest in Europe. Ireland & Germany send more of their sons & daughters to this country than all other nations beside.

"A most pleasing incident occurred the other day respecting the Lemmon slaves, of whom I have already informed you. A young man of colour, a fugitive slave from Virginia had found his way to Cleveland, Ohio, and had employed himself as a waiter in the American Hotel at that place. One of the waiters was reading one of our 'penny' papers to his confrers (everybody here reads newspapers) that contained an account of the examination of the Habeas Corpus case by Judge Paine that resulted in the liberation of the slaves. The young man immediately exclaimed, 'That's my aunt—that's my sister!' He sent a telegram to one of the Committee, whose name he learned at the office of the *Free Democrat,* and in a few days presented himself here in person. He went to the house where his sister and her child were, and as he entered the joyful woman exclaimed, 'My brother!' They had not seen each other for two years. 'Well,' said Richard, for that is his name, 'I have other news to tell you—your husband is in Canada!' This was joyful intelligence indeed. The result is, as the young man brought with him letters testifying to his good character and capacity, it has been arranged that the whole party, under Richard's escort, proceed this evening to Amherstburg, C. W., with suitable letters, there look out for a good location, and when it is decided ᵘᵖon, draw from the fund raised here for their benefit, about eight hundred dollars. Thus you see both parties are well pleased. Mr Lemmon has received nearly double the amount his slaves were worth in Virginia, from the supple merchants in this City who trade with the Southern merchants, and the *Johnson Family* are emancipated with a snug little fortune in hand to enable them to settle down in the dominions of Queen Victoria. The 'Cotton' merchants are making a great clamor on account of the 'robbery' of Lemmon, and threaten to move in the matter until the law, granting instant freedom to all slaves brought into this State by their masters is repealed. But it will not be repealed. The electors of the rural districts will not thus stullify themselves to promote the trade between this city & the Slave States.

"A most capital article has just appeared in the 'New-Englander,' a quarterly magazine, published at New Haven, Conn. *On the Literature of Slavery,* ascribed to *Leonard Bacon,* D. D. It is a review of *Uncle Tom's Cabin* and several of the pro-slavery tales which that gem of Tales has brought into being. The New-York *Observer* and other publications that have falsely represented Mrs Stowe's work as prejudicial to religion, exaggerated in its statements &c meet with indignant censure. Mrs Stowe has in the press, *A Key to Uncle Tom's Cabin,* being a pamphlet of about 100 pages, double columns, 'being a complete refutation of some charges which have been made against her on account of alleged over statement of facts in Uncle Tom.' It will 'present original facts and documents, most thoroughly establishing the truth of every statement in her book.' [291] The fact is, Mrs Stowe *under*-stated the facts, and fair-minded men at the South have acknowledged it. Her 'Key' will be a file which the pro-slavery vipers can bite if they see fit.

"An edition of Uncle Tom 'for the million' has just issued from the press of John P. Jewett & Co, Mrs Stowe's publishers in paper covers, at 37½ cents. They announce also an edition in the German language, translated by Prof. *Hutton,* one of the most distinguished German scholars in this country. A splendid 8 vo. edition is also

[291] Other attempts were made or projected to establish the authenticity. A certain E. F. Quant, of Braintree, wrote to Bolton, October 26, 1852, seeking financial assistance in publishing a book that should vindicate "Uncle Tom's Cabin." He was prepared to show from evidence published by the American Anti-Slavery Society in 1839 that "just such things do happen and have happened in the South."

in the press, with steel portraits of Mrs *Stowe* and *Little Eva,* and illustrated with 100 original designs by *Billings,* engraved in the highest style of Wood Engraving, by ten (two?) of the most distinguished artists in America. It is very gratifying to the friends of freedom, as it is extremely annoying to our secular and religious pro-slavery papers, to hear of the immense sale of this work in England and other European countries, and the extraordinary interest the work excites. The citadel of Human Slavery is at length invested by a woman, whose missiles are doing execution on an unprecedented scale.

"Your's truly

"LEWIS TAPPAN"

"P.S. to my last letter to the Ed. of the Reporter.

The Congress of the United States commenced its session on Monday, the 6th. The President's Message and the Reports of the Heads of Department fill the newspapers. The country is represented as being in an unusually prosperous condition. Think of the twenty millions of dollars in the Treasury, & a national debt of small amount. The members of Congress appear to be in great harmony, feeling probably as did the Americans and Mexicans after the capture of Mexico. Such an unexpected & signal victory on the part of the Democrats, and such a complete overthrow on the part of the Whigs make both parties quite good natured, while the vote given for *Hale* & *Julian,* the candidates of the Free Democracy, as the Free Soil party is now called, 150,000, considering that these voters are men of unflinching principles & determined zeal, inspires the friends of Liberty with courage and hope.

NEW YORK, January 8th. 1853.[292]

The fact that the Dutchess of Sunderland, [sic] and other British ladies, have addressed [293] the ladies of this country on the subject of slavery, has excited reciprocal feelings on the part of the truly estimable of their sex among us, and I doubt not the expostulation of the women of England will be responded to in a becoming manner by the women of the United States. There are those however, chiefly among the *harder* sex, who seem disposed to retaliate by pointing out to the fair memorialists the misery, desti-

[292] Published with at least one correction, "Frazier," in B. & F. A-S. *Reporter,* Feb. 1, 1853, pp. 28–29.

[293] For the text of the "Stafford House Address" and some replies thereto, see Introduction, pp. 40, 41, 42, footnotes 33 and 34.

tution and crime of their own country. One professed *religious* newspaper, the *New York Observer* has wantonly indulged in this strain.[294] It is deeply to be regretted that, in the address, intimations are made that it is not the duty of masters immediately to emancipate the slaves. *Gradualism* should find no favor with British philanthropists, especially after the experience had of the Apprenticeship system in the British West India Colonies. The true doctrine should be everywhere proclaimed whether offenders comply with it or not.

Mrs. Stowe has in the press a "Key to Uncle Tom's Cabin," a work of about the same size as the work to which it is a sequel. Her object is to substantiate the statements and illustrations in reply to carpers on both sides the Atlantic. I hope it will be worthy of the gifted author. It may prove that facts are stronger. than fiction, or rather that unadorned facts do more execution than fiction founded upon facts. It is rather a perilous thing for so popular an author to venture so soon upon a second attempt. But she writes to do good and will write until the old Bastile crumbles and falls, if her life and health are spared. From the avails of her first work on slavery she has built a cottage for her own family, and is about erecting one for her aged parents in the same village. The article in *Frazier's Magazine*, respecting the Beecher family, is substantially correct, but there are several errors of greater or less importance.[295]

The Lemmon [296] freemen have safely arrived at the Elgin settlement in Canada, where they will purchase 100 acres of land, and cultivate it. Meantime our courts will try the appeal of the slaveholder. The partisans of the slaveholders will endeavor to get the laws of the free States, giving freedom to all slaves brought into them by their masters, repealed, so that slaves, *en route*, for other slave States may pass through the free States unmolested. The democratic governor of Pennsylvania has recommended to the legislature such a measure. The democratic governor of this State, just elected, warily omitted all reference to the subject in his

[294] Issue of January 8, 1853.

[295] "Some Account of Mrs Beecher Stowe and Her Family" by an Alabama man, in *Fraser's Magazine for Town and Country*, November, 1852, pp. 518–525. The article was favorable to the family, the author confessing himself to belong to the Tappan school, opposed to colonization, and friendly to "Uncle Tom's Cabin."

[296] "The Lemmon Slave-Case," B. & F. A-S. *Reporter*, Jan. 1, 1853, pp. 3–6.

message to the legislature, but a political partisan has made a motion notwithstanding. If the decision of the question depended upon the members from our large cities no doubt the laws would be repealed, and any thing almost done to propitiate the southerners, gain their custom and support. But the country members who do not represent rotten principles, nor rotten boroughs, will not be quick to make Slave avenues of free territory.

Since the passage of the Fugitive Slave Act about fifty colored persons throughout the free States have been arrested as fugitive slaves. How many of them have been remanded into slavery I cannot say, but not so many are seized and returned as under the old law. The Act will soon become a dead letter or, if enforced, will do more to arouse the people to anti slavery sentiment & action than any other measure that could be adopted.

William Goodell has recently published a work entitled "Slavery and Anti-slavery a History of the Great Struggle in both Hemispheres." It contains 600 pp. with a full Index and a copious table of contents. It is a valuable repository of facts and executed with ability. He has another work, of about half the size, prepared on the "Slave Code" or the Law and Facts of Slavery.[297] It will contain a large portion of the laws & decisions, historically arranged. Such a work will be useful and much sought after, in England as well as in this country.

During the last session of Congress between two and three hundred thousand copies of anti-slavery speeches, by members of Congress, were printed & sold at Washington and widely circulated throughout the country. Twenty five thousand copies of the *National Era* are published weekly, by the same printers! This was the paper in which Uncle Tom's Cabin was originally published. You will see from the statement of these facts, that the slavery question continues to be *agitated* in this country, and that the *finality* so much spoken of by the framers and supporters of the infamous Fugitive Slave Act, and their allies & abettors has not yet taken place.

The diplomatic correspondence between the special agent of this country, young Walsh, son of our late Consul at Paris, and the government of Hayti, has been lately published.[298] It seems that

[297] Goodell, William, *The American Slave Code in Theory and Practice; Its Distinctive Features Shown by its Statutes, Judicial Decisions, and Illustrative Facts* (New York, A. & F. A-S. S., 1853).

[298] Another illustration of the international aspect of slavery.

France, England and the United States had representatives at Haiti, who, by order of their governments, united in an attempt to coerce the emperor Soleaque [sic] to refrain from making war upon a portion of his refractory subjects. The attempt was repulsed, but the publication of the correspondence on the part of our functionary has filled the minds of generous and high minded men with disgust. His insolence toward the sable emperor showed that he was a mere minion of the Slave-Power. I regret that the British government should bear a part of the disgrace attached to such *braggardise*.

The correspondence between our government and Spain, respecting Cuba, also reflects little honor upon our diplomacy or philanthropy. This country, as to its aggressive, belligerent spirit and conduct may not be worse than some other countries, whose wars and military chieftains are subjects of the highest eulogy, but all such do not publish their manoeuvres in diplomacy nor their nefarious attempts to aggrandise themselves at the expense of public communities. I wish they did, that the world might know how much villiany is meditated or practised by those who advise in the councils of nations.

It is a matter of devout thankfulness that your men of war have been so successful recently, in the capture of several slavers about to enter the ports of Cuba, with their living cargoes. Apropos: Why does not your government *enforce* the observance of her treaties with Spain? How many years more must it spend in diplomatic correspondence before the suit shall be terminated, judgment rendered, and execution issued? THE WORLD EXPECTS IN THIS MATTER THAT ENGLAND WILL DO HER DUTY.

I am informed from a reliable source, that a slaver was recently fitted out, from this port, for "parts unknown." Our laws are such that it is almost impossible to convict parties of their piratical offences before some *overt act* has been committed. I hope your fleets will snap up this rascal and all his *confreres*.

Rev. Asa Rood, of Philadelphia, has published at length his correspondence with Rev. Joel Parker, that took place several years since in which the sentiment quoted by Mrs. Stowe in Uncle Tom's Cabin was alluded to, and for uttering which Mr Parker threatened her with a suit for libel, laying the damages at £4000 sterling. The readers of this correspondence will find sufficient in Dr Parker's letters, clearly showing that if he did not utter the precise words attributed to him by Mrs. Stowe the ideas were not very dissimilar.

Jewitt & Co, the publishers of Uncle Tom's Cabin, generously offered to pay any damages Parker might obtain, if he sued Mrs. Stowe, and begged her not to expunge the sentiment imputed to him, but she felt able to be not only upright but magnanimous. Her opponent has not sued, nor will he. He has not gained the £4000, nor any part of it, but is *minus* some reputation. Once he professed to be an abolitionist!

A week or two since nine missionaries left this port for Sierra Leone, to join the mission at Kaw-mendi, in the interior. They are sent out by the "American Missionary Association," an anti-slavery Missionary Society, the officers being chiefly members of the American & Foreign Anti Slavery Society. They will preach an anti-slavery gospel, establish schools, teach the natives agriculture & the mechanic arts. They will also inculcate the principles of Peace and Temperance.

Intelligence has been received by a *telegram* this morning that General Pierce, our newly elected President, has met with a great misfortune, owing to the overthrow of a car, in the sudden death of his only son, a promising lad of twelve years of age. Mr & Mrs Pierce were in the car, and both were bruised. Great sympathy will be felt for the distressed family. A niece of mine who resided several years near General Pierce, says, "whatever may be said of him, as a public man, in private life, he is most estimable."

A public meeting is advertised to be held this evening at the Metropolitan Hall (the largest in the city) "for the purpose of expressing the sympathy of the Christian community, and of the Friends of Religious Liberty, with the 'Madiai' family and others, imprisoned in the Grand Duchy of Tuscany, for possessing and reading the Scriptures, &c." [299] The notice is signed by twenty four of our leading conservative citizens, of different religious denominations. This is well. Rev. Dr *Cox* and others are to address the meeting. There is not a man among the signers who would affix his signature to a call for a meeting to express sympathy with the *three millions* of Americans called Africans, most of whom are *bereft* of the Scriptures by merciless tyrants. The inhabitants of Tuscany are prohibited from possessing & reading the Bible, and great deserved sympathy is excited, but the colored inhabitants of fifteen of the American States are thus prohibited, and

[299] *New York Observer*, January 13, 1853, pp. 10–11.

little sympathy is expressed by the conservative members of our metropolitan churches!

YOUR CORRESPONDENT.

After studying the Anti-Slavery question in America, John Scoble sent back the following summary:

"NEW YORK, 14 feb, 1853.

"TO THE COMMITTEE OF THE BRITISH & FOREIGN ANTI-SLAVERY SOCIETY,
"Dear Sirs,
        "A variety of circumstances. have hitherto prevented my carrying into effect my design of writing you a series of letters on the Anti-Slavery question; but I hope now that I have become a little more settled, to be able to write you a monthly letter, giving you the result of my observation and experience, which, I trust may prove both acceptable & useful, (Before, however, I enter upon the subject I have selected for my present communication, allow me to discharge a most agreeable duty, namely, that of returning you, collectively and individually, my warmest thanks for all the confidence and kindness you have shown me during a long period of years, in the various relations in which I have stood to the Anti-Slavery cause, both at home and abroad. With some of you I have acted for more than twenty years past, and you have made the duties I have had to perform most pleasant by the manner in which you have encouraged and aided me in their discharge, and I will venture to say, that, whenever the history of the abolition of slavery is written, you will be enrolled amongst its earliest, most earnest, and self-denying friends: To me it was most painful to part from you, but a sense of growing infirmities, among other reasons, seemed to render the step I have taken not only desirable but necessary: You may be assured, however, that, so long as I am favored with health and strength and opportunity, I shall still continue my Anti-Slavery labour, and feel that I am still associated with you in the great work you have in hand—the universal extinction of Slavery and the Slave-Trade. Permit me also to add my grateful acknowledgments to those kind friends who have so generously and spontaneously contributed to the testimonial fund which is to be presented to me; and to assure them that I value it not only as the token of their good will, and the estimate they have

been pleased to put on my poor services in the cause of suffering and oppressed humanity, but as a means of enabling me to be of still further use to that cause.)

"I propose, in my present communication, to glance at the various agencies now at work, in this Country, to promote the abolition of Slavery, or at least to prevent its extension on this Continent, and to relieve the General Government from the responsibility of ministering to its support.

"THE AMERICAN ANTI-SLAVERY SOCIETY.

"This Society was formed in the year 1833: It was nobly designed, based on the highest principles, and for several years conducted in a spirit worthy of the great cause it was intended to promote: Its success was more than proportionate to the great efforts it made to diffuse right views of the Anti-Slavery question; and to beget right action in relation thereto. But WILLIAM LLOYD GARRISON, one of its chief leaders, had imbibed new views in reference to Women's rights, Human Government, Non-resistance, the emancipation of Mind etc, which led him to subordinate the Anti-Slavery cause, properly so called, to these doctrines. In pursuance of his object and aided by those who sympathized with him, he 'sifted' into the '*Liberator,*' against the remonstrances of many of his fellow-labourers these opinions, and finally brought them on the Anti-Slavery platform: This led to the breaking up of the Society in 1839–40, and to the formation of the *American and Foreign Anti-Slavery Society.* The course which Mr. Garrison's party have pursued since that period has been such as to alienate from them the great body of Abolitionists throughout the Country, whilst the Agencies they have employed and the spirit in which they have prosecuted their work have earned for them, and I think justly, the name of 'Infidel Abolitionists.' They have but few Auxiliaries. and certainly not more than half a dozen papers, and they but of comparatively small circulation, to advocate their peculiar views, or sustain their movements. And yet they pretend to be the only true Abolitionists in their Country. I am thankful to say that they form but a fragment of the noble army of Anti-Slavery Men who are to be found in the United States; and my impression is that, before long, many of the foremost men of the party will either break away from it, or, in the exercise of their private judgment, act in direct opposition to Mr. Garrison's most cherished views in the matter of political action, and the support of proper Candidates to Congress.

"The American and Foreign Anti-Slavery Society.

"This Society is the true successor of the American Anti-Slavery Society. It has adopted all the distinctive views of that noble Organisation, and a comparison of its Constitution with that of the *British (&) Foreign Anti-Slavery Society* will show that they completely harmonize in principles, object, and modes of operation. Among its leading friends are *Arthur* and *Lewis Tappan,* and *Judge Jay,* men every way worthy of the position they occupy, and of the confidence which is reposed in them as the zealous, devoted and self-denying friends of the Slave. I need scarcely say that the Agencies which this Society has employed in carrying on its work, have been christian, and that whilst it has been faithful in exposing all that was pro-slavery in the Church and the State, it has not forgotten the dignity of its mission; nor offended against the spirit of the Gospel. It will, I trust, shortly, greatly enlarge the sphere of its operations by the multiplicating of its Agencies, and give the right tone in every part of the Country to Anti-Slavery.

"In connexion with this Society I would mention the 'Vigilance Committee,' whose operations are directed by its Members principally: It is doing a good work, not only in forwarding fugitives to Canada, but in defending the rights of captured Slaves, and otherwise helping this suffering class of our fellow-men. But more particularly would I draw attention to the American Missionary Association which has grown out of the A & F. AS. Society. This noble institution, at its sixth Anniversary held in September last year, reported its income to be 31,134 dollars, and its expenditure at 30,233 dollars. The whole number of Missionary laborers under its care was then 140, of which 74 were employed in the Free and Slave States and Canada, and the remainder in Africa, Siam, the Sandwich Islands, and Jamaica. All these are sent forth to preach an Anti-Slavery Gospel and to form Anti-Slavery Churches, and all of them may be regarded as Anti-Slavery Agents wherever they are placed. I send on with this certain documents which will give you interesting details, and a part of which I should like to see inserted in the columns of the '*Reporter.*'

"Conventions of Christian Abolitionists.

"These have been held in several parts of the Country and may be regarded as a protest against the Garrisonian Body of Abolitionists, and a vindication of the Gospel from the injury attempted to be inflicted on its spirit and teachings, by the pro-slavery sections of the Church in this Country. These conventions uniformly take the highest ground, on the Anti-Slavery question, and their influence has proved most salutary in various directions. I trust they may be multiplied, for I am satisfied that if ever Slavery be abolished in this Country, it will owe its downfal to the prevalence of Christian principles, sympathies and prayers crowned by the Divine blessing.

"Conventions and Mass Meetings of a general kind.

"These are not unfrequently held, and are usually well attended, and, as the vehicles through which Anti-Slavery sentiments are conveyed, and Anti-Slavery action promoted are most important auxiliaries of the Anti-Slavery Cause. There is no lack of spirit or energy manifested at these gatherings, though, perhaps, except in particular cases, their influence is more local than general.

"CONVENTIONS OF COLORED PEOPLE.

"Though these Conventions are usually held to promote some great object connected with the elevation and welfare of the people of Color, there are two subjects which are never lost sight of at these Meetings, namely, Slavery and Colonization. The free people of Color, with few exceptions, are true to their brethren in bond, and determine to remain by them whatever it may cost them. They will not hear of Colonization in Africa, and regard the American Colonization Society as their deadliest enemy, and the greatest obstruction to the cause of abolition. It is very satisfactory to observe that the number of educated colored men is increasing, that there are many among them of excellent abilities, great eloquence and superior character, and that the manner in which they conduct their public proceedings secures from [sic] the respect of the unprejudiced, and the support of every friend of Humanity and Freedom. They may fall into some errors at times, but not more frequently than do their white fellow-citizens.

"THE LIBERTY PARTY, or rather THE LIBERTY LEAGUE.

"The Liberty party was first organized in 1840. Neither of the old political parties, the Whigs and the Democrats, could be depended upon to give effect to Anti-Slavery principles in Congress, and hence the formation of this third party. This party nominated for the Presidency and the Vice-Presidency of the U.States the Hon. *J. G. Birney* and *Thomas Earle*, Esq., and, in 1844, gave them 60,000 Votes, a most encouraging fact. In 1845, the Liberty League was formed, and at its head may be found *Gerrit Smith,* a man worthy the highest respect and confidence. The platform of this party may be briefly stated as follows—The League maintains that Slavery is unconstitutional in the United States, and that, consequently, it has not, and never can have any proper legal existence in the Country. It contends, therefore, that Congress has the power to abolish it in every one of the Slave States whenever it shall think fit. The League has also adopted as part of its platform, Free Trade, gratuitous distribution of public lands; limitation of land ownership; the inalienable homestead; retrenchment of public expenses; free suffrage; and the abolition of all legalized monopolies and Castes. Whilst, however, the League will seek to realize all the measures comprehended in its platform, its chief attention will be directed to the abolition of Slavery.

"THE FREE SOIL or FREE DEMOCRATIC PARTY.

"This party was organized in 1848, at Buffalo, and among its most earnest and zealous supporters were some of the most advanced abolitionists of the Country. They however, suffered themselves to be made the tools of certain politicians at the time, and gave their strength as the sequel proved, to men who proved unworthy of their confidence. They are not likely however, to be taken in the same snare again. The Free Soil Party has now adopted the name of the Free Democracy, and at Pittsburgh, N.Y. on the 12th of August, 1852, adopted a platform which declares 'That Slavery is a sin against God, and a Crime against Man. which no human enactment nor usage can make right, and that Christianity, Humanity, and Patriotism, alike demand its abolition. That the Fugitive Slave Act of 1850 is repugnant to the Constitution, to the principles of the common law, to the Spirit of Christianity, and to the sentiments of the Civilised World. We therefore deny its binding force upon the American people, and demand its im-

mediate and total repeal. That no permanent settlement of the
Slavery question can be looked for, except in the practical recognition of the truth, that Slavery is sectional and Freedom national,
by the total separation of the general Government from Slavery,
and the exercise of its legitimate and constitutional influence on
the side of Freedom, and by leaving to the States the whole subject
of Slavery and the extradition of fugitives from service.' The sum
of their Platform is summed up in the following words—'We in-
scribe on our banner *Free Soil, Free Speech, Free labor,* and *Free
Men,* and under it will fight on and fight ever, until a triumphant
victory shall reward our exertions.' The Conventin (sic) at Pittsburgh, nominated the Hon. John P. Hale, of New Hampshire, now
in the Senate of the United States, and George W. Julian, of Indiana, to the Presidency and Vice Presidency, and on the day of
election cast upwards of 150,000 Votes for these gentlemen. This
powerful organization, composed of earnest Men, will, if their measures be fully carried out, soon have the balance of power in their
hands. The Whigs, as a party, called the Conscience Whigs, may,
hereafter, join the Free Democracy, and it is understood that not a
few of the Democratic party, now in the ascendency, are disatisfied
(*sic*) with the terms on which their chief, General Pierce, has been
elected to the Presidency, and may be led to join a purer organization.

"Speaking generally I should say that there never was a time in
the United States, when Anti-Slavery exertions were more needed,
or would yield more precious results. I am, however, convinced
that it is above all things necessary that the great distinctive features of the Anti-Slavery Cause should be kept permanently before
the public mind, for there is a constant tendency to sacrifice principles to expediency whenever it becomes mixed up with politics,
or is taken hold of by mere political men. My anxiety is that the
American and Foreign Anti-Slavery Society should put forth all
its strength, should multiply its agencies, and be the salt of this
great question. That it will be sustained by the sympathies and
prayers of British Abolitionists I have no doubt, and that its triumph may be speedy I most earnestly pray.

"The number of Newspapers, more or less devoted to the Anti-
Slavery Cause, is upwards of seventy, with a constant tendency to
increase. These papers represent the different sections of the Abolitionists, but all, with the exception of the few under the immediate

control of Mr. Garrison and his party, sustain the Free-Soil movement. Some of them are edited with great ability, and, among
those may be specified the 'National Era' published at Washington,
which has now a circulation of 28,000 Copies weekly. The 'Independent' published in New York, has a circulation of upwards of
10,000 weekly, 2,500 of its subscribers being Ministers, chiefly of
the Congregational body. I mention these two not to disparage
others, but simply because I happen to know more about them.
'Uncle Tom's Cabin' is doing a mighty work here, as well as in
Europe. It has penetrated into the Slave States, for the people
there will read it as well as in those that are free; and though it is
attacked with virulence by the pro-slavery party, and its truthfulness denied, it maintains its ground against all opposition, and
when the 'Key' is published, which it shortly will be, a sensation
equal to that of the original work, will, I am persuaded be created.
Slavery will then be seen, not as depicted in the soul-stirring story
of Uncle Tom, but in its naked and hideous reality.

> "I am, my dear Sirs,
> "Yours faithfully,
> "JOHN SCOBLE."

> "NEW YORK, February 15th 1853.[300]

"At last the whole world is talking or reading about American
Slavery. The popularity of Uncle Tom's Cabin and the White
Slave [301] have compelled the Booksellers to advertise them. And
the many pro-slavery pamphlets, got up on the emergency, to divert
public attention from the great works alluded to, have utterly
failed to effect that object. New standard works on the 'accursed'
system, as the sainted WILBERFORCE, in a letter to ARTHUR TAPPAN,
once denominated it, are announced and will have a rapid sale.
Mrs. Stowe's 'Key,' of which I spoke in my last, will be published
this month, as will Goodell's 'American Slave Code: its Theory and
Practice.' Mr Stroud's sketch of the 'Slave Laws,' [302] published

[300] Published in B. & F. A-S. *Reporter*, April 1, 1853, pp. 77–78.

[301] Hildreth, Richard, *The Slave; or Memoirs of Archy Moore* (3d edition,
Boston & New York, 1840 [first published in 1836]).

——, *The White Slave—Another Picture of Slave Life* (1st English edition,
1852).

——, *Archy Moore, the White Slave; or Memoirs of a Fugitive* (New York,
1855).

[302] Stroud, George McDowell, *A Sketch of the Laws Relating to Slavery in
the Several States of the United States of America* (Philadelphia, 1827). In

about twenty years since, has long been out of print. The new work is vastly superior to it in design and execution. Judge JAY says of it, 'Your book is as impregnable against the charge of exaggeration as Euclid's Geometry, since, like that, it consists of propositions and demonstrations. It is not only true, but it is *unquestionably* true.' [303] Another volume of Poems by WHITTIER, our quaker Poet, is announced. You may be sure it will contain some exquisite anti-slavery sonnets. I have seen the *MS* of a pamphlet, written by a gentleman who has resided at the South more than ten years, which gives FACTS corroborative of the scenes depicted in Uncle Tom's Cabin, with others of still greater atrocity. In WASHINGTON's mansion at Mount Vernon, hangs a glass case containing the veritable key of the Bastile presented to our renowned *Pater Patria* by LAFAYETTE. The world has now got the 'Key' of the American Bastile, and we call upon the friends of freedom everywhere to aid in demolishing the hateful prison-house, and letting the poor inmates go free. If, as is said, the British king compelled his subjects on this continent to sustain slavery, let the people in both nations now unite to compell king 'Slaveocracy' to give up his victims.

"A pamphlet has just appeared entitled 'Indian Missions and the American Board' which contains the Slave Code of the Choctaw and Cherokee Indian nations, and the countenance for a long time past and now given to slaveholding by the missionary churches in these nations gathered and sustained by the *American Board of Commissioners for Foreign Missions*. This Board is sustained by a large number of the most prominent men of different denominations & political parties in the country. Another Society, called the *American Home Missionary Society*, also patronized by 'men of property & standing,' sustains missionaries over fifty churches in the Slave States, to many of which slaveholders are admitted. The great body of American Christians of the Presbyterian, Dutch Reformed, and Congregational faith sustain these Societies, and

the Preface is the author's acknowledgment to James Stephen of London, "to whose comprehensive work," *The Slavery of the British West India Colonies Delineated*, he was indebted for the suggestion of his own and to which "I am," said he, "largely indebted for much valuable information." A second edition, revised and enlarged, of Stroud's work came out in 1856.

[303] From letter, William Jay to William Goodell, dated New York, January 25, 1853, written on the occasion of his returning the MS. submitted to him for perusal. Goodell's *Slave Code* came out in its third edition within six months.

thus the iniquitous system of slavery is propped up and kept in countenance. Take away these props and it would fall. And yet such estimable men as Leonard Bacon, D. D., Rev. Joseph P. Thompson, Richard S. Stows, Jun., Albert Barnes, etc. support them, seemingly content that these Societies should be the hand-maids of the system they abhor, write and preach against. Alas, for such inconsistency! Judge Jay, I learn, is preparing a Letter to the *American Tract Society* on the support it gives to the American Bastile. Meantime, the work, months since announced, on the Mutilations and Expurgations of American and British Literature to please the slave-holding people of the South, is in progress.

"A few days since a converted Syrian called on me. He is a native of Bethlehem, and a preacher in his own country. At his house in Palestine Americans have often lodged, and he has enter-tained one or more of the Secretaries of the above mentioned A.B.C.F.M. a week at a time; and yet (will it be believed?) until his arrival a few weeks since at Boston, where he fell in with an anti slavery friend of mine, he had never heard of the existence of *slavery* in this country! He is amazed, considering that we have made such political and religious pretensions. The first book he has read here is Uncle Tom's Cabin, and he has commenced translating it into the Armenian language. American Missionaries in foreign countries, are, it is believed, very slow in acquainting the heathen, and the people of the oriental countries, that Slaveholding and Caste prevail in this country, and that the churches of nearly all denominations are contaminated with the polluting system.

"In a late letter I strongly commended a Review of Rev. Dr. Bacon in the New Englander. On the spur of the moment I did it, not having read the article, on the very warm recommendation of a clerical friend in whose judgment I thought confidence could be placed. That eulogism I wish to take back at least in part. The Review is admirable in many respects, but it does injustice [304] to the abolitionists of the country and especially to the author of

[304] "In the year 1839, the American Anti-Slavery Society—then in the most prosperous period of its operations—published a volume of 224 closely printed pages, entitled 'American Slavery as it is: Testimony of a thousand witnesses.' With the spirit of such a book as that is, we have no sympathy. It is compiled and digested for the purpose of showing the darkest side of slavery, and nothing else; and it is therefore as unlike as possible to the representation of southern life given by Mrs Stowe" (*The New Englander*, November, 1852, pp. 588–613).

'American Slavery, as it is,' a book that was written by an able writer,[305] with the kindest feelings, which has done eminent service to the cause, the statements of which have never been refuted and of which, Mrs. Stowe, in her forth-coming 'Key,' has availed herself largely.

"Soon after the address of the 'Women of England' appeared in this country, a reply was published in one of our rank pro-slavery morning newspapers, the *Courier and Enquirer,* purporting to be the reply of some thousands of American women. It was the coinage of the editor or one of his correspondents. Everybody here deemed it a hoax. But it seems that many on your side the ocean have believed it a genuine document, and among them, Lord *Shaftsbury,* (*sic*) whose reply is before me. It would seem remarkable, did not the best part of our people know the mendacity of the point alluded to, that, notwithstanding its portraiture of the misery of the poor of England, in a subsequent number of the paper, the editor published a most appalling account of the destitution, suffering, and misery of a portion of this city, that equals anything that has been ever published of the physical and moral degradation, poverty and distress of any part of London.[306] Fully sensible of the sufferings of our own poor, and of the many noble charities for their relief, we also know the miseries of the poor in your metropolis as well as the many excellent institutions for their benefit, which in the language of *Burke,* stand, as so many moral lightning-rods to avert the wrath of heaven.

"The friends of humanity are greatly indebted to the authors of the articles in the 'Westminster Review' and 'Blackwood's Edinbrough Magazine,' on American Slavery.[307] These publications are read in all the principal cities and towns in the Southern as well as the Northern States, and these articles will find numerous readers throughout this country. We earnestly hope that all your periodicals, that are not under time-serving influences, will, in temperate and faithful essays, address the conscience, the humanity, the religion of this country on behalf of the down-trodden Americans

---

[305] Theodore Dwight Weld.

[306] Tappan steadfastly refused to be drawn into a controversy on the conditions of the poor man in England and America.

[307] "American Slavery, and Emancipation by the Free States" in *The Westminster Review,* January, 1853, pp. 125–167; "Slavery and the Slave Power in the United States of America" in Blackwood's *Edinburgh Review,* January, 1853, pp. 1–20.

called Africans. Mrs. Tyler, wife of Ex-president Tyler, has been
induced to affix her name to a masculine production, called a response to the Dutchess of Sutherland.[308] A Mrs Howard, also,
representing herself to be an American woman, travelling in Italy,
has with several of her country-women addressed the ladies in
England, who signed the address adopted at Stafford House.
These letters emanate from slave-holders or their abettors and are
unworthy of serious consideration. If all they say of England is
true, they do not touch the merits of the question.[309] 'You sustained slavery and abolished it; We sustained slavery and ought to
refuse to listen to your admonitions because you have not abolished
every other evil.' This is logic worthy of knights of cat-o-nine-tails.

"The pressure on the slave-system, from both sides of the Atlantic, is extending anti-slavery feeling and sentiment, and causing
the slave holder to wince. The important Concession has recently
been made by the *Richmond* (Va) *Examiner,* which admits that if
the negro race is capable of rising to as high a point of intelligence
and usefulness as the white race the moral question, as to the right
of holding the negroes in bondage, would be decided forever. 'One
set of men,' it says, 'have no right to keep another set of men down
by force or law, to a grade of moral excellence and intellectual
power, lower and more confined than that of which they are capable.
Hence the enslavement of one portion of the white race by another
would be a moral wrong.'

"Our colored countryman, Rev. Dr. PENNINGTON, has recently
been elected moderator of the Third Presbytery in this City, a body
composed of a large number of the most influential Presbyterian
ministers among us. This is a sign of the times.

"Several of our periodicals are endeavoring to prejudice the
public mind against the DUTCHESS OF SUTHERLAND by intimating
that this distinguished lady, in the exercise of despotic power,
ejected from her estates the Scotch Gaelic population in 1811, when
Marchioness of Stafford, thereby confounding the present Dutchess
with another person bearing the same title. And one of them ex-
claims: 'The enemy of British Wages—Slavery has a right to condemn negro-slavery; a Dutchess of Sutherland, a Duke of Athol, a

[308] *The Christian Times,* February 25, 1853, p. 114; see Introduction.

[309] They also missed the point, of all points the most important to the
Evangelicals and especially to Lord Shaftesbury who refused to consider
physical welfare as of value without the benefits of religion.

Manchester Cotton-lord—never!' I have heard explanations of the course pursued by the predecessor of the Dutchess in 1811, that have satisfied a portion of the good people of Great Britain, but it would be well if Lord CARLISLE, or some one who is conversant with the facts, would state them once more for the information of those in this country who reverence him and his accomplished relative.

"The new President will, on the 4th. of March, take the oath of office. General PIERCE has been officially noticed of his election, and will, this week, proceed to Washington. It is not known, as yet, whom he has selected as Heads of Department and of course, his Constitutional advisors. His recent bereavement of an only child must have a happy effect upon the mind of an affectionate father, and lead him, one would think, to moderation and an abiding consciousness of his accountability. We hope and pray that his administration will be just, peaceful, honorable, prosperous; and that both he and the *members* of his administration will remember that 'RIGHTEOUSNESS EXALTETH A NATION; BUT SIN IS A REPROACH TO ANY PEOPLE.' ''

[LEWIS TAPPAN]

"NEW YORK, Feb. 15/53.

"PETER J. BOLTON, ESQ.

"My dear Sir,

"Enclosed is another letter for the Reporter, from your 'N.Y. Correspondent.' The february Reporter has not come to hand. Why?

"Rev. W^{m}. Goodell has written an excellent work on the Amer. Slave Code. I send you a table of contents & 48 pp. of the proof. The whole number of pages will be 432, including Index & Table of Contents. I wish you would immediately confer with Mr. Clark, publisher of Uncle Tom's Cabin, with a view to have it published simultaneously in London. We will not publish here until we hear from you, & by next Steamer will forward the balance of the proof sheets. You can make such an arrangement as you think best. I hope you will be able to secure ten per cent on the retail price for the benefit of the anti Slavery cause in this country, but whether you are able to do this, or obtain a less sum, or even nothing we shall be pleased to have the work published in London. We shall have it neatly bound in muslin, & part of the edition in Lawcalfe for the legal profession. In this way—perhaps in 8vo form —the price will be enhanced.

"I thank you for the newspapers you sent & as before stated shall be glad of every work, Review, paper &c on the anti S. question, subject, of course, to a charge for the expense.

"Will you send me a copy of Mr. Buxton on the African Slave Trade, Part 1st. I have the 2[d] part, viz. the Remedy, but believe you have both complete in one volume. I will also thank you to send me a few copies of 'Slavery & the Internal Slave Trade in the U.S.' [310] published by your Society. If you have in pamphlet form Lord Denman,[311] etc. on Uncle Tom please send them to me. I have rec[d]. Nos. 24 & 25 of the 'Slave,' [312] published at Newcastle Upon Tyne, I believe. Can you send me all the other nos?

"Very truly your's
"LEWIS TAPPAN."

"NEW YORK, Feb. 22/53.[313]

"PETER J. BOLTON, ESQ.
"Dear Sir,

"Mr John Wiley, Bookseller of this city, has rec[d]. from me & agreed to forward to Trubner & Co, 13 Paternoster Row, two par-

[310] *Slavery and the Internal Slave Trade in the United States* (London, published by the British and Foreign Anti-Slavery Society, 1841).

[311] Denman, Thomas (Lord), "Uncle Tom's Cabin, Bleak House, Slavery, and Slave Trade"—Six Articles reprinted from the *Standard* with "An Article Containing Facts Connected with Slavery" by Sir George Stephen, reprinted from the *Northampton Mercury* (London, 1853). Lord Denman argued against the *Times* reviewer of *Uncle Tom's Cabin.* Sir George Stephen reviewed both *Uncle Tom's Cabin* and *The White Slave.*

[312] *The Slave,* a monthly anti-slavery journal, published at Newcastle-upon-Tyne, was issued, beginning with January, 1855, from London, under a new editor, Elihu Burritt.

[313] Between this and the next Tappan letter, one of date May 17, might be placed two Scoble letters, written from America, the earlier of them having been addressed to Peter Bolton and the later to the B. & F. A-S. Society Committee.

(a)   "I cut the enclosed slips from the '*New York Daily Times*'—they have reference, as you will perceive to the slave-trade at Rio and the Havana. My object in sending them to you is that the attention of the Committee should be specially called to what appears to be the fact, that the British Government appear to be in earnest in urging upon the Spanish Authorities in Cuba the fulfilment of the treaties in our sense of the term. Now if this be so, the C[ee] should place itself in immediate communication with Lord Clarendon, now I understand Minister for Foreign Affairs, with a view of strengthening the hands of Government in this respect. If I were at home, I should suggest that a Deputation should wait on Lord C. & that in addition to the members of our C[ee], Samuel Gurney, Dr. Lushington, Sir E. N. Buxton, and as many Members of

cels (in one), the first containing 100 pamphlets, 'Indian Missions,' written by myself, and the second various publications for Mr W. E. Forster. I have paid the freight, duty & all expenses to Trubner & Co, so that you will have to pay only porterage from their establishment to your office.

"Enclosed is a list [314] of names, to whom the pamphlet should be sent, prepared by Mr Scoble. The others you will please distribute at your discretion. Please acknowledge the receipt & mention the distribution.

"I have already sent 48 pp. of Goodell's 'American Slave Code,' with a view to have it re-published in England. By this opportunity I send you the whole work. Let me know how much postage you pay on it, for use to us here hereafter. I have paid as far as I could, viz. to Liverpool—56 cents. I hope you will be able to

> Parliament as you could command, should be invited to accompany them, in the interview— I am sure public sympathy will be with you in such a . . . . I would further recommend that petitions to both Houses of Parliament embodying our views should be immed[y] presented, Lord Brougham would take that for the Lords, & would be aided by the Bishop of Gloucester & Lord Denman. Do see that this is followed up with spirit . . ." (Scoble to Bolton, March 8, 1853).

(b) In the second letter, Scoble after announcing that he and Mr. Tappan have heard that the Canadian Anti-Slavery Society is sending over the Reverend Samuel R. Ward, "a pure negro," to plead in Great Britain the cause of his oppressed brethren in the South, adds,

> "Mr. Garrison is not of the School of Mr. Ward— You need therefore be under no apprehension that Mr. W. will compromise you with any of the sentiments of his school— If there be any one point in which I differ from Mr. Ward, or rather which (I) have regretted in one or two of his addresses, it has been a tendency towards a belligerent spirit . . ." (Scoble to the B. & F. A.-S. Society Committee, April 7, 1853).

Of this second letter, only an extract is given here for the reason that only one page of it was found among the files at Denison House. What was the complete letter, presumably, is to be found in B. & F. A.-S. *Reporter*, New Series, I, 98–100. A memorandum on the surviving page at Denison House is as follows:

> "N. B. If this letter be published by the C*ee*, please send slips to the 'Patriot,' 'Banner,' 'Nonconformist,' 'Christian Times,' 'Wesleyan Times,' the 'Morning Advertiser,' and any other Journal that will be likely to insert it; and allow me to ask of you to forward early Copies, in slips, to Rev[d] Jno. Burnet, Rev[d] Wm. Brach, and Rev[d] J. H. Hinton, with my kind regards. *This requires immediate attention from the Committee.* Should the C*ee* decline using it, then please hand it to my son Richard who will be good enough to see it inserted in as many papers as possible & act upon my wish."

[314] Missing.

effect something with some bookseller for the benefit of the author & for the good of the cause.

"The Reporter for February (the parcel) has just been brought into the office, before the single copy by post! How is this? The Reporter looks well & I hope it will obtain a good circulation.

"When you requested me to write regularly you promised to write me, monthly, I think. Have you fulfilled this engagement? Are you the editor? How long I shall continue to send you letters I cannot say. Are they such letters as please your readers? On what day of the month must you have them to ensure publication in the next Reporter?

"I am grateful to you for the Addresses you sent, and for the newspapers I regularly receive. Do you wish me to send regularly a copy of all the anti Slavery publications published here? I will send them if you wish it very cheerfully. We desire your's— everything pro and con.

"Very truly your's

"LEWIS TAPPAN.

"Please send Jos. Sturge Esq a copy of 'Indian Missions.' "

"Office of the American & Foreign Anti S.

COPY.
Office,

"New York, May 17/53.

"Louis Alexis Chamerovzow,[315] Esq.

"Dear Sir,

"Your notes of April 15th and May 3d were duly received. I think I remember you at Exeter Hall, June, 1843. It is my earnest hope that you will be able to conduct the Reporter with the ability & fidelity to the cause that distinguished your predecessor, & to give satisfaction in your new office. I have but little confidence in efforts not conducted on Christian principles. It will give me satisfaction to interchange letters with you & to cooperate in advancing the interests of the cause in which we are engaged.

[315] G. W. Alexander, Joseph Cooper and Henry Sterry, empowered as a sub-committee to seek a successor to John Scoble (*Minute Books*, III, minute 667) in the office of secretary to the B. & F. A.-S. Society, were able to report at a meeting of the Committee, December 3, 1852, that L. A. Chamerovzow had been engaged for six months at the rate of £150 per annum (*idem*, minute 683). He was permanently engaged at a salary of £200 in July, 1853 (*idem*, minute 833).

"The re-print of Goodell's Slave Code and the copies of the Address to Xtian Chhs,[316] are received.

"Mr. Bowditch [317] has not yet published his work on the Slave laws. He is preparing a pamphlet or book, to contain the laws, decisions &c. I presume it is to be a law-book.

"It will be sometime yet before the publication of (?) &c appears. It is a work of much labor. We may print it in parts.

"I shall be greatly obliged for the *Magazines* that contain articles on Slavery, & for articles in Newspapers &c that are of interest.

"There have been two great political parties in this country, the Democratic and Whig, beside the Liberty party & the Free Democratic party. Last year in one of my letters to the London Patriot they were described. You will find there all that will be useful to you I think. The first of these letters appeared about a year since.

"As Mr. Scoble has now taken up his abode in Canada West you had best look to him for information respecting the colored fugitives. Rev. Samuel R. Ward,[318] now in England, can give you ample information also.

"Should not the publisher refund to you the sum paid for postage on proofs of Goodell's book? If not, charge it to our Society, & also whatever should be charged hereafter on books, etc.

"I suppose you receive the *National Era*, N.Y. *Standard* & Boston *Liberator* & *Commonwealth* regularly. These papers (weeklies) will inform you what is going on in the Anti Slavery cause, in addition to the letters I may send you. You take the N.Y. *Tribune* also I believe. Do you not?

---

[316] At a special meeting of the B. & F. A-S. Society Committee, March 23, 1853, the Secretary read a rough draft of this "Address to Christian Churches." It was approved and ordered to be printed in April (*Minute Books*, III, minute 739). B. & F. A-S. *Reporter*, April 1, 1853, pp. 85–87; May 2, pp. 108–109.

[317] William Ingersoll Bowditch had published, in 1849, a work entitled *Slavery and the Constitution*.

[318] The B. & F. A-S. Society Committee had had cause before hearing from either Scoble or Tappan to know something of the reputation of S. R. Ward. At its meeting, March 5, 1852, the Secretary had laid before it a letter from Dr. Willis, requesting aid to assist the Canadian Anti-Slavery Society in securing Ward's services in forwarding the cause. Hiram Wilson made a similar appeal with reference to another man. Both cases were held over for further consideration (*Minute Books*, III, minute 602). At this meeting one of Tappan's letters was laid before the Committee.

"The *Anti Slavery Advocate* [319] has been sent to me to 1st April. I shall be glad to receive them regularly. Have rec^d May no.

"Mr. (not Dr) Prime [320] is acting editor of the N.Y. Observer & a delegate from the American Bible Society. How Mr. Scoble could have said he went from the A. & For. Bible Soc. (a Baptist Soc) I do not understand. Doubtless it was an inadvertence, for he must have known the Soc. that deputed him. Mr. P. left here for England & intended to go, I believe, to Jerusalem &c. You say the Bible Soc no doubt concluded it was safer to announce that he (Mr. P) had not reported himself &c. Am I to understand from this that the Soc. did announce &c?

"I do not know of any overt act of Dr. Vermyle's [321] against the Anti-Slavery cause. He belongs to the large class of American ministers who stand aloof. I suppose Mr. Scoble named him in order that you sh^d not take it for granted that Dr. V. was an Anti-S. man, & if he should profess to be that you might interrogate him thoroughly. You ask me to keep you always promptly informed of the movements of pro-slavery clergymen from this country. I met with such poor success in advising the British public last year, and was so brutally attacked by Dr. Campbell in his *Banner,* that I had nearly made up my mind to let your editors & ministers find out the characters of visitors from this country, without a prompter. Dr. C. defended Mr. Chickering as a genuine Anti-Slavery man & abused me for advising to the contrary & when he had learned his mistake he had not the magnanimity to acknowledge it. Dr. V. has never to my knowledge, taken any part against the cause, as Chickering had, but has not that I can learn ever done anything to advance it.

"I send you two copies of Bibb. [322] You ask for other similar works. None have been printed lately. You have, I suppose, Henson's [323] Douglass' [324] & Clarke's. I will send you a catalogue of publications in the Depository connected with our office.

[319] *The Anti-Slavery Advocate* (October, 1852, to December 1, 1862) was a monthly, published in the Garrison interest. R. D. Webb was a leading spirit in it.

[320] The Reverend Samuel Irenaeus Prime.

[321] Dr. Thomas E. Vermilye, an American Presbyterian minister.

[322] Bibb, Henry, *Narrative of the Life and Adventures of an American Slave* (written by himself).

[323] Concerning the fugitive slave, Josiah Henson, who became pastor of the missionary settlement at Dawn in Canada, the following are of some slight interest:

"When you come to see our Annual Report for the past year you will have an accurate & concise statement of the progress of the Anti-Slavery cause during that period. Domestic matters have delayed it this year, but I hope to be able to complete it in a few weeks. Should our Society conclude to publish a monthly paper your wishes will be answered respecting information that I could give you. I have a great deal to do however that does not get into the paper. For example I have been several days engaged in Court attending to a kidnapping case, & it may consume several days more. Our committee are not particularly anxious to have all their labors published to the world, nor all their expenditures. Members of our Committee publish considerable Anti-Slavery matter in various papers of the day, anonymously. This is particularly the case with Judge Jay and myself. Much of my time is devoted to correspondence, furnishing facts &c to lecturers, writers &c. I am also treasurer of an Anti-Slavery Missionary Society, the income of which is $40,000 per annum. It employs 100 Missionaries and teachers, who all inculcate an Anti-Slavery gospel. This Society was founded chiefly by Members of our Committee & is sustained by those who sympathise with us. You know too, I suppose, that our Committee established the *National Era* at Washington (now owned by Dr. Bailey) of which 28000 copies are published weekly.

(*a*)   "BOSTON, Mar. 30, 1851
     "D^r. Sir
          "Y^r. favor of the 14th inst is rec^d by wh. I am glad to learn that Mr Henson has some prospect of substantial relief to his colony. We have great confidence in him, & take a lively interest in his success. It is from this cause, that besides the sums of money given to him at various times, Mr. Sam. A. Eliot, Mr. J. J. Bowditch & myself lent him temporarily a considerable sum, to be repaid from the proceeds of lumber to be shipped from his settlement to this port. He has exerted himself faithfully to perform his part of the contract, but there remains about $2700 or $2800 still unpaid.
          "I do not know of any other debts due from the Institution nor from Henson nor have I any copy of their deed of Trust.
                              "Respectfully
                                   "Y^r. Obt Ser^t
                                        "AMOS A. LAWRENCE.
     "John Scoble Esqr
     "London."

(*b*)   "He (Josiah Henson) had been a chained and manacled slave, but now he could stand on a platform in London, and a real English nobleman condescended to shake hands with him! And the British audience applauded him to the echo" (a satirical reference from the *New York Observer*).

³²⁴ Douglass, Frederick (1817–1895), *Autobiography*, originally published in 1845, but rewritten in 1855, and later

"We had an excellent Anniversary. The proceedings were printed in the Tribune. I send you a copy, tho. I suppose you receive the paper otherwise. Mr. Douglass made a magnificent speech. The account of the business meeting in the N.Y. *Herald* is a mere caricature. At this meeting an *Outline of Effort* was reported, and pledges made of about $14,000 to carry it out.

"Dr. & Mrs. Bailey expect to sail from this port for England on the 28th. Your rule about not publishing the names of your correspondents appears to be a good one, except in special cases.

"I propose that we pay here postages on all letters &c to your office, & that you do the same on communications to us. Sometimes, I fear, postage has been paid twice.

"L.T."

"New York,
"June 16 [325]/53

"L.A.CHAMEROVZOW, ESQ
"Dear Sir,
          "Since my last I have been very busy attending to the case of Jane Trainer,[326] a colored child of 9 years of age who was brought from Mobile in the State of Alabama, under the pretence of going to California on the part of the woman having her in charge, against the wishes of the child's father, a freeman of color who had followed the woman from Mobile in quest of his little daughter. The various legal steps taken have been reported in the New York City newspapers during the last five or six weeks. We were beaten before the first legal tribunal, but on bringing the case before a Judge in the adjoining County (King's Co) a significant name you may think, we succeeded & the child has been restored to its father. The decision of the Judge may be found in the paper of the 14th. It is an admirable paper. The whole pro-slavery influence of the press, the bar, the community, backed by a party of notorious bullies were arrayed against us. Great credit is due to E.D.Culver, Esq, the able counsel of Charles Trainer, and to Judge Barculo, for their noble conduct in the matter.

"Long & unwearied attention to this case has prevented me from

[325] Summarized with other matter in B. & F. A-S. *Reporter*, August 1, 1853, pp. 186–188.

[326] At the meeting of the B. & F. A-S. Society Committee, July 1, 1853, "Mr. Sturge read a letter from Lewis Tappan detailing some particulars of the rescue from Slavery of a little girl named Jane Trainer."

writing out the Annual Report. When I shall be able to finish it I cannot say.

"The Committee have issued an Appeal for the establishment of a weekly anti-slavery newspaper in the German language at the City of Washington.[327] A copy is enclosed. There are four millions of persons in the U.S. who speak that language constantly half of them being immigrants & half the descendants of immigrants. A large portion of their newspapers are edited by men who have little sympathy with either the Anti-Slavery cause or Christianity. A family paper in their own language, conducted on Christian principles & aiming to engage their support of the Anti-Slavery cause is, you will at once perceive a matter of great interest.

"We have just published an edition of 5000 copies of Jay's Letter to the Tract Society.[328] I received the beautiful copy of the English edition you sent me.

"The 3d edition of Goodell's American Slave Code is in the press.

"Ten thousand copies of Uncle Tom's Cabin have been sold at the Depository connected with our office, beside large numbers of other Anti-Slavery publications.

"Jewitt (Jewett?) & Co, the original publishers of Uncle Tom have in contemplation to publish a series of illustrated juvenile anti-slavery publications.[329]   "Very truly yours,
                                         "LEWIS TAPPAN.

[327] This project was endorsed by S. P. Chase, Charles Sumner, and Charles Francis Adams. The paper was to be *Der National Demokrat*, a weekly, and edited by Frederick Schmidt, formerly editor of the *Kirchenzeitung* of Pittsburgh.

> "The principal design . . . is to circulate among our vast German population a family newspaper, advocating Christian and Free Democratic principles . . . among the friends of genuine liberty and of the rights of man" (A. & F. A-S. Society *Annual Report*, 1853, p. 208).

[328] Jay, William (Judge), "Letter to the Reverend R. S. Cook," Corresponding Secretary of the American Tract Society. This was first published in the *Tribune* early in the spring, then in pamphlet form, and republished in London under the title, "The American Tract Society; withdrawal from by the Hon. Judge Jay, on the ground of its alliance with the slave power; proved by the expurgation of all anti-slavery sentiment from its publications, and its refusal to bear any testimony and opposition to the sin of slaveholding." Note also Jay's "Letters respecting the American Board of Commissioners for Foreign Missions and the American Tract Society."

[329] This company issued, during 1852 and the first half of 1853, no fewer than "four hundred and twenty-eight thousand volumes of anti-slavery publi-

"I have read the proceedings of your anniversary with much interest. A succint statement of the Trainer case will appear I suppose in next week's no of F. Douglas's Paper.[330]

"I have sent to Mr Jos. Sturge an interesting letter about Flax Cotton with specimens."

"NEW YORK,
"November 19/53

"L.A.CHAMEROVZOW, ESQ,

"My dear Sir,

"I hope you received the copies of our Annual Report that were sent to you. For the copies of your Report please to accept our best thanks, & also for the copies of the Review. Both are valuable documents.[331] I have distributed them to influential friends of the cause & you may be assured they will do great good.

"We have issued a Circular [332] on the subject of petitioning Congress, and hope that numerous petitions will be poured in. This will stimulate the anti-Slavery members of Congress to agitate the subject of Slavery in the National Legislature, and the reflex influence will be Salutary upon the public mind. If I do not send you one of these Circulars you will see it in the N.Era and other Anti-Slavery newspapers.

"The German newspaper established at the City of Washington under the auspices of our Committee has met with good success. It is ably edited, & is well received by a large portion of the German population. Have you seen the paper? I shall send you one.

cations." These included, in addition to *Uncle Tom's Cabin* and the *Key*, Jay's *Miscellaneous Writings on Slavery*, Giddings' *Speeches in Congress*, Mrs. Stowe's *Two Altars*, Sumner's *White Slavery in the Barbary States*, and also *Autographs for Freedom* (A. & F. A-S. Society *Annual Report*, 1853, p. 131).

[330] At this time the eighth volume of this paper was in course of completion. It was a weekly anti-slavery journal, published in Rochester, N. Y., devoted to the interests of the free colored people.

[331] The A. & F. A-S. Society *Report*, its *Thirteenth Annual* (1853), is especially valuable for a survey of the attitude of American churches and missionary societies towards slavery (see pp. 66–130).

[332] See *National Era*, December 1, 1853, p. 189. The Circular pronounced against slavery in the District of Columbia as being unconstitutional, discreditable, and wrong in itself; against the slave trade, coastwise and internal; against slavery in new Territories and wherever, under the Constitution, the Free States are responsible for it; and, finally, against the Fugitive Slave Act, demanding its repeal.

"Your note of 2d Sept was duly rec^d. I have read the proceedings of the Convention at Edinburgh [333] with much interest, and the discussions, and result, of the friends of the Anti S. cause. They were marked with much wisdom.

Private. "Enclosed is a note for Mr Hemming.[334] Please ask him to show it to you. I want you to understand fully his relations to the cause here. When he proposed going to England he offered to use his influence with the members of his own denomination, to receive whatever pecuniary aid they might put into his hands to be used by our Committee. I encouraged him in this matter but when he spoke of more extended operations I advised him that the Com. were not prepared to commission him to act publickly in England for them. Since then he has written to me most enthusiastically about a plan entered into by British abolitionists to raise a large amount of money & to give our Society a portion of it, saying he has been engaged to lecture &c, &c,. Please inform me how far all this corresponds with your views—what Mr H. has done & contemplates doing in G.B. &c, &c

"By & by I intend to write to you at greater length. Meantime I am very truly yours,

"LEWIS TAPPAN.

"Your name was unfortunately spelled wrong in the Reporter owing to the carelessness of the proof-reader."

[333] See B. & F. A-S. *Reporter,* October 1, 1853, p. 228.

[334] At its first of July meeting, the B. & F. A-S. Society Committee had considered the substance of a communication from the Reverend Mr. Hemming soliciting "co-operation to promote the object of his visit to England, namely to raise funds for the American & Foreign Anti-Slavery Society to aid an anti-slavery mission amongst the various religious bodies of the United States. . . . It was thought desirable to communicate further with Lewis Tappan on the subject, which Mr. Joseph Sturge undertook to do" (*Minute Books,* III, minute 860).

A letter from Sturge reveals the next step in the case,

"I am obliged by thine of yesterday and return herewith Lewis Tappan & Geo. Thompson's— With regard to the former I quite think that if Henning [sic] does not shew thee Lewis Tappan's letter we sh^d. let our Manchester Friends know that he has represented himself in a position with regard to the American & Foreign Anti-Slavery Society which the facts do not warrant. I greatly fear if they entrust their movement to him he will shipwreck it, though doing his best to promote it— I am confirmed in this view from what Lewis Tappan says he has written to him . . ." (Sturge to Chamerovzow, December 8, 1853).

"NEW YORK, February 14, 1854.

Queries About expurgations.

How many Slaves in 1852 & 1853
got across to Canada.

"L.A.CHAMEROVZOW, Esq.

"Dear Sir,

"Your letter of Dec.30th. was received
while I was in Massachusetts. It was my intention to have replied
to it before, but numerous engagements have prevented; and now,
I find that your letter is mislaid, so that I shall have to depend upon
my recollection of its contents or postpone writing to you. I choose
the former alternative & throw myself upon your candour. The
past year has been one of peculiar trial and unusual labor. Bereavement & sickness in my family have occupied much of my time, and
the rest has been engrossed by labors in the anti slavery and missionary enterprises. You know I suppose, that in addition to my
duties as Cor. Sec. of the Amer & For. Anti S.Society I am Treasurer of the Amer.Missionary Association, a Society founded chiefly
by the officers & friends of the A & F. Anti S.Soc. This Association was founded about seven years since, on anti-slavery principles,
& has arisen from small beginnings to its present condition. We
have sent forth nearly 200 missionaries & teachers into the Western
States, into two Slave States, to Jamaica & other foreign countries.
All inculcate an anti-slavery gospel, & our missionaries in slave
States have founded anti-slavery churches & employ coporteurs
[sic] to circulate anti-slavery & other tracts. For a time I had the
labour of editing a monthly paper for each of the Societies. The
missionary Society has now two Secretaries, issues a monthly paper
of which it circulates gratuitously 18,000 copies, and the income the
past year was forty two thousand dollars. The donors are chiefly
anti-slavery in their sentiments & sympathise with the Amer. & For.
Anti Slavery Society. I mention these things to shew you how
much is doing by anti-slavery Christians in this country, and how
greatly my time is occupied, and not from any egotistical or selfish
motive as by some I am slanderously reported. Labor in this cause
brings its own reward, & it would evince anything but a due appreciation of it to boast of one's labors or extol those with whom you
are privileged to labor. Considering the magnitude of the work &
the feeble efforts of man in its prosecution it becomes us all to
acknowledge that we are but unprofitable servants, & unless the

Divine blessing accompanies our laborers [*sic*] they will all be in vain or worse than in vain.

"I think you have done right in making the Reporter a register of anti-slavery facts, and notices of anti slavery efforts, irrespective of the different branches of the anti slavery body. The *National Era,* at Washington, founded by our Committee, has not devoted much space to a record of the doings of the Society of which Mr Garrison is President, because the editor, Dr Bailey, is averse to *polemic* abolition. For the same reason, our Society, while it refrains from censure of the other Society, avoids all needless reference to it, being content to fulfil its own mission, and not obstruct others in their mode of promoting the anti slavery cause. We have aimed to conduct our operations on Christian principles. The consequence has been that some, unenlightened or prejudiced on this subject, stigmatise us as *bigots,* while they complain of being called, by not a few, *infidels.* Let candid men judge of both parties by what they do, and what they circulate, and let professed anti slavery men refrain from hurling at each other abusive epithets. Were the abolitionists in your country & ours united, in heart & judgment, and striving for the downfal of slavery as their principal object, greater progress would undoubtedly be made.[335] Whether

---

[335] Much this same idea was expressed by Thomas Sturge, who objected to the B. & F. A-S. Society's taking its stand on the principle that slavery was a sin. He deplored the schisms that it would occasion and said,

"I think that the British & Foreign Anti-Slavery Society ought instead of limiting the number of those who are desirous of helping to remove oppression to have opened wide the doors to all without distinction or restriction of creed" (Thomas Sturge to Chamerovzow, November 24, 1854).

Of the whole anti-slavery period this was the part of it when animosities— many of them largely personal—were most rife within the anti-slavery ranks. This was true of Great Britain as of the United States, although in the latter country the spirit of the extremist was far more uncompromising than in the former. Perchance, it was the large Quaker element in British philanthropy and the Quaker spirit, firm yet gentle, that enabled Britain to be spared the ugly personalities that so disgraced the cause in America. Much of the factional bitterness did, however, extend itself beyond the confines of the United States and sympathizers in England, Scotland, and Ireland took up one American dispute after another. For one instance of this and one account, see Quincy, Edmund, *An Examination of the Charges of Mr. John Scoble and Mr. Lewis Tappan against the American Anti-Slavery Society* (London, 1852). The Scoble-Tappan charges were three in number, viz., that the Amer. A-S. S.

1. Has abandoned its original ground of political action
2. Has changed its original policy of church action
3. Is infidel in its tendencies and instrumentalities

this be practicable with you I know not, but it is not practicable here while such different views prevail, & while so much unholy temper predominates. Thousands are kept from open advocacy of the anti Slavery cause, or identifying themselves with those associated to promote it, on account of these bickerings, calumnies, and contentions; and it [is] believed by many that the anti Slavery enterprise would prosper more, far more, than it now does were all existing anti Slavery Societies in this country disbanded.

"The sum contemplated to be secured previous to setting in operation the Plan announced in the last Annual Report has not been raised. I have not been able to devote much time to it, & various causes have retarded the effort to raise the needful sum. I have almost dreaded the success of the scheme, fearing that the amount of labour that might be required of me would, considering my state of health, age & pressing avocations, be beyond my ability and strength. In this connection I will reply to your questions about Rev. F. Heming, who is now in England, & supposed by some to be an agent of our Society for the purpose of raising funds. Mr H. is a worthy Wesleyan minister, an Englishman by birth, who has resided in this country some years. He has been sustained in his pastoral labors in part by the *Amer.Missionary Association.* Being about to sail for England, as a delegate to his denomination in your country, *he suggested* that he might be offered funds there or be able to raise them, for the promotion of the anti slavery cause in this country. I told him *our Society had always been averse to soliciting money abroad for such a purpose,* but if any persons of his denomination or out of it in England, should *offer* him money, in a private way, to be used here, he might receive & transmit it. In furtherance of *his views* I gave him a letter of recommendation, *but our Ex.Com. have never appointed him agent,* nor have they been informed that he has ever acted in that capacity. I have no doubt that Mr. Heming is a good man, and is actuated by good principles. Whether he has been discreet in all his movements abroad those who have witnessed his course can better judge than myself. He has been the subject of censure I learn, and it has probably proceeded from those who do not understand or are willingly prejudiced against a simple-hearted & ardent Christian man who can not coincide with them in all their plans and feelings.

George Thompson, R. D. Webb, F. W. Chesson, and others entered the lists in defence of the Garrisonians.

"Mr O. Johnson, the enterprising editor of the *Standard,* an anti slavery weekly paper published in this City, of the Garrison School, has, with the aid of those agreeing with him, got up a series of anti-Slavery lectures in the Broadway Tabernacle. Gentlemen of different views and affinities have been invited to give lectures. I have attended all the lectures except those delivered in my absence from the City, and, in general, have been much gratified, not only with the good attendance & perfect order, of the meetings, but with the large amount of anti-slavery truth uttered by the lecturers. A similar course of lectures has been begun at Boston by the orthodox ministers of that City, and three gentlemen of this City, two of them laymen and one a minister, are to take part in them. Both these series will, I trust, do good, and extend a knowledge of the principles of the anti Slavery body.

"There is a subject now before the Congress of the United States of transcendant importance. A bill, called the Nebraska bill, has been introduced into the Senate by Mr Douglass, [*sic*] who, although he represents in part the free State of Indiana is said to be, in the right of his wife, the owner of a slave plantation at the South. This bill has for its avowed object the organization of the vast territory east of the Rocky mountains & beyond the limits of the States & Territories of the Union into one or more territories with a view to their becoming states in the Confederacy at some future day, leaving the question open, whether Slaveholders may move into & hold slaves in the new territories. Mr Douglass, an aspirant for the Presidency, is, with his adherents, pushing the bill forward with indecent haste, in hopes of getting it passed by both houses of Congress before the people in this extensive Republic can be aroused to a consideration of the enormity of the scheme, and by their remonstrances, defeat it. The territory referred to is large enough to make twelve States of the largest class. Momentous will be the results whether the bill becomes a law or not.

"The deputation [336] from the Society of Friends to present an Address [337] to the President of the U.S. and to each of the governors of the States have nearly completed their philanthropic labors. They have been received generally, it is said, with the attention due to their character & to the important matter they had in charge.

[336] The deputation was from the London Yearly Meeting and consisted of William Forster, his brother Josiah, John Candler, and W. Holmes.

[337] B. & F. A-S. *Reporter,* March 1, 1854, pp. 53–54; April 1, 1854, p. 84.

Their friends here are greatly distressed to learn that one of the deputation, the venerable and good WILLIAM FORSTER,[338] has sunk under the fatigue to which he has been exposed, and has died in East Tennessee. His services have been invaluable, and he was great(ly) beloved not only at home but in this country. 'Precious in the sight of the Lord is the death of his Saints.'

"Mr E. Barritt [339] is now here prosecuting his Ocean Penny Postage enterprise with very encouraging success. This 'Citizen of the World' is everywhere received with the attention due to his character & to the importance of the object he has in view.

"You ask me to renew my correspondence for the Reporter & desire to know whether you may affix my signature to my letters. It will give me pleasure to write to you occasionally & I have no objection to my name being put to what I may write.

"Most heartily do I wish you & all who are engaged in the great work of promoting human freedom abundant success in all good efforts.
"Very truly yours
"LEWIS TAPPAN.

"*Private.* Should you publish my letter I prefer to have it published entire.

"I have mislaid Mr Heming's address. Please forward the enclosed note to him."

"NEW YORK, 8th April, 1854.
"My dear Sir,

"The bearer is Mr Alexander Macdonald, a member of our Ex. Com. & a sound abolitionist.

"I send you several publications recently published by our Society or written by members of the Ex. Com.

Dr. Perkins's [340] Sermon is doing great good in this country. He is a highly esteemed missionary of the 'American Board of

---

[338] William Forster, who had married Anna Buxton, sister of Sir Thomas Fowell Buxton, had made two previous visits to the United States, one in the early 'twenties and the other in 1845, on business connected with the Society of Friends. His son, William Edward Forster, was, like him, early identified with the anti-slavery cause and aided Bright and Cobden in behalf of the North in the American Civil War, and was the author of the Education Act of 1870, virtually providing for universal elementary education in England.

[339] Elihu Burritt. See ante, footnote 200, for a sketch.

[340] Justin Perkins (1805–69). In another letter of the same date Tappan says that a large edition of Perkins's discourse was published. Perkins was a missionary in Persia.

Commissioners for Foreign Missions.' His rebukes will be felt in the right places.

"Mr Goodell's Prize Essay,[341] written at the request of a church of converted heathen, is a timely & able production.

"Judge Jay's 'Examination of the Mosaic Laws of Servitude' [342] is the best treatise that has ever been published in this country on the subject. Will you put them into the hands of some of your able men & get a Review of it in some of your quarterlies?

"Drayton's Memoir [343] will interest you.

"I send you a splendid copy of Senator Sumner's admirable Speech in Congress, entitled 'The Landmark of Freedom.' [344] Also a few copies of Mr Goodell's new paper entitled 'American Jubilee.' [345] You will find that instead of considering that the Constitution of the U.S. is pro-slavery he takes higher ground & contends that the execrable system is both unconstitutional & illegal.

"I have just had the pleasure of conversing with Mess[rs] Forster and Candler whose visit to this country has done much good.

"I send you a catalogue of our anti slavery publications. If there are any you want for the Society's Library please inform me.

"The recent elections have shown the administration that the People are indignant at the prospect of establishing Slavery in Nebraska. "Your's truly
"L. TAPPAN.

"L.A. Chamerovzow, Esq.
    "London."

                    "BROOKLYN, NEAR
                "NEW YORK, 20th April 1854.
    "My dear Sir,
            "Being four miles from Mr. Murray's I was not able, during the storm, to call on you the day or evening before

[341] For Goodell's (1792–1878) career, see "Memorial of William Goodell" (1879).

[342] Jay, William, *An Examination of the Mosaic Laws of Servitude*—"The Statutes of the Lord are right"—Psalm xix. 8 (New York, 1854).

[343] Drayton, Daniel, *Personal Memoir of*, for four years and four months a Prisoner (for Charity's sake) in Washington Jail; including a Narrative of the Voyage and Capture of the Schooner Pearl (Boston, 1855).

[344] Sumner, Charles, "The landmark of freedom"; Speech of, against the repeal of the Missouri prohibition of slavery north of 36° 30', February 2, 1854.

[345] *The American Jubilee* anticipated the creed of the New York City Abolition Society that slavery was "inconsistent with the Declaration of Independence, and contrary to the Constitution of the United States." B. & F. A.-S. *Reporter*, June 1, 1855, p. 123.

you left in the Atlantic. I went to the ship, however, the next morning & deeply regretted not being able to get near to you & to give the parting hand to yourself & your esteemed associates. I handed a brief note to a passenger, with a book & letter for our friend Jos. Sturge which I hope were given to you.

"The weather has been so tempestuous since your departure that I am apprehensive you have had an uncomfortable time. I trust however that under the care of a kind Providence you will have arrived home in safety.

"I thank you for the documents you sent me from Burlington. Should you, or either of your associates print anything further I shall be pleased to receive a copy. Or should any Memoir of our deceased friend & brother William Forster be published I hope to have a copy sent to me.

"It is my earnest hope that the visit of the deputation to this country will be attended with happy results.

"With respects to your family I remain, my dear Sir, Very truly your's

"Lewis Tappan.

"Josiah Forster, Esq
    "England"

                         "BROOKLYN,
                     "NEAR NEW YORK,
                          "Oct 29/54.[346]

"L.A.CHAMEROVZOW, ESQ.
  Sec. of the B. & F. Anti S.Soc.
"Dear Sir,

      "A day or two since I received your note of the 10th in which you ask for a variety of information, relating to the position & prospects of the Anti-Slavery cause in this country, and expressing a wish that an answer should be returned by the first steamer for November. The information you request can not be furnished with accuracy in so short a time. It would take a month's hard labor to collect & arrange it, and to work out the reflections that should accompany it. As I expect to go into a neighboring State to attend to some important business, on the morrow, and to be

[346] Between this date and the preceding, the only letter found was a short one, May 1st, introducing the Reverend James B. Walker of Ohio, "a true-hearted abolitionist and a gentleman greatly esteemed," who "visits England for literary & other purposes."

much engrossed with it for some weeks to come I am necessitated to write you at once & give you such information as lies in my mind.

"Your first inquiry is, How British abolitionists can promote the Anti-Slavery cause in the United States. I answer 1. By promoting the disuse of American cotton. 2. By able essays on the impolicy, wickedness, and unprofitableness of Slavery. 3. By non-fellow-shipping slave holders. 4. By discriminating between the active and lukewarm friends of freedom when they visit England. 5. By correspondence. 6. By aiding self-emancipated slaves who seek refuge in Canada. 7. By aiding the emancipated in the British West Indies. 8. By affording pecuniary assistance to unexceptionable Anti-Slavery efforts in this country & in other countries. 9. By influencing your Government and the governments of other countries to do all they can for universal emancipation. 10. By influencing the British people to cherish and diffuse civil and religious liberty, and to be an example to this and every nation worthy of imitation, and 11. By prayer to Almighty God that Freedom, physical and mental, may prevail throughout the world.[347]

"You next inquire about the various religious denominations and associations, slaveholding or pro-slavery which refuse to take

[347] A large order this. Its all-embracing and widely diffuse character would seem to lay Tappan open to the charge that he, the A. & F. A-S. Society and the B. & F. A-S. Society made against the Garrisonians of uniting with the one great cause of anti-slavery, alien issues. It also exemplifies the patronizing and almost dictatorial attitude that he, in his letters, so often assumed towards those, who, across the Atlantic, were working in a far bigger, broader way than he, with his complicated domestic situation, was able to do; but no offence seems ever to have been taken at the superiority and self-righteousness of his tone and the acceptance of his suggestions was generous in the extreme. Some of the responses are indicated in our Introduction, one other may, with advantage, be given here. It is taken from the article on "American Slavery," already referred to, which appeared in the *Westminster Review*, January, 1853, and which was considered so admirable that, at Mr. W. E. Forster's own request, steps were taken by the B. & F. A-S. Society Committee to re-publish it in pamphlet form along with his *British Philanthropy and Jamaica Distress* (*Minute Books*, III, minutes 803, 873).

"... Is the only practical sympathy we can give sympathy with the cotton-planters, in fear for our cotton-mills? Alas, There is but little that we can do. We can think the truth, and speak it; we can say that Slavery is a sin and an evil. ... But all this is but mere words or thoughts; as to deeds, America must do them herself—one nation cannot do the work of another" (pp. 165–166). Continuing and with the prospect of an Anglo-American alliance in mind, the author said,

"Let that fight once be finished, let but America herself be free,—then, and not till then, England and America together will shield the oppressed against the despots of the world" (p. 167).

action against slavery &c,. All these denominations and associations in the Slave States refuse to take any action against the system or the practice of slaveholding. There are associations belonging equally to the Free and Slave States that by the mutual consent of their members ignore the claims of the slave. I instance the Episcopal church & the Presbyterian church. In the Annual Report of the Amer. & For. Anti-Slavery Society for 1853 you will find all the information that I can now furnish, except that the N.S. Presbyterians have, since that date, refused to entertain the question of slavery & a relaxation has taken place in one or two portions of the Episcopal church on the subject of Caste. I have not time to prepare a tabular statement, as you request.

"3. You ask for information respecting national religious institutions, such as Bible Societies &c. that refuse to take action against slavery or expurgate anti-Slavery sentiments from their publications.

"The Amer. Bible Society once sent an agent to Exeter Hall to announce that every family in the United States had been or soon would be furnished with a copy of the Holy Scriptures, when it had not taken any step towards supplying the slave population with the Bible. Soon after the Amer. Anti Slav. Soc. (before the division of the anti-slavery body) proffered to the Bible Soc. $5000 to aid in supplying the slaves with the sacred volume, every five slaves to be considered a family. But, although seven denominations were represented in the Committee that made the proposition it was churlishly rejected. Since then the Bible Society has invited contributions for the Slaves, as if it had a fund for that special object, and though funds were contributed to such supposed fund, all the money received has been put into the general fund, and no special effort has been made to supply the slaves with Bibles. In the usual meaning of the term it is therefore a pro-slavery institution, managed by men who take no interest in the anti-Slavery movement. On application the Society does make grants of Bibles to the fugitives in Canada, and to the destitute everywhere, yet it does not use exertions to circulate the Bible among the slave population. The plea has been that the slaves can not read, & that the laws in Slave States forbid them to learn to read. And yet the Christian anti-Slavery missionary Society, the 'American Missionary Association,' of which I have the honor to be Treasurer, does supply slaves with Bibles in Slave States thro' the agency of its colporteurs and missionaries. These facts are known, or should be (for they have again and again been published to the world) to the officers of the British & Foreign Bible Society, and yet that venerable institution has never to my knowledge, lifted up its voice in remonstrance against the cruel neglect of three millions of my countrymen in chains who have been shut out from the possession of the sacred volume.

"The 'American Tract Society' wielding an annual income of nearly a hundred thousand pounds sterling, and scattering its publications over the whole country, has never published a syllable on the sinfulness of American Slavery. Nay, it has systematically and perseveringly expurgated every American or English Work it has published of every denunciation of Slavery, while it has not failed to publish tracts against dancing, intemperance, lewdness, desecration of the Lord's day, theatrical entertainments, etc,.

"The 'American Sunday School Union,' another large & influential national institution, which scatters publications for the young in the form of Sunday School books over the country has intended scrupulously to refrain from touching the subject of Slavery, and has, at the dictation of its patrons in Slave States, suppressed one of its most popular works containing a mild definition of Slavery and alluded to one of its abuses which had accidentally found a place among its standard works.[348]

"These Societies are patronized by ministers and Churches of every evangelical denomination, North and South, & but few, except technical abolitionists, protest against the practices alluded to.

"4. You want information respecting the effects of the Nebraska and Kansas Bill & a sketch of the proceedings in Congress in relation to it. These proceedings have been widely published. The effect has been that a revival of the anti-slavery spirit has taken place—the members who voted for the iniquitous measure have generally been defeated when candidates for re-election—and tens of thousands of citizens from the free States are emigrating to the New Territories, determined to plant the standard of freedom there and defend it at all hazards. Most signally has the Almighty caused the wrath of man to praise Him in this matter.

"5. You request a statement of the real obstacles which slave

[348] Tappan, Lewis, "Letters respecting a book" "dropped from the catalogue" of the American Sunday School Union in compliance with the dictation of the slave power (New York, 1848).

holders & the apologists of the system say exist to complete and immediate emancipation.

"It is said that the negro is an inferior being, incapable of self-government; that his ignorance disqualifies him for exercising the duties of a freeman; that emancipation would fill the nation with colored paupers, endanger the lives of the white population on whom the Slaves would wreak their vengeance; that Slave labor is indispensable to the cultivation of the low ground in the Southern States; that God has ordained the perpetual servitude of the African race; that slavery is the corner stone of a republican edifice; that slavery has brought thousands & millions under the influence of the gospel who would otherwise have been lost; & that emancipation has signally failed in the West Indies.

"6. In all the Slave States restrictions exist upon free people of color, and every Slave State except Kentucky & Missouri prohibits emancipation in the State.

"7. Every Slave State prohibits the teaching of slaves to read. I send you a copy of the 'American Slave Code' that you may see all the laws on this and other subjects referring to slaves.

"8. The internal slave trade is carried on constantly between the old & the new States, and thousands and tens of thousands are annually sold to the 'far South.'

"9. The free colored people are subject to many disabilities in the slave States, & laws are passed from time to time to induce their emigration. In the free States a kinder feeling prevails generally than in previous years. Still they are not allowed the same privileges as are the white population; and a cruel prejudice still prevails founded upon condition and color, making a distinction as universal & onerous as exists in England between masters and liveried servants, and subjecting the free people of color to far greater inconveniences.

"10. You ask what are, so far as can be ascertained, the avowed projects of the Slave-power? They avow their intention to preserve an equality of political power in the government of the country by the admission of slave States equal to the number of new free States; they aim to procure a decision of the Supreme Court of the U.S. that the Constitution allows slaves to be taken into all the States of the Union the same as other 'property'; they advocate the repeal of laws forbidding the African Slave trade; they intend to annex Cuba, the Sandwich Islands, Central America

& Mexico, and by treaties more favorable to England than to the
U.S. prevent the annexation of Canada. The recent elections demonstrate that the people of the free States are aroused in opposition
to the new doctrines avowed by Slaveholders, and strong hopes are
cherished by the friends of freedom that the slave power is check-
mated.

"11. You next inquire what measures the anti-slavery body
contemplate taking to defeat the projects of the slaveholders. The
number of abolitionists in this country, that is those who advocate
immediate emancipation, is comparatively small. In the Congress
there are eight or ten perhaps who are called abolitionists, but most
of them go no farther than to contend that slavery should be
divorced from the general government. They & most of the anti-
Slavery people of the country concede that, under the Constitution,
the States have the exclusive right to manage slavery according to
their own policy. But, by the anti-Slavery body, I suppose you
may mean those who are enrolled in the Amer. Anti-S.Soc. or the
A. & For. Anti-S. Soc. These bodies, as you know, differ materially
in principle and action. The former contends that slavery is allowed by the Constitution & they advocate a dissolution of the
Union. Thus many think they are playing into the hands of the
slaveholders, who contend for the same thing, only the latter argue
that the institution of slavery ought to be protected by the people
of the U.S. while the former justly scout that notion. The Amer.
Anti-S. Soc. are, of course, doing nothing directly to defeat the
projects of the slaveholders. The Amer. & For. Anti-S.Soc. have,
from the beginning of their existence, used moral & political efforts
to withstand the Slave power & bring about emancipation, believing
that the Constitution is an anti-Slavery instrument.

"Within a few years a new political party has arisen called the
Free Soil party. They contend for a deliverance of the general
Government from all support of slavery, for excluding it from the
Territories of the U.S., for the prohibition of new Slave States, &c,.
This party has recently taken the name of the Republican party
with a view to add to their large numbers from the Democratic &
Whig parties who have got tired of their parties & who are desirous
of enlisting under the banner of Freedom. This party is now
rapidly increasing & hope to have a majority in the next House of
Representatives, or at least weight sufficient to control a majority.

"The 'anti-slavery body' then may be considered as including at the present time all the friends of freedom, all who aim to prevent the extension of Slavery, to divorce it from the general Government, and by moral & political means to circumscribe & annihilate slavery in this country, so far as it can be done under the Constitution.

"12. In Alabama & perhaps one or more other slave States intimations have been thrown out that some relaxation of the slave code might be advantageously made, but I have not heard of any legislative measure to that effect. No doubt the suggestion was prompted by the pressure of public opinion in the free States. There is not, I think, evidence that any sincere intention exists to ameliorate the condition of the slave, in any of the Slave States.

"13. You ask what are the real and peculiar difficulties which abolitionists consider to stand in the way of emancipation? The greatest difficulty undoubtedly is, next to the hardness of heart engendered by slavery, that slaveholders find a ready market in England for their cotton. The next is the two great political parties of the country, by forming, in turn, an alliance with the slave power obtain the control of the government with the offices in the gift of the administration & the disbursement of the revenue of the country. Another difficulty is the prevailing opinion that a compromise was made by the framers of the Constitution by which Slavery was to be forever under the control of the states where it exists, & that the Gov. of the U.S. is obligated to return fugitive Slaves to their masters. Another difficulty has existed in a majority of the ministers of the gospel and members of churches claiming that slavery is not sinful *per se,* that slavery existed among the Jewish people & is not forbidden by the Gospel. The Fugitive Slave Bill & the Nebraska & Kansas Bill have opened the eyes of the clergy and the laity in the free States, on these subjects, & a vast change has taken place in public sentiment.

"You express a wish to know what the Amer. & For. Anti-Slavery Society is doing. I frankly reply, very little. Its mission is about ended. The whole northern country is now awakening to the evils, encroachments and desperation of slavery and a continuance of the old societies for the promulgation of anti-Slavery sentiments or for anti-Slavery measures seems needless. Conventions will be held from time to time and associations formed for special purposes. The anti-Slavery cause will move on. Politicians will urge it on in their way; religious men will prosecute (*sic*) it in their associations and those who were early in the field may aid the various plans on foot according to their ability and pleasure.

"Those who have conducted the affairs of the Amer. & For. Anti-Slavery Society feel that they have acted on the principles of the first association, formed twenty years since, and of which they claim to be the legitimate successors; that they have diffused far and wide a vast amount of anti-slavery intelligence; that they have contributed essentially to the prevalence of the anti-slavery sentiment now extensively prevailing in the free States; that the *National Era* was established by them, out of which proceeded Uncle Tom's Cabin and other influences greatly exceeding in magnitude the effect of all other anti-slavery papers in the country; that several standard anti-slavery works have been published under their auspices; that the American Missionary Association with its 200 missionaries and teachers all inculcating Christian anti-slavery sentiments has been founded by them & exists with increasing prospects of usefulness; and that the anti-slavery enterprise as conducted by them has been commended to the religious feelings of the people throughout the country.

"I notice the remarks you have made respecting the lack of 'vital energy' in our Society. We do not incline to boast of what we have done. There is such a thing as making an ostentatious display and yet accomplishing very little good. Under the circumstances of the country, the division of abolitionists, and the state of religious and political parties we have done what was deemed wisest & best, with the means at our disposal. I suppose that no abolitionist in the United States has done more, if so much, than Judge Jay, one of the Vice Presidents of our Society & a member of the Ex.Com. Large quantities of anti-slavery publications have been circulated from our Depository, and the correspondence has been extensive, in addition to what has been previously related of the doings of the Society & the principal members of the Ex.Com. If others have done more we are glad of it. We have not laboured for applause, but to do good, & therefore do not wish to institute a comparison between what has been essayed or accomplished by others & ourselves.

"I am not disposed to enter into a discussion, suggested by your remarks respecting the Amer. Anti-S.Soc. Those who have read their papers for ten years past and heard their lecturers or read the reports of their lectures & addresses, both in England & in this country, should be able to form a pretty accurate judgment of their merits & how far they have advanced the cause of freedom in this land. For one, believing that no real or permanent good can be achieved for the anti-Slavery cause where its advocates do not found their principles upon the Bible I have believed and do believe that much of what has passed for anti-slavery discussion in this country instead of advancing the cause has retarded it—greatly retarded it.

"You say 'I am aware that there arose some years ago a fierce & a bitter feud between them (the old organisation) and yourselves.' And you think 'that there would be found no difficulty—were the attempt resolutely made—to unite all abolitionists in your country (the U.S.) to cooperate on a common basis &c,.' Our Society was formed because some leading men in the old Society foisted upon it views & measures not originally contemplated by its founders & departed from some of those adopted by these who established the Society while they took unusual & extraordinary measures to obtain a majority of votes to carry the objects they had in view. The new Society as has already been intimated, determined to carry out the views of the original founders of the Amer. Anti-Slavery Society, & they have done so, with calmness, good-temper & without any bitterness towards those from whom they felt bound to separate. The 'bitter feud,' so far as it has existed, has been altogether on the other side. You are greatly mistaken in supposing that all the professed abolitionists of this country could unite on 'a common basis.' The principles & modus operandi of the two divisions are diametrically opposed to each other. Still, I think the papers conducted by those belonging to the old organisation have been, of late, less bitter than formerly towards our Society.

"If the anti-slavery body had been true to the original principles of their association, and kept united, their influence would have been far more powerful than it has been. The separation, after the course pursued by the present leaders of the old organisation, was unavoidable unless the cause had been surrendered to those who had other objects in view & whose course alienated from them the evangelical Christians of the country. A tremendous responsibility has thus been taken by those who caused the division. Divine Providence will, I doubt not, raise up another band of abolitionists to carry the great work to a consummation. The seed has been sown though it has been amidst storms and dissentions. It has sprung up & will yet yield an abundant harvest when perhaps the original sowers are passed away and forgotten.

"You may be assured that no slight differences divided the Anti-Slavery body here, as you seem to suppose. But I must close. Your letter seemed to call for an expression of my views on the various topicks alluded to in it, & they have been expressed with frankness but without any unkind feeling toward any laborer for the slave. I wish you abundant success in all that you wisely do for the downfall of slavery & shall continue to labor in this cause (?) to my strength and ability.

"Faithfully yours,
"LEWIS TAPPAN.

"P.S. I send you thro' the agency of John Wiley, Bookseller, a copy of Goodell's [349] 'Slavery & Anti-Slavery' & a copy of the 'American Slave Code' with one of the catalogues of books in the Depository."

"NEW YORK, Nov. 24/54.

"L.A. CHAMEROVZOW, ESQ
"Dear Sir,

"I send you a letter [350] for the editor of the Nonconformist. Please read it. I am anxious to have it published in that paper—in the Banner—London Patriot—and Reporter. Can you bring this about?

"I had thought of sending it direct to Mr Miall, with whom I have been acquainted, but have thot it best to send it to you to seal & send to him if you think that the best mode, or to hand it to him personally. The subject is very important as it relates to the Anti

---

[349] Goodell, William, Slavery and Anti-Slavery: A History of the Great Struggle in Both Hemispheres (1852); The American Slave Code (1853).

[350] This Tappan letter of date, November 23, 1854, appeared in the B. & F. A-S. Reporter, January 1, 1855, pp. 15–18. Tappan here dealt with the reputed character of the A. B. C. F. M., giving full details on its connection with the Choctaw Mission in Indian Territory, and ventures the opinion that when the British read this letter of his,

"They will say . . . that the Abolitionists of America have not only to contend with the slave power, with a proslavery government, with ecclesiastical bodies and national Societies in complicity with Slavery, but with a large body of ministers, editors, and church members, in the free States, who style themselves anti-slavery people, and yet afford aid and countenance to the iniquitous system, by their apologies, mystifications, glosses, and misstatements."

Slavery cause in this country, & it is important that British Christians should not be misled by the attack of the 25th Oct. in the Nonconformist.[351]

"Use your best skill & judgment in the matter & advise me.

"Yours Truly,

"Lewis Tappan"

"Boston, February 22ᵈ. 1855.

"L.A. Chamerovzow, Esq.

"My dear Sir,

"Your letter of January 26th was duly received but not before I left New York for this vicinity where I have been some weeks on a visit to a sick relative.

"I have sent you a copy of the Annual Report of the A.B.C.F.M. for 1848,[352] agreeably to your request. I hope it will reach you through the Post safely. That letter [353] of Mr Treat, made so famous by circumstances since it was written, will puzzle you to understand it. When it first appeared it was hailed with much gratification by the anti-slavery body of the U.S. because it was almost the first move in a right anti-slavery direction the Board had ever made, and because it contained so many admirable things. You will find that while it speaks decidedly against the system of slavery it tolerates slave holding. If a slaveholder is a reputable

[351] This attack in the shape of a letter was largely compiled from extracts from the *Independent* and against Tappan's counter accusations, that paper defended itself, asseverating that it (*The Independent*) had done more than any other paper against slavery for the last five years:

"We are quite content to risk the reputation of *The Independent* against the sign-manual of Mr. Lewis Tappan. We would not convey the least intimation against the respectability of the name or to the reproach of the gentleman who wears it. He has done good service in many ways to the cause of freedom. We trust that he will live to rejoice in the triumphs of a cause to which he has given so freely of his money, his time, and his labors. We are only sorry that a sincere but misdirected zeal should lend his name to the unworthy office of misrepresenting his Christian brethren, even though this should lead to a fusion with Mr. Parker Pillsbury. . . . Mr. Tappan ought by this time to know that intelligent Christians in England are beginning to regard the claims of the two rival cliques of Abolitionists in this country to a monopoly of the Christian Anti-slavery sentiment of the land, as about upon a par with the claims of Adventists and Latter-Day Saints to all the faith and piety of the times" (*The Independent*, March 8, 1855, p. 76).

[352] For a discussion of the American churches and slavery, see the *Annual Report* of the A. & F. A-S. Society for 1853, referred to above.

[353] The A. B. C. F. M. was under fire from anti-slavery leaders for many years.

member of a Church & not scandalously cruel he may be fellow-shipped &c. This is the earnest sentiment at the present time of a majority of the Churches of nearly all the religious denominations in the country.

"I have not seen a very full account of the proceedings of the Anti-Slavery Conference,[354] but hope soon to see the copies you speak of. It will give me pleasure to circulate them. The *Independent* of New York, last week, had a scorching notice [355] of Mr. Pillsbury's and Mr Vincent's remarks about the A.B.C.F.M. Whether any injustice is done to those gentlemen or not I cannot tell until I see a copy of the proceedings. That Mr. P. should be extravagant and intemperate in his statements does not surprise me; but I had hoped Mr Vincent would keep himself free from improper remarks. I greatly fear that he too has made assertions respecting the Board that can not be justified, either in spirit or truthfulness.

"I have not seen the *Advocate*. Will you have it sent to me if you think it will be advantageous to the cause for me to read it regularly? At least, please send a number now & then if anything appears of peculiar interest. I have not seen the copy of the *Empire* [356] to which you allude, but presume it is at my office in New York.

[354] B. & F. A-S. *Reporter*, Jan. 1, 1855, p. 12 ff.

[355] The "scorching notice" was as follows:

"It is not always easy to draw the line exactly between knavery and insanity; nor is it always necessary. When Mr. Parker Pillsbury affirms that the American Board of Foreign Missions 'is a slave-holding body; that its treasury is constantly replenished by the price of the bodies and souls of men; sold like beasts in the market; that its missions to Africa are sustained by the money raised from the sale of Africa's daughters, sold in the American shambles to grace the seraglios of southern debauchees' . . . that the religious bodies in America have 'furnished the means of sending delegates to the churches in Great Britain by the sale of babes in the market'—we have no occasion to judge whether he speaks under the hallucination of frenzy or with a full consciousness that he is lying" (*The Independent*, February 15, 1855, p. 52).

[356] The first number of *The Empire*, a weekly with which Tallis's *London Weekly Paper* had been incorporated, came out on Guy Fawkes' Day, 1853. Its expectation was to stress *empire* news and regular colonial correspondents were to be appointed. It came to be usual for most of the American news to be copied direct from American papers. Its attitude towards slavery was revealed in one of its very early editorials. It was an editorial on President Pierce's message, December 5, 1853 (*Richardson*, VI, 2740 ff.).

"But, notwithstanding the polite silence of the President, that dark and deadly stain (slavery) on the American escutcheon is present to the

"You say, 'Mr. Pillsbury stated at the Conference that 19,000 slaves' (I have copied your figures exactly, but do not understand whether they mean 19000 or 9000, but am inclined to suppose you meant 19000.) 'were introduced from Africa every year' into the U.S. This is a very extraordinary statement! So far as I know none are introduced, nor have been for many years. The statement seems to carry its own refutation on the face of it. Our manufacturing establishments would hardly be willing to see foreign goods smuggled into the country. Neither would slaveholders, who sell their slaves for $800 to $1200 each be willing to have their neighbors smuggle them into the country. But, to make the matter more sure I addressed a note to Judge Jay, than whom no man in the whole country is more attentive to facts & rumors in regard to Slavery, to ascertain what he knew on the subject. In his reply he says: 'I have seen nothing & heard nothing that leads me to believe that within the last twenty years one single slave has been landed in the United States from Africa. Before the annexation of Texas I did hear that a large number of slaves had been imported into that State from Cuba, but I have no means of knowing how far the report was true.'

"I find an increased anti-slavery sentiment in this, my native State, that is remarkable and cheering. As evidence of it Mr. Loring,[357] the magistrate who sent the alleged fugitive Burns [358] from this city into slavery, under the Bill of 1850, has been rejected as a Lecturer in the Law School of Harvard University, and there is a prospect that he will soon be removed from the office of Judge of Probate by the Governor & Council on application of the Legislature of Massachusetts, now in Session.

"I am in correspondence with Mr Treat [359] respecting his letters to Mr Young,[360] extracts from which were published in the Anti-Slavery Reporter last received. He alleged that 'most untrue'

eyes and mind of every civilized community, and sooner or later it will have to be effaced. . . . This wound will rankle in the body politic till a day of retribution arrives, and it is not at all improbable that the 'majestic union' may be torn at no distant period into two conflicting empires by the influence of this fatal controversy. . . . We must blush, as Englishmen, for the land of our descendants, who allow of such a frightful domestic institution, and perpetuate so indelible a disgrace'' (*The Empire*, December 24, 1853, p. 8).

[357] Edward Greely Loring.
[358] Anthony Burns.
[359] S. B. Treat, Secretary of the A. B. C. F. M.
[360] Rev. C. G. Young.

charges had been made against the A.B.C.F.M. in the organ of the American Missionary Association. He now says he did not intend to say that anything had been designedly said that was untrue, &c.

"Truly yours
"LEWIS TAPPAN."

"I wish you to publish this letter in the Reporter.

"NEW YORK, March 20 [361]/55.

"L.A. CHAMEROVZOW, ESQ.

"My dear Sir,

"Yesterday I rec^d Mr Bolton's note written on your behalf. On the 22^d Feb. I wrote to you in reply to yours of Jan 26th, in which I gave Judge Jay's remark about Mr Pillsbury's extraordinary statement respecting the importation of slaves into the U. States & my own views of the same subject.

"I respectfully called upon him again for a specification of the American Board of Commissioners for Foreign Missions, to furnish evidence that 'most untrue' charges had been made in the 'American Missionary' against the Board, as he alleged in his letter to Rev. C.G. Young, extracts from which were published in the Reporter of January 1st 1855; but he declined pointing out such alleged charges, saying: 'I did not aver that "the official paper" of that Society had designedly made any "untrue statement." I merely affirmed that it had made "charges" which were "very severe," and which were also "most untrue," adding that we had "let them pass," because we disliked "controversy" with a "missionary body." Such being the case, I can not feel that I am under any obligation to point out the statements in the American Missionary which we regard as untrue.'

"I respectfully called upon him again for a specification of the charges which he had asserted were 'most untrue,' and he replied:

" 'Were I to accede to your wishes, a protracted correspondence would be very likely to ensue; for this I have neither time nor taste. I respectfully decline, therefore, a compliance with your request.'

"The public will judge how far it is correct for the Secretary to make such an assertion respecting a sister missionary Society, and then decline furnishing proofs of the correctness of the allegation. The truth is, 'very severe' remarks have been made in the *American*

---

[361] The B. & F. A-S. *Reporter*, April 30, 1855, pp. 108–111, published a part of this letter in connection with a lengthy article on the subject of S. B. Treat and the American Board.

Missionary respecting the conduct of the Board in its Indian missions &c., but nothing that was 'untrue.'

"The *Independent*, of the 15th had a calumnious article,[362] respecting my letter to the *Nonconformist*, published in the *Reporter* of the 1st January, and attempted to shew that there was a conspiracy (or in the classical language of the editor, a *fusion*) between the American Anti-Slavery Society (Mr. Garrison's) the American & Foreign Anti Society, Rev. J. Vincent, Mr. Pillsbury and myself to denounce the American Board. The unfairness of this is apparent. There is no 'fusion' between the two Societies, and neither Mr. Vincent's nor Mr. Pillsbury's remarks & statements in England respecting the American Board, so far as they were violent, uncharitable or incorrect have met with any approval on the part of the committee or members of either the A.&.F. Anti Slavery Society, the American Missionary Association or myself. *The Independent* joined the names of the Societies and individuals together, in its unjust phillipic, to throw odium upon the A & F. Anti Slavery Society and myself. It is welcome to all the reputation it may gain by this procedure.

"You will see in *the Independent* of the 15th and 22d instant, paragraphs, relating to the article referred to, published at my request. Taken together they carry their own meaning. While, on many accounts, I approve the course taken by this able and influential paper on the Anti Slavery subject, and on other subjects, yet I am constrained to believe that with regard to its upholding the American Board, in its complicity with Slavery at its Indian missions, it has done great injury to the Anti Slavery cause, acted very inconsistently with its professions, and deserves the rebuke of all true-hearted abolitionists, both in this country and in England.

"Respectfully & truly your's,

"Lewis Tappan.

"New York, March 20, 1855.

"☞Please send me No.12 of the B & F. Anti Slavery Report."

"Brooklyn, N.Y. April 3d 1855.

"L.A. Chamerovzow, Esq

"My dear Sir,

"Yours of the 9th March was duly rec^d. I send you by this mail the 49th Report of the A.B.C.F.M. which

[362] The article appeared on March 8th, 1855, p. 76, and is quoted p. 537, note 349.

contains the proceedings at the last annual meeting. In the hasty examination I have been able to make I do not find the article you have written for, but the official proceedings will be interesting & valuable to keep. I shall write to Boston to know if there has been published any other pamphlet & if so will soon send it to you. I will also send you the copy of the *Independent* that contained the proceedings at Hartford.

"A distinguished minister at the West is reviewing Mr. Treat's letter of 1848 in the *Congregational Herald* printed at Chicago. It will be a thorough review & shew the connection the American Board, for many years, has had with Slavery. I give you an extract from one of the numbers. 'The Antrim petition was presented to the American Board some twelve years ago. It was signed by ministers from New Hampshire, disavowing abolitionism, and asking, in effect, that the Board would relieve its friends & silence its enemies by reviewing & if necessary reforming its relations to Slavery in its Indian Missions. The results of the discussion occasioned by this and other petitions was the Brooklyn Report of 1845; adopted after a full discussion and never since *rescinded, qualified or repealed,* but often since referred to as containing *the* doctrines of the Board touching Slavery. This celebrated Brooklyn Report (which was adopted) *distensibly and in terms recommends the reception of slaveholders into church-relation,* without specifying any distinction as to any particular kind or sort of slaveholding, & prescribing no condition but such as applies to non-slaveholders, such as evidence of "spiritual regeneration," etc. Of course the Board's Missionaries continued, as before, to receive all the slaveholders, being otherwise unobjectionable, who applied for membership in their churches. *They do so still!* (1855.)'

"Judge Jay has assured me that he has no knowledge of slaves having been introduced into the Southern States from any foreign country. Some members of Congress may have made such a statement, but Judge Jay never quoted it with his sanction or belief of the statement. You can deny the statement made in England absolutely.

"Recently I revised the list of names to whom your Reporter is sent. I will send you a copy soon. It has been the practice to send them immediately after being received; and as evidence of their being rec^d. the editors (pro slavery & all) to whom some of them have been addressed have regularly sent me their papers in exchange.

"Enclosed is a bill from the *Tribune* office for papers sent to your office. I paid the five dollars & charged it in a/c.

"Very truly your's

"LEWIS TAPPAN.

"I have seen Judge Jay since writing this letter. He says he has not written, spoken or published anything going to shew that slaves have been imported into the U.S. the past twenty years. He says there may be some allusion to the importation of slaves formerly in his 'View' [363] or 'Inquiry.' [364]—"

"BROOKLYN, N.Y. April 13/55.

"L.A. CHAMEROVZOW, Esq.

"My dear Sir,

"Referring you to my last letter of the 3ᵈ. I would now inform you that no pamphlet or publication has issued from the office of the A.B.C.F.M. respecting the motion to elect Lord Shaftesbury & other gentlemen in your country corresponding members of the A.B.C.F.M. Dr. Cox, without consulting anyone it is believed made a characteristic speech & offered a resolution respecting the election of those gentlemen. It was referred to a Committee, but no report was made, and it is not probable that any will, as the duties of such committees expire at the adjournment.

"In my last I gave you an extract from a Review of Mr. Treat's letter of 1848, by a Western Minister, in the Chicago *Congregational Herald*. I now send you a pamphlet entitled, 'Missionary Boards in relation to Slavery, Caste, & Polygamy from the *American Missionary*, Extra, May 1854'—with an article annexed taken from the *Congregational Herald,* sometime since, being a communication from Rev. S.G. Wright on 'Missions and Caste.' This pamphlet & the Reports of the Board for 1848 and 1854, which have been sent to you, will furnish all the information you have requested.

"Rev. James Vincent has sent me a copy of his pamphlet published in London entitled 'American Slavery Defeated in its attempts &c.' It contains a good deal of valuable information, and asserts principles that are undoubtedly correct; but I regret the spirit in which it appears to have been written, and several assertions which seem to me quite reprehensible. The conduct of the

[363] Jay, William, *View of the Action of the Federal Government in Behalf of Slavery.*

[364] Jay, William, *Inquiry into the Character & Tendency of A. C. & A. Anti-S. Societies.*

A.B.C.F.M. in regard to the slavery question, has been bad enough, but no good cause can be advanced when the advocate speaks the truth even in unrighteousness. As a sample of the expressions alluded to is the following on page 10. 'The Amer. Board of Missions has employed on those stations (the Indian) men to whom God never gave a commission to preach the Gospel, who ought never to be tolerated on earth, and who, in my opinion, never will be in heaven.' I regret that such a man should have been sent out as an agent of the Amer. Reform Tract & Book Society, and I know that many other friends of that Society also regret it. The Society, if I am not greatly misinformed, do likewise. Some persons here have supposed that Mr Vincent was authorized to represent in England the 'American Missionary Association,' but he was not. Mr V. is scarcely known hereabouts. I am told he is an Englishman. If so, all I need say, further, is, it is rare that a minister from your country gives just offence to anti slavery men here by the style of his remarks on subjects connected with American slavery.

"A new anti-slavery Society has been organized, called The Abolition Society of New York City and vicinity. Its object is to secure the immediate and unconditional abolition of American Slavery. Its leading sentiments are these: Slave holding is sinful, illegal, and unconstitutional; it is the duty of the Federal Government, in all its departments, to suppress slave holding throughout the United States, &c.[365] The great majority of those who have professed anti slavery principles in this country have conceded that neither the people of the U.S. nor the Gen. Government had any right to meddle with slavery in the States. While they have united in asserting that all support of the iniquitous system on the part of the General Gov^t was unconstitutional they have admitted that slaveholding in the States could only be reached by moral suasion. The party of which Mr. Garrison is the head have contended however, that the Constitution of the U.S. is pro-slavery, and on this ground they have desired a dissolution of the Union. Meantime the slaveholding oligarchy have adopted the same principle, although they advocate a continuance of the Union except, in special cases, when by threatening a dissolution of the Union they can by fright-

[365] The constitution of the new society is in the B. & F. A-S. *Reporter,* June 1, 1855, pp. 123–124. The name of the society was soon changed to the American Abolition Society. Its official publication was the *Radical-Abolitionist.*

ening the North carry some favorite political measure to strengthen slavery.

"Those who formed the Amer. and For. Anti S. Society conceded that they could not constitutionally touch the slavery question in the States except by agreement and persuasion; but in the progress of its history not a few began to believe that something more could be done, that slaveholding was not only sinful but illegal and unconstitutional, and within the power of the people of the U.S. through the national legislature and judiciary. Lysander Spooner of Massachusetts, a lawyer of great acuteness, has, for several years, been urging these views, and his publications [366] have been gradually increasing in popularity. William Goodell, of this state, one of the ablest ethical writers in the country, has advocated them with much ability. You have doubtless seen his articles in the *National Era*.[367] He edits *The American Jubilee*, a monthly paper

[366] John Quincy Adams presented a Lysander Spooner (1808–1887) memorial to Congress as early as 1840. *Memoirs of John Quincy Adams*, X, 295, 298, 300. Spooner was active in the fight for cheaper postage. His chief works on slavery were the "Unconstitutionality of Slavery" (1845) and "A Defence of Fugitive Slaves" (1856).

[367] The letters of William Goodell on *The Legal Tenure of Slavery* began to appear in *The National Era* in 1853, continued irregularly throughout 1854, and ended with the thirty-ninth, November 8, 1855. In his last letter, the writer asserted that in the two years,

"the leading statesmen of the South, its prominent editors, and, finally, the great mass of southern slaveholders, have been in process of shifting their legal basis of slave tenure, from that of local, positive, municipal law (where their own courts and the Federal courts had always placed it,) to that of natural and common law, on the same footing with the tenure of property in domestic animals and inanimate objects. . . . On no other basis can the new tactics concerning Territories be justified. On no other plea *is* it attempted to justify it. Slavery was to be pushed into the Territories, without positive local law, on the pretence of universal, natural, common law. And the legal basis of Slavery in the Territories had to be adjusted accordingly. On the same basis reposes the pending lawsuit of Virginia versus New York, to reverse Judge Paine's decision liberating Mr. Lemmon's slaves. On the same basis rests the decision of Judge Kane. The proposed Federal legalization of the African slave trade, and consequent protection of slaveholding in all the States, completes the programme, and follows of course! The Nebraska bill, overriding the Missouri restriction, determined all the rest! Who would have believed a prediction of all this, two years ago? *But here we are!*

"The unavoidable issue now is—a Federal Government protecting Slavery in all the States, or a Federal Government prohibiting Slavery in all the States. If this be consolidation, there is no help for it. . . . The slaveocrats have forced the alternative upon us. Let them abide by it, as they indeed must. If 350,000 slaveholders can outrage and overawe the country, with its twenty-four millions of inhabitants, the victory will be theirs. If not, they are to be defeated, and must yield the controversy.

"The point reached by our discussion of 'The Legal Tenure of Slavery,' including its relation to the Constitution and the Federal Govern-

devoted to the advocacy of these doctrines. A majority of the
Ex.Com. of the Amer. & For. Anti S. Society have adopted them,
and will, I think become members of the new Society. If so, it is
probable that the A and F. Soc. will henceforth have only a nominal
existence.

"Some of our ablest lawyers who have never identified themselves with the anti slavery cause acknowledge privately that they
believe that slaveholding in the U.S. is both illegal and unconstitutional. It is thought that the number would be greatly increased
were they thoroughly to examine the question, and were they sufficiently independent to avow their belief before the world. Other
lawyers, of no mean ability, who call themselves anti slavery men
& are thought to be thoroughly so, avow that were they judges and
a slave should be brought before them on a writ of habeus corpus,
they would set him free under the common law. Judges might do
this, some of them say, but it is not the province of the Congress to
do it. But if it be a righteous thing, and it can be done through the
action of the judiciary, it seems to be incumbent on the Congress to
effect it through the agency of the judiciary. The Constitution
does not limit the number of judges; one can be appointed, if need
be, in every city, every ward, every town, & every village in the
country. Congress can pass a bill for the creation of judges and
the President with the concurrence of the Senate can appoint them.
But I will not pursue the subject. The press will be employed to
give circulation to the views of the new Society, and however
strange they may appear to those who have set [sic] down in despondency, thinking there was no remedy for Slavery should the
Slave-power be unyielding, they will, I predict, receive the attention
of numerous readers & result in a marked change in public sentiment.

"I have thought it my duty to resign the office of Corresponding
Secretary of the Amer & For Anti Slavery Society, and to accept
office in the new Society, though, at my age, I do not anticipate that
my health & strength will long continue so as to allow me to act
very efficiently in the cause so dear to my heart.

"Truly yours
"LEWIS TAPPAN.

"P.S. I send you a copy of an excellent Tract just published by
the Tract & Book Society & sent in large numbers to Kansas."

ment, is precisely the point needed by the necessities of the times. If any
other theory of the Constitution be admitted, it affords us no adequate
basis of political action against Slavery, now and henceforward."

"BROOKLYN, N.Y.

"L.A. CHAMEROVZOW, ESQ "April 18/55.

"My dear Sir,

"I send you by Dr Burchard [368]

"1. Phelps's Letters to Prof. Stowe.[369] This book is worth your perusal, as it will throw much light upon the controversy with the A.B.C.F.M. & its leading supporters in 1845.

"2. A Tract [370] by Mr Goodloe, late of N.C. now of Washington City (a lawyer) respecting Slavery in Kansas.

"3. The April no of the 'Jubilee,' containing the Constitution &c of the new Anti S⁷ Society.

"4. A list [371] of the persons to whom your Reporter has been sent from our office.

"5. An article from yesterday's daily Tribune respecting the Amer Tract Society.

"Truly Your's

"L. TAPPAN"

"BROOKLYN, N.Y.

"L.A. CHAMEROVZOW, ESQ "Oct 9/55.

"My dear Sir,

"I recᵈ your note enclosing one for Mrs Legrand,[372] which I send to her. I have not seen her for several weeks & do not know how she is getting along.

"I sent the $200 per Philip Bailey to Wᵐ S. Peira, Esq. of Philadelphia & he is in treaty for the free papers. But as counsel for Passmore Williamson he has been very busy & the matter had to be delayed. I hope soon to receive them.

"In haste

"Your's truly

"L. TAPPAN."

"The package of Books is sent to Trubner & Co No 12 Paternoster Row.

[368] The Reverend Samuel D. Burchard, to whom Tappan gave one of his letters of introduction.

[369] Phelps, Amos A., "Letters to Professor Stowe and Dr. Bacon."

[370] Goodloe, Daniel Reaves, "Is it expedient to introduce slavery into Kansas?" A tract for the times by, of North Carolina. Cincinnati, published by American Reform Tract and Book Society, 1855. (For more about Goodloe, see Bassett, J. S., *Anti-Slavery Leaders of North Carolina.*)

[371] The list has been omitted as of slight importance.

[372] Caroline Legrand, formerly Caroline Douet de St. Pons.

"BROOKLYN, N.Y. Nov. 10/55.

"L.A. CHAMEROVZOW, ESQ.

"My dear Sir,

"Yours of Oct. 12th was duly rec^d.

"The letter you addressed to me for Mrs. Le Grand was sent to her lodgings in this city. I did not know that she had left the city until the receipt of your note. Poor thing! I hope she will get along in Philadelphia. She ought to have gone to some *French* island.

"I have sent you two Syracuse newspapers entitled *'The Reformer,'* which will give you an account of the Convention of Radical Abolitionists in Boston.[373] An article in the *'National Era'* (by L.T.) will also give you some information. The *'Liberator'* affects to sneer at the Convention. But we had a good meeting. The Hall was about as large as your Hall of Commerce. It was half filled during the day Sessions & in the evening quite filled. The Garrisonians did not enter into the discussions though many of them were present & invited to discuss with us. H.C. Wright ventured to question Gerrit Smith, but he was silenced by Mr S's reply. They are aware that the success of the principles will prove the destruction of their Society & they prudently avoid a public discussion.

"Mr John Wiley of N.Y. bookseller, sends for me to-day by a packet ship 2 copies of Douglas's Life for you I paid for them both $1.50, wholesale price. I also send you a pamphlet of rare merit entitled 'Letters on Slavery, by O.S.F.'[374] You will find that it

---

[373] On January 16, 1856, the executive committee of the American Abolition Society addressed a letter to the committee of the American Anti-Slavery Society, asking for a debate in New York on the legality and constitutionality of slavery in the states. The reply, February 7, 1856, stated that, "We deem the constitutionality and legality of Slavery as generally understood, and the exclusive jurisdiction of the slave-States over it within their limits, to be justly regarded by the whole nation as self-evident and axiomatic facts: as much so as the existence of Slavery, or of the Constitution itself. . . ." And as revealing the antagonism between anti-slavery men, ". . . we, apprehend, from the antecedents of a majority of the Committee through which you have communicated with us, that, should we meet you in the way proposed, we might seem to recognise as genuine Abolitionists and honourable antagonists, men in no wise entitled to be so regarded, ..." B. & F. A-S. *Reporter*, July 1, 1856, pp. 146–148.

[374] Freeman, O. S. (pseudonym for Edward Coit Rogers), *Letters on Slavery*, addressed to pro-slavery men of America; showing its illegality in all ages and nations—its destructive war upon society and government, morals and religion (Boston, 1855).

is one of the best works ever published here on the subject, and that it corroborates the position taken by the new Soc. formed at Boston, by the Radical Abolitionists.

"Your's very truly
"LEWIS TAPPAN.

"Please send me 'Anti S.Recollections' by Sir Geo. Stephen,[375] London, Hatchards

"Observe the beauty of Dr Smith's Introduction to Douglas's Life & F.D's modest & dignified letter in the Editor's Preface

"I send the drawings by Mrs. Le Grand in one of the pamphlets sent in a packet by Ship this day.

"Will you send me 25 penny stamps & charge them to me? If this letter is not within the postage I pay charge the excess to me.

"By the Tribune today I see that Mrs Le Grand is still in this city.

"Has Ex. gov. Hammond of South Carolina ever paid for the *Reporter* sent him. He asked me to subscribe for it some years since & promised to pay. Has he done so? If not, send me his a/c.

"I send a copy of 'Letters on Slavery' for my son who is in France. Please deliver it when he sends for it. When you write to me please inform me the rate of postage on letters & pamphlets between England & France."

"BROOKLYN, N.Y. 24th. July, 1856.

"L. A. CHAMEROVZOW, ESQ
   27, New Broad St.
     London

"My Dear Sir,

"Your note of the 11th. was received this day. I have forwarded the letter [376] for Hon. Ch. Sumner to Hon. J. R. Giddings, M.C. to be forwarded. Mr Sumner is at some watering place, I know not where, to recruit his health. The Address I have forwarded to the editor of the 'National Era,' Washington, requesting him to publish it. Other papers will probably copy it. The 'sympathy & encouragement' of our British friends will be gratefully rec^d by the abolitionists of this country.

[375] Stephen, Sir George, *Antislavery Recollections.*

[376] For B. & F. A-S. Society "Address of Sympathy for Charles Sumner," see B. & F. A-S. *Reporter,* August 1, 1856, p. 179.

"You speak of my letter to you of 29 Dec. 1855, which remains unanswered, and of the money you were to send per the a/c in said letter. You ask me how you can transmit the money. Numerous Bankers in both countries supply applicants with drafts on request.

"In my letter of Dec 29/55, referred to above, I stated the amount due to be $33.22. You will see that there was a mistake in adding up of one dollar, so that the amount due is $34.22, which at the present rate of Exchange is equivalent to £6.19.8 stg. I do not know of any other sums for which I am liable on your a/c or that of the B. & F. Anti S. Soc.

"A moral & political battle is now waging in this country that may decide the fate of Slavery.

"Your's truly
"LEWIS TAPPAN"

"NEW YORK,
"20th April, 1858.

"L.A.CHAMEROVZOW Esq.

Secretary &c.

"My dear Sir,

"I have your note of 16 March. I did not ask you to send my Reporter to the Brooklyn P.O. but not the packet for distribution. Hereafter I shall be glad to have all letters papers &c sent to my address here.

"I hope that ere this you have received Mr Olmsted's [377] work on Texas, but if you fail to receive it I will forward you another copy. Messrs Witey and Halsted of this city, Booksellers will forward to their correspondent in London the Books named below. Perhaps you have seen some of them before. Do you wish me to send for your Committee a copy of each Anti-Slavery Book published in this country? Or shall I wait to hear from you before sending any & send such as you see advertised & desire to have.

"I have forwarded a second copy of the A.M. for March agreeably to your request.

"I forward you a copy of the Weekly Evening Post. The price per annum is (see paper). It contains nearly all the reading matter in the daily evening paper. A large part of the daily is devoted

[377] Olmsted, Frederick Law, *A Journey through Texas;* or a saddle-trip on the southwestern frontier; with a statistical appendix (New York and London, 1857).

to advertisements. W.C.Bryant, the Poet, is senior editor of the paper, but John Bigelow, junior editor, writes, with his assistants, most of the editorials.

"It will give me pleasure to aid you in the plan you propose for being a correspondent of one of our papers here.

"I have recᵈ a note from you of later date than that of 16th March, but unfortunately have left it at my house at Brooklyn so that I cannot refer to it in writing this letter. You speak of sending me a Morning Star, sent, as you say, by the same vessel that took your letter. Three or four weeks since I recᵈ a copy of the Morning Star from some unknown person. It is lost but this could not be the copy, I think, to which you alluded. I think the best way will be for you to send me a letter for one of our papers here just such a letter as you would write if you had been engaged to write it. It need not be addressed to any particular paper. I will then take it to some of our leading editors & endeavour to get a proposition from one of them to send you.

"You asked about the Report that slaves have been introduced into Mississippi from Africa. There is such a rumor, but I cannot learn that it is founded upon facts. The South foiled in their attempt to make Kansas a slave state may be desperate in measures to uphold southern slavery but the Lord and an increasing interest of the people of the U.S. against them. The Lord reigneth.

"Your's

"L.TAPPAN.

"When you write next please send me 50 penny stamps and charge them to me on a/c.

"Books sent: Picture of Slavery—G.Smith in Congress [378]—The impending Crisis [379] and God agᵗ Slavery; [380] all for $2.65."

"...

[378] "Gerrit Smith in Congress" is the speech which he made on December 20, 1853, contrasting the lot of a Hungarian refugee, Martin Koszta, with that of a fugitive slave. B. & F. A-S. *Reporter*, February 1, 1854, pp. 43–46. The *Reporter* confuses the two houses of Congress. *Appendix to the Congressional Globe*, 1st sess., 33d Cong., Dec. 20, 1853, pp. 50–52. Smith is perhaps best known as the friend of John Brown.

[379] Helper, Hinton Rowan, *The impending crisis of the South: how to meet it* (New York, 1857).

[380] Cheever, George Barrell (1807–1890), *God Against Slavery*. He was an ardent temperance reformer as well as an anti-slavery advocate.

"New York, June 23/58

"L. A. Chamerovzow, Esq

"My dear Sir,

"I have rec^d. your note of the 11th. and a copy of the Morning Star of the same date & the pamphlet entitled 'The West India Labour Question &c.' [381] Also the stamps. Accept my thanks for your attention.

". . .

"You ask me to inform you respecting Delegates sent to London by the Churches & Societies on this side. Do you not remember my correspondence with the 'Banner'? A Rev Mr Chickering from Portland, State of Maine, went to London, stop^t with Dr Campbell & professed to be a thorough anti Slavery man. I wrote to Dr C. about his antecedents. He (Dr. Campbell) abused me in his paper & when I sent him documentary evidence that Mr Chickering *was* pro slavery here he did me injustice again. It was while Mr. Scoble was Secretary, but I suppose you have seen the pamphlet published in London, at the time, on the subject. The conduct of Dr Campbell discouraged me from giving the antecedents of our pro Slavery clergymen &c. to English correspondents. I will bear in mind your request, though in these days of steamer enterprise ministers and others go to Europe & return often without having been missed.

"I think I sent you a 'National Era' of May 27th. containing a speech of mine, containing Dr Cheever's speech. He has recently delivered 3 speeches, two of which have been published in pamphlet form. These will be sent to you. They are up to the mark. One of the daily papers in Boston volunteered to publish the Address before the Amer. Miss. Asso. at length.

"A new weekly paper in this City, 'The Witness' did the same. Dr C. writes & speaks like an ancient prophet. He writes for the Independent. His articles are usually on the 1st. page & have the signature of C.

"Very truly your's

"Lewis Tappan

"Does Hon. J. Hammond of S.C. owe your Society. He took the paper for a time. If he owes anything please send me a bill."

[381] B. & F. A-S. *Reporter,* September 1, 1857, pp. 209 ff.; July 1, 1858, pp. 162–163.

"NEW YORK,
"3d Sept. 1858.

"L.A.CHAMEROVZOW Esq,
London.

"My dear Sir,

"I send you today's Evening Post. In it you will see my letter respecting 300 Africans captured by a U.S. man of war & carried into Charleston, S.C. I send the *Tribune* of today to Mr Whipple, yʳ care. In this paper you will see some particulars about these Africans & the article in the Richmond Enquirer to which my letter is a reply. Are my statements all correct? Please send me as soon as you can some information about the Mixed Courts number of liberated Africans & especially about the apprenticeship system. Is it continued now? to what extent? Let the British people know the sin our Slaveholders make of the fact.

"In the *Tribune* of August 31st. (I think) you can see my letter to Dr Hopkins, respecting the complicity of the Amer. Board with Slavery. Much of it is taken from a pamphlet Mr Whipple prepared in 1854.

"If Mr *Whipple* is in London please hand him the note for him. If he is away I wish it sent to him. I wish the letter to my daughter sent to her. Mr W. probably knows her address. If he is away & you do not know where she is please enclose it to care of Mrs Blodgett, 153 Duke St. Liverpool.

"Has Mr Scoble returned to England to reside? I have neither seen nor heard of him for a long time, only Mr Whipple mentions seeing him in London.

"It is very easy now getting Anti-Slavery articles into our daily Press. The Times, Tribune, & E.Post—Secular & the Independent & Evangelist & Examiner (Baptist) religious are Anti-Slavery.

"The letter for Africa to be sent, care Day & Charden, Sierra Leone.

"Very truly yours,
"L.TAPPAN."

CONCLUSION

The letters here come to a somewhat abrupt end; but there is no good reason to suppose that the correspondence itself did.   There is some evidence to the contrary and, with further research, additional Tappan, Leavitt, Whittier, Jocelyn or Jay letters may yet come to light.   Towards the end of our period, George B. Cheever contributed to the sources of overseas information and, upon the basis of his letters as well as upon some of Josiah Forster and John Bevan Braithwaite authorship or ownership, it may with certainty be claimed that British interest in the great cause of the Negro suffered no diminution.   Some later study may show how variously it expressed itself and how it continued on through the years of the *War Between the States,* working eventually through a Freedmen's Aid Association, which had been promptly organized by the philanthropists of New Broad Street.

Advantage may now be taken of the opportunity which the ending of the present study affords of making a few general reflections upon the character of the period embraced by it.   It was a period of increasing intercourse between Great Britain and the huge republic that had developed out of her revolted colonies and, although it included at least one of the so-called anti-British periods of American history, it was, on the whole, rich in circumstances that made for a better understanding between the two English-speaking peoples.   Much of the bitterness left by the *War of Independence* had entirely disappeared, while that left by the *War of 1812,* never of equal intensity throughout the country, had gradually spent itself. Greatly contributing to this state of affairs was the exchange of visits between British people and Americans; for American visits to the Old World were more than balanced, in those days, by visits to the United States of British sportsmen interested in the big game of the West, of British Quakers interested in their Society or in general philanthropy, and of British literary men and women. As a matter of fact, visitors came and went on every conceivable errand, making many friendships, of which that of Carlyle and Emerson is, perhaps, the most famous.

In commerce, the United States exported wheat [1] as well as cotton so that the North as well as the South had a powerful economic tie with England, while British capital and thousands of British emigrants, answering to the call of the West, moved across the Atlantic to help in the development of a new country.

In intellectual and humanitarian interests, Britain and America found much to draw them together. The letters here published exhibit one great and striking instance of this and hint at several others. The letters, too, illustrate how the British public was urged to be active in American affairs. In them appears an amazing dependence upon British help and sympathy and an almost abnormal sensitiveness to British opinion. Of all the things, however, for which coöperation was solicited anti-slavery was, of course, the greatest. The anti-slavery enthusiasm was very general throughout the United Kingdom and, considering that this was the case, it must be doubted whether, without it, Britain would have remained neutral throughout the American Civil War, particularly as free trade and cotton were two weighty factors in the cementing of her relations with the South.[2] In a few individual instances, British official sympathy was with that section when war came and it took the commonalty of the United States a long time to understand and to realize that the heart of the nation was on the side of liberty. Outside of official circles, in England, there were some rather puzzling instances of sympathy with the South, Charles Dickens presenting the most surprising of the cases, surprising, however, not because he was the

---

[1] Scoble to Alexander, February 23, 1845, *ante*, p. —.

[2] On the British attitude towards the American Civil War, see Adams, Charles Francis, *Trans-Atlantic Solidarity*, Oxford, 1913.

author of *American Notes,* in which he depicted the essential barbarity of slavery, but because he was himself, in reality, a social reformer. How the American people were, after long years, to appreciate the difficulties of the British position and to make allowances for it was early commented upon by the Reverend Joseph P. Thompson who, in a letter to Richard Cobden, January 2, 1862, said:

"In our generous appreciation of the English people as the friends of popular freedom under a constitutional government, we had overlooked the strength, energy and persistence of that party in England which favors oligarchy in State and Church; and we were at first confounded with their voice as the voice of England! We had also assumed that the English were unanimous in their moral conviction against slavery; forgetting that, since the abolition of slavery had ceased to be a practical question in the British dominions, commercial and manufacturing interests, closely interlinked with slavery in the South, *might* pervert or overrule conscience in England, as they had already to some extent in our Northern States." [3]

But conscience overrode economic interest in many instances. It overrode it for John Bright who championed the cause of the North with a fervor but little short of that of Abraham Lincoln himself, so that the London *Times* suggested "that it seems a pity Mr. Bright's energy and unscrupulous determination do not rule in the White House. . . ." [4] A quotation from his famous Rochdale speech of December 4, 1861, delivered during the crisis of the Trent affair, may well conclude this study, anticipating as it did present-day discussions of American continental prosperity and political self-sufficiency. In many respects, it sets before the western world an ideal not yet reached and, in yet other respects, endorses the isolation doctrine with no foreshadowing of its selfishness on the one hand and its utter impracticability on the other.

[3] *The Rebellion Record,* Supplement, First Volume (New York, 1871), January 7, 1862, p. 15.

[4] *Idem,* p. 13.

"There cannot be," said Bright, "a meaner motive than this I am speaking of . . . that the United States should be severed, and that that continent should be as the continent of Europe is, in many States, and subject to all the contentions and disasters which have accompanied the history of the States of Europe. I should say that if a man had a great heart within him he would rather look forward to the day when, from that point of land which is habitable nearest to the Pole to the shores of the Great Gulf, the whole of that vast continent might become one great federation of States—that, without a great army and a great navy, not mixing itself up with the entanglements of European politics—without a custom-house inside through the whole length and breadth of its territory, but with freedom everywhere, peace everywhere—would afford at least some hope that man is not forsaken of Heaven, and that the future of our race might be better than the past." [5]

[5] Moore, Frank, *Speeches of John Bright, M.P., on the American Question*, pp. 47–48. There are several editions of this Rochdale speech with slight verbal variations.

INDEX

A

Aberdeen, George Hamilton Gordon, Earl of, memorial to, n., 9, 17, 57, 113; deputation waits upon, relative to Mendian Negroes, n., 52; Scoble reports interview of deputation with, 84–87; correspondence with, relative to extradition clause, n., 94; Committee of B & F A-S. Society in communication with, n., 113; address to, n., 119; answer of, to Lord Brougham, 152; letter to, to be drafted expressive of unabated interest in the Texan question felt by B & F Committee, n., 165; address to, on annexation of Texas, 207–208; reply of, through Addington, 208–209; declines doing more than advise Mexico, 240.

Abolition, of slave trade, a practical part of creed of all Britons, 12; recognition of Texan independence would be a blow to the cause of, n., 16; possible effect of, upon Texas, n., 17, 18; within possessions of East India Company, n., 18; by Mexico commended, n., 19; Britain preaches and practices, 35; work of Madden on, n., 12; efforts being made to form an, party in U. S., 62; in District of Columbia, 119; immediate, without compensation recommended to France, 138; movement of British Government in favor of, in Texas is exciting slaveholders, 144–145; in Texas ought to be a condition of recognition of independence by Gt. B., n., 113; should Gt. B. acquire Texas, the theory of, would be speedily reduced to practice, n., 114; new code regarding petitions on, 167; H. of R. adopts abstract resolutions against, 117;

missiles hurled against the sacred cause of, 197; work of Hancock on, n., 212; hope of, in all other civilized countries when slavery ceases in U. S., n., 213a; Dr. Bailey opposed to *polemic*, 336.

Abolitionists, n., 27; views of Thompson-Garrison group of, 35–36; number of, in U. S., 62; Tappan determined not to abuse those who differ from him, 70; duties of British, outlined by Birney and Stanton, n., 37; many would prefer postponement of convention, 111; President and Faculty of Dartmouth College are, 120; Amer. A-S. Society opposed to British, who sympathize with its rival, 121; Tappan writes concerning, 131; Garrisonian, absented themselves from Convention of 1843, n., 108; S. P. Andrews has publicly identified himself with, 177; Clay generally preferred by, 184; Torrey one of the most active of, 185; O'Neall very severe against, *ibid.*; the political future of, 186; untiring vigilance on part of, needed, 188; of Gt. B. and Ireland commend work of Torrey, &c., n., 148, 149, 150; American, have generally voted for Birney, 199; address to the, of U. S., n., 163; sentiments of both British and American, spoken, 208; remonstrance addressed to, n., 176; change in popular attitude towards, 227; American, strengthened by British, n., 206; N. Y. *Courier and Enquirer* formerly took decided ground against, 246; Sturge thinks a public meeting to express sympathy for, would be appropriate, n., 233; Dr. Cox abuses, 263; Turnbull